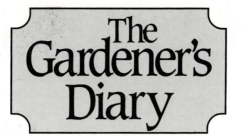

# The Gardener's Diary

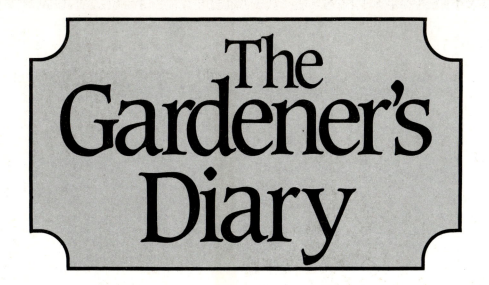

# The Gardener's Diary

CONSULTANT EDITOR
## ALAN TITCHMARSH

GENERAL EDITOR
## PETER McHOY

BLANDFORD PRESS
POOLE    DORSET

First published in the U.K. 1982 by
Blandford Press, Link House, West Street,
Poole, Dorset, BH15 1LL.

Copyright © 1982 Blandford Books Ltd.

Distributed in the United States by
Sterling Publishing Co., Inc.,
2 Park Avenue, New York, N.Y. 10016.

**British Library Cataloguing in Publication Data**

McHoy, Peter
   The gardener's diary.
   1. Gardening
   I. Title
   635            SB450.97

ISBN 0 7137 1267 8

Set in Monophoto Apollo by
August Filmsetting, Warrington, England.

Printed by Fakenham Press, Fakenham,
Norfolk.

# Contents

# Introduction

It is very easy to worry about the garden. There it sits in all weathers looking vigorous and overgrown or bleak and windswept—there always seems to be a need to do something about it, but many people are unsure of what. Here, then, is the book to take the worry out of gardening, for it will tell you just what to do at any time of year to perk up your plants and, with luck, your spirits.

Do not become agitated if you cannot fit in all the jobs mentioned; it is far better to tackle a part of the garden and to enjoy it rather than vainly trying to keep up the show in every corner when you just have not got the time. That does not mean that you should let the ground lie fallow (although it might be an attractive thought). Plan your plot instead to be a labour-saving haven, with areas that need little attention other than an occasional sweeping or a gentle hoeing or mowing.

To help you to get the best out of your patch of earth there are sections on garden planning, tools and equipment, controlling weeds and pests and diseases, buying plants and a host of other topics written by experts who have learned the hard way. Specialized plants such as alpines and water plants, roses and bulbs, trees and shrubs also get sections to themselves, as do fruit and vegetable growing. Delve into these chapters for basic subject information and use the diary section as an aid to memory.

Unlike many hobbies, with gardening you cannot easily do what you want when you want. More than most leisure activities, you are at the mercy of the seasons. You either sow or plant at the right time, or wait another year. For these reasons a reminder at the right time can make the difference between failure and success. The second part of the book is designed to ensure that you do not miss the opportunities, and to help you get the most from your garden.

For each week of the year you will find seasonal reminders of jobs to be done, seeds and plants to be ordered, and things to look out for in the garden. Because every year is different, and the climate so variable from one part of the country to another, you should always adapt the advice to suit your own area—and the season.

The reminders are based on a normal season in the midlands or south. If you live in the north, or in Scotland, you will need to delay most jobs by about two weeks in the spring—but *advance* them by a week or two in the autumn. In favourable areas you might be able to advance many jobs by a week or two in the spring.

Except at critical times, most of the week's work can be advanced or delayed by a week with no particular risk, so make a point of glancing through the weeks either side of the current one. It will give you a better idea of the seasonal work to be done, and give you a chance to obtain plants, seeds and materials ready for when you need them. You then have a better chance of fitting the jobs in to suit the weather.

Do not sow or plant if the weather or soil is not suitable. In spring in particular, a delayed sowing can easily overtake seedlings sown too early and that have received a check to growth. Remember, soil temperature can be more important than air temperature for sowing, so do not be taken in by a few isolated sunny days. A soil thermometer is a worthwhile investment. For half-hardy plants the last frost date is important, and you must be guided by local conditions when planting out tender subjects.

If you find yourself at a loose end at any time of year you will find that the weekly projects will keep you out of mischief and produce something to show for your efforts, and with any luck the diary might jolt you into trying a few flowers, vegetables or fruits that you have not experimented with before.

If the words do not inspire you then most probably the illustrations will. There are line drawings to make practical operations crystal clear, and plenty of colour illustrations to convince you of the the beauty of many garden plants.

With this book to hand, you might still worry a little, but at least you will know what you *should* be doing to turn your plot into a garden for all seasons.

ALAN TITCHMARSH

# PART ONE

# Principles of Gardening

# Site and Design

Garden design requires not artistic brilliance so much as sensible planning.

Whether you are starting from scratch or simply carrying out modifications to an existing layout, the advantages of working to a plan are several. In this day and age economy must come near the top of the list, and if you are able to implement construction over a reasonable period of time a budget can be planned accordingly. A well thought out design will also help to control not only that irresistible urge for spontaneous purchases at nurseries and garden centres but also those spasmodic flurries of activity in the garden when you are tempted to construct anything from a patio to a pergola and most things in between. It is in fact this tendency towards piecemeal development that spells disaster to many a garden layout. When it comes down to it, simplicity is the key to all good design.

Before even thinking of working out a design it is sensible to gather together as much information as possible, and this will fall into two categories. Firstly we shall need what we have got in the way of existing features, and this means carrying out a simple survey. Using a long tape, start by measuring the house itself, checking the external dimensions, the position of doors and windows and the distance of the building from the boundaries. Note any existing features, whether or not you think they are worth keeping, such as trees, shrubs, pools or steps. Changes of level are of course important, and if not too great the vertical differences can be easily measured. What sort of boundaries are there—fence, hedge, wall or nothing at all? Are there any good or bad views that might need emphasizing or screening? How about prevailing winds or an annoying draught that always blows down a side alleyway? In other words jot down everything you can think of and do not forget that all-important north point, or where the sun shines in relation to the house. Once you have this information translate it into a scale drawing on a sheet of graph paper, using a scale of 1:50 (6 mm–30 cm; $\frac{1}{4}$ in–1 ft) or 1:100 (3 mm–30 cm; $\frac{1}{8}$ in–1 ft).

Now and only now should you consider what you want, and possibly the best way to do this is to make a list. This might include a terrace or patio, barbecue, built-in seating, pond, sandpit, swings, slide, lawn, fruit and vegetables, shed, greenhouse, shrubs, trees and annuals. Do not worry at this stage if the list seems endless; you can easily prune it down later. On the other hand it is far more difficult to try and work in a forgotten feature once the garden is built. Remember, too, that the garden is not just for adults. Children and pets will be very much involved and will almost certainly make more impact than grown-ups!

A garden must also house the unsightly as well as the beautiful—such items as dustbins, oil tanks and fuel bunkers need sensible siting, possibly within a purpose-built enclosure that can be softened by climbing plants.

Before we look at a specific scheme it is worth considering some of the more common design problems and how these can best be solved. Perhaps the most awkward garden is that long narrow shape that seems to stretch away for ever. The golden rule here is not to emphasize the length by running a path, or anything else, straight down the middle; this simply makes matters worse. Instead, why not create a number of separate garden 'rooms', each one having a different theme and being separated from the next by wings of hedge or planting. If the site is sloping, steps will sensibly link each area, these being broad and generous as all garden steps should be. Paths should echo this being well laid and wide.

In a rectangular garden it is often a good idea to turn the whole design at an angle of say 45° to the house and boundaries. This immediately attracts attention away from the inherent shape of the plot and can set up all sorts of possibilities for patios, lawns and borders.

Areas close to the house are often best planned in crisp, rectangular shapes, to link with the line of the building. Do not be tempted to use too many different paving types; one or two carefully chosen materials will be far more effective than a wealth of contrasting colours and textures.

Curves in a garden should be positive. Use a pair of compasses when working out the design and transfer these shapes onto the ground by swinging a line from a stake that acts as a radius point. Such shapes will look just right when softened and surrounded by mature planting.

If a view is important the boundaries must allow this to flow in; in such a situation a post and rail, cleft chestnut paling or simple trellis fence would be ideal, but remember that these will be ill equipped to provide privacy or shelter. If the latter are needed something more solid is necessary.

As gardens become smaller the pressures placed upon them by an active family are correspondingly greater. In the illustration is shown a very typical plot measuring 15 × 18 m (50 × 60 ft). It is assumed that the house is new and the site is surrounded by a stark panel fence. The survey has pinpointed a number of important factors, which include two old trees, a slight change of level where the ground slopes up towards the bottom right-hand corner, and the benefit of a south-westerly aspect. The views outside the boundaries are not particularly good or bad, but the garage is very dominant and needs disguising in some way.

Moving away from the house ample room for sitting and dining has been provided, the brick paving acting as a visual link with the building and softening the neat precast slabs. A built-in barbecue and seat are practical features and also help visually to contain the area, and the line of the garage is broken by climbers that have run over a carefully sited pergola. Herbs are close to the kitchen and the brick dustbin store is convenient for the back door and dustmen alike.

Near the house the design is architectural, and rightly so, but as soon as you move from the terrace, the path, which provides easy access for feet, barrow and wheeled toys, sweeps away in a strong flowing curve, immediately leading the eye away from those rectangular boundaries. The trees act as pivots to the path, which pauses at the seat, acting as a focal point at the bottom of the garden. A 23 cm (9 in) brick retaining wall corrects that awkward slope in the corner, and this part of the garden, partially screened by the garage, would be ideal for a small vegetable plot, neatly flanked by espalier fruit. A lean-to greenhouse fits snugly against the sunny garage wall, while the path continues on the lower level leading back under the pergola.

As we have said, children demand a lot of a garden. A stout limb from the old

tree would make an ideal host for a swing, whereas the raised bed on the terrace could start life as a sandpit, with a fitted wooden cover to discourage nocturnal visitors.

Planting is of course vital to any scheme, softening and surrounding the composition as well as disguising raw walls and fences. Remember that the colour and texture of foliage can be every bit as important as flower and also that evergreens will be vital during those long winter months, to provide screening, shelter and also an attractive display. As a general rule keep hot colours, reds, yellows and orange close to the house, grading your planting scheme away to include blue, pink and that great harmonizer, grey. By doing this you will create a restful pattern and increase the visual depth of your garden.

In the final analysis a design should never be lifted complete from this or any other book. Set your own criteria, work out both what you want and what you have got and remember that the simple things work best of all.

# Tools and Equipment

Having the right tools makes for more enjoyable gardening. This means picking the kinds that will save you most effort, and ensuring that they are strong, well balanced and reasonably light. Many will last for a gardening lifetime, so choosing is worth some care.

Fortunately, there are just a few really essential tools. The rest can be added as particular needs arise. The important thing is to have a good idea of what you want before visiting the hardware shop or garden centre, and then to handle alternative makes to compare weight and balance. Look for a smooth comfortable handle.

## Tools for digging and cultivating

*Spades* The basic choice is between a full-size digging spade and a border spade. The former has a blade measuring about 29 × 19 cm (11½ × 7½ in). Border spades measure 23 × 14 cm (9 × 5½ in). Men generally prefer the larger blade, though a smaller one saves effort on heavy soil and is a wise choice for anyone with back trouble. Border spades are more likely to appeal to women, and in any case are handier for working between plants.

Stainless steel blades are an expensive alternative to the usual carbon steel. Remaining rust-free and smooth, they reduce friction on heavy, sticky soil.

Whatever the metal, a turned-over tread prevents damage to footwear and is easier on the feet.

*Forks* Most of the comments made about spades apply also to digging and border forks, although these do not have treads. Forks made especially for potato lifting have broader flatter tines, but a digging fork does the job quite well.

*Rakes* A lightweight head with about a dozen teeth is a good choice for most average soils. Some of the best rakes have flattened, angular teeth, and handles of either plastic-coated aluminium or ash. The most expensive have stainless steel heads.

*Tined cultivators* Hook-tined cultivators are invaluable for loosening heavy soil that has become compacted and for inter-row cultivations on the vegetable plot.

They are less useful on light soil. Most are made with either three or five tines, some having removable tines so that the tool can be adjusted to suit different conditions.

*Dibber* This is a tool for vegetable growers. The firm planting needed by brassicas, such as cabbages, is best achieved by punching a hole with the point, inserting the plant and then pushing in the dibber again alongside to firm the soil against the stem.

Steel-tipped dibbers are the best, or you can fashion your own wooden dibber from the handle and shaft of a broken spade.

*Garden line* A strong line (nylon for preference) is needed for cutting a straight lawn edge, sowing and setting out vegetables or fruit bushes, erecting fencing, and so on. A wind-up spool makes for easier handling.

*Trowel and hand fork* A trowel is essential for planting seedlings and bulbs. A similar-size fork is handy, though less vital, for loosening the soil when weeding and tidying-up. Look for sturdy tools that will not bend.

*Hoes* The basic long-handled types are the Dutch hoe, which has a flat blade used with a pushing action, and the draw hoe, which is pulled backwards. Both are effective, but the draw hoe is liable to bury some of the weeds instead of exposing them to wilting. Several excellent patent hoes, such as the Swoe, derive from the Dutch hoe.

The short-handled onion hoe is useful for weeding close to plants and for thinning rows of seedlings.

## Tools for lawn care

*Edging knife* With its half-moon blade, this tool cuts a neat, vertical lawn edge. (A spade leaves a scalloped edge.) When cutting, use a garden line as a guide; or lay out a hosepipe to mark curves.

*Long-handled shears* There are two types. Edging shears, with blades set at right angles to the handles, are for trimming lawn edges; lawn shears, with blades aligned with the lawn surface, are for trimming grass in places where a

mower cannot be used. Hand shears will do both jobs, but at the cost of bending or crouching.

*Lawn rakes* Fan-shaped rakes with wire, plastic, bamboo or rubber teeth are ideal for collecting leaves and cut grass, or for scattering wormcasts. Wire or bamboo tines have a scarifying action and will loosen moss and dead grass. Plastic and rubber teeth do not penetrate so well but allow effortless collection of material.

*Aerators* One type has rows of steel spikes, mounted on a rotor, which penetrate the surface when the device is pushed along. For more drastic treatment, when a top-dressing of soil or compost is to be given, there are hollow-tine aerators which remove and collect plugs of turf.

## Tools for pruning and trimming

*Secateurs* There are two main types of secateurs, sometimes called pruners: those which have curved blades and cut with a scissor action, and straight-bladed types which have a single sharpened edge cutting against a flat anvil. Both are satisfactory provided that they are kept sharp, and easier to use than a pruning knife, the vital point being to buy a tool large enough for your needs. Excessive pressure on inadequate secateurs may damage the blades or joint. Do not attempt to cut stems of a thickness greater than your finger.

Flower-gathering secateurs have a springy grip to hold the cut blooms.

*Long-handled pruners* Loppers and long-handled pruners are, in effect, heavy-duty secateurs with extended handles for extra leverage. They are especially useful for disabled gardeners unable to grip one-handed secateurs.

*Pruning saws* Though secateurs will take care of routine pruning, a purpose-made pruning saw is needed for removing larger branches. A bow saw will do at a pinch, but is less convenient where other branches restrict working space. The blade of a pruning saw is usually curved, or set at an angle to the handle.

*Hedging shears* Many shears have blades about 22 cm (8½ in) long, but women may prefer lightweight shears with a 19 cm (7½ in) blade. Wavy-edged blades are designed to give an improved grip on the material being cut. Some shears have a pruning notch for cutting thick twigs.

*Hooks and scythes* Short-handled grass hooks, used with a wristy action, are useful for trimming overgrown banks and patches. Alternatively, there are several makes of miniature scythes and scythettes which perform the same function without the need to stoop. A vital accessory is a carborundum stone to keep the blade sharp.

## Equipment and machines

An abundance of mechanical gadgets does not necessarily make for an easier life, but there are certain basic aids, a barrow and a mower, for instance, that are virtually essential. To save pointless expense, take time to consider your real needs before selecting from the many makes and models available.

*Barrows* A single-wheel, galvanized steel barrow is still the best buy for most gardeners. Pay the extra for one with a pneumatic tyre and strengthened body if you plan to do constructional work involving heavy loads. Low-slung two-wheel barrows are easy to use and do not have to be lifted, but they are suitable only for fairly light work.

*Mowers* For cutting lawns, the choice lies between cylinder, rotary and air cushion types.

Cylinder mowers have curving, horizontal blades which shear the grass against a fixed bottom blade. This calls for careful adjustment. They give a close cut and, when mounted on rollers, leave the lawn with a striped finish. There are hand-pushed, electric and petrol models, with cutting widths about 30–60 cm (12–24 in).

Rotary lawn mowers have two or more high-speed blades revolving under a protective deck. They cut by slashing rather than shearing and do not need fine adjustment. Rotary mowers do not give quite such a close cut as cylinder mowers but will deal with longer, overgrown grass. There are both petrol and electric types, with cutting widths of 30 cm (12 in)

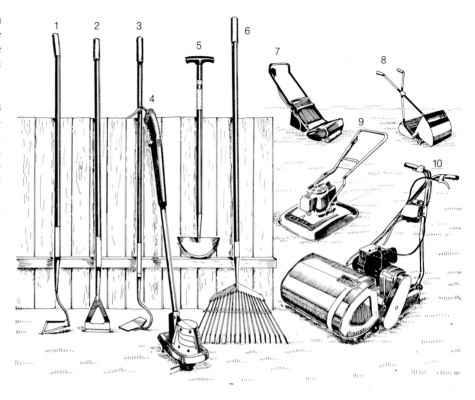

1 Swoe   2 Dutch hoe   3 Draw hoe   4 Nylon line-trimmer   5 Half-moon edger
6 Lawn rake   7 Electric cylinder mower   8 Hand cylinder mower
9 Hover mower   10 Petrol cylinder mower

upwards. Those mounted on rollers give a striped finish. On all but the smallest mowers, cut grass is blown into a collecting box.

Air cushion mowers work on the rotary principle, but support themselves on a downdraught of air instead of wheels or a roller. In addition to cutting lawns, they will deal with overgrown grass and will mow on slopes and beneath overhanging plants. Only one or two models collect the cut grass. There are petrol and electric versions.

For cutting really long grass and weeds there are more powerful and rugged rotary grass cutters, mostly petrol-driven, and heavy-duty air cushion mowers. If only occasional use is required you could consider hiring one.

*Nylon line-trimmers* Powered by an electric motor or a miniature petrol engine, twin nylon lines are whirled at high speed to cut grass and weeds right up to fencing, paving, tree trunks and other obstructions—places where no mower can reach.

*Sprayers* A hand-held, trigger-action sprayer holding perhaps half a litre (about 1 pint) is essential for controlling insect pests and fungus diseases on small groups of plants.

For large-scale applications (on potatoes or fruit trees, for instance) a pump-up pneumatic sprayer, holding up to 8 litres (14 pints) is needed. Alternatively, a continuous-action syringe, fed by a hose from a bucket, may be used.

*Watering equipment* Sprinkler hoses, sold in lengths of about 5 m (16½ ft) upwards, dispense a mist-like spray through dozens of perforations. They are ideal for use between rows of vegetables or along the edge of a border.

Spike-mounted sprinklers, which have no moving parts, cover a circular area, as do rotating sprinklers, which have a spinning head. Pulse sprinklers, too, have a circular action but throw the water further than rotating sprinklers.

Oscillating sprinklers cover a rectangular area, the size of which can be varied on some models.

# Soil Care

Very few of us have ideal soil, but it is almost always possible to improve it no matter what the problem. Good cultivation and the addition of suitable manures and fertilizers can do much to improve a poor soil.

Sandy soil sounds an attractive proposition. Although the top spit is certainly easy to dig, however, there is often a hard pan (layer) beneath it that can be extremely hard to penetrate. The real drawback of a sandy soil, though, is its lack of moisture-retaining capacity, and the fact that there is usually only a small reservoir of nutrients. The only real solution is to incorporate as much organic material into the soil as you can spare, and you will have to be prepared to feed and water generously when necessary.

Clay soils present the other extreme in workability, and with these it is well worth double-digging to improve drainage and incorporate humus into the bottom spit as well as the upper layers. Again the regular application of humus-forming materials will gradually improve the structure. Liming is another traditional way of improving a clay soil, but never add lime without checking the pH first (see p. 17).

## Digging

There are some gardeners who claim to achieve good results without digging, and the prospect of avoiding one of the most physically exhausting gardening chores is an attractive one. This type of cultivation, however, calls for a special approach and often cultural methods that vary from those described in this book. For most of us the reality is that some digging really is necessary, although, by incorporating plenty of humus, using mulches and avoiding soil compaction, much can be done to minimize it.

Old gardening books are full of advice on trenching and double-digging, but such energetic activities can be reserved for reclaiming new land or preparing for special crops that will benefit from the extra work involved. Most crops will grow perfectly well if only the top spit (spade depth) is turned over—this is usually known as single-digging.

*Trenching* This involves digging three spits deep. A dedicated exhibitor of sweet

Green manuring: rye grass and mustard

peas or runner beans may think it is worthwhile, but such earth-moving exercises are guaranteed to put the beginner off what is supposed to be a relaxing hobby, and perfectly satisfactory crops can be grown without recourse to such action.

*Double-digging* This is particularly useful for breaking up the bottom spit if a hard pan has formed, or if you want to incorporate compost into the bottom spit for deep-rooted plants. The drawing below illustrates the principle involved, but it is important to work in strips at least 60 cm (2 ft) wide, otherwise there will be insufficient room to manoeuvre in the bottom of the trench.

*Single-digging* This is straightforward, but you should always take out a small trench at one end first, placing the soil at the opposite end of the plot to fill in the last row—or if the plot is wide you can simply divide it into two halves as shown below, placing soil from the first trench to one side to fill in the last row.

## Manures and fertilizers

Soil is more than a mere inert anchor for plants: it is a provider of nutrients and moisture, and home to millions of insects and micro-organisms both beneficial and

harmful. It is a finely balanced biological world that needs tending. If the balance is upset the results can have a profound effect on the plants we grow. A strongly acid soil will suit camellias, but if you make it more alkaline, perhaps by adding lime, the same plants will become sickly and yellow. This same shift would improve the growth of your cabbages, however, and go a long way towards eliminating that plague of Brassica crops—clubroot—which simply does not like an alkaline soil. Other diseases, however, such as potato scab, will thrive in a neutral or slightly alkaline soil, yet almost cease to be a problem on an acid soil.

Too little nitrogen and growth will be stunted and the leaves pale (in brassica crops the lower leaves turn pinkish-orange instead of yellow). Too little phosphorus and the roots will grow poorly with leaves tinged purple or bronze. Not enough potassium and plants are likely to fruit poorly. Even those minerals known as trace elements, because they are normally required in minute quantities, can cause profound problems if there is a deficiency. Boron is required in only minute traces, yet if it is not there in sufficient quantity the consequences can vary from brown hearts in cauliflowers, and discoloured hearts in swedes and turnips, to deformed apples.

All the major and minor nutrients must be available to the plants in the right quantities, but the roots must also have air and moisture, and it is the *structure* of the soil that can mean the difference between good growth or poor growth. Although the structure of the soil is largely a matter of what you inherit, the bulky organic manures can do much to improve it.

*Bulky organic manures*  Manures do more than add nutrients (indeed these are often very low in comparison with straight fertilizers), they also improve the structure of the soil. Clay becomes easier to work, sandy soils become more moisture-retentive, and many of the organisms that contribute towards a fertile soil are encouraged.

Horse manure is excellent, and pig and farmyard manure (which may be a mixture) is also very good.

If fresh animal manure is not readily available it is worth considering spent hops (clean and pleasant to handle, if rather smelly, but often only available locally) or spent mushroom compost. Mushroom compost usually contains farmyard manure and plenty of straw, but as it is also likely to contain limestone do not use it on chalky soil or around acid-loving plants.

There is, of course, garden compost. This gives you an excellent opportunity to recycle a lot of waste material—but if the garden is large, supply may not keep up with demand.

If only a little compost or manure is available, it is best to concentrate it in a limited area so that you can really improve that bed, rather than spreading it too thinly with little noticeable benefit.

*Green manuring*  If you do not have enough organic material to improve soil structure, green manuring is one way of overcoming the problem for an open area of ground such as a vegetable plot. Green manure is a quick-maturing crop such as rape, mustard or annual lupins, or even rye grass, which is dug in before the flowers produce seeds and preferably before flowering. This introduces valuable organic material into the soil. With the exception of lupins and other leguminous crops whose roots are able to 'manufacture' nitrogen which will later be released, green manuring will not contribute much in the way of nutrients but it will provide humus, which will in turn help soil structure.

*The major nutrients*  The three essential plant nutrients, required in comparatively large amounts, are nitrogen, phosphorus and potassium. These are commonly abbreviated respectively as NPK (the chemical symbols for these elements).

*Nitrogen* (N) encourages leaf growth and gives the plant a lush appearance. A deficient plant will grow more slowly and have pale, yellowish leaves (although a shortage of iron or magnesium could produce similar leaf symptoms). Although plenty of nitrogen produces a lush-looking plant this is not always a good thing; too much can lead to few flowers and little fruit.

Nitrogenous fertilizers may be especially necessary on heavily cropped land deficient in decomposing organic matter. The cheapest and most widely available nitrogenous fertilizers are sulphate of ammonia, nitrate of soda, and Nitro-chalk. All these are inorganic and quite rapid in action. Organic sources such as dried blood and hoof-and-horn tend to be much more expensive, and hoof-and-horn releases the nitrogen more slowly over a longer period (which may be desirable).

Because leafy growth is undesirable in winter, nitrogen is usually used in spring, or as a booster during the growing season.

*Phosphorus* (P) (normally available as phosphate) encourages root growth, and deficient plants grow slowly, with the dull leaves taking on a greyish-bronze tinge. An overdose is unlikely but too much can affect the availability of other nutrients.

Phosphatic fertilizers are particularly useful for young plants, when a good root system is being built. The most widely available inorganic source of phosphates is superphosphate of lime (usually just called superphosphate). This contains a lot of readily soluble fertilizer which is soon available to the plants. Basic slag was once another popular source (it is a by-product of the steel industry), but this is slower acting and the analysis can vary, so you need to check this to know how much you are really paying for the actual fertilizer.

How to apply lime (*see* p. 17).

# Soil Care

The most popular organic phosphatic fertilizer is bonemeal. Here the fertilizer is released slowly over a long period, which makes it particularly useful when planting bulbs in autumn or when planting shrubs. A slow-acting fertilizer can also be especially useful for vegetables with a long growing season, such as Brussels sprouts and some of the winter cabbages.

Steamed bonemeal has the advantage of having been treated in such a way that there is less likelihood of contracting a disease such as anthrax or salmonella poisoning. Even so the risk is very small, but if it worries you make sure you wear a pair of gloves and wash your hands afterwards. Bonemeal also contains a small amount of nitrogen.

If you use a quick-acting type such as superphosphate, apply it close to the plants (but not touching); the fertilizer will also remain in a quick-acting form for longer if the pH is maintained in the region of 6.5–7.

*Potassium* (K) can be regarded as a counterbalance to nitrogen, producing tougher, hardier growth and being particularly useful in promoting the formation of flowers and fruit. A deficiency is not easy to identify as symptoms can vary, but a fairly positive sign is the edges of older leaves turning yellowish then bronze or greyish-brown. An excess of potassium can lead to a shortage of magnesium.

*The minor elements* Although it is the three major nutrients that have to be replenished most frequently, some soils show a deficiency in one or more of the minor or trace elements (so called because only a trace is required). Although trace elements should not normally be applied as a routine measure, a few of them may be required in abnormal circumstances, particularly magnesium and iron (calcium —lime—is dealt with separately).

Magnesium deficiency, which shows itself in the form of yellowish, mottled leaves with green veins, can be a problem on sandy soils (but remember that other problems can cause similar symptoms). This can be put right with Epsom salts (magnesium sulphate) applied at 35 g to 10 m² (1 oz to 10 sq yd).

Iron deficiency is most likely to show itself on very alkaline soil, although the leaves of many acid-loving plants soon turn yellow even in moderately limy soil. Often the problem is not a lack of iron in the soil but the fact that it has become 'locked up' by the lime and is unavailable to those plants; so simply applying sulphate of iron may not solve the problem. For this reason it is usually applied as chelated (or sequestered) iron in the form of 'iron sequestrene'.

Many foliar feeds contain trace elements, and this is a good way to give your plants a boost if you suspect a trace element deficiency.

*Buying fertilizers* All the fertilizers mentioned on this page are readily available from garden shops and centres, usually in small packs as the largest amount is usually applied as a compound or general fertilizer. Most of the products have a standard concentration of active ingredient and it is easy to compare value, but a few of them can vary significantly (in basic slag and bonemeal, for instance). You can easily work out which is the best buy if you calculate the unit price: simply divide the percentage of the active ingredient into the cost of the packet (assuming that they are of the same size).

You will have most need for individual fertilizers for special applications, perhaps giving a leafy crop such as cabbage a boost of nitrogen, or providing slow-release phosphorus throughout the winter and spring by giving autumn-planted bulbs a dressing of bonemeal. For the main fertilizer application, however, it is always best to use a balanced fertilizer that will provide all the major nutrients.

It is possible to buy fertilizers specially formulated for crops such as roses and chrysanthemums, but an all-purpose fertilizer will be adequate for most vegetables and flowers, and it is more sensible to buy a large quantity of an all-purpose fertilizer than smaller quantities of several kinds. The cost can be brought down considerably if you buy a quantity from a horticultural society. Sometimes it is possible to buy a sack of agricultural fertilizer from a merchant, and this can be a good buy if you remember that it is likely to be stronger and the application rate may differ.

It is best to buy a special lawn fertilizer, but be careful to apply one suitable for the season. Spring and summer lawn fertilizers have lots of nitrogen, but those

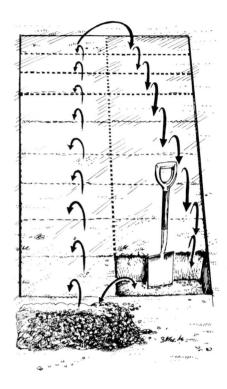

Single-digging

designed for autumn application should have the emphasis on phosphorus.

Mixing your own is a tempting idea, but it is a messy job and you are quite likely to end up with a surplus of some ingredients, which can increase the cost of usable fertilizer. If you do attempt your own recipes, do not mix lime or basic slag with sulphate of ammonia, Nitro-chalk or superphosphate.

Do not overlook liquid feeds, for lawns, flowers and vegetables. It is undoubtedly more trouble to keep mixing cans of fertilizer regularly, but the results can often be quick and dramatic, and can be invaluable for giving plants a quick boost in summer. The whole job is made easier if you use a feed that can be applied through a hose-end dilutor.

*Applying fertilizers* A few fertilizers, such as bonemeal and basic slag, and some lawn fertilizers, can be applied in autumn, but the majority of them should be applied during the growing season. If it does not rain a day or two after applying a lawn fertilizer, it is always worth watering it in. For other plants, it is important

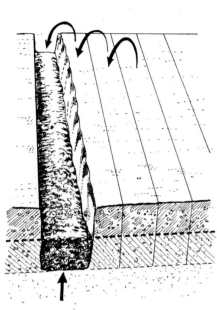

Double-digging.

Forking second spit.

not to get the fertilizer on the leaves, otherwise it might scorch them.

You can waste a lot of fertilizer by spreading it carelessly. The weeds may appreciate it but it will not do the plants much good if you spread it around on mainly bare soil rather than around the root area of the desirable plants. Where established plants are growing in rows, such as many vegetables, the most effective way is to sprinkle it either side of the row, close to the plants, and lightly hoe or hand-fork it in. For trees, shrubs and herbaceous plants, it is often most effective to sprinkle it around individual plants and hoe or water it in.

For lawns and an area being fertilized before planting or sowing, the difficulty is usually one of achieving an even spread. If you have a large area to fertilize regularly, a fertilizer spreader is a worthwhile investment, otherwise it is worth dividing the area up into 1 m (1 yd) strips, and applying only half the quantity first, making a second pass to make up the total amount. Ideally you should spread half in one way and the remaining half cross-ways.

*pH and its effect* The acidity or lime content of the soil can have an effect on plant growth as great as any of the major plant nutrients. Some soils are naturally acid or alkaline, and nature has adapted some plants to grow and thrive in one extreme or the other. Camellias, rhododendrons and many heathers are examples of plants that need a strongly acid soil; carnations are an instance of a plant that prefers neutral to alkaline conditions. If you give these plants a soil that is too alkaline or too acid they simply will not thrive.

The degree of acidity or alkalinity is measured on a pH scale, which ranges from 0 at the acid end to 14 at the most alkaline, with 7 as neutral. In horticulture few soils fall outside the range 5–8. Horticulturally 6.5–7 is considered neutral; the majority of plants grow satisfactorily within this range.

If your soil is too acid it is easy to put it right by adding lime, but an alkaline soil is more difficult to adjust.

The amount of lime you need to add will depend on the type of lime (hydrated lime per m² (10 oz and 7 oz per sq yd) will

you need less of it than ground limestone), and the type of soil (clay soils will need more than sandy soils), but as a guide 300 g of ground limestone or 200 g of hydrated lime per m² (10 oz and 7 oz per sq yd) will probably increase the pH by about one step.

It is best to apply lime in the autumn or after the soil has been dug during the winter, simply leaving it on the surface or hoeing it in. Do not apply it at the same time as other fertilizers or farmyard manure. If you use hydrated lime it is best to wear gloves and keep it away from eyes and mouth.

If you want to make your soil more acid, use as much peat as you can afford, and use acidic fertilizers such as sulphate of ammonia (but obviously not more than the plants need). For a more radical change, you can apply flowers of sulphur about 140 g per m² (5 oz per sq yd). Retest occasionally and apply more if necessary. To increase the acidity around ornamental plants aluminium sulphate can be useful, but it tends to be expensive for a large area, and it is poisonous.

### Testing your soil

You can have your soil analysed by a laboratory, but it is expensive, especially if you have a large garden and need a number of samples analysing. A laboratory test is accurate, however, and you will probably be told how to correct any deficiencies. Alternatively you can buy a kit and do it yourself.

Checking the pH is the easiest and most accurate of the tests you can do at home. The kits vary from indicator papers that change colour according to the acidity or alkalinity of the soil, to 'test tube' kits in which you add an indicator solution to a sample of soil (and sometimes something to settle the particles in the soil) and compare the resultant liquid against a colour chart.

Most of the pH kits are inexpensive and it is well worth buying one.

The kits that enable you to test for NPK (nitrogen, phosphorus, potassium) are also quite simple to use but not so dependably accurate in results. In the absence of a laboratory report, however, they are better than no guide at all. They work on the same principle of comparing a colour against a chart.

# Weed Control

The control of unwanted plants can be one of the most time-consuming jobs in the garden. However, if tackled in the right way, it can be reduced quite quickly to a minimum and then, with skilful planting and planning, there need be no weeds at all, unless you wish it.

A weed is sometimes defined, as far as gardeners are concerned, as a plant in the wrong place. The majority of weeds consist of such plants as dandelions, nettles, couch grass, chickweed and so on, nearly all of them native or wild plants. Occasionally a cultivated plant becomes a nuisance—bluebells, poppies or alstroemeria are examples. Weeds are usually strong vigorous plants which colonize the ground rapidly, all the while absorbing moisture and nutrient from the soil, and taking up space and light. Some act as hosts to pests or diseases, and provide shelter for small mammals. Few of them are considered ornamental or useful.

Against these drawbacks, it should be remembered that beneath a low cover of weeds the soil will remain moist for longer than when exposed to prolonged hot sun, and the leaves and stems provide good compost heap material. The roots penetrate to different levels of soil than those reached by garden plants, so that more of the useful mineral nutrients, or different ones which might otherwise remain an untapped source of food for many years, become available after decomposition in the compost heap.

Weeds can be roughly divided into two groups: annuals/biennials and perennials. The former reproduce largely by seed, and it is vital to destroy them before they flower. Some annuals are what is known as ephemeral, and these have the nasty habit of completing a life-cycle in six or eight weeks. This means that a plant germinating in April can die in June, and the seed from it germinate a few days later, to die down in its turn in August, to be followed by a third infestation before the autumn.

The perennials concentrate their survival capacity mainly on their roots. Some have extremely tenacious roots which spread widely beyond the crown of the plant; some have deeply penetrating or bulbous roots which have a large food reserve in the form of starch or other carbohydrates. Some have roots which are actually underground stems, capable of sprouting from buds all along their length. Practically all of them can regenerate from pieces of root broken off and left in the soil.

Some perennials increase by putting out long stems lying on the ground which root at all the leaf-joints, or which develop plantlets at the ends, to root in their turn.

One particularly pernicious weed, *Oxalis acetosella*, produces ten or more loosely attached bulbils round the top of its taproot, each of which will become a new plant. Its clover-like leaves appear in early summer, and its tiny bulbils are easily missed when weeding as they are soil-coloured.

Some perennial weeds hit below the belt by producing vast quantities of seed, as well as being tough-rooted, e.g. dandelion, dock and perennial nettle.

If you find you have a lot of a weed which remains small and has many fine, fibrous roots, it is likely to be an annual. The cheapest control method is hoeing with a Dutch hoe, when the weed is a seedling, with only two tiny seed leaves and perhaps one true leaf just developing. The blade of the hoe will cut it in half, and lift its roots into the air, and if this is done every week, weather permitting, it is quick and easy, and can virtually eliminate a species within one growing-season. The vegetable garden, flower borders and rock gardens are places where this kind of weed is most likely to appear.

Smothering by mulching is a good control, and in fact a preventive, if the mulch is put down on to clean, moist soil; for shrubs and flower borders, processed bark is an excellent and good-looking cover which lasts two or three years.

If the annuals have grown large, because of circumstances beyond your control, the chemical weed-killing mixture of paraquat and diquat can be called into use. These two chemicals affect the chlorophyll of plants so that it is no longer manufactured and the plants die rapidly, turning yellow within a few days. A solution is sprayed or trickled on to the leaves and stems of the weeds but, because of the way it works, will have no effect on the roots of cultivated plants. Hence surplus solution dripping into the soil will not be damaging; it is only necessary to prevent it contaminating the leaves of garden plants. It also follows that planting or sowing can take place within a few days of application. Although paraquat and diaquat will affect perennial weeds, they will not completely kill them.

Perennials can be treated in the same way as annuals while they are small, but where they are established will need more forceful methods. Digging rather than hoeing is the best cultural method, when complete root removal is necessary. Mulching will only be effective if all the top growth of the weed is completely covered and all light completely excluded, but this may mean an unacceptably thick mulch.

If time does not permit thorough digging and fallowing alternately for a season, chemical control is the only answer. Weedkillers for perennials must necessarily be extremely phytotoxic, and so must always be used with great care.

There are two sorts: those for leaf absorption, and those for root absorption. Into the first category come glyphosate, ioxynil, and the group containing the hormone chemicals, 2,4-D, 2,4,5-T, MCPA, dalapon, mecoprop (CIPC), fenoprop and dichlorprop. Glyphosate is the most recently produced, and is mostly applied in dilution as a spray. It works within a week or two, and areas treated with it can be planted or sown as soon as the weeds are dead. Most perennial weeds are killed by one application; a few need a second. Even such a previously chemically-immune weed as oxalis is vulnerable; perennial nettle appears at present to be the most difficult to eradicate with glyphosate, and several applications are necessary.

Ioxynil is a specialist chemical for speedwell control on lawns, without harming the grass; it is also applied to kill weed seedlings germinating with grass seed in a newly-sown lawn.

The hormone weedkillers have an effectiveness of the order of parts per million; the various chemicals encourage the cells of the growing tips of stems and roots to multiply many times more rapidly than usual. The familiar distortion and curling of leaves, stems and flowers is followed by blackening and death of the plant. MCPA, 2,4-D and 2,4,5-T are general hormones affecting a good many broad-leaved weeds; dalapon deals with couch and other grasses. Mecoprop, fenoprop or dichlorprop are useful for clover and other small-leaved

Red Clover

White Bindweed

Dandelion

Couch Grass

Horsetail

Groundsel

Daisy

Hairy Bittercress

Shepherd's Purse

Annual Nettle

lawn weeds. 2,4-T and 2,4,5-D combined are suitable for woody plants (saplings, brambles, ivy and bushes) and are contained in the so-called brushwood killers.

The root absorption chemicals include sodium chlorate (a potent total weed-killer), simazine, dichlobenil and propachlor. All are applied to the soil, the first two in solution, the last-named dry, as powders or granules. They will damage all plants whose roots absorb them, so mostly have to be restricted to paths, drives or areas which are to be cleaned before planting. The only one that can be used close to cultivated plants is propachlor—this kills weed seeds as they germinate, but is not strong enough to kill the plants specified in the directions on the container. Dichlobenil remains effective for four to eight months, sodium chlorate for at least six, and simazine for twelve months. Simazine also has the advantage that it does not move sideways in the soil, whereas sodium chlorate is likely to do so. Use this last-named weedkiller only in exceptional circumstances where complete soil clearance is desirable. Obtain a type treated with a fire depressant, for ordinarily the crystals are highly inflammable.

A quick method of removing surface weed cover is to burn it off with a flame gun. This will also kill some weed seeds in the top couple of inches of the soil and destroy some roots, but is not a complete control.

Lawnsand, which contains sulphate of ammonia and iron, is primarily for use on moss and certain weeds of lawns. Its action is to blacken and burn leaves and stems, and it is useful for the more obstinate lawn weeds, such as pearlwort, yarrow and other small-leaved species. It also acts as a nitrogenous fertilizer for the grass.

There are various methods of applying weedkillers, many similar to those used for pesticides. Watering-cans with fine roses or trickle-bars fitted are quite satisfactory. Hand sprayers, knapsack sprayers and wheeled devices can be obtained; foaming aerosols are useful for spot weeding. Glyphosate is formulated as a gel as well as a wettable powder and can be applied to individual weeds with a brush. The lawn herbicides are often combined with a fertilizer; there is a wax bar impregnated with hormone chemicals also for use as a touch-weeder on lawns.

# Pests, Diseases and Disorders

Blackfly.

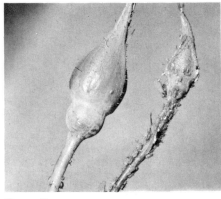

Greenfly.

Capsid bug.

## Pests

*Aphids: Greenfly and Blackfly* Greenfly and blackfly are also known as aphids; blackfly are very partial to broad bean plants and some other vegetables. Greenfly are liable to infest any plant, usually feeding on the shoots above ground level, although there are those that attack the stem at ground level and the roots. At certain times of the year the small insect produces wings so that it can fly away to other plants to feed and reproduce itself so that other colonies establish. Aphids suck sap from plants causing stunting and twisting of the young shoots; much of the sugary sap taken from the plant is not required by the aphid and is passed through the body and deposited on the leaves as a sticky substance called honeydew. This deposit attracts black sooty moulds to grow on the plant, and although the sooty mould is not harmful in itself it does make the plant look unsightly, it cuts out light and is difficult to remove from edible crops. Another reason why aphids should be avoided is that they transmit virus diseases from plant to plant. Several insecticides including malathion and gamma-HCH will control aphids; pirimicarb kills aphids without harming beneficial insects.

*Capsid Bug* Another pest that sucks sap is the capsid bug, often called the bishop bug because the shape of its body resembles a bishop's mitre. When the capsid punctures the plant tissue to remove the sap it causes malformed growth: in the case of flowering plants, like the chrysanthemum, the flower bud becomes lopsided and more often than not the petals do not mature properly on one side of the flower. The leaves may also be mal-

formed with brown constrictions. Tree fruits like apples and pears are among other plants that are attacked by capsid; in their case the skin of the fruit has roundish raised pimples. Capsid bugs are controlled with fenitrothion, rotenone (derris), or pirimiphos-methyl.

*Sawfly* Rose leaves rolling downwards are a sign that they could be under attack by the leaf-rolling sawfly maggot. The symptoms appear in spring when the new leaves are growing, and quite often two or three leaves of the shoot grow away satisfactorily and then for no apparent reason the next ones curl downwards. The adult sawfly lays eggs on the rose leaf, and when they hatch the small maggots, which are hardly large enough to be seen with the naked eye, feed on the leaf. The female injects a chemical at egg-laying time which causes the leaf to roll downwards. This benefits the maggot because it is then protected from heavy April showers that may wash it from the plant. What is required here is an insecticide that will pass through the leaf to reach the pest below: systemic insecticides such as dimethoate, and pirimiphos-methyl are both effective.

*Woolly Aphid* Fruit trees and others and frequently hedgerows of beech are sometimes invaded by woolly aphid. Small areas of white fluffy wax can be seen on the twigs. In addition to reducing the vigour of the plant, the feeding punctures made by the pests allow diseases like canker to enter the tree. The woolly aphid is well protected by its waxy coat and it is essential to spray the plant thoroughly. Malathion or pirimiphos-

methyl are satisfactory and spraying the trees during the dormant season with a tar oil winter wash is recommended.

*Mealy Bug* Waxy marks on leaves and stem of houseplants usually indicate the presence of mealy bug, a pest that is often confused with woolly aphid. An aerosol of pirimiphos-methyl and synergized pyrethrius is usually most convenient to use in the home.

*Scale Insects* Scale insects resemble minute tortoises and the majority of them have a very tough protective shell which resists many liquid insecticides. The pest sometimes attaches itself to the flat part of a leaf so that it may be removed with a fingernail; more usually it is inclined to find shelter in the area where the leaf grows away from the stem. Scale insects will soon weaken a plant by sucking out its sap and the plants should be treated with pirimiphos-methyl, malathion or a systemic such as dimethoate.

*Red Spider Mite* One of the problems we face as gardeners is that over a period of time some pests build up a resistance to some pesticides. This may come about by applying understrength sprays or perhaps by using the same type of insecticide for a number of years. The red spider mite is a good example of a pest that has become resistant to many chemicals that are available. This is most unfortunate because the mite establishes itself very quickly, especially during the spring and summer months. Most types of plants are attacked including tomatoes and others in the greenhouse and home, fruit and flowers. The mites themselves are very

# Pests, Diseases and Disorders

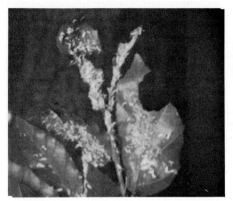

Whitefly.

Leaf miner.

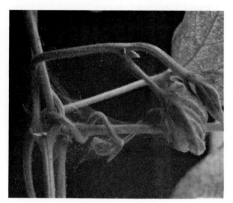

Red spider mite.

small, although they can be seen with the aid of a magnifying glass crawling on the underside of the leaves. The symptoms to look for are silvery dots on the leaf. These dots eventually join up and cover the complete leaf which turns silvery bronze and eventually dies. When the mites become established, they form a web that covers the leaves and shoots of the plant and that makes it even more difficult to control the pest because the webbing acts like an umbrella. The fruit tree red spider mite overwinters in the egg stage and can be seen in clusters on the twigs. Greenhouse red spider mites hibernate in crevices from the end of September until more favourable conditions prevail in March or April the following year. One type of greenhouse red spider mite remains active during the winter months, feeding on the sap of plants like carnation, chrysanthemum and some pot plants. Control can be difficult and thorough repeated spraying with rotenone, pirimiphos-methyl, or malathion is recommended. A predatory mite called *Phytoseiulus persimilis* can be used to control red spider mites in the greenhouse. This method of biological control can be successful in spring and summer, provided that the predators are introduced properly and the correct temperature is maintained.

*Whitefly* Until recently, the whitefly was considered to be the number one pest, especially on plants growing under cover. It still is a formidable pest when allowed to become established. Plants become covered with sticky honeydew and sooty mould; when the leaf of a plant is touched, a cloud of small white flies rises to land on other plants nearby.

Permethrin is very effective in controlling whitefly and it has the advantage that crops can be picked and eaten the same day as spraying. Permethrin with heptenophos is another new insecticide which is efficient, although there is a time lag between application and eating the crop. Biological control is sometimes used in the greenhouse and a number of chalcid wasps feed on whiteflies. The wasp used, mainly by commercial growers, is *Encarsia formosa*. Again, as with the red spider predator, introduction and environmental control is important.

*Other pests* All of the pests dealt with so far live by sucking the plant's sap; the pest is small and does not move very fast, if at all once it has become attached to the plant. Other pests obtain their food by eating holes in the plant, and these pests are usually much larger.

Caterpillars cause considerable damage to a wide range of plants by eating holes in the leaves, stems, flowers and fruit. Vine weevil adults eat parts of the leaves of some pot plants and shrubs: the damage usually takes the form of notched holes around the outside of the leaf. The vine weevil maggot attacks the roots of pot plants (particularly cyclamen) and others too. Serrated edges of broad bean leaves is a sure sign that the pea and bean weevil has been active, especially during mild spells in winter and spring. Cockchafer grubs can do a considerable amount of damage to shrubs and other plants by feeding on the roots; the adult is like a large beetle and eats leaves when it is active during the summer. Woodlice can be very destructive particularly where young seedlings are concerned and they will also feed on leaves of larger plants.

These chewing pests are generally easier to control than the sap suckers; they are easier to detect so that remedial action can often be taken sooner. Prevention is accomplished by spraying or dusting the plant just before the pest is active; for example with permethrin or gamma-HCH when the apple sawfly and gooseberry sawfly is on the wing in spring time, and treating brassica plants with rotenone or permethrin in late summer when cabbage white butterflies and moths are searching for egg-laying sites.

*Ground pests* Several garden pests spend a good deal of their time in the ground. Ants disturb roots and cause plants to wilt and die, and they bring soil to the surface of the lawn, making mowing difficult and causing bare patches. Borax or sodium tetraborate ant baits are good control measures. Moles tend to do much the same sort of damage as ants but on a larger scale. Trapping is a sure way of disposal, provided that the trap is set in a main communicating run, and mole smokes are available. Various other methods are often suggested, such as planting caper spurge (*Euphorbia lathrus*), or placing strips of rag soaked in eucalyptus oil in the run under mole hills and pushing moth balls into the soil. If you are surrounded by farmland you will, sadly, have to live with the problem of moles.

Leatherjackets are dirty grey creatures like caterpillars without legs. They feed on grass roots causing yellow patches on the lawn, and birds usually announce them by tearing at the turf. Gamma-HCH or pirimiphos-methyl dusts may be used to control leatherjackets. These are useful against other soil-borne pests.

# Pests, Diseases and Disorders

Mildew on marrow leaves.

Peach leaf curl.

Black spot on rose leaves.

## Diseases

Plant diseases can be very destructive by killing the host outright, or at least by feeding on the plant and causing weak, spindly growth. Sometimes the disease causes unsightly spots on the leaves and stem, at other times attacking other parts of the plant. When a disease attacks the root system of a plant the whole plant is affected because water and plant foods are taken up less easily, if at all. Infected stems restrict the movement of moisture and plant foods up into the plant. When leaves are attacked they cannot function properly to take in daylight, exchange air or keep the plant cool by transpiration.

Conditions favourable to the disease are necessary for it to establish and survive. For example, continual wet weather during summer provides the ideal conditions for potato blight to attack the leaves and stems of the crop and, if the disease is not checked, then tubers will also be attacked and rot. Here we have a combination of dampness and temperature leading to high humidity, and the same conditions often occur in the greenhouse where insufficient ventilation is given: when tomatoes are grown, potato blight can be a problem as can other diseases like leafmould and grey mould. Grey mould is a good example of a disease that can gain entry through a wound caused by careless handling of the plant, or perhaps by insect damage.

Irregular watering and allowing the roots to go dry, or too much water causing a check to growth that way, can cause plants to be put under stress and make them more susceptible to disease attack. Mildew can often be avoided by keeping those plants growing in containers or in the greenhouse uniformly moist, so that they are never too wet or too dry; garden plants should be watered as necessary and a layer of bulky organic material such as garden compost, peat or composted bark placed on top of the soil around the root zone will help to retain moisture during dry periods and it will also suppress weeds that compete with crop plants for available soil moisture and nutrients.

Some plant diseases like plants themselves have a preference for an acid soil: club-root which attacks the cabbage family is a good example. Part of the answer in that case is to apply lime to the soil, although such diseases often require other remedies in the form of fungicidal dressings and crop rotation too. The soil can in some cases be too chalky and scab on potato tubers is always more of a problem in alkaline soils compared with more acid conditions.

One cause of disease attack usually overlooked is the lack of plant food in the soil. Lawns in sandy areas are prone to a disease which causes the grass to turn brown; on close examination the leaf will be seen to have a red cotton-like thread growing from it. The red thread disease is aggravated by low nitrogen level and one or two applications of high nitrogen lawn food during the growing season will help to correct the problem.

We have seen some of the reasons for diseases gaining entry into the plant, but how do they get there in the first place? The vast majority of diseases produce minute dust-like spores and they are really like the seeds of a plant. The spores are often air-borne and carried by the wind; they can be carried by insects or other animals from plant to plant and soil clinging to footwear can carry disease spores too. One of the most common sources of infection so far as the greenhouse and other plants growing in containers is concerned is water taken from a rainwater butt or water left in the can from one application to another. When soft rainwater is essential, as in the case of the azalea pot-plant, it is most important to keep the water butt clean and provide a lid.

Dirty seed trays, pots and other containers should be avoided because they often harbour diseases carried over from the previous plants growing in them, or they may have been contaminated in the mean time. The growing medium itself may be a source of infection and that can often be avoided by using John Innes composts or proprietary peat-based potting composts rather than soil taken from the garden. In the open garden itself, plant crops should be rotated so that the same type of plant is not growing on the same site too frequently; details of crop rotation are given in the vegetable section on page 48.

Prevention is far more effective than control so far as plant diseases are concerned. The reason for this is that once the symptoms can be seen, the problem is already inside the plant tissue and harm has been done; having said that, there is no reason why precautions should not be taken even at that late stage to stop the disease from spreading. Certain diseases that attack fruit trees and roses have an overwintering stage that stays on the plant or on the ground below, during the dormant winter period. This is fortunate because strong sprays like tar oil washes can be applied then, whereas their application during the growing season would damage the leaves and buds of the plant.

*Grey Mould* The most common disease attacking plants above soil level is called grey mould (botrytis) and the common name is a good description of what it looks like on the plant: grey fluffy patches appear on leaves, stems, fruit or flowers. Grey mould gains entry through a wound made by careless handling, for example by leaving tomato sideshoots too long before removing them so that a large wound is made that does not heal quickly; insects cause damage by puncturing the skin of the plant, again allowing the dust-like spores to settle and germinate. Plants that remain wet for too long will be prone to the disease because the skin becomes soft and loses its resistance. In addition to avoiding damage to the plant and controlling pests, atmospheric conditions in the greenhouse can be improved by providing more ventilation and by giving some heat where it is available. Plants can also be protected by using a fungicide like benomyl; tecnazene smokes are convenient to use in the greenhouse and have the added advantage that they do not increase the atmospheric humidity.

*Mildews* Various mildews attack a wide range of plants from those growing in pots in the home to roses, apples and many others outside. Leaves and shoots look as if they have been dusted with a fine white powder, and mildew can attack fruit as well. Trees and bushes that are affected may be pruned so that the diseased shoot is cut away. This should be done in the winter when the twigs will show the characteristic silvering. Tar oil winter wash should be sprayed over the fruit trees and bushes when they are dormant in winter, followed by fungicide sprays

like bupirimate with triforine or dinocap when the leaves appear.

*Leaf spots* Leaf spots appear in various shapes, sizes and colours. Those attacking plants late in the season just before leaf fall do not cause much harm, because the leaf has more or less finished its work. A cold wet spring or summer can lead to early infection and some areas are prone to certain leaf spot diseases every year. In these cases it is worth applying a preventive spray so far as rose black spot and apple scab are concerned and the same materials as suggested for mildew above give good control. In addition to spraying, infected leaves should be gathered as they fall from the plant and burned.

*Damping-off Diseases* Damping-off diseases cause small plants and seedlings to rot off at soil level. These problems are usually associated with using dirty containers, over-thick sowing and planting in unsterilized soil; irrigation water may also be contaminated and there is a very good case for using only mains water for that purpose. Seedlings should be watered with a solution of Cheshunt Compound (copper sulphate and ammonium carbonate), a liquid copper fungicide or tecnazene smokes can be used in the greenhouse.

*Rust* Yellow spots on the top of the leaf with blisters below usually indicate the presence of a rust disease: the malady was given its common name because of the colour of the spores that come from the pustule. The majority of rusts are very difficult to control, especially those that attack roses and pelargoniums. Bupirimate with triforine has given some measure of control in some areas against rose rust and it is active against the rust attacking blackcurrants. Mancozeb and Liquid Copper Fungicides will also control some of the rust diseases.

*Root diseases* Diseases attacking the root can cripple the plant in a short space of time. Foot rot of plants growing in containers should be treated in the same way as those precautions taken for damping-off, above. Greenhouse border soil may be treated with a tar oil formulation or the plants may be grown in beds isolated from the infected soil below. This is easily done

Grey mould on strawberry.

Rust on hollyhock leaves.

Pear rot.

# Pests, Diseases and Disorders

when growing bags are used and they can be purchased from garden centres and stores. Alternatively, isolated beds can be made by removing some of the soil to form a shallow trench, placing a sheet of polythene in the trench, then filling with sterilized loam or fertilized peat. Plants growing out of doors and attacked by foot rot should be treated with Cheshunt Compound or copper; in the case of trees and shrubs, the problem is more difficult. Long black strands like bootlaces attached to the roots of an ailing shrub or tree indicate that the plant is infected with honey fungus and the plant should be removed with roots and soil and burned; there is a formulation of tar oil which the manufacturers recommend for the control of honey fungus.

Fungicides, as with insecticides, can be obtained as liquids, granules or powders to be mixed with water and sprayed onto the plants or soil. Smoke cones are convenient for use in the greenhouse and puffer packs containing dust to puff onto plants is also another convenient method. It is most important to read the manufacturer's label on the container before using the product.

## Disorders

There are occasions when plants begin to go wrong for no obvious reason; no pests or diseases can be seen and yet perhaps the leaves are crinkling up or the fruit is growing into an odd shape. Disorders of that nature could be caused by cultural discrepancies or abnormal weather conditions: certainly frost at strawberry blossom time will damage part of the young fruit causing malformed growth, and in severe frost the young fruitlet will be killed. This can happen to other fruits, including tomatoes, and the condition is often called 'cat face' due to the strange markings. Overwintering lettuce plants are often affected by low temperature and the leaves pucker and thicken; plants usually grow away as the weather improves, although they do appear to be more susceptible to mildew disease.

Rose leaf rolling sawfly will cause downward rolling of the leaves and the period of attack often overlaps with the time of year when warm days can be

Magnesium deficiency in raspberry.

followed by cold nights. The irregular growth pattern causes the leaves to roll downwards; usually the problem resolves itself as the nights become warmer and the shoots produce normal leaves. Blind shoots in roses can be caused by low temperatures too, especially when associated with wind. In fact cold winds are responsible for a number of problems, including brown edges to the leaves of a wide range of plants; pear leaves and shoots are particularly prone to wind damage. It is not only seaside areas that are vulnerable to salt spray damage. There are cases where salt has been carried by strong winds 35 miles inland, still in sufficient quantity to cause damage to sensitive plants. The symptoms of salt spray damage show as brown markings on the leaf and corky areas on the skin of fruit. Before leaving cold temperatures, however, we should remember that it is really asking too much for seeds to germinate in temperatures that are not high enough; in some cases, for example with beetroot, the young plants may grow and then run to seed prematurely without forming a root crop. Beetroot varieties resistant to the low temperature problem include 'Avonearly' and 'Boltardy'.

Although some plants are encouraged to flower earlier, others like chrysanthemums and poinsettias find it difficult to produce flower buds when the temperature is too low. Chrysanthemum

Effect of sooty mould on tomatoes.

enthusiasts will know that a period of low temperature is important for the stock plants to produce proper shoots for cuttings; otherwise the shoots remain stunted. Numerous seeds require a period of freezing temperature before they will germinate at all. On the other hand, very high temperature brings its problems too, especially when combined with strong sun.

The majority of plants growing under glass look for some form of protection from strong sunlight. Brown crumpled leaves are usually a sign that the plant has had too much sun, especially if the roots have been allowed to dry out and insufficient moisture has been available to keep the leaves turgid. Considerable quantities of water are taken up by plants during sunny weather and it is interesting that a mature tomato plant uses up to 2 litres (3½ pints) during a very bright day in summer. Fruit like the grape and tomato that is growing in a greenhouse is inclined to scald when it is too near the glass: soft skin goes brown, and in the case of tomatoes some varieties are susceptible to produce hard green skin around the shoulders, a disorder known as 'greenback'.

Weather conditions prevailing in the open can produce some unusual features. Perhaps the tree struck by lightning is not so extraordinary; the same problem can strike sprout plants and others causing

# Pests, Diseases and Disorders

Frost damage to potato.

Sun scorch through glass.

brown marks down the stem and on the leaves. Hailstorms can tear leaves to shreds and many summers bring forth the odd storm strong enough to cause brown spotting of leaves and fruit; the latter may easily be confused with scab or a disorder known as 'bitter pit' of apples. This is a condition where the flesh just below the skin has brown marks and it is associated with dry soil conditions around the root and too much nitrogen. Calcium deficiency is also thought to be associated with the problem. Trees should be kept watered in dry weather and an application of lime around the root zone would not come amiss if the soil is at all acid.

Bud drop in many plants can be traced

Wind damage to *Choisya ternata*.

back to dryness at the root when the buds were being established. This could be some months before, as with the camellia whose buds are initiated during the July before flowering in the following spring. Plants growing in containers and the greenhouse border like figs and peaches fall into the same category: the young fruits will drop if the soil becomes too dry around the root. Other reasons for bud drop include poor light due to overcast sky or overcrowding as in the case of tomatoes grown inside; that plant will also drop buds when the atmosphere is too dry and runner beans shed flowers for the same reason. Alternatively, when the atmosphere is too moist, especially when the night is cold and the root wet, plants show their disagreement in a number of ways: pelargoniums produce small swellings under the leaves, a form of oedema; tomato fruits are inclined to crack for the same reason.

The cost of fuel for heating has encouraged many of us with a greenhouse to put up insulating material such as polythene. Considerable savings can be made, although it is important not to cover the ventilators: plants require a change of air for many reasons, not least of which is to let fumes from the heater escape. Severe scorching can be caused to plants subjected to the build-up of sulphur fumes given off by paraffin heaters. Leaves and young shoots of plants can be twisted by

carbon monoxide due to insufficient combustion of the fuel because of a lack of ventilation.

Oxygen is also required by the roots of plants. The disorder known as 'black heart' in some root crops, and wilting of plants in general, is often caused by insufficient oxygen at the root. Overwatering is often the real problem here, or possibly the ground is poorly drained and subject to flooding.

Plant disorders associated with a lack of certain plant foods show in a variety of ways: nitrogen deficiency produces smaller leaves which are often pale or yellow. Yellow leaves can be caused by a lack of magnesium and in that case the veins remain green. When the young leaves at the top of the plant only are yellow, the plant is most likely suffering from a deficiency of manganese or iron. This can be rectified by an application of sequestrene and it is usually a sign that the soil is too chalky. Boron is another plant food required in very small quantities and is usually only lacking when the plant is growing in the same loamless compost for a considerable time, or again if the soil is too alkaline. Symptoms vary from plant to plant but usually the leaves are brittle and snap easily, tomato fruits have a rough corky skin and carnation plants produce a large number of shoots from around the leaf joint. Complete plant foods including trace elements contain boron, but should a separate application be made one teaspoon of borax watered in over an area of 1 m² (1 sq yd) would be sufficient.

Phosphate is required by plants in large quantities; a deficiency causes stunted growth with dull greyish coloured leaves in most plants. Potash is another major plant food, required for general health, flower and fruit development, and a lack of potash usually takes the form of leaf margins going yellow and then brown. This is followed by the production of smaller fruit with less flavour. The flowers are smaller with less intense colour and the plant takes longer to produce its flowers — an important point when we are aiming for a special occasion.

Generally, most of the disorders that occur in cultivated plants can be avoided by careful growing and consideration of the plants' needs (*see* Soil Care).

# Lawns

Lawns of one sort or another have been part of the British way of life for many hundreds of years. The slender-bladed close-mown turf is delightful to see in early morning dew, and acts as the foil to house and flower beds and borders. At home in the open, or in shade, on light or heavy soils and in both wet and dry situations, the grass family is exceedingly large and most versatile, but gardeners have selected for lawns a relatively small number of grasses to meet their general needs.

The percentages are chiefly governed by the actual number of seeds per kg, since these vary considerably. Surprisingly, the mixture just suggested will do quite well on a variety of soil types, but should give best results when used on sands, gravels and loams. For mixtures for other soil types, see the table opposite.

## Creating the lawn

Having selected the most suitable species, there are basically two methods of making

Effect of selective weedkiller.

*Some useful lawn grasses*

| Botanical Name | Common Name | Mode of growth |
|---|---|---|
| Agrostis tenuis | Browntop, common bent | Rhizomes and stolons* |
| Festuca rubra rubra | Creeping red fescue | Rhizomes |
| Festuca rubra commutata | Chewings fescue | Tufted |
| Festuca tenuifolia | Fine-leaved sheep's fescue | Tufted |
| Poa pratensis | Smooth-stalked meadow grass | Rhizomes |
| Poa trivialis | Rough-stalked meadow grass | Sparse stolons |
| Poa nemoralis | Wood meadow grass | Tufted |
| Phleum pratense | Timothy | Tufted |
| Cynosurus cristatus | Crested dogstail | Tufted |
| Lolium perenne | Perennial rye grass | Tufted |

*Rhizomes—underground stems; stolons—surface rooting stems

Although the actual choice of creeping grasses is limited you can indeed have a lawn of only one grass species, the fescues, and yet still have both creeping and tufted sorts. This is important, for these are the true needle-like grasses with very narrow inrolled leaves which produce the finest turf. Many of the best lawn mixtures are made up of selected varieties of the following sorts.

| 20% (by weight) | Agrostis tenuis |
|---|---|
| 40% | Festuca rubra rubra |
| 40% | Festuca rubra commutata |

the lawn of our choice: laying ready-made turf, or sowing the correct grass seed mixture. Each method of covering the surface will demand a similar programme of site preparation. There really is no short-cut to the beautiful, lasting lawn, but all the effort is so rewarding when you have done the job properly and can sit back after mowing and really *enjoy* the view.

To have a fair chance of success, the grasses used in lawn turf formation need not less than 10 cm (4 in) depth of *fertile* topsoil, and preferably 15 cm (6 in), since they are capable of producing roots to

this depth. A stunted root system will lead to a sparse sward of grass and invites nature to fill in the gaps with the natural flora.

*Site preparation* Seldom is there a perfectly clean, level, weed-free site, and there are usually relatively large stones, pieces of rock and even perhaps builder's debris on or near the surface. The debris must be removed, as must all stones over 2.5 cm (1 in) in diameter (leave the smaller ones to assist drainage), and, of course, all vegetable matter, roots, rhizomes and such-like. It will mean a lot of raking and forking to clear the site; indeed if weeds and/or coarse grasses are numerous it may be necessary to use the appropriate chemical treatment well in advance of sowing.

If you are to be successful with ready-made turf, this should be laid when the grasses are making natural root growth (autumn, winter and early spring), so the site should be prepared during the previous spring and summer. Where seed is to be sown this can be done during spring, summer and autumn. For a spring sowing the ground should be basically prepared in the previous autumn, and for an autumn sowing in the previous spring.

Having disposed of weeds, plant roots, debris and stones, the site must be levelled, so that there will be no humps or hollows, and mowing will not result in scalping on the high spots and unmown grass in the depressions. Ascertain the average depth of topsoil (the darker coloured layer) and endeavour to finish

| For clay soil | *Agrostis tenuis* (browntop, common bent), *Festuca* spp (fescues), *Poa* spp (meadow grass) and *Lolium* (rye grass) |
|---|---|
| For peaty soil | *Phleum pratense* (timothy), *Poa trivialis* (rough-stalked meadow grass), *Lolium perenne* (perennial rye grass), *Festuca* spp (fescues) and *Agrostis tenuis* (browntop, common bent) |
| For chalky soil | *Cynosurus cristatus* (crested dogstail) |
| For sandy soil | *Poa pratensis* (smooth-stalked meadow grass) |
| For shade | *Agrostis tenuis* (browntop, common bent), *Festuca rubra rubra* and *F.r. commutata* (creeping red and chewings fescue), *Festuca tenuifolia* (fine-leaved sheep's fescue), *Poa trivialis* and *P. nemoralis* (rough-stalked and wood meadow grass) and *Lolium perenne* (perennial rye grass) |

the levelling with an even depth of topsoil over-all. This may involve stripping and stacking the topsoil whilst you carry out major levelling on the subsoil (usually paler in colour). When such levelling is complete and the surface has been firmed the topsoil may be replaced evenly over the area. This too will need firming and the best result will be obtained by treading with a rocking motion (heel and toe) in one direction over the area and raking at right angles, carrying out both operations alternately in changing directions until the surface is firm enough to leave only the imprint of heel and toe when walked over. The fine grasses need a firm surface.

Spread a good balanced pre-seeding (or turfing) lawn fertilizer at the recommended rate (usually 100–140 g per m²; 3–4 oz per square yard) and gently rake this in. Wait a few days and then you are ready either to lay purchased turf or to sow a grass seed mixture.

*Turf* Good quality turf is relatively expensive and it is pointless to use anything but this for a really good lawn whether it is purely for show or for the children to play on. Turf should be laid rather like the bricks in a wall, the pieces being pressed firmly side by side. When all of the turf is laid give the area a light dressing of finely sieved soil or compost and brush this in to fill the cracks. Finish the job with a light crosswise rolling.

*Seed* Sowing is decidedly less expensive than using good quality turf, and you can indeed choose the grasses to be used, and be sure of a lawn of those sorts only. The work is less laborious in that you merely have to sow the seed evenly at from 30 to 60 g per m² (1–2 oz per square yard). Best results are achieved when half the seed is sown in one direction and the rest at a right angle to it. Lightly cross-wise rake it into the top 6 mm ($\frac{1}{4}$ in) and then crosswise roll to complete the job. Seed that has been treated with a substance repellent to birds is available and should be used in preference to other types. As an extra precaution, however, it is wise to have some bird scarers as well.

A lawn turfed in late autumn or winter should root satisfactorily by the following late spring/early summer and take a reasonable amount of traffic. A seeded lawn completed in early autumn should similarly be ready for use by the following late spring/early summer. A spring-sown lawn given proper treatment can well be in use by the following autumn.

## Care of the lawn

Whether you have laid or sown your own lawn, or simply inherited an established one, it is important that you care for it properly. If the lawn is regarded as an outdoor carpet composed of millions of individual grass plants growing in very close proximity, the need for frequent attention will be appreciated. Each plant must have adequate moisture and food throughout the year. In addition, like most other subjects in the garden, grasses are susceptible to both pests and diseases, and these account for most of the discolorations which occur.

A well-kept lawn is a fine feature.

# Lawns

*Mowing* Depending upon the local climatic conditions, grasses normally make leaf growth from early spring until late autumn. Any mowing programme must take the seasons into account in regard to the amount of foliage you remove. Leaves are essential and sufficient foliage must be left to allow the plants to breathe, take in carbon, give off moisture and process food throughout the year.

The finer grasses give of their best when mown no closer than 13 mm ($\frac{1}{2}$ inch from the surface, but with care can be cut down to 6 mm ($\frac{1}{4}$ in) during the summer, although it is not usual for ordinary garden lawns to be mown closer than 13 mm. Regularity in mowing is essential; never allow the grasses to grow 'long' and then shave them down to the surface. Mow once or twice a week from spring to autumn. Start the mowing year by *gradually* reducing the height of cut-down to 13 mm ($\frac{1}{2}$ in) by late spring.

The box on the mower should be attached at all times to catch the grass cuttings, except when the weather is very dry, when a layer of cuttings left on the lawn will help to retain moisture.

The lawn can be mown in strips in order to give the well-known striped effect, but the direction of the stripes should be changed at each mowing to run at 90° to the previous line of direction, so that ridges do not form.

*Levelling and trimming* Bumps and hollows can be eradicated by removing the offending piece of turf (using a half-moon edger and a turfing spade), placing it upside down in a wooden box and either removing excess soil with a scythe blade or adding soil as appropriate. The turf can then be replaced in the lawn. Alternatively, make several cuts in the lawn and peel back the turf on each side of the bump or hollow. Soil can then be removed or added as required, and the turf folded back.

Straight edges to the lawn can easily be achieved by laying a plank along the desired line and trimming with a half-moon edger along the plank. Thereafter the edges should be trimmed with a pair of long-handled shears.

*Watering and feeding* Grasses take much of their nourishment in liquid form and when the lawn loses colour during

Levelling the ground in preparation.

drought it is suffering from starvation as well as thirst. Use an efficient sprinkler and apply the water in the early morning or late evening and give not less than 5.5 litres per m² (approximately 1 gallon per sq yd).

It is simple to make the grass *look* green by using quick-release nitrogen, but this does not supply the other essential plant foods: phosphorus and potash. Apply a properly balanced lawn fertilizer in the spring to provide a gradual supply of food.

Many excellent lawn fertilizers are on the market both for spring and autumn use; the latter will encourage healthy root development. You should encourage foliar development in spring and summer and the grass plant should make new roots during autumn and winter. The density of the sward will depend upon the amount of root development the plants have made.

Top-dressing with well-rotted garden compost is most beneficial and assists in the rooting down of stolons and keeps the surface healthy. This is a spring or autumn job and the material should be spread at about 1.5 kg per m² (3 lb per sq yd) and worked in with the back of a rake.

*Rolling and aeration* Lawns seldom require rolling. After heavy frosts the turf may 'lift' and resettling can be effected by *light* cross-wise rolling before the first mowing in spring. Heavy rolling is both unnecessary and harmful.

Over-consolidation from traffic can have an adverse effect on both grass and soil life and structure. To compensate for

Treading in the topsoil.

this, aeration is necessary in spring or autumn. One method of aerating involves raking and scarifying to remove any surplus leaves or other unwanted matter, and then spiking or slitting the surface of the lawn with a garden fork or a small spiker. This also serves to improve drainage after a wet spell. In autumn, a light top-dressing should be applied after aerating.

The mosses will soon colonize lawns in need of aeration, and although proprietary dressings will destroy these unwanted growths the condition of surface or soil must also be improved to prevent future colonization.

*Scarification* This operation involves the raking of the lawn very vigorously in order to remove dead grass and mosses and to scatter wormcasts. A wire lawn rake is used first one way across the lawn and then at right angles. This is usually done in spring or autumn to improve the aeration of the turf, and to prevent the spread of fungal diseases.

*Weed control*   In a healthy sward of grass there is little opportunity for weed invasion. There are a number of natural agencies which are responsible for carrying weed seeds from place to place and weed control becomes necessary even in the best-kept turf. Many weeds are easily controlled by the artificial hormones which we call selective weedkillers, but these must always be used with care.

Rolling after the seed has been sown.

These are growth-regulating substances and must be used when weeds and grasses are actively growing. Such work should be done from spring to early autumn, avoiding periods of drought or heavy rain. Selective weedkillers are easily applied in solution by watering-can or sprayer, but one must avoid spray drift on to surrounding beds, or borders. Some are embodied in weed-and-feed lawn fertilizers in a dry form, but need rainfall or irrigation to become effective.

Weed grasses such as *Poa annua* (annual meadow grass), the grass which actually produces flowers and seed heads even under very close mowing, and *Holcus lanatus* (yorkshire fog grass), with wide leaves of pale green colour and hairy surfaces, are more difficult to control than dandelions, buttercups, plantains and such-like. Once established it is

exceedingly difficult to eliminate annual meadow grass, whereas yorkshire fog can be removed as single plants and colonies can be cut out and replaced with sound turf. (*See also* pp. 18–19.)

*Worm control*   The earthworm is regarded as the gardener's friend, and these creatures are indeed natural aerating machines. They can prove a nuisance, however, when their activities are evident in lawns. There are many species of earthwork and most never come to the surface. Some do, however, and leave their casts—small heaps of fine soil on the grass sward. Such casts are unsightly and messy and when flattened by feet or mowers can be harmful to the turf. When dry they should be carefully removed by brushing.

There are a number of excellent proprietary worm killers which can be applied if wormcasts are too numerous to be swept off regularly, and the best time for carrying out treatment is spring or autumn when the creatures are working near the surface.

*Pests*   The root zone of many lawns is the nursery for soil-inhabiting creatures, especially the grubs of various flies. Their larvae have a staple diet of grass root and a high population of grubs can consume the entire root system in a few months, causing death of the plants. Patches of dying grass in early summer are often traceable to the activities of grubs during the previous autumn and winter and the culprits have either moved on to 'pastures new', or pupated according to their life cycles.

The crane fly or daddy longlegs (*Tipula* spp) is on the wing in late summer or early autumn and deposits its very numerous eggs just below the grass foliage. The eggs are very fertile and hatch into greyish/brown legless grubs with enormous appetites. These creatures have a 12-month cycle and treatment in autumn with suitable insecticides is necessary if damage to the turf is to be prevented. Evidence of past occupation by these creatures can be found in the form of their pupae cases protruding through the surface in the summer or autumn which accounts for their common name of 'leatherjackets'.

Members of the chafer beetle family in

the grub stage can prove harmful to the turf, since they will feed upon the roots. The larvae have creamy white, soft bodies and lie in a curved position. The grubs have large brown heads and they have six legs on the front segment of the body. Some species remain in the soil for only about eight months and others for up to three years. Chafers go further down than leatherjackets and are, therefore, difficult to control. (*See also* pp. 20–21.)

*Diseases*   Small circular patches of collapsed foliage of a brownish colour are indicative of *Fusarium nivale*, a fungal disease which kills the affected turf. Certain types of fungus mycelium develop around the edges of the affected patches and serve to spread the infection. It is usually called fusarium patch. Outbreaks are often induced by stimulatory dressings of quick-release nitrogen too late in the season. To control an attack use the appropriate turf fungicide as soon as possible after diagnosis.

Grass seedlings are susceptible to 'damping-off', especially when wet weather follows germination. A number of soil organisms are responsible, and some may attack before there is any visible sign of plant growth, often when the seedlings are 25–50 mm (1–2 in) high. The seedlings turn red or yellow in colour and collapse. These diseases spread very rapidly, so urgent spraying with a fungicide is necessary. (*See also* pp. 22–23.)

*Fairy rings and puff-balls*   These are usually in the form of whole or part circles where the grass grows lush and toadstools or small puff-balls develop around them. The rings are caused by the activities of fungi within the soil releasing soluble nitrogen, and the fungi do not actually attack the grasses. Fairy rings become larger each year and barish areas develop inside the stimulated zone. The very dry soil in the bare ring will be permeated with white 'threads' of the fungus and will have a musty smell. The only effective answer is to cut out the whole ring including at least a 30 cm (12 in) band outside the area which the mycelium will already have penetrated. Make sure no white threads remain, introduce fresh soil and re-turf or resow.

The excavated area should be sterilized before the new soil is introduced.

# Pruning and Training

Everyone wants to make the most of their trees and shrubs and this means doing more than just planting them and then leaving them to get on with it. They need training and pruning to give them an attractive shape, to keep them in good health and to ensure that they flower and crop well.

The object of all training and pruning is to encourage the plant to make the best of itself. Correct training in the early stages will ensure good long-term prospects, but pruning, sometimes twice a year, will inspire success each year.

Careful pruning increases the size and numbers of flowers and fruits, encourages attractive foliage and stems, keeps plants healthy and disease-free and enables you to create the size and shape of plant that you would like.

There is some pruning which must be done every year to all woody plants, but especially shrubs and fruit bushes. The first thing is to remove all dead wood. Dead twigs and branches harbour pests and diseases which can spread to healthy growth and badly damage the plant. Cut dead wood out every spring, pruning back to healthy, live wood if possible. Anything that is obviously diseased should be removed at the same time.

On all except weak plants which you are trying to nurture back to strength, cut out feeble, spindly growth as well. This is usually unproductive and susceptible to disease. The final thing to do is to remove all rubbing and crossing branches.

The type of growth that a plant makes will influence exactly what and how much you remove. A mature hypericum, if not pruned hard, will have a large number of thin shoots coming from near the base. In this case the removal of an occasional older piece to encourage new younger shoots is helpful, though thinning the shoots out is pointless. With roses, however, it is easy to spot the spindly shoots that will not flower and cut them out, together with those that rub or cross.

## Shrubs

When you buy shrubs from a nursery or garden centre they should have been trained to a good shape by the nurseryman—if they are very uneven or straggly, do not buy them. Slightly imbalanced plants can be evened up by cutting one or two shoots back to buds facing into the space that needs filling, and leggy ones can be shortened generally to encourage them to bush out. The best plan, though, is to try and buy well-shaped plants in the first place.

Shrubs fall into two main types. There are those that flower on shoots made earlier the same year—the summer flowering ones such as buddleia, caryopteris and hypericum—and there are those which flower on shoots which have grown the year before. Forsythia, winter jasmine and flowering currant, flowering in spring, are well-known examples.

Those in the first group are best pruned just as they are starting into growth in spring. Cut them fairly hard leaving just a few buds at the base of the previous year's shoots. Do not cut into older wood unless really necessary. The basal buds will then grow out strongly and produce large attractive flowers later in the year.

Shrubs flowering on shoots which grow during the previous year need a different treatment. If pruned in spring most of the shoots bearing flower buds will be cut off. The answer is to wait until the flowers are over and then cut out as many as possible of the shoots which have carried flowers. This will leave plenty of space for new shoots to grow.

There is also a much smaller group, the most familiar of which is chaenomeles, also known as japonica or cydonia. Those in this group produce flowers on the same short, stubby shoots, called spurs, year after year; apples flower and fruit in the same way. The best way to encourage spurs and to get the most flowers from them is to shorten new growth in summer and then to cut back the resulting side shoots in winter. Chaenomeles is usually grown trained on a wall, in which case any shoots growing towards or straight outwards from the wall will have to be removed.

Pruning lavender after flowering.

Clematis can sometimes be confusing as the varieties are split between the first two of these general groups. Those in the first group, which flower in summer on growth made the same year, include varieties such as 'Hagley Hybrid', 'Ville de Lyon' and *C. x jackmanii*. Prune these in late winter by cutting back all the stems to 23 cm (9 in). As a refinement and to ensure that flowers are spread over as great a height as possible, cut the stems to a range of heights between 23 cm (9 in) and 90 cm (3 ft).

Spring varieties that flower on shoots which have grown the previous year include 'Nelly Moser', 'The President', *C. montana* and *C. macropetala*. These are best left unpruned, but as some are rather vigorous they may need to be restricted. Immediately after flowering cut out all those shoots which have carried flowers and spread out the remaining ones to cover the required area. If drastic reduction is needed, the plant can be cut back hard in spring in the same way as summer flowering varieties but one season's flowers will be lost.

*Roses* Of all the shrubs, roses respond best of all to regular pruning. If planting in winter cut the tops back to about 23 cm (9 in), and trim the roots of bare root plants if they are over-long or damaged. In spring cut back hybrid tea varieties such as 'Peace', 'Grandpa Dixon', 'Fragrant Cloud' and 'Alec's Red' to 2–4 buds and floribundas like 'Iceberg', 'Evelyn Fison', 'City of Leeds' and 'Elizabeth of Glamis' to 3–5 buds.

In following years cut out all dead, diseased and crossing shoots and then cut back hybrid teas to 4–6 buds and floribundas to 6–8 buds. Weaker shoots that must be retained can be cut harder, and as the plants get older remove the occasional old branch at the base to stimulate vigorous new growth. This pruning is best done in spring as growth begins, but roses are best cut down by about half in autumn to prevent winter winds rocking the roots. Standard roses are pruned according to their type but are usually cut a little harder.

Climbing roses should be trimmed lightly on planting and the shoots, there should be three or four, trained evenly over the area to be covered. Keep these shoots, with their extension growth, as

Dead-heading roses to encourage flowering.

long as possible, pruning laterals back to three buds every spring. In later years remove an older branch near the base every so often to stimulate fresh new growth.

Ramblers are rather different. They produce strong shoots from the base during the season and flowers form on these the following year. Tie them in loosely as they grow. Pruning consists simply of removing the long shoots low down after flowering and tying in the new shoots in their place. If few new shoots appear, retain some of the old ones and prune the laterals to three buds.

Container-grown roses can be planted at any time and are sometimes even planted in flower. There is no need to trim the roots and if you are planting in winter or early spring the plants should be already pruned. If not, prune them in the same way as bare root plants. Summer planted roses need no pruning till autumn.

An important aspect of rose care is dead-heading. The removal of old flowers as they fall to pieces encourages a further crop of new flowers and so should not be overlooked. Cut off each individual flower as necessary, and then when the whole head is finished cut it off just above the first full leaf below.

# Pruning and Training

Those shrubs grown for their winter stems, cornus and some species of salix, are best pruned in early spring. Cut them down to within a few inches of the ground. This will encourage the strong growth from the base that has the best stem colour. For foliage plants like variegated privet spring pruning is again the best bet as this will stimulate the finest foliage during the following year.

Careful watch must be kept on variegated plants in case they revert—that is, throw up plain green shoots. It is vital that these be removed as soon as possible as they will be more vigorous than the rest of the plant and tend to swamp it.

Pruning has quite an influence on the size of plants. The old saying that growth follows the knife has a lot of truth in it: the more you cut the more growth will be stimulated. Plants are best reduced in size not by vigorous hacking, or by cutting back hard all over leaving a bun-like shape, but by removing the longest branches at a point within the bulk of the plant. This will ensure that the plant retains its natural shape.

## Fruit

Fruit pruning is a little more complicated as the various fruits all need different treatments.

Summer-fruiting *raspberries* are pruned immediately after the fruit is picked by cutting out at ground level all those canes which produced fruit and tying in new canes for fruiting the following year. In spring these canes are tipped back to just above the top wire. Autumn fruiting varieties like 'Zeva' and 'September' are cut down completely to about 7.5 cm (3 in) in early spring.

*Blackberries* are treated in a similar way although the method is adapted to cope with the extra vigour. While the plants are flowering and fruiting strong new growth will be coming through, and unless this is controlled the result will be a tangled mess. The best solution is to train all the growth in one year to the left-hand side of the support system, and while this is fruiting train all the new growth to the right-hand side. After picking the fruit all the shoots on that side are cut back and the others left for the following year.

*Blackcurrants* are cut back to about 7.5 cm (3 in) on planting in winter. The following spring remove the weakest shoots leaving the others well spaced around the plant. These will fruit that year. In following years between a quarter and a third of the old wood is cut out at the base at any time when the plant is dormant. This older wood is easily recognized as it is dark in colour whereas young shoots are straw-coloured. Also make sure to pick off any 'big buds' infected with gall mite, or if most of the shoot is affected cut it out altogether.

*Gooseberries* should be cut back by about half on planting then six evenly spaced shoots selected and these cut by half the following winter. All other shoots are cut to 7.5 cm (3 in).

Continue in this way—leaders by half and laterals to 7.5 cm at the end of each winter. For extra good crops pinch out the top third of all shoots in July. Some varieties tend towards a drooping habit and to counteract this it is a good idea to reverse the normal procedure and cut to an inward- or upward-facing bud. Upright types can be cut to an outward facing bud as normal.

Many *apples* are now grown as dwarf trees on single stems known as cordons (*see* p. 54). Cordon trees are best bought ready trained. Pruning is basically a matter of cutting back laterals to four or five leaves in August while shoots growing from old laterals can be shortened to 3 leaves.

Bush trees of *apples* and *pears* will need some training. If you start with a tree with just one shoot cut it back to 60 cm (2 ft) on planting. The following winter cut the new shoots back by half and remove any weak ones crowding stronger growths. Carry on in this way in following years but also prune lateral shoots to three buds; leaders can be cut less severely as the years go by. The result will be a dwarf tree of manageable proportions.

A few varieties will not respond well to this type of pruning as they bear their fruit at the tips of the previous year's shoots. 'Bramley Seedling' and 'Worcester Pearmain' apples are the commonest varieties of this type. They tend to make large trees, and the simplest way of dealing with them is to thin out the whole tree removing crowded and crossing branches and aiming for an open-centred tree with an even distribution of branches.

too ragged

not near enough to bud

cut should slope away from bud

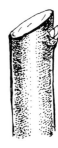

correct

# Pruning and Training

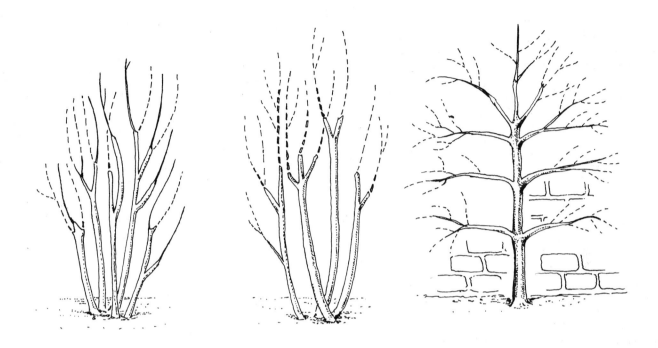

Shrub pruning. Left: early-flowering type, for example forsythia - remove year-old shoots after flowering in spring. Centre: summer blooming on new growth, for example buddleia - cut down all flowered shoots to older wood in spring. Right: wall-trained flowering shrubs - shorten laterals back to main branches after flowering.

An old neglected tree which needs rejuvenating is sometimes inherited. After removing all the dead wood and weak, diseased, crossing and rubbing branches your tree will look very different. It will still probably be crowded. Start by removing some of the central branches to leave it more open. Take out one or two each year as low down as possible and when the centre is well opened up thin the outer branches as well. The fruiting spurs may be crowded and unproductive too so these can be thinned out by up to half over two or three years.

When it comes to *plums* there is a bit of a risk. The disease silver leaf enters through the pruning cuts and can be very serious. The solution is to prune the tree in spring, removing as little as possible and to do what must be done when the tree can heal quickly. This helps to keep out the spores. So remove any dead, diseased and crossing branches by mid-July

at the latest. For larger trees that will suffice but smaller trees and those trained on walls can have laterals cut back to about 7.5 cm (3 in) in July and the resulting shoots cut back again after the fruit is picked. Morello cherries can be treated in the same way.

*Sweet cherries* are best grown against a wall where it is easy to contain them. The basis of pruning is to pinch back new growth to five leaves in summer and then in winter further to shorten the shoots to three buds.

The actual technique of making a pruning cut is important. Always cut just above a bud with a slightly slanting cut running away from the bud. Do not leave a long snag as this may rot and infect the rest of the shoot. Always cut above an outward facing bud so that the centre of the plant does not get too tangled.

Remove larger branches in stages. First

make a cut one third of the way through the branch from underneath about a foot from the main stem. Now cut right through the branch a little nearer the main stem leaving a short stump. Lastly cut the stump off flush with the main stem. This method avoids any possibility of the bark tearing.

After pruning, all wounds over 13 mm ($\frac{1}{2}$ in) should be painted with a wound paint. Remove all prunings and burn them and fork over any ground that has been trampled.

Do not forget that plants pruned regularly will need regular feeding too. The best way to do this is to apply a mulch each spring when the ground is moist. Use well rotted compost or manure if possible though it is usually more convenient to use a general fertilizer such as John Innes Base for shrubs. There are many feeds on the market designed for use on specific varieties of tree.

# Bedding Plants

There are two seasons in the year when bedding plants are used: summer and spring. Most bedding plants are usually annuals, i.e. plants that grow from seed, produce their flowers and leaves and die in one growing season. They may be classified as hardy, in which case they can be sown in the positions where they are to flower, or half-hardy, which means they will need to be sown and kept as seedlings in protected conditions, such as a greenhouse, and then hardened off before being planted out when all danger of frost is over. There are very many hardy and half-hardy annuals listed in seed catalogues.

Other plants for bedding include hardy biennials, which are raised from seed one year in order to flower the next, before they die, such as cheiranthus (wallflower), some dianthus (sweet williams), myosotis (forget-me-nots), digitalis (foxgloves), lunaria (honesty), some campanulas (Canterbury bells), polyanthus, primrose, and some papavers (poppies); half-hardy perennials, like many chrysanthemums, pelargoniums (geraniums), some begonias, impatiens (busy lizzie) petunias, antirrhinums (snapdragons), nemesia and ageratum (a number of these plants are treated as annuals as they do not flower well a second time) and bulbous subjects, for example dahlias and tuberous begonias (which are both half-hardy), as well as the ever popular tulips, daffodils, crocus, hyacinths and muscari (grape hyacinths), which are hardy but often used in spring bedding schemes and moved to another part of the garden when not in flower.

## How best to use summer bedding plants and hardy annuals

Both are ideal for giving a mass of summer colour, especially in a new garden where there has not been time for permanent planting. They can be grown in beds and borders on their own, and magnificent displays and designs created by a little forethought and planning. Equally, they can be used most effectively as 'fillers' to give colour where there are gaps among trees, shrubs and herbaceous plants. They are excellent for containers, window-boxes, tubs, hanging baskets and such like, where areas near the house require colour or a focal point is to be created in a

special part of the garden. Taller types can even be used for temporary hedging and screening purposes, and rows of them in a spare corner of the garden can be used purely for cutting for indoor flower decorations. There is even a group of annuals called 'everlastings' (e.g. helichrysums, helipterum, moluccella, limoniums and some grasses), whose flower spikes can be dried and used for indoor arrangements in winter.

## Use of spring bedding plants

Spring bedding plants fulfil many of the same purposes as do summer ones, and can be planted to give colourful displays from winter until late spring. Unfortunately, however, there is nothing like the same range of plants from which to choose and most frequently seen are combinations of daffodils, narcissi, tulips, wallflowers, forget-me-nots, polyanthus and small bulbous subjects for edging the beds. Nevertheless, careful choice of varieties will make a colourful addition to any garden, especially if visible from the house windows during wintry days.

A point to remember is that the biennial types are destroyed after flowering, but that the bulbous plants, in particular, should be dug up carefully and planted elsewhere in the garden, either for re-planting again in the autumn where they are to flower or for naturalizing, in which case new bulbs are purchased for the next spring bedding scheme.

Spring bedding schemes are created in late autumn, and the plants usually lifted during the following May to allow the soil to be prepared for summer plants.

## Buying plants and seeds

Whenever possible raise your own bedding plants and hardy annuals from seed. Not only is the choice of varieties far greater than with plants available from retail outlets, but it is cheaper if any great quantity of plants is required. Half-hardy annuals and perennials will need raising from seed sown in heated conditions, usually between January and April, March being the most common month. In order to save heating costs, do not sow too early. Equally, half-hardy plants such as dahlias, fuchsias, abutilons, canna lilies and pelargoniums will require over-

wintering in heat sufficient to prevent frost. (Most bedding dahlias and many pelargoniums are now seed-raised.)

Before any of these half-hardy plants are set out for summer bedding, they must be hardened off thoroughly. This means gradually lowering temperatures until the pots and boxes are placed in a cold house or frame, and finally in a sheltered position in the open. Planting out at the end of May is usually quite early enough, except in the most sheltered parts of the country where mid-May is possible.

If half-hardy bedding plants are to be purchased, do not buy them too soon before planting time, even though they may be on sale in April for summer bedding. Choose only healthy looking plants: those that are sturdy, a good green colour, do not have too much root showing through the containers, and are not smothered in flowers already. If no flowers are showing or you do not know the colour of the varieties you are buying, ask your supplier, otherwise your colour scheme could go badly awry.

Hardy annual seeds are usually sown in April in the positions in which they are to flower. Biennials are sown in summer for transplanting later the same year or late spring the following year.

## Preparing the ground for sowing and planting

Fork the areas where seeds are to be sown or plants are to be set out to a depth of about 10 cm (4 in), adding well-rotted garden compost and a general-purpose fertilizer at the manufacturer's recommended rate at the same time. Tread the soil firmly by shuffling the feet over the dug area, then rake it in several directions to break down any lumps, remove large stones, and to create a fine surface. If the soil is dry, sprinkle it with water thoroughly at least 24 hours before sowing or planting.

## Planning planting schemes

As a general rule, set the tallest plants at the back of the border, or in the centre of an island bed, and gradually reduce height with the lowest plants forming the edging. Alternatively, the bulk of the plants can all be of approximately the

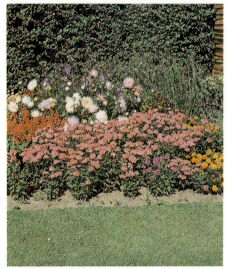

A bed of hardy annuals.

Assorted pansies for spring colour.

Summer bedding plants in full bloom.

same height, though still with low-growing edging ones to give a neat finish, with tall-growing 'dot' plants, e.g. abutilons, cannas, standard fuchsias and kochias, set at intervals to catch the eye and give a raised effect and added interest.

Colour schemes are very much a matter of personal taste; some people like harmonizing effects, others prefer contrasts. It is certainly worth mixing the types of plants, however, to give additional interest in shape and form, e.g. spiky antirrhinums and penstemons contrast well with bushy *Cineraria maritima* or compact growing begonias and marigolds.

## Sowing hardy annuals and biennials

Having prepared the areas for sowing seeds of hardy annuals where they are to flower, mark out with a stick irregular areas where each batch of seed is to be sown. Scatter the seed very thinly and lightly rake it in. Label each area. Alternatively, make shallow drills and sow the seeds thinly in these and lightly cover with soil; this method makes for easier weeding. When the seedlings are about 2.5 cm (1 in) high, thin them to the recommended distance and firm the soil disturbed by thinning.

Biennial seeds, or those hardy annuals which can be sown in the autumn of one year to flower the next, are sown similarly in rows in an area of the garden reserved for the purpose, generally a seed bed. Space the rows about 15 cm (6 in) apart.

When large enough to handle, move the young plants to a nursery bed, prepared like the seed bed, and space them 15 cm (6 in) apart each way. Keep them weeded and watered as necessary until required for planting in their flowering positions.

## Setting out plants

Before setting out young plants, ensure that their root balls are moist. If not, water the nursery beds and containers 24 hours in advance of planting. Start planting at the back of a border or centre of a bed, setting the plants according to your previously designed plan. Place the plants at the recommended distance apart and use a trowel to make a hole of the correct depth to take the roots without cramping them. Firm in the young plants with the fingers or handle of the trowel. When all planting has taken place, lightly hoe the bed to remove feet marks. Do not overcrowd the plants and do not set them out when the soil is very wet or very dry. After planting, turn on a sprinkler to settle the plants thoroughly into their new soil. Repeat as necessary until they are growing away strongly.

*Selection of half-hardy annuals and perennials for summer bedding*
Ageratum, amaranthus (love-lies-bleeding), antirrhinum, aster, begonia (fibrous and tuberous-rooted), celosia (cock's comb), *Cineraria maritima* (silver leaves), cosmos, dahlia (bedding type), dianthus (pinks), heliotrope, impatiens (busy lizzie), kochia, lobelia, marigold (African, French and Afro-French), mesembryanthemum, nemesia, nicotiana (tobacco plant), pansy, pelargonium (geranium), penstemon, petunia, *Phlox drummondii*, rudbeckia (annual coneflower), *Salvia splendens*, stocks, tagetes (dwarf marigolds), verbena and zinnia.

Dot plants include: abutilon, canna, fuchsia standards, phormium and taller-growing bedding plants, e.g. antirrhinum, kochia and penstemon.

*Selection of hardy annuals for direct sowing*
Alyssum, bartonia, calendula (pot marigold), *Chrysanthemum carnatum* (syn. *C. tricolor*), clarkia, delphinium (larkspur), eschscholzia (Californian poppy), godetia, helianthus (sunflower), iberis (candytuft), lavatera (mallow), linaria (toadflax), linum (flax), lychnis (campion), mignonette, nasturtium, nigella (love-in-a-mist), papaver (poppy), scabious, sweet peas (dwarf types) and Virginian stock.

*Some biennials for summer bedding*
Bellis (daisy), campanula (Canterbury bell), dianthus (sweet william), digitalis (foxglove), lunaria (honesty) and some papaver (poppy).

*Selection of spring bedding plants*
Cheiranthus (wallflower, biennial), crocus, hyacinth, muscari (grape hyacinth), myosotis (forget-me-not, biennial), narcissus (daffodils and narcissi), polyanthus (biennial), primrose (biennial) and tulip (early and mid-season types).

# Buying Seeds and Plants

There are two ways of buying seeds and plants. You can study catalogues and order the seeds or plants to come by post, or you can buy them in a garden shop or garden centre.

## Seeds

Seeds nowadays are no problem. The large seed houses supply good quality seeds, whether by mail order or in garden shops. If they did not, they would soon be out of business, so fierce is the competition. Another safeguard for the customer is the legal requirement that for the most important vegetable seeds the percentage of germination must be above a prescribed minimum.

Of course with seeds of some of the more unusual plants, shrubs, trees and alpines for example, germination may be problematical, but usually this is due to unfavourable conditions at harvest time resulting in premature loss of viability which the seedsman could not be expected to foresee. Also some seeds, mostly of alpines, need a long period of cold weather before they will germinate. Keeping such seeds in the domestic refrigerator for two or three weeks will often hasten germination (but they do not usually tell you this on the packet!).

## Plants

The firms that still issue tree, shrub, bulb, hardy plant and other catalogues are almost all highly reliable. Would that the same could be said of some of the firms that advertise amazing bargains in the national press—and sometimes regrettably in the technical periodicals. Ideally you should be able to see the plants you are going to buy, either in the nursery or in a garden centre. There are many excellent garden centres but there are also those where the quality of the plants leaves much to be desired.

Here are some points to look for if you go to a garden centre. Check that the plants look 'happy', that is that the foliage is uniformly of good colour throughout a given batch of plants, and that there are no dead branches, discoloured, or spotted leaves. If the soil on top of the containers is covered with moss or weeds and if the plants look starved, as they probably will be, leave them alone. They have been in

the container too long.

Another point to consider is the question of the difference between container-grown plants and 'containerized' plants. A container-grown plant has been in its container, a plastic pot of some kind, for several months and has already made a good mass of roots. A 'containerized' plant has been put into the container quite recently and has had no time to make an adequate root system, and therefore should be avoided.

A good garden centre will have someone available to advise about the plants on sale. The labels should give information about the ultimate height of a plant and maybe about its tolerance or otherwise of acid or alkaline soil. If in a garden centre this information is not provided on the labels, and if you are attracted by a plant but know nothing about its height and spread or soil requirements, ask to speak to the proprietor. If he cannot give you the answers, leave the plant alone until you have been able to look it up in a good gardening book.

It seems that so-called 'bare-root' plants, trees and shrubs lifted from the open nursery and wrapped in hessian or plastic, are becoming more popular again. (Do not confuse these with 'balled'

plants—plants with a ball of soil wrapped in hessian or plastic.) These plants are fine if you can pick them up at the nursery or garden centre or if they are delivered swiftly. Indeed it may be that with some plants these will be better specimens than you might be offered in containers.

Beware of the practice in shops and garden centres of offering tender plants far too early in the spring. We see tomatoes, cucumbers, marrows, petunias, geraniums, zinnias, salvias, dahlias, ageratums and other plants which are killed by frost on sale even as early as the end of March or the beginning of April. This is all right if you have a heated greenhouse in which to grow them on, but it is not safe to plant out tender plants in the south of England until the last week of May, or the second week of June in the north and in Scotland.

As with plants in containers, look for bedding or vegetable plants that are sturdy, of good rich green colour, and not 'drawn' or spindly. All these plants planted later when the soil has warmed up and the nights are warm will catch up and surpass those planted earlier—even if the early plantings have escaped damage by frost.

Far too many people are disappointed with their crops and the growth of plants generally because they do not apply water, early enough, often enough, or in sufficient quantity. To grow well plants need sunshine, good soil and adequate water. Sunshine we have. Soil we can improve and we can supplement the plant food in the soil with soluble fertilizers. Too often, however, gardeners do not apply water until plants are showing signs of stress (flagging) and by that time the check to growth can be serious.

Do not be taken in by old gardeners' tales that you should not start watering because once you start you have to keep on. This nonsense has been handed down from the days before we had hose-pipes and gardeners used to have to push round 30-gallon water butts on wheels.

The golden rule is to water before plants begin to suffer and keep on watering as and when necessary. Begin to think about watering as early as April. If little or no rain falls in a 10-day period in April and early May it would probably pay to put on say 7 litres (1½ gallons) of water to the square metre (yard). From mid-May onwards twice this amount would be needed or even three times as much in high summer if you really want maximum growth.

Always put on 4.5–7 litres per m² (1–1½ gallons per sq yd) each time you water. It is far better, if you have to carry water in a can, to give part of the borders or vegetable rows a good soaking every day rather than giving a useless sprinkling over a larger area. If you use a watering can only, have the rose turned up if you wish to give newly planted plants a freshen up. Use the rose face down when watering rows of seedlings or individual plants, or even without the rose around large recently planted shrubs, roses or other plants.

With shrubs, draw a few cm of soil away in a circle say for about 30 cm (1 ft) around the plant, fill the hollow with water and push the dry soil back again to prevent evaporation.

If you mulch any part of your garden with peat, compost, straw or leaves always allow 4.5 litres (1 gallon) of water to the square metre (yard) to wet the mulch before putting on the dose for your plants.

Ideally you should water all plants as and when necessary, but peas respond to water when the pods are setting and again about 10 days later. Soft fruits need plenty of water once the fruits have set. All brassicas, cabbages, cauliflowers, Brussels sprouts and the like need regular watering in dry spells. Potatoes especially respond to watering, giving much higher yields, and runner beans should always be given plenty of water. Sweetcorn and tomatoes and all salad crops benefit from regular and adequate watering.

Today applying water to a garden from the smallest patch to acres of ground is really simple and labour-saving if you are prepared to invest, as and when you can afford it, in some modern equipment.

Any good garden shop or garden centre should be able to offer a good range of equipment, or if they have only limited stocks should be able to supply the addresses of the various firms that specialize in sprinklers, hoses and fittings which enable us to install the various watering systems that save so much time and labour.

For a small garden a 'through feed' hose reel is a godsend. You clip it to a wall or post. A length of hose goes to your tap and you then pull off as much of the hose from the reel to reach the part of the garden you wish to water—no weary and dirty business of uncoiling and coiling an ordinary length of hose.

Next you have to decide which is the best way of applying water. There is the choice of small sprinklers covering a circle of say up to 6 m (20 ft) diameter, impulse or 'flip flap' sprinklers, which will cover up to a 18 m (60 ft) diameter or even more if there is enough water pressure, and the oscillating sprinklers which may be adjusted to cover a narrow or a wider strip, or a square of up to 15 × 15 m (50 × 50 ft).

Then for really large areas—say the size of a tennis court—there are 'travelling sprinklers'. These are really excellent for larger gardens as you just lay the hose along the area you wish to water, place the travelling sprinkler on it and it will work its way along very slowly. When it gets to the end of the hose it switches itself off.

For any garden of a reasonable size, however, the ideal irrigation system is a 'ring main'. You lay a length of plastic hose down one side of your garden, if it is a long rectangle, or around the outer edge of the garden if it is of any other shape. The hose is of course attached to a main water supply. (It is wise to check with your local water authority about the type of fittings permitted.) At various points, you may fit in a 'water stop'. This is a take off point in the hose length and is also a tap. Then all you need is a short length of lightweight plastic hose with a sprinkler which you can pick up with one hand and move from point to point as you may wish—rather like plugging in an electric fire in your home.

*Approximate weekly water losses from a garden in Great Britain*

| Area | April/September | May/August | June/July |
|------|-----------------|------------|-----------|
| Northern Scotland | (9 mm) 0.35 in | (12 mm) 0.5 in | (18 mm) 0.7 in |
| Southern Scotland Northern Ireland Northern England | (10 mm) 0.4 in | (14 mm) 0.55 in | (20 mm) 0.8 in |
| Midland England Wales | (11 mm) 0.45 in | (16 mm) 0.65 in | (22 mm) 0.9 in |
| Southern England | (12 mm) 0.5 in | (18 mm) 0.7 in | (25 mm) 1.0 in |

(By courtesy of Diplex Ltd.)

# Border Plants

No garden is complete without a selection of plants which come up year after year to flower in due season from early spring to late autumn. Such hardy perennials are a permanent asset to any garden. There exists an infinite variety from which a selection can be made for every soil and situation. Some make a bright splash of colour, others have charm in form and subtler aspects of beauty. There are kinds which can be used in conjunction with shrubs, or other purposes such as cutting, and they can become a fascinating alternative to annual bedding.

The conventional herbaceous border, however, with its backing of wall, hedge, or fence often proved troublesome. Plants unduly cramped for light and air grew lankily and needed staking and so often it contained kinds which were far too tall for the narrow confines of the border. In recent years the 'island bed' idea has caught on. This reduces staking to just a few kinds, such as delphiniums, simply because the plants in an island bed grow more strongly but less tall.

This is not to say that the one-sided border for perennials is inevitably troublesome. The most vital factor towards trouble freedom is that of choosing the best kinds for a given site. A narrow space calls for dwarfish plants and something growing to 2 m (6 ft) tall in a border only 1 m (3 ft) or so wide is incongruous.

1 Galega    2 Echinops    3 Viola
4 Crocosmia    5 Filipendula
6 Sidalcea    7 Fuchsia    8 Erigeron
9 Festuca    10 Solidago
11 Coreopsis    12 Molinia
13 Erigeron    14 Campanula
15 Coreopsis

Such kinds overhang and spoil the beauty of lowlier subjects, and there should always be regard to outward spread as well. Perennials with a rapid growth spread should not be planted next to others with a slow rate of growth.

Such factors are worth a little study in advance of planning, and information is easily obtained from books or specialist catalogues on such matters as spacing according to height and spread, as well as special preferences in the matters of soil type, moist or dry, shade or sun, together with height and flowering period.

Bearing in mind that a selection can be made and procured for any given site, the majority of perennials though reasonably adaptable prefer an open position. The most limiting is in dark, dry shade under overhanging trees, but even so some kinds such as lamium, vinca (periwinkle), bergenia and symphytum (comfrey) will survive and flower, especially if planted in autumn.

Having judiciously chosen a site, or having decided to overhaul an existing but unsatisfactory herbaceous border, the first task is to ensure that all perennial weeds are dead. In an old border some flowering plants may themselves have become weedy, and having taken out any worth keeping then make sure all else is forked out or killed off. Apply humus, if the soil is poor, and dig thoroughly. Add sharp sand if it is sticky or hard with clay, and if possible let winter frost break down the clods. Do not rush the job of preparation, bearing in mind that thoroughness ensures long lasting success.

The most pernicious weeds are couch, ground elder, creeping thistle, mare's tail, bindweed and creeping sorrel. It takes a dose of strong systemic weed-killer to avoid more than one forking over, and it should be applied during the growing season (*see* pp. 18–19). Whilst waiting for it to do its job or in between spells of digging, however, make a list of plants which appeal and which are suitable for the chosen site. By noting against each the height, colour and flowering time as well as growth rate, and the sun/shade/soil preferences, if applicable, a balanced list can be achieved. The choice is yours as to favourite colours, types of flower, and whether you prefer maximum continuity to a display at any given season, from March to October.

The width of a border or an island bed should be the determining factor concerning the heights of its contents. The one-sided bed must have its tallest subjects at the back, with the dwarfest along the front. A safe guide is to avoid using kinds which grow taller in height than about half the width of the border, allowing for the root spread of a hedge or trees. So, for a border 2 m (6 ft) wide the tallest plants should be about 1 m (3 ft), grading down from the back to about 30 cm (1 ft) along the front. This guide can also be used for island beds, but with them the tallest kinds should be in the centre part. When such beds are planned pay heed to suitability of shape. Most garden plots are rectangular and it would be out of keeping to have a bed of some irregular shape unless the surroundings are informal.

The size of a bed or border will have some bearing on the selection. The larger it is the greater the variety of plants it will hold. Variety is of course the key to continuity. In small beds or borders variety and continuity can be achieved if single plants of different kinds are chosen. Where a more spectacular and colourful display is preferred, however, then use three or more of a kind in groups together. The average spacing for perennials is about five plants per square metre or yard, but because of variations in height and vigour spacing too may vary between ten and two or three per square metre. Always allow a little more space around a group than between member plants of the group.

There need be no upper limit for size in either an island bed or a conventional border. Such infinite variety exists both to fill the largest possible, and to choose dwarf, slow-growing kinds which will be a joy in a very restricted space. There is no clear division between border perennials and what are usually classed as alpine or rock garden plants. Many of the latter are quite adaptable for frontal or edging positions, including dwarf species of achillea, campanula, dianthus, veronica and viola. For shady but not too dry soil a different but no less attractive range exists, but obviously some advance study is advisable as in selecting subjects for a permanently damp spot.

Perennials vary greatly in habit and form as well as in height and season.

Back row plants 90-135 cm

Middle row plants 45-90 cm

Front row plants 15-45 cm

Spacing plants in the border. Plants of the same kind should be planted in groups of three 38–50 cm apart, with 60 cm between groups. Spiky plants should be interspersed with those of rounded habit.

Herein lies much of their attraction. To make the most of such variations, spike-forming kinds should be interspersed amongst those with a more rounded or flat headed appearance. Most members of the daisy family (Compositae) are in the latter category, including achillea, helenium and aster. Spike-forming kinds, such as anchusa, delphinium, lupin, sidalcea and veronica should be used to give a more pleasing natural effect. Kniphofia (red-hot pokers) and hosta, having good foliage as well as a show of spikes, should be given a position where their overall 'architectural' value is appreciated. Even if they exceed the height/width guidelines, their shape-lines make an attractive focal point.

Staking is a chore no one enjoys. If showy, but weak-growing or top-heavy kinds are chosen, one must be willing to give them supports. Pea sticks, or specially made wire supports through which stems can grow, should be in position well before flowering time. Delphiniums, oriental poppies and a few more invariably need supporting. Quite often, these are the kinds which need to be cut hard back after flowering. Most of the taller hardy geraniums are also apt to flop, and these too should be cut back so as to encourage new basal leaves to fill in what otherwise would be an untidy gap.

Some subjects, including delphiniums, will flower a second time if old spikes are severed at ground level when they have faded.

In a general way, dead-heading is a matter of choice—whether or not dead flowers or spikes offend the eye. If the foliage below the flowers remains green, as with peonies, let it remain until winter comes, but with some spiky plants, such as lupins, *Salvia superba* and its varieties, removal of the upper main spikes when over will encourage more side spikelets to prolong the display. It is also a matter of choice, or convenience, when the final cut-back and clean-up is undertaken. Any time between November and early March will do, for this and for lightly forking over between the plants, so long as the soil is not sodden or frostbound. Early spring is the time to apply fertilizer, preferably a good organic mix, followed by the first hoeing of the year. 55 g (2 oz) per $m^2$ (sq yd) is ample.

To some, the task of planning in detail (arranging a selection in a bed or border) might appear quite daunting; but it need not be a deterrent. Some specialists' catalogues include a stereotyped plan or two, but these cannot fill everyone's need. The size, shape and subject offered could suit only a few, and most satisfaction comes to those who can draw up a plan of

their own, using the guidelines already given here. All you need is some graph paper, and on it outline the bed or border in relation to existing garden features. Make out a list of subjects from a good specialist's book or catalogue, and fit them in. Give each a kind of reference number, and use this on the plan rather than the full names. Having done this to your satisfaction, order the plants, and assuming that the site is prepared place sticks or labels marked with the name or reference number of each in position according to the plan. These can be juggled to fit if need be—a job best done before the plants arrive.

When they do arrive, they can be planted with no problem, though if the soil is very wet or sticky you may have to wait a day or two, or use a couple of planks on which to stand to avoid jamming down the soil. Autumn planting is best, with early spring only slightly second best. If plants arrive when conditions are very bad, heel them in sand or peat till later, even if it means waiting for a few weeks till winter gives way.

Perennials can be a permanent joy. Making your own plan and choosing the plants will stimulate interest. They can create a new dimension to your gardening as you get to know and love them, and it will be very rewarding.

# Propagation

Propagation is one of the most satisfying aspects of gardening—the sight of a row or box of newly germinated seedlings, the sense of wonder at a new plant arising from a leaf cutting, the thrill when a graft takes—all bring rewards greater than the mere production of new stock. Raising new plants is fun. It also makes economic sense.

All plants can be propagated somehow, but the methods are many and the ease with which plants respond is varied. Some will root without any effort on your part: some bryophyllums will produce new plantlets whether you want them or not, whereas tradescantia and impatiens (busy lizzie) cuttings will root in water. Others, however, remain a challenge even to the experienced with all the modern propagating aids.

Although most gardeners have tried rooting a few cuttings or sowing seeds, there are usually a few techniques still to try. Not so many will have tried budding their own roses or raising lilies from 'scales'.

This chapter can only describe basic techniques; it cannot give you a recipe for success with particular plants. You may need to consult reference books for the way to propagate an individual plant, but be prepared to experiment too. It is fun to try new techniques, and often rewarding too.

*Tools and equipment*  The tools you need are few; a knife will do. The equipment *can* be elaborate and expensive, although you can usually improvise.

You can manage to take most cuttings with a razor-blade (or secateurs for woody plants), but it is dangerous and not to be recommended. A sharp knife is well worth buying. Choose one of medium weight for most jobs, but a heavier one would be useful if you plan to do a lot of grafting. A special budding knife (which has a wedge-like section at one end to prise open the flaps of bark) is not really worth considering unless you plan to do budding on a fairly regular basis.

Sharp secateurs are useful for hardwood cuttings, but you are almost sure to have these anyway.

The most expensive equipment is likely to be a garden frame, greenhouse, or propagator—maybe even a mist propagation unit. All are essential for anyone raising a wide range of cuttings commercially and nice to have at your disposal as an amateur. Fortunately you can usually manage without them if you only want to raise easy plants or do not mind a few more failures.

A garden frame and greenhouse are useful because they provide both protection and warmth. Nevertheless if you have a suitable windowsill indoors, or do not mind delaying your sowing until the warmer weather arrives, you can often manage without these.

A mist unit can increase the chances of rooting difficult cuttings considerably, but a polythene bag over the pot (suitably supported on canes or wires to prevent it touching the plants) will sometimes produce the same effect.

The one piece of equipment well worth buying, whether for seed-raising or rooting cuttings, is a propagator. This will provide both warmth and a humid atmosphere—an ideal combination. Most propagators are electrically-heated, but you can buy some to place over a paraffin heater.

*Compost*  If you are sowing seeds, always use a suitable compost. John Innes *seed* compost is ideal (the potting composts are likely to inhibit germination because they contain too much fertilizer), but try to make sure that it is fresh: chemical changes take place after several weeks and can affect the germination rate of some seeds.

Some composts are based only on peat, rather than loam, peat and sand as in the John Innes composts. Many of these peat-based composts are 'all-purpose' and you should be able to use these for seed-sowing. Others have a separate formulation for seeds and cuttings, so check on the bag.

For cuttings use a proprietary seed compost or a mixture of equal parts coarse sand and sieved peat. Vermiculite and perlite (two inert and sterile media) also root cuttings successfully, but the rooted plants must be potted up into a proper nutritious compost as soon as possible.

*Rooting hormones*  Hormone rooting preparations (most are powders but you can buy a liquid) are an aid, but not a magic recipe for success. Some plants will root just as readily without them, and they will not produce roots on material incapable of forming roots. What they will do is improve the root formation on many difficult subjects.

Unless you take a lot of cuttings, use a 'universal' preparation—one you can use on all cuttings regardless of their firmness. If you take a lot of cuttings, it may be worth considering one formulated for softwood or hardwood types, according to your needs. Do not use these preparations on root or leaf cuttings.

## Cuttings

Cuttings are usually taken from stems, but sometimes leaves and roots can be used.

*Stem cuttings*  Although there are various kinds of stem cuttings, the basic preparation is the same for most of them. Take a shoot about 7.5–10 cm (3–4 in) long (but be guided by the plant—a cutting of an alpine will obviously be smaller, that of a tree or shrub longer), and place it in water unless you are going to insert it immediately. Most cacti and succulents, however, should be left exposed to the air for a few hours before insertion.

Always remove the leaves (and any conspicuous associated buds) that will be below compost level when the cutting is inserted. Take the opportunity to remove any damaged or diseased leaves at the same time.

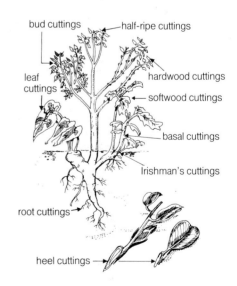

bud cuttings — half-ripe cuttings

leaf cuttings

hardwood cuttings

softwood cuttings

basal cuttings

Irishman's cuttings

root cuttings

heel cuttings

Trim the end at a node (the point where a leaf arose from the stem), taking care not to cause bruising.

If you want to use a hormone rooting powder, just dip the end into the powder or liquid. Dipping the end into water first will help the powder to stick (but do not coat the stem); most of the hormone is taken up through the cut surface, and too much on the stem can be detrimental.

If you have just a few cuttings, insert them around the edge of a small pot, using a dibber. This ensures good drainage and spaces the cuttings out so that you can get quite a few to a pot, but there is no reason why you should not insert them in deep boxes, into compost at the bottom of the garden frame if they do not need much heat, or even in a sheltered (not too sunny) part of the garden if they are hardy. If the soil is heavy in the garden it is always worth taking out a shallow, V-shaped trench and sprinkling sand along the bottom.

Water with a fine-rosed watering-can, and moisten the leaves occasionally to maintain humidity. Most cuttings are bound to flag a little after they have been inserted, but do not overwater. As they have no roots there is a limit to how much water they can take up, and they will rot if kept too wet.

Many hardwood tree and shrub cuttings benefit from mist propagation (provided by a device that sprays the air with a fine mist of water as soon as the atmosphere becomes too dry), but this is luxury equipment for most of us. As a substitute you can place the pots in a deep box and place a pane of glass over the top to maintain humidity, moistening the atmosphere occasionally with a hand sprayer. For a few plants on a window-sill, you can use a polythene bag as already described.

*Softwood cuttings* are taken from new growth in spring and early summer. Dahlias, chrysanthemums and impatiens (busy Lizzies) all provide softwood cuttings. They usually root readily.

*Semi-ripe cuttings* are usually taken in late summer when the current season's growth is becoming thicker and harder. Shrubs such as ribes (flowering currants), deutzias and forsythias are usually propagated from semi-ripe wood. A hormone rooting powder is usually beneficial.

*Hardwood cuttings* are taken from the

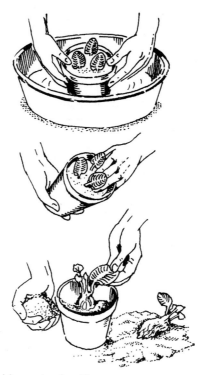

Taking a leaf cutting.

mature stems of trees and shrubs, while the plant is dormant. They are best taken soon after the leaves fall and can be inserted outdoors in a sheltered spot immediately. Unlike softwood and semi-ripe cuttings, they are sometimes stored before insertion. They should be bundled together and almost buried in a bed of sand in a sheltered spot (ideally a frame) for the winter, then spaced out to root as soon as the ground is suitable in the spring.

Most hardwood cuttings can be 15–23 cm (6–9 in) long when prepared. Remove the softer tip with a slanting cut above a bud, and cut directly below a bud at the base of each cutting.

It is best to rub out the lower buds of some plants (redcurrants and gooseberries are examples) to ensure that they do not send up shoots from beneath ground level. Hardwood cuttings are usually planted quite deeply: half to two-thirds their length.

*Evergreens* are treated in a similar way, and are usually taken during late summer and early autumn. It may be worth cutting large leaves back by a third, to reduce the surface area that will be losing moisture. Try to keep them humid.

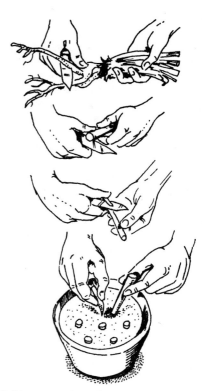

Taking a root cutting.

*Heel cuttings* are popular for some woody plants, but are most frequently used for subjects that take some time to root, as the 'heel' offers some protection to the base of the cutting in the meantime. To take a heel cutting, simply pull the shoot off and bring with it a sliver of the main stem. Trim the 'tail' and dip the cut surface in a hormone rooting powder.

*Leaf cuttings* Fewer plants can be raised from leaf cuttings, but those that can include some popular house and greenhouse plants, such as saintpaulias (African violets), *Begonia rex*, and streptocarpus (cape primrose).

*Leaf petiole cuttings* (petiole is a technical word for stalk, so it just means leaves with the stalk left on) are used for saintpaulias and *Peperomia caperata* among others.

Select a healthy young leaf, and trim off the stalk about 5 cm (2 in) from the leaf blade. Insert the stalk into a hole made with a dibber, so that the blade just rests on the compost, in an upright position. Keep the cutting in a propagator or polythene 'tent' until the plantlets begin to form.

# Propagation

*Midrib cuttings* are best for streptocarpus and can also be used for gloxinias. Cut the leaf into narrow strips about 2.5 cm (1 in) wide, across the main midrib vein. If inserted upright, so that the cuttings stand on end, they should produce plantlets at the base. Keep the atmosphere humid, and provide adequate warmth.

*Sansevieria trifasciata* (mother-in-law's tongue) can also be propagated from slices of leaf inserted vertically in the compost. Unfortunately the variety 'Laurentii' with yellow variegation is unlikely to produce variegated offspring.

*Leaf blade cuttings* use only the blade, which is placed on a flat surface while the veins are cut through with a knife or razor-blade in several places. If the leaf is laid flat in contact with a suitable compost, plantlets should form at the sites of the cuts. You will need to hold the leaf in contact with the compost with bent wire 'pegs', and keep the atmosphere humid at all times until the plantlets have formed. This method is often used for *Begonia rex*.

*Root cuttings*  Root cuttings are a useful way of propagating a number of herbaceous plants (including anchusa, *Papaver orientale* and phlox), and alpines such as *Primula denticulata* and pulsatillas. Several trees and shrubs can also be propagated from root cuttings.

Root cuttings are best taken when the plant is dormant. You will probably have disappointing results at any other time.

Wash the roots free of soil, and choose young roots. For most plants, the cuttings should be about the thickness of a pencil, but some, such as phlox, only have thin roots, so be guided by the plant. Each cutting should be about 5–7.5 cm (2–3 in) long. Cut the top end of the root at right-angles, but make a sloping cut at the bottom—otherwise you might forget and plant them upside down. Insert thick-rooted kinds vertically, with the top just below the surface. Thin roots can be laid horizontally and lightly covered with compost.

## Layering

Layering is a useful method for plants such as carnations, and many shrubs.

Select a suitable, low-growing branch that can be pegged into the ground. Remove the leaves and sideshoots for about 15–60 cm (6–24 in) behind the growing tip, and peg the shoot down into a prepared hole 10–15 cm (4–6 in) deep. The leafy tip should be just above the soil level. To encourage root formation, make a shallow cut on the lower side of the stem where it will be pegged down. Be careful not to cut more than half-way through the stem. Return good compost or a mixture of soil and peat into the hole and keep the ground well watered.

Once the layer has rooted and is growing away well, sever it from the parent plant.

*Air layering*  Some shrubs, such as lilacs and magnolias, can be air layered, but the technique is most popular for houseplants such as *Ficus elastica* (rubber plant) that have become too leggy. In this case it is more a method of obtaining new for old, rather than a way of increasing the number of plants.

To make an air layer, make an upward slit in the stem with a sharp knife at the point which will be the new base of the plant. Take care not to go further than half way through the stem. Tie a piece of black polythene about 2.5–5 cm (1–2 in) below the wound, then pack damp sphagnum moss or peat around the stem. Enclose this with the polythene, then tie or tape it at the top to seal the pack. Sever the new plant from the parent once sufficient roots have formed. A rubber plant will sometimes root within a month or so in a warm and humid atmosphere, but usually the operation takes several months. Hormone rooting powder dusted into the cut may help to speed things up.

*Tip layering*  This is an easy way to propagate plants like blackberries and logan-

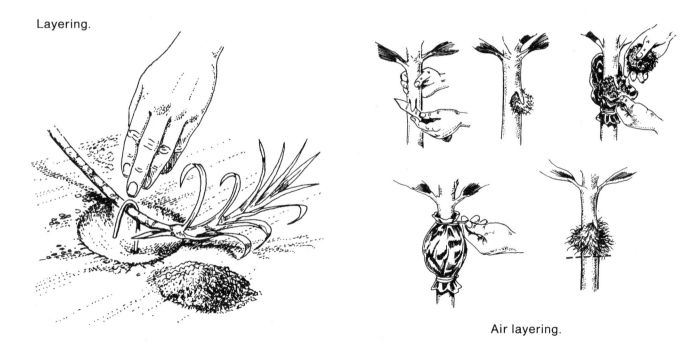

Layering.

Air layering.

berries that have arching canes with tips that root easily in contact with the soil. Simply pull down a stem in summer and peg the tip down in a hole about 10 cm (4 in) deep, cover with fine soil and peat, and water well. New plants should grow from the tips. Sever from the parent plant, and transplant once the leaves have fallen, at the end of the season.

## Offsets and runners

An offset is a small plant that has developed from its parent on a lateral stem, above or below ground. Bulbs and corms sometimes produce a kind of offset, but they are then known as bulbils and cormlets.

Offsets can simply be pulled away from the parent and potted up. They soon form roots and grow away.

Perhaps the best-known plant propagated from runners is the strawberry, but mother-of-thousands (*Saxifraga stolonifera*) is another good example. Simply peg down the plantlets formed on the runners, preferably into small individual pots, and sever them from their parent once they are established.

## Plantlets

Apart from runners and offsets it is hard to imagine an easier method of propagation than that provided by some of the bryophyllums (also known as kalanchoes). Both *B. daigremontianum* and *B. tubiflorum* produce plantlets on the edges or tips of the leaves. These will drop eventually and probably take root where they fall. *Tolmiea menziesii* also produces new plants on its leaves (but only one to a leaf, and you will need to pot it up carefully).

## Division

The advantage of division is that it gives you a reasonably-sized plant immediately.

Herbaceous plants are best divided in spring by prising an old clump apart with two forks back-to-back or chopping a clump apart with a spade. It is best to replant outer portions and discard the old centre.

Houseplants such as saintpaulias (African violets) are simply teased apart by hand.

*Bryophyllum daigremontianum.*

## Bulbs, corms, tubers and rhizomes

Bulbs can seem infuriatingly slow to increase, and young corms also take years to flower, but in fact the time from propagation to flowering is often much less than you would be prepared to wait for a shrub, so do not be deterred from trying. Tubers and rhizomes provide a useful means of propagation, and the results are more immediate.

*Bulbs* The bulbs most of us think of first are those whose layers of 'leaves' or 'scales' are closely packed and enclosed in a kind of skin—such as onions, daffodils, and tulips. There are also 'scaly' bulbs such as lilies and fritillarias. Propagation is different for the two kinds.

Most 'ordinary' bulbs will increase themselves slowly by producing new bulbs alongside the old ones, and it is simply a matter of lifting and separating them during the dormant season, and then growing them on in a spare piece of ground if they are too small to flower.

Hyacinths are so slow to produce more bulbs (they tend to get larger instead) that it is usual to 'help' them. The simplest way is to score the base with a sharp knife, making a cross with two cuts about 6 mm ($\frac{1}{4}$ in) deep, at the end of the dormant season. Leave the bulbs in a warm, dry place for the wound to heal (it is worth dusting the wound with a fungicide). Store in the airing cupboard with the bulb supported upside down on damp sand.

*Bryophyllum tubiflorum.*

Once bulblets have formed on the surface, plant the whole bulb in compost, still upside down, just covering it. At the end of the season, simply separate the small bulbs and grow them on for about three years, until they reach flowering size.

'Scaly' bulbs are easier to multiply. Just separate a few outer segments. Dust them with a fungicide and place them in a polythene bag containing damp peat and sand (vermiculite is also good). Close the top, ensuring the bag is inflated, and leave in the airing cupboard until bulblets form at the base of the scales. Simply pot these up, still attached to the scale, and gradually harden off. Separate and plant out once the leaves have died down.

A few lilies freely produce bulblets naturally above or below the main bulb, and these can just be detached and grown on.

Bulbils are tiny bulbs that form on the *stem*, where a leaf joins it. These can be detached after the plant has flowered and potted up until large enough to plant out. Unfortunately not many plants produce bulbils, but *Lilium bulbiferum* and *L. tigrinum* are examples.

*Corms* Most corms multiply themselves rapidly enough for most people, but if you want to speed things up, you can divide a corm by cutting it into pieces—but make sure each has a bud. Dust cut surfaces with a fungicide.

Some corms (gladioli for instance) produce a lot of cormels (miniature corms) between the old and new corm. These can

# Propagation

be saved and grown on in a spare piece of ground. They should start to flower after about two years.

*Tubers*  Tubers are really swollen stems, and provided that you retain an 'eye' on each piece they can be divided into several pieces. The potato is an example, where even a piece of peeling with an eye may grow. It is always worth dusting cut surfaces with a fungicide.

Apart from tubers proper (which are modified stems) there are also tuberous roots, as on dahlias and begonias. With these you cannot just cut the tuber up into a lot of pieces. Each one must have at least one crown bud. In the case of the dahlia, it means cutting along the old stem in order to be sure of a relatively undamaged crown.

*Rhizomes*  Rhizomes are thick stems that usually grow horizontally along or in the ground. Mint and couch grass demonstrate how effective this can be. Bearded irises are at the desirable end of the scale.

Simply lift a clump of rhizomes (usually after the plant has flowered), cut away and discard any old rhizomes and replant pieces of the current season's growth at about the same depth as they were before lifting.

## Grafting

Commercially, grafting is an invaluable method of propagation. It involves uniting a shoot which will form the stems of the plant with one which will act as the root system and control size, vigour and cropping or flowering ability. It enables apples, cherries and pears to be grown on trees compact enough for small gardens or suitable for intensive training. They will also come into fruit sooner than on their own roots. Among ornamental plants, there are rhododendron rootstocks that tolerate a less acid soil, and a variety of rose rootstocks can be used to suit soil types and plant habit.

For most amateurs, grafting is more an interesting experiment than an important method of propagation.

The most likely form of grafting amateurs are likely to tackle is budding, a useful technique for roses. This is described in detail in the chapter on roses, on pages 76–77.

*Splice grafting*  If you want to try ordinary grafting, the splice graft is the easiest for the beginner. It is useful for fruit, broom, roses and clematis.

The two parts to be joined are known as the 'stock' (the root part) and the scion (the part you want to flower or fruit). Grafting is usually done in early spring, but the scions are collected and stored in December or January. Simply tie them in bundles and heel them in the ground in a cool place, perhaps against a north wall or fence. They should be cut from the previous year's growth and have four or five good buds after removing the soft tip from the stem.

When you are ready to graft, cut the scion down to a length of three buds, and make a long, slanting cut (see illustration). The rootstock, which should be the same thickness, is prepared with a matching cut, so that the two parts can be brought into direct contact.

Traditionally grafts were tied with raffia, but the special grafting tapes you can buy are much easier to use. The drawback of this method of grafting is lack of support until the graft unites, so tie both parts to a cane, or use split-canes as 'splints'.

*Whip and tongue grafting*  This is the most common method of grafting. It is practised most often on deciduous subjects, including roses and fruit trees, usually in the spring. An oblique cut about 4 cm (1½ in) long, with a nick or 'tongue', is made in the centre of the wood on a rootstock no more than about 7–8 mm thick. A similar cut is made in the scion, which is then matched up with the rootstock and securely fastened to it with grafting tape. The tape should then be covered with grafting wax to avoid drying out.

## Seeds

Even gardeners who never take cuttings or bother to increase their own perennial plants usually sow seeds. The vast majority of vegetables are raised from seed, and all annuals (whether hardy or half-hardy) are seed-raised. Beyond these 'everyday' subjects, however, do not overlook the possibility of raising houseplants, alpines, herbaceous plants, and even trees and shrubs from seed. It is

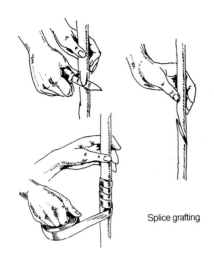

Splice grafting

cheaper than buying plants—and more satisfying if you have the extra patience needed.

Most seeds will germinate readily if the soil is warm enough; but many 'exotic' seeds are likely to need special treatment.

There are thousands of different kinds of flower and vegetable seeds readily available, and many of them will have special needs when it comes to germination. Some need to be exposed to light, others must have darkness; a lot will benefit from 'pre-chilling' in a refrigerator, a few need considerable warmth to break dormancy; some need 'washing' or soaking to remove a germination inhibitor, a few need 'nicking' or chipping to allow moisture to penetrate the hard coat. Over-riding many of these is the effect of temperature (too much warmth can be as detrimental as too little).

Because the permutations are so vast, you should be guided by the instructions on the packet or in the catalogue. Nevertheless, these are not always comprehensive or detailed, so be prepared to learn from experience too.

*Sowing seeds outdoors*  Most of the seeds sown outdoors are vegetables, and these are conventionally sown in shallow furrows known as 'drills' in straight rows. There is a tendency today to move towards closer spacing than used to be recommended, with plants grown in beds or blocks, but whatever spacing you opt for the basic techniques for sowing remain the same.

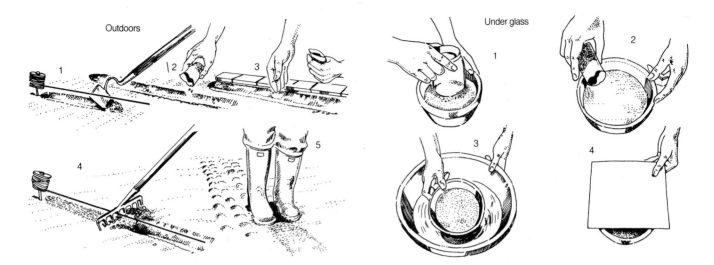

Outdoors

Under glass

The soil should always be crumbly and worked into a fine tilth free from weeds. If it is dry, water the ground well *before* sowing. Unless you can apply sufficient water from a sprinkler to penetrate significantly, apply the water to the drills before sowing (if you water afterwards you are likely to compact the soil and displace the seeds if you apply enough water to penetrate to a sufficient depth).

Take out a drill with the corner of a draw-hoe, Dutch hoe or a rake, using a garden line to keep the row straight.

Sow *thinly*. Sowing too thickly not only wastes seeds and money, it makes work when you have to thin the seedlings.

There is much to be said for sowing at 'stations'—the correct spacing for the plants after thinning. If you do this, you will need to sow about three seeds in each position, and thin first to two and then to one plant.

Cover the seeds by drawing soil over the drill with the back of a rake.

All thinning should be done as soon as the seedlings can be handled. Never attempt to thin to the final spacing immediately; there are inevitably some losses during the early weeks. Thin to the final distances at the second or third session.

Some vegetables are sown in seedbeds, to be transplanted later. You can sow broadcast for this, but there is much to be said for sowing in close rows. Broadcast sowing involves raking the ground so that very shallow depressions are created. The seeds are then scattered over the soil which is then raked in the opposite direction to cover most of the seeds.

Flower seeds for cutting also tend to be grown in rows, but annuals for a general display are best sown in 'drifts'. It is wise to mark out the areas with sand first. You can then sow broadcast within each area and rake the seeds in, but sowing in close rows will make it easier to decide which are the plants and which are weeds in the early stages.

Pelleted seeds have a coating that makes them larger and easier to handle, and offers some protection from diseases. Because they are large, accurate spacing is easier so you will waste fewer seeds—but they are more expensive, and germination can still be a problem.

Biennials and herbaceous perennials are usually sown in a seedbed in late spring or early summer, thinned out, then transplanted in a nursery bed until autumn or the following spring (perennials may be left longer).

*Sowing under glass* Most bedding plants are best sown in seedboxes (with the advent of plastic, they are increasingly known as 'trays'). Where just a few seeds are involved (or if they are very fine) there is much to be said for sowing in pots or pans (a kind of a cut-down pot).

There is no need for 'crocks' (broken pots) at the bottom of a plastic seed tray. Most seeds will germinate equally well in John Innes seed compost or one of the peat-based composts (but make sure it is a seed or dual-purpose type—not one designed *only* for potting).

Fill to within about 13 mm ($\frac{1}{2}$ in) of the top of the tray, and then press the compost down with the fingers. To produce a firm, level surface, use a piece of wood as a firmer (in a pot you might find a jam-jar or the base of another pot useful). Water *before* you sow.

Cover lightly with sieved compost— unless the seeds are very fine, or need light.

Unless you are using a propagator, try to cover the box or pot with a sheet of glass. This will conserve moisture and should reduce the chance of having to water again before the seeds germinate. Most seeds will benefit from sheets of newspaper or brown paper over the top of the glass, but do not cover seeds that need exposure to light (although these should still be protected from direct sun). Turn the glass daily to reduce condensation drips.

Above all, try to maintain the right temperature. Once they have germinated, most seedlings will tolerate lower temperatures, but adequate warmth is usually vital for quick and successful germination.

Prick off the seedlings as soon as they can be handled: pot plants into pots, most bedding plants into boxes. Always try, however, to give bedding plants that resent root disturbance (such as zinnias) individual pots.

Bedding plants and vegetables for planting outside must always be hardened off thoroughly (gradually introduced to lower temperatures), preferably in a garden frame.

# Container Gardening

Just because you do not have much of a garden, it does not mean that gardening has to be totally abandoned. A balcony, patio, back yard, the steps up or down to a flat, a windowsill, even a roof if it is flat, can be used to stage a flowering display. The difference is, of course, that all the plants must be grown in containers.

These come in natural and artificial materials and in a wide variety of shapes and forms. Natural materials fit into the garden best but stone, earthenware and lead are all expensive, although you pay for something that will last for years if treated well.

A good imitation of natural stone can be made at home. The secret is to use an old white enamel sink as a base and to cover it with 'hypertufa'—a mixture of cement, fine grade peat and sharp sand in equal proportions plus a little water to bind it together.

Clean the sink off, score it all over with a wire brush, then paint it with a resin-based (PVA) adhesive. Next simply slap the mixture on the sides, the top and 5 cm (2 in) of the inside. When it is set you will have a sink that looks like stone and which will be ideal for small rock plants or for bedding.

Reconstituted stone is now used to cast urns and troughs and this is the only widely available stone material. It contains a high proportion of stone dust. Some types weather very quickly and give an antique effect in a short time, and they are quite reasonably priced alternatives to stone.

Wood is very popular but deteriorates quickly unless looked after. Wooden containers should be treated with preservative (not creosote which damages plants) two or three times before planting up, and are best used for temporary displays of bedding plants. They can then be emptied every year, scrubbed down thoroughly, left to dry, then repainted with preservative before planting.

Fortunately wood is reasonably cheap and containers can be made to fit exactly the space available. When making up troughs yourself always treat the wood after sawing but before putting together, and it is a good idea to use brass screws or galvanized nails which will not rust. Paint is a less effective protection than preservative as plant roots and water can get into the smallest crack and lift the

Hanging baskets can make a very attractive feature.

paint off; preservative actually soaks into the wood.

Concrete is commonly used for cheaper troughs, pots and urns and is often textured to look like stone. Some are rather garish and rather obviously concrete, but when cast in contemporary designs they fit very well into modern town gardens. Take care, though, when choosing them for Victorian back yards or cottage style gardens as they can look out of place.

Plastic containers are hardly affected by the weather at all, so they last very well. Nevertheless, they always tend to look shiny and new and they do not fit comfortably into the garden scene. Plastic is best used for window boxes where trailing plants will soon cover it up. Choose a box a few inches shorter than your windowsill so it can easily be lifted out, and make sure it is at least 20 cm (8 in) deep to give the plants plenty of root space. If you have no outside sills, fix boxes on steel brackets.

Hanging baskets come in galvanized or plastic covered wire mesh, either round for hanging from a bracket or half round for fixing to a wall. They also come in solid plastic, sometimes with a water tray. These, of course, cannot have plants put in the sides.

Growing bags have become very popular for tomatoes and other vegetables over the last few years but they are just as good for bedding displays. Water them regularly as they are very difficult to re-wet once they have dried out. They are very convenient on balconies where carrying pots and compost through the house can be messy, and after use the contents can go on your, or your neighbour's, garden.

Drainage is vital to all containers, so if yours have no holes in the base it will be necessary to make some yourself. Half-barrels, for example, can easily have three holes bored in the base, but be sure to treat the cut surfaces with preservative before filling.

Containers impossible to equip with holes can still be used—they can hold a number of smaller pots. You will need a layer of gravel or coarse peat in the bottom, and you will need to watch the watering carefully as small pots dry out very quickly. It is easy with this system to replace plants when they get past their best with something more attractive.

Always raise containers slightly off the ground on bricks or tiles to allow free drainage, and those which are to be hung on a wall must be fixed securely. Drill and plug masonry and make sure the bracket

# Container Gardening

is strong enough to hold a considerable weight; wet soil is very heavy.

Correct choice of compost is very important. For all containers except hanging baskets John Innes Potting Compost Number 2 is ideal. If good quality J.I. is not available pick one of the peat-based composts; never use ordinary garden soil as this will be full of diseases and weeds. It also tends to set in a solid lump. Peat composts are very light in weight (and so ideal for baskets) but once they dry out they are difficult to re-wet thoroughly.

There is a choice between temporary displays (spring and summer bedding) and permanent displays of rock plants, shrubs or conifers. Summer bedding is planted in late May or early June but if you have a greenhouse or conservatory plant up tubs a couple of weeks earlier to give them a head start and move them out when danger of frost is passed. Spring bedding goes in when summer bedding is over.

Shrubs and conifers which will be in tubs for some years can be planted from pots at any time but in summer must be carefully looked after to ensure that they do not dry out.

Try to get your container into position before planting. Plastic window boxes can be put in place after filling, though wooden ones sitting on brackets should be secured first.

First put a layer of crocks in the bottom, cover this with medium grade peat or gravel, then add the soil. Allow a few centimetres or more of drainage in tubs but in window boxes and other shallow containers use less.

Do not put all the compost in at once but fill in stages firming as you go. When planting bulbs fill to the level at which the bulbs should be planted, space them out on the surface, then carry on filling.

Plants from pots should be set in place as you fill up and those from trays put in last. Do not crowd them in—they need plenty of space to develop.

Hanging baskets need lining before filling. Use sphagnum moss, from your garden centre, or try felt carpet underlay. Fill as you plant putting plants through the sides as well as round the rim and finishing off with a large plant in the centre at the top. Once the basket is established the best way of watering is to lower it into a large bowl of water.

All containers should be checked for dryness regularly, some may need watering twice a day. Give them a good soak whenever they need it. Keep watering until the water drips through the drainage holes.

If you have a number of similar tubs or troughs or a few growing bags try a semi-automatic system. The simplest of these consists of a length of fine rubber tubing into which nozzles are fitted wherever you need them. Run the tubing amongst the pots, with a nozzle for each, connect to the mains and you can water the whole lot with one turn of the tap. Remember that earthenware pots dry out quickly and need watering more frequently than other containers.

Although both John Innes and soilless composts have fertilizer in them it is a good idea to feed every week or so with a liquid fertilizer to encourage strong healthy growth and intense flower colour. Follow the maker's instructions and do not overdo it. Containers permanently planted with shrubs or conifers can be top-dressed every spring. Remove the top 5 cm (2 in) of compost and replace it with compost of the same type.

Keep a constant look out for pests and diseases, for they can build up very quickly, and keep an aerosol spray handy to treat infections as they appear.

Another thing you can do to keep your tubs looking good is to dead-head them regularly. As soon as flowers fade, pinch them off. This will encourage the production of more. Only by regular dead-heading will you get a blazing display right through the season.

*Plants for hanging baskets*
Ageratum
Alyssum
Begonia
Geraniums (zonal and ivy-leaved)
*Helichrysum petiolatum*
Fuchsia
Lobelia
Petunia
Tagetes
Verbena

*Bulbs for tubs*
Acidanthera
Agapanthus
Crocus
Narcissi and Daffodils
Hyacinths
Muscari
Tulips

*Shrubs for tubs*
Acer (Japanese Maples)
Aucuba
Camellia
Eleagnus
Euonymus
Heathers
Lavender
Rosemary
Yucca

In town-houses, well-planted window boxes can provide much-needed colour.

# Vegetables

## Introduction

Unless you can devote a lot of time and space to vegetable growing, you are unlikely to save very much financially by growing your own: the cost of seeds, pesticides, fertilizers and cloches rapidly eats into profit margins! Where you gain immeasurably, however, is in quality and satisfaction. Shop vegetables may be bigger and unblemished, but in terms of flavour, freshness and nutritional value, nothing can touch those you pick from your own garden just a few moments before you eat them. This applies especially to leafy vegetables like spinach and salad crops. So if your space is limited concentrate on these, and buy root vegetables such as potatoes, carrots and beetroot, which are usually cheap, and perhaps brassicas such as cauliflowers and Brussels sprouts, which require a fair amount of space and take a long time to reach maturity.

## The vegetable garden

Unlike annual flowers, which can give a splendid display even on poor soil, good vegetables can only be grown under good conditions. Give them the most fertile piece of ground you have, and build up and maintain the soil fertility by adding generous quantities of bulky manures or compost, if possible annually at the rate of about 5 kg per m² (10 lb per sq yd).

If you are starting from scratch in a garden which is virtually builder's rubble, clear debris and remove perennial weeds, then spread a thick layer of bulky manure (spent mushroom compost, for example) on your garden in the first autumn and leave it over the winter. It can be up to 23 cm (9 in) thick. It is surprising how fast worms will pull it down and start creating a worthwhile garden for you.

It is very important that the vegetable plot is well drained. If the surface looks mossy, or if water fails to seep away after heavy rains, make small trench drains across the lower end of the slope to absorb surplus water. Make them about 30 cm (1 ft) wide and 60–90 cm (2 to 3 ft) deep, and fill the bottom half with rubble before replacing the soil. If the problem persists make a more elaborate system. (*See* Week 50.)

Vegetables like an open site in the sense that they need maximum sunlight and should not be overhung by trees or tall buildings. However if the garden is very exposed some kind of windbreak is needed. The ideal windbreak is about 50 per cent solid so that it filters the wind rather than forming a rigid barrier. A large exposed garden can be protected by planting willows, poplars or fast-growing conifers around the edge. On a smaller scale erect fences or windbreak netting, making sure they straddle any narrow gaps between buildings which funnel the wind in a particularly devastating way.

Recent research has shown that if you shelter plants from even light winds it can increase their yields as much as 30 per cent. This is why cloches and low polythene tunnels are invaluable in vegetable gardens. By providing shelter bigger and better quality crops can be obtained, and in addition the season can be extended by sowing and planting earlier and harvesting later under cloches.

Wherever possible rotate crops in your garden to avoid the build-up of those soil pests and diseases which attack certain plant families. In practice rotation is difficult in small gardens, but try to avoid growing the same crop in the same place year after year. Try especially to move potatoes and tomatoes, peas and beans, brassicas (all the cabbage family as well as turnip, swedes, kohl rabi) and onions and leeks to a different position each year.

*Seed* Most vegetables are raised from seed, which can be bought from garden shops or through mail order seed catalogues, which often offer a wider range. Seed deteriorates with time, especially in damp or hot conditions, so should be stored somewhere cool and dry, preferably in airtight tins or jars.

In choosing varieties suitable for your area by guided by local experience and information in seed catalogues, gardening magazines etc. Several modern developments are useful for vegetable growers, and should be considered when buying seed.

*Air-sealed foil packets* keep seed in prime condition until opened, though once opened seed starts to deteriorate normally.

$F_1$ *hybrids* are specially bred varieties which produce exceptionally vigorous and high-yielding plants. Such seed is generally worth the extra cost.

*Pelleted seeds* are made by coating individual seeds with a hardened paste. They are easily handled and so can be spaced out accurately to avoid thinning. Keep them well watered as they may fail to germinate under dry conditions.

*Seed treatment and disease resistance.* Some seed is treated against common seed-borne diseases (e.g. celery against celery leaf spot), while some varieties have been bred with useful resistance to particular diseases.

*Sowing* Vegetables are either sown direct where they are to grow or are sown 'indoors' (in a greenhouse or frame), or in special seedbeds outdoors—in both cases being planted into their permanent positions as young plants.

In general the less hardy vegetables such as tomatoes, sweetcorn and green peppers are raised indoors. They are then ready for planting outdoors as soon as warm weather comes. They are sown in the same way as bedding plants, being moved finally into deep seedboxes or small pots. Before planting out they must be hardened off by being gradually exposed to colder temperatures. Alternatively plants which are ready for planting can be bought from garden centres etc.

*Sowing outdoors* Seed is normally sown outdoors in drills, which are narrow slits made in the soil with the edge of a hoe or trowel. Prepare the soil first by breaking down any clods with the back of the rake, then rake backwards and forwards to remove stones and make a smooth surface. Use a garden line to mark a straight line, and make the drill to the depth required. Fine seeds such as lettuce need a drill about 13 mm ($\frac{1}{2}$ in) deep, larger seeds like peas 2.5 cm (1 in) deep, and so on. Sow the seed in the bottom of the drill as thinly as possible. For most seeds it is a good idea to 'station sow', i.e. sow two or three seeds together then leave a gap before sowing a few more. This makes thinning very much easier. Press the seeds gently into the drill before covering them with soil.

Seedlings grow fast and must not become overcrowded. As soon as they are large enough to handle start thinning by nipping out the tops of surplus seedlings about an inch above the ground, so that each remaining seedling stands just clear of its neighbour. Thin in stages until plants are the recommended distance apart for each vegetable.

To save space vegetables such as brassicas, leeks and lettuces are often sown in small outdoor seedbeds, and transplanted into their permanent positions when a few inches high. Sow thinly in rows about 13 cm (5 in) apart, thinning to 5 to 8 cm (2–3 in) apart.

*Planting* Planting is a shock to plants and everything must be done to minimize the shock. If the plant is in a seedbed, box, or pot, water it well *before* uprooting it. Make a hole in the ground just large enough to accommodate the roots and hold the plant by the stem while filling in the soil around the roots. Using the fingers firm it in well after planting, watering again if the soil is dry. In hot weather the plant will wilt initially, but 'sunhats' can be made from newspaper to protect them until the roots have become established.

*Spacing* Traditionally vegetables were planted fairly close in rows that were relatively far apart. Weeding between the rows with a hoe was easy, but a lot of space was wasted. Research has shown that higher yields can be obtained by equidistant spacing, in other words planting lettuces, say, 25 cm (10 in) apart in each direction. In the early stages it is necessary to weed between the plants by hand; but later the leaves will cover the soil completely, so preventing further weeds from germinating.

*Weeds, pests, diseases* An established vegetable garden can be kept weed-free by hoeing and hand weeding, rather than by using chemical weedkillers, which can easily damage vegetables. However weedkillers can prove useful in clearing derelict ground of perennial weeds, which otherwise have to be dug up by hand.

The main pests and diseases which attack vegetables will be mentioned under the various crops, but the important thing to realise is that healthy, well-grown plants are much less likely to be attacked or seriously damaged than poor plants. So make sure your soil is fertile and well drained, thin seedlings

early, plant only strong healthy plants, avoid sowing and planting when the soil is cold and wet, and keep the garden as clean as possible, burning any diseased material and clearing away garden rubbish, old cabbage stalks etc, all of which provide hiding places for pests and encourage disease.

Slugs and birds are common problems in vegetable gardens. If you do not want to use slug pellets, go out on a muggy night with a torch, and catch the slugs while feeding. It works! Young seedlings can be protected from birds like sparrows by running a single strand of *strong* black cotton an inch or so above the row, and nets stretched over hoops help to protect mature vegetables from large birds such as pigeons.

*Hints on watering vegetables*
1) Always water as gently, as steadily and as thoroughly as possible. In summer water towards the evening to minimize evaporation losses.
2) With growing and mature vegetables a few heavy waterings (about 9 litres per m² or 2 gallons per sq yd), are *far* more beneficial than frequent light waterings.
3) There are 'critical stages' in growth when plants particularly benefit from water. With 'fruiting' vegetables such as peas, beans, tomatoes and marrows this is from the time of flowering onwards. Leafy vegetables such as cabbages, spinach and lettuce require water throughout growth, but respond particularly to watering 10 to 20 days before harvesting.
4) If root vegetables such as radishes and turnips are *over*watered they produce leafy tops rather than swollen roots: so only water if the soil is in danger of drying out.
5) Conserve water in the soil by mulching, i.e. covering the surface around plants with a layer several inches thick of something like manure, compost, straw or seaweed, or with white or black polythene film. Slits can be cut in the film and growing plants pulled through.

*Storage* Root vegetables like Jerusalem artichokes, celeriac, parsnips and Chinese radishes are hardy enough to leave in the soil in winter, but cover them with straw or bracken to make lifting easier in heavy

frost, and mark their position so you can find them in snow! Lift beetroot, carrots, turnips and swedes during the autumn and winter, and store them in boxes between layers of moist peat or sand in a shed. Potatoes can be stored loose in sacks, but must be in frost-free conditions. Onions, shallots and garlic should be dried off well in the summer sun and hung in plaited ropes, nets or nylon stockings in a well ventilated, frost-free shed. Always handle vegetables for storage extremely carefully, as rots start where they have been bruised or cut.

## Individual vegetables

In this section the spacing recommended is for *minimum* distances between plants. In small gardens it is often practical to adopt equidistant spacing: so, for example, where spacing of 20 cm (8 in) apart is suggested between plants in the row, the rows *themselves* can also be 20 cm apart. Where for some reason wider spacing between rows is necessary, a separate figure is given.

*Globe artichokes* are perennial vegetables grown for their delicious flower buds. Buy rooted offsets (suckers), plant 60–90 cm (2–3 ft) apart between February and April, in fertile, well-drained soil. Some will be ready the first autumn. Protect with straw in winter in cold areas. Replace plants every 3 years. (Raising from seed is unreliable.)

*Jerusalem artichokes* are extremely hardy, the knobbly tubers being a useful winter standby. They can grow over 3 m (10 ft) high, in any type of soil. Buy tubers (from a greengrocer if necessary, plant 10–15 cm (4–6 ins) deep, 30 cm (12 in) apart, between February and May. Trim back tops to 1½–2 m (5–6 ft) in mid-summer and cut stems back to ground level in autumn. Lift as required during winter, keeping a few tubers to plant the following spring.

*Asparagus* does well in any well-drained soil, provided that it is not acid. Prepare the bed by digging thoroughly and working in well-rotted manure. Plant *one* year old crowns about 10 cm (4 in) deep, 45 cm (18 in) apart in March and early April. Weed the beds carefully by hand, cut

# Vegetables

back the stalks just about ground level in late autumn, and apply a top-dressing of general fertilizer each spring. Start cutting moderately in the third season after planting.

*Aubergines* (egg plant) only succeed in southern England and are best grown in greenhouses, under cloches, or in very warm positions outdoors. Sow indoors in gentle heat in March and April, plant indoors April/May or outdoors after frost 38 cm (15 in) apart in fertile soil. Keep well watered, stake if necessary, nip out the tops when 38 cm (15 in) high and feed with tomato fertilizer when the fruits start to swell. On indoor plants watch out for red spider, greenfly and whitefly.

*Broad beans* are one of the earliest vegetables. In mild areas sow in October and November, elsewhere February to April. Sow 4–5 cm ($1\frac{1}{2}$–2 in) deep in drills or holes made with the dibber, about 15 cm (6 in) apart in single rows, or 23 cm (9 in) apart in double rows or blocks of several rows. Support tall varieties with wire netting or canes and twine, nip out the tops when in full flower to forestall black-fly attacks, and in dry weather water heavily when flowering to increase yields.

*French or kidney beans* are normally dwarf, though climbing varieties are available. The pods are eaten whole, though mature beans can be dried for winter. Sow outdoors in a sheltered position between April and early July, early sowings preferably under cloches. Or sow March/April indoors, planting out when 6 cm ($2\frac{1}{2}$ in) high. *Never* sow in cold wet conditions. Sow 3–5 cm (1–2 in) deep, 15 cm (6 in) apart. Water heavily once flowering, keep picking to encourage cropping, and protect with cloches in autumn to prolong the season.

*Runner beans* are decorative, productive and vigorous, growing $2\frac{1}{2}$–3 m (8–10 ft) high. They do badly in cold areas and like a sheltered site. Prepare the soil thoroughly the previous autumn, digging in plenty of manure. Sow as for French beans from March (indoors), until the end of June. Plant 15 cm (6 in) apart in double rows 60 cm (2 ft) apart. Erect very strong supports, allowing the plants to climb up strings, canes or poles. Water heavily once

flowering and pick regularly to prevent stringiness.

*Beetroot* can be used fresh, or pickled, or stored for winter. It likes rich, light, but not freshly manured soil. Early sowings are made outdoors in March and April (preferably under cloches), using 'bolt resistant' varieties which do not run to seed. Use any varieties for sowings from May to July. Soak seed for $\frac{1}{2}$ hour before sowing to aid germination. Sow in rows 15 cm (6 in) apart, thinning in stages to 5–15 cm (2–6 in) apart, the closer spacing for small salad beet, wider spacing for storage beet.

*Purple and white sprouting broccoli* are amongst the hardiest and most prolific winter and spring vegetables. Four plants are adequate for most families. Sow in a seedbed from mid-April to mid-May, starting with the early varieties, and plant 60 cm (2 ft) apart from June to mid-July. Earth up and stake the mature plants as they are top heavy. Snap off the sprouting shoots when 10–30 cm (4 to 12 in) long.

*Brussels sprouts* need to be grown in firm, fertile, but not freshly manured ground. Sow in a seedbed from mid-March to mid-April, starting with the earlier varieties. Plant from mid-May to early June, dwarf varieties 60 cm (2 ft) apart, taller varieties up to 90 cm (3 ft) apart. Earth up the stems and stake plants to prevent them 'rocking' in winter. Pick from the bottom of the stem upwards. Take precautions against club-root and cabbage root fly in spring, and watch out for mealy aphid in summer.

*Cabbages* can be available all year round by using appropriate varieties. Plant firmly in fertile soil into which manure has been worked several months previously. Watch out for club-root and cabbage caterpillars, and place felt discs around the base of the stem when planting to forestall cabbage root fly attacks.

Sow *spring cabbage* in a seedbed end July/early August, either planting mid-September to mid-October, or over-wintering in frames and planting out in spring. Protect with cloches in cold areas. Plant 15 cm (6 in) apart, using intermediate plants first as unhearted 'greens'.

A wide range of vegetables may be grown in even a small patch.

Drying onions. 'Get Set Red' and 'Sturon'.

Sow *summer cabbage* from February or early March (under cloches) to early May (in a seedbed) for planting from late April to June. Plant 35 cm (14 in) apart to get small heads, 45 cm (18 in) apart for large heads. Work in a general fertilizer before planting.

Sow *winter cabbages* from the end of April to mid-May, planting in July and early August 50 cm (20 in) apart.

*Carrots* prefer rich, but not freshly manured, light, sandy soil. Sow outdoors in succession from late February and March (preferably under cloches), to May and early June, starting with the smaller early types and progressing to the large storage and maincrop carrots. Sow *very* thinly (to minimize thinning which attracts carrot fly), in rows 15 cm (6 in) apart, thinning in stages to about 5 cm (2 in) apart. Where carrot fly is serious use insecticides if essential; try sowing in May to avoid the worst attacks, burn all thinnings, and lift storage carrots by early September.

*Cauliflowers* require fertile soil and plenty of moisture throughout growth. Sow in seedbeds, then plant firmly, working in a general fertilizer before planting. Where cabbage root fly is a problem use stem discs. (See *Cabbage*.) Sow *summer cauliflowers* from March (in frames) to May, planting from May to June, 54 cm (21 in) apart. Sow the *Australian autumn and early winter cauliflowers* in mid-May, planting in early July, 60 cm (24 in) apart. In mild areas sow *winter and early cauliflowers* in early May, planting late July, 65 cm (26 in) apart; elsewhere sow overwintering cauliflowers in late May, transplanting in late July 90 cm (3 ft) apart. These will be ready the following spring.

*Celeriac* has a turnip-like root which is a useful winter vegetable. It requires rich soil and plenty of moisture throughout growth. To get large roots sow indoors in gentle heat in February or March, planting in May 30 cm (12 in) apart. Keep well watered and feed with liquid fertilizer during summer. Tuck straw around the plants in late autumn, or lift and store in sand, keeping a tuft of leaves on the root.

*Celery* is grown in trenches, the stems being blanched for use around Christmas. Prepare a trench 30 cm (12 in) deep and 38 cm (15 in) wide the previous autumn, working in plenty of manure and filling to within 10 cm (4 in) of ground level. Sow seed in late March in gentle heat indoors, and plant in the trench end May/early June, 23 cm (9 in) apart. When plants are 30 cm (12 in) high, draw soil 8 cm ($3\frac{1}{2}$ in) up stem to blanch. Repeat twice at 3-week intervals until only the tops are exposed.

*'Witloof' chicory* is forced and blanched to produce white 'chicons'. Sow outdoors in rows 30 cm (12 in) apart in late May/early June, thinning to 15 cm (6 in) apart. Between late October and December lift the roots, trim off the leaves to 2.5 cm (1 in) above the crown, and lay them flat, in layers in moist sand, until required. To force plant 3 or 4 roots in damp soil in a large flower pot, covered with a pot the same size with the drainage holes blocked to exclude light. Put somewhere dark and warm (at least 10°C, 50°F) for about 3 weeks until chicons develop.

*Courgettes*, see *Marrows*.

*Cucumbers*. 'Greenhouse' and 'frame' varieties are long and smooth, whereas the rougher, hardier 'ridge' cucumbers are grown outdoors. In all cases prepare the soil beforehand by digging in generous quantities of well-rotted manure and straw. For heated greenhouses (min. temp. 20°C, 68°F), sow single seeds in small pots in gentle heat in February and March, planting 45 cm (18 in) apart 4–6 weeks later. Train the growths up wires to the top of the house. Keep the atmosphere moist, watch out for red spider attacks, and unless 'all female' varieties are grown, remove male flowers which cause swollen and bitter fruit.

For unheated greenhouses and frames sow in late March, planting late April/early May. Nip out the tips of frame cucumbers after 5 leaves, and train the lateral shoots to the frame corners before nipping off their tips. Outdoor cucumbers are sown *in situ* in mid-May, preferably under jars or cloches. Allow them to grow naturally, but if possible train them up off the ground on supports.

# Vegetables

*Endives* are used in salads or cooked. Although it is not essential, they are generally blanched before use to make them less bitter. Either sow in seedbeds and transplant, or sow *in situ* from April until July, thinning to 30 cm (12 in) apart for curly types or 38 cm (15 in) for broad-leaved types. Make a late sowing in August to transplant into frames or under cloches for winter. Blanch mature plants by tying up the leaves, then covering the plant with a box or bucket for about 10 days.

*Garlic* likes a sunny position and light, well-drained, rich but not freshly manured soil. Ideally plant between September and November, otherwise between February and March. Plant single cloves 4 cm (1½ in) deep, 10 cm (4 in) apart, with tips just above the soil surface. When the foliage dies down in summer lift and dry off well in the sun. Store in a well-ventilated frost free place for winter.

*Kales* are exceptionally hardy, so invaluable for winter greens. Eat the leaves of the curly kales or borecoles, and the young shoots (in spring mainly), of the smooth-leaved kales. Sow in seedbeds from late April to early June, planting firmly in July and early August, the dwarfer varieties 45 cm (18 in) apart, taller varieties 68 cm (27 in) apart. Give a top dressing of general fertilizer in spring to stimulate growth.

*Kohl-rabi* is a brassica which swells just above ground level. It grows rapidly, has considerable resistance to club-root, and does best on fertile, light soils. Sow very thinly from late February (in mild areas), to early September, in rows 30 cm (12 in) apart. Start thinning early or growth is interrupted, the final distance being 23 cm (9 in) apart. Used when no larger than tennis balls, the flavour is delicious.

*Leeks* are available from September to May. Make the soil rich by working in plenty of manure or compost. Start sowing indoors in heat in February for planting in May; sow outdoors in seedbeds from March to early May, planting when 20 cm (8 in) high from June to early August. Plant 10 to 15 cm (4 to 6 in) apart, dropping the leeks into 14 cm (5½ in) deep holes made with the dibber.

Allow the earth to fall back in naturally. Water in dry weather. If very white stems are wanted earth up during growth or use collars. (See Week 28.) Lift as required, using early varieties first.

*Lettuce* can be available all year round using appropriate varieties, although heated greenhouses are necessary for mid-winter crops. Lettuce needs rich soil and plenty of moisture throughout growth. Sow *in situ*, or in seedbeds or seed-boxes for transplanting. Average spacing is 30 cm (12 in) apart. For *late May/early June* crops sow indoors late February/early March, planting in greenhouses, under cloches, or somewhere sheltered outdoors end March/early April. For *June* to *October* crops sow from late March to early June, sowing *in situ* from mid-May onwards, as transplanting is less successful in summer. For *November to March* crops sow appropriate winter varieties outdoors from late August to early October, planting in heated or unheated greenhouses or frames in late autumn. *Hardy overwintering varieties* are sown August/September, thinned to 7.5 cm (3 in) apart in October and planted out in spring to crop May/June. Cloche them during winter.

*Marrows* and *pumpkins* are raised like cucumbers (q.v.) and need well prepared ground into which plenty of manure has been worked. Bush marrows, which are most suitable for small gardens, are planted 90 cm (3 ft) apart; trailing marrows and pumpkins 120 cm (4 ft) apart. Courgettes are immature marrows picked when only a few inches long; pick regularly to encourage further cropping. In cold summers marrows sometimes need hand pollination. (*See* Week 22.)

*Melons* are raised like cucumbers (q.v.) but must be grown in greenhouses, frames or cloches. Plant 90 cm (3 ft) apart, allowing one per Dutch light frame. Nip out tips after 5 leaves, training 4 side shoots to the frame corners; train one shoot each way under cloches. In greenhouses train 3 or 4 shoots up strings. If bees are scarce hand pollinate. (*See* Week 22.) 'Stop' growths two leaves above fruits. Fruits become scented and crack when ripe.

*Onions* and *shallots* need well-drained, fertile, but not freshly manured soil. Sow

*summer and storage onions* between February and April (once the soil is warm), in rows 23 cm (9 in) apart, thinning to 8 cm (3½ in) apart. Use the thinnings in salads. (Apply insecticide at seedling stage if onion fly is serious.) Alternatively sets (tiny bulbs) can be planted in spring 5 cm (2 in) apart, their tips just above ground. *Very early onions* are obtained by sowing Japanese overwintering varieties in August, thinning them in spring. For green *'spring' onions*, in summer, sow between March and June; for early spring onions sow hardy overwintering varieties in July and August. No thinning is necessary. *Shallots* are grown from sets planted 15 cm (6 in) apart, in December or January in mild areas, February and March elsewhere. For onion and shallot harvesting *see* page 00.

*Parsnips* are very hardy root vegetables, and need deep, well-cultivated but not freshly manured soil. Sow from March (provided the soil is warm) until May, in rows 25 cm (10 in) apart. Thin to 7 to 15 cm (3–6 in) apart, the wider spacing to get larger roots. Always use fresh seed as parsnip seed deteriorates rapidly. Lift roots as required during winter.

*Peas* require well-drained fertile soil into which plenty of manure has been worked. The 'early' varieties mature faster than the 'maincrop', but bear less heavily. Start sowing in warm areas in late February under cloches, then sow in succession until early July. In mild areas sow overwintering varieties in October and November for very early crops. Peas are generally sown 3–4.5 cm (1–1½ in) deep in flat bottomed, 23 cm (9 in) wide drills, spacing seed 5 cm (2 in) apart. Guard against mice and birds (*see* p. 49). As soon as tendrils appear, support the plants with pea sticks or wire netting. If dry, water heavily once flowering.

*Peppers* (capsicums or sweet peppers) are normally eaten green, as they only ripen into fully mature red or yellow fruits in very warm summers. Grow them like aubergines (q.v.) using $F_1$ varieties which mature earliest.

*Potatoes* require a lot of space; in small gardens concentrate on growing the faster growing 'earlies'. Buy seed potatoes

# Vegetables

*Radishes* must be grown quickly with plenty of moisture, or they become 'woody'. They need light, rich, but not freshly manured soil. Start sowing under cloches in February, sow in succession outdoors until September, and under cloches or in cold greenhouses in September and October. Sow very thinly in rows 15 cm (6 in) apart, thinning to 2.5 cm (1 in) apart. Giant *winter radishes* are sown in July and August in rows 25 cm (10 in) apart, thinning to 13 cm (5 in) apart. Lift these as required during winter.

*Rhubarb* provides the first fruit each season. It needs well-drained, fertile soil into which plenty of manure has been dug. Plant bought sets (or divide old crowns), between November and March. Plant at least 1 m (1 yd) apart, the buds just below soil level. Do not start pulling until the second season. Apply heavy dressings of manure every autumn, and lift, divide and replant crowns every 5 years or so. For forcing *see* Week 1.

*Spinaches and leaf beets* (which include perpetual spinach and chards or seakale beet) need fertile soil and plenty of moisture throughout growth. Sow *summer spinach* from late February to May, in in rows 30 cm (12 in) apart, thinning to 15 cm (6 in) apart. Sow *winter spinach* in August and September, in rows 30 cm (12 in) apart, thinning to 23 cm (9 in) apart. Sow *leaf beets*, (which are more productive and easier to grow than ordinary spinach), from March to August, in rows 40 cm (16 in) apart, thinning to 30 cm (12 in) apart. *New Zealand spinach*, an unrelated, sprawly plant thriving under dry conditions, is sown in May in rows 45 cm (18 in) apart, thinning to 45 cm (18 in) apart.

*Swedes* often succeed where turnips fail. Manure the soil for the previous crop, sow from late April until early June in rows 38 cm (15 in) apart, thinning early to 28 cm (11 in) apart. Dig as needed until Christmas, when they should be lifted and stored or they become woody.

*Sweetcorn* is normally only successful in the south. Select a sheltered, well-drained, reasonably fertile site. Sow the seed indoors in small pots in gentle heat, thin to one seedling per pot, and plant out,

preferably under cloches, in late May/early June. Seed can also be sown *in situ*, under individual jars or cloches, in mid-May. To assist wind pollination plant sweetcorn in blocks or squares, the plants 36 cm (14 in) apart each way.

*Tomatoes* can be grown in a warm sheltered position outdoors, or in frames or under cloches, or in heated or unheated greenhouses. Move to a fresh site every 3 years. Prepare the soil by working in well-rotted manure or compost. Sow outdoor tomatoes in gentle heat indoors mid-March to April, planting out end May/early June. Sow indoor tomatoes 2 weeks earlier, and heated greenhouse tomatoes between mid-January and March. Plant in double rows, tall varieties, which need to be staked, 38 cm (15 in) apart, bush varieties 48 cm (19 in) apart. With tall varieties take out sideshoots and 'stop' growing points after about 4 trusses outdoors, or 6 trusses indoors. Keep indoor tomatoes well ventilated, and feed with tomato fertilizer when fruits start to form. Spray outdoor tomatoes against tomato blight in damp summers.

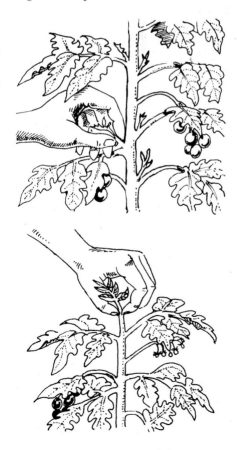

in February, and stand them upright to chit (sprout) in boxes, in a light but cool room, until the shoots are 2 cm (¾ in) long. Plant upright in very fertile soil from April onwards, in drills or holes about 12 cm (4½ in) deep. Plant earlies 30 cm (12 in) apart in rows 56 cm (22 in) apart; maincrop 38 cm (15 in) apart in rows 75 cm (30 in) apart. When plants are about 23 cm (9 in) high, draw earth up around stems to prevent surface potatoes greening and help control weeds. Or cover them with black plastic after planting, later pulling the stems through slits cut in the plastic.

# Fruit

## Soil

Fruit in general will grow on a wide range of soils, which is fortunate, for the home gardener can do little to change the nature of his own soil. However, he can obtain maximum results by choosing the most suitable fruits to grow.

All fruits need good drainage. Provided topsoil drainage is reasonable, however, the fruits most able to cope with doubtful drainage below are cooking apples, blackberries, currants, gooseberries, pears and plums. Most fruits thrive best in a slightly acid soil, whereas blueberries and cranberries require very acid, but still well-drained, conditions. If the soil is alkaline, various mineral deficiencies will be troublesome. On chalky land never bring the chalk to the top. If there is less than 30 cm (1 ft) overlaying the chalk it is better not to grow fruits other than possibly strawberries, except in containers and raised beds. The latter can also help to solve indifferent drainage problems.

Fruit will do best on a deep and well-drained soil of a loamy nature but the average garden which has been well cultivated in the past will be quite rich enough, without preparation other than digging, for tree fruits. Soft fruits need richer conditions and plenty of organic matter in the soil to retain moisture during the summer months.

Over-acid soils may be improved by careful liming. Alkaline soils can be made more fruitful in the short-term by watering with a preparation of chelated iron, magnesium and manganese in mid-winter. Long-term improvement can be secured by dressing with flowers of sulphur annually, 25 g per $m^2$ (4 oz per sq yd) for sandy soil, 50 g per $m^2$ (8 oz per sq yd) for heavy loam.

## Choosing the site

In selecting a site for growing fruit in the garden, try to arrange a single plot for the fruit. This makes manuring, cultivation and protection from birds easier. At the same time do not neglect the protection offered by wall space for suitably trained trees. Group the nitrogen-lovers together (notably blackcurrants, pears and plums) and the potash-lovers (dessert apples, gooseberries and redcurrants).

Cordon pears.

Full sun will make for higher yields and better quality. In exposed areas, look for shelter from winds but avoid planting near trees or hedges where their roots will compete—and win.

Apricots, figs, grapes, peaches and nectarines, and some of the choicer varieties of pears and gage plums are most in need of full sun. Blackberries, raspberries and other soft fruits will best tolerate partial shade.

Blackberries, red and white currants, gooseberries, loganberries and morello cherries will grow against north-facing walls. East walls will do for early varieties of plums and pears. Reserve a south-facing wall for apricots, figs, grapes, peaches and nectarines. West-facing walls will give shelter for gages, pears and early peaches and nectarines.

## Choice of shape

Having decided you want to plant some fruit trees you have to decide what shape to buy. This will depend mostly on the intended site and space available. These notes should assist you in your choice.

*Standard and half-standard* Trees with a trunk of about 2 m (6½ ft) or 1.4 m (4½ ft) respectively before the first branch. Too large for the ordinary small garden, spreading up to 11 m (36 ft).

*Bush* This has a trunk of 50–75 cm (20–30 in). Even these are large for the average garden requiring to be 3.5 to 5.5 m (12–18 ft) apart for apples, pears, plums or peaches.

An espalier pear.

*Dwarf bush* With a trunk of 45–50 cm (18–20 in) and pruned to a goblet shape, makes an excellent tree for the small garden. Suitable rootstocks are available for apples which should be spaced 2.5–3 m (8–10 ft) apart. The smallest bush pear tree, grafted on Quince C rootstock, needs to be planted 3–4.5 m (10–15 ft) apart.

*Cordon* This has a single central stem with fruiting spurs springing from it. Apple and pear cordons are usually planted at an angle of 45° to restrain growth and economize space. Plums do not take kindly to cordon training. Red and white currants and gooseberries are often grown as vertical cordons and can be trained not only as singles but in a U-shape, or with three or four stems as two Us (multiple cordons). Apple cordons should be 75–90 cm (2½–3 ft) apart, pears 60–90 cm (2–3 ft), red and white currants and gooseberries 30 cm (1 ft) apart for single cordons, 60 cm (2 ft) for U-cordons, 90 cm (3 ft) for trebles and 120 cm (4 ft) for double Us.

A row of apple or pear cordons needs 90 cm (3 ft) clear on either side of it, unless trained on a fence or wall. Soft fruit cordons in rows should be 1.5 m (5 ft) apart.

*Espalier* This form of tree is flat-trained with a vertical central trunk and horizontal branches in pairs, one on either side. This system is popular for training pears against walls or fences and can also be used for apples or pears trained in the open to border a path or divide one

A fan plum.

How to train a blackberry.

portion of the garden from another. Apples will take up 3–4.5 m (10–15 ft), pears 3.5–6 m (12–20 ft).

*Fan* Another form of flat training but with the branches radiating from the centre like the ribs of a fan, more difficult to train and look after than the forms previously mentioned. Can be used for apple and pears, popular for peaches, nectarines and apricots. Fan-trained apples should be 3–4.5 m (10–15 ft) apart, pears 3.5–6 m (12–20 ft), plums, apricots, peaches and nectarines 3.5–5.5 m (12–18 ft).

*Pyramid* This has a vertical central stem with tiers of branches radiating all round it. Dwarf pyramids are useful where space is restricted. Apples, pears and plums are grown in this way. Allow 1–1.2 m (3½–4 ft) for apples, 1 m (3½ ft) for pears with 2 m (6¼ ft) between the rows. Pyramid plums on St. Julien 'A' rootstock should be 3–3.5 m (10–12 ft) apart each way, but if grafted on the new Pixy rootstock 3 m (10 ft) is sufficient even on good ground.

*Soft fruits* Plant red and white currants and gooseberry bushes 1.5 m (5 ft) apart each way, blackcurrants 1.8 m (6 ft). Set raspberry canes 45 cm (1½ ft) apart in rows 1.8 m (6 ft) apart and strawberries 45 cm (1½ ft) apart with 75 cm (2½ ft) between rows.

*N.B. Where two figures are given above, the lower is for poorish soil, the higher for very fertile soil.*

## Cross-pollination

Most apples and pears and many plums and gages need to have their blossom fertilized by pollen from another variety before they will set fruit. A few apples and pears, several plums, all peaches except 'Hale's Early', and all soft fruits except blueberries, are self-fertile and will set a crop with their own pollen. However, all tree fruits will set bigger crops when cross-pollinated.

Outdoors the pollen is transferred by the movements of bees and other insects, and their activity is necessary for self-pollination as well as cross-pollination, for which reason cloched strawberries should be well ventilated at blossom time.

Under glass, where insects may be scarce, the fruit-grower must assist by transferring pollen on a wisp of cotton wool or a small camelhair brush.

Where cross-pollination is necessary you must have in your or the next door garden a variety with good pollen flowering at the same time as your tree. If you are in doubt, the supplier of your tree will advise. Most catalogues give some guidance on flowering times.

Note that certain varieties of tree have no good pollen and so you may need another tree to pollinate it and yet a third tree to fertilize the pollinator.

Where you have room for only one tree you can either plant a 'family tree' with two or more varieties grafted on one stem, selected by the nurseryman to pollinate each other, or choose from one of the following.

In apples 'Ellison's Orange' and 'Laxton's Superb' are both reasonably self-fertile but both tend to bear biennially (every other year), especially the latter, a tendency which may be corrected by drastic blossom thinning.

In pears 'Conference', 'William's Bon Chrêtien' and 'Louise Bonne of Jersey' are partially self-fertile.

Among the plums several varieties will give reasonable crops on their own. These include the dessert varieties 'Denniston's Superb', 'Early Transparent Gage', 'Oullin's Golden Gage', 'Reine Claude de Bavay', 'Severn Cross' and 'Victoria'. These cookers are also self-fertile—'Czar', 'Marjorie's Seedling', 'Merryweather Damson', 'Monarch', 'Pershore' (also called 'Yellow Egg'), 'Purple Pershore', 'Shropshire Damson' and 'Warwickshire Drooper'.

## Staking

Preferably, stakes should be put in before planting to avoid subsequent root damage. All tree fruits will need support in their early years and dwarf trees on non-vigorous rootstocks will require a stake throughout their life unless in a very sheltered garden. Stakes should always be set on the prevailing windward side (usually the south-west) to provide some protection.

Buy substantial treated stakes or soak all that part which will be in contact with the soil with a copper-based preservative. It should be noted that creosote or tar may injure roots.

Stakes should be long enough to be inserted 45 cm (18 in) in heavy soil, 60 cm (2 ft) in light, and come up to just above the first branch. If you use cord for tying, twist it several times at right angles to the main tie, to form a buffer between tree and stake. Patent plastic fasteners are better, because they are easily adjustable as the girth of the trunk increases.

For cordons provide three horizontal wires on the support system: 3.15 mm (gauge 10) for the upper, 2.50 mm (gauge 12) for the others, with a straining bolt at the end of each to keep it always taut. Posts should be about 3 m (10 ft) apart and tall enough for the lower wire to be 75 cm (2½ ft) above the ground and the others at 60 cm (2 ft) intervals. To these wires a cane is tied for each cordon.

# Fruit

## Planting

The fruit planting season extends from November to March or April, but the earlier you plant the better. The soil should be moist but quite friable. Should the trees or plants arrive when the soil is too wet or frozen, heel them in. Dig a small trench with one side sloping and lean the stems against that. Cover the roots and make reasonably firm. It is worth covering a sheltered spot so that trees can be heeled in whatever the general soil conditions. If the roots are dry, soak them for an hour and trim back any broken or damaged roots.

Take out the planting hole at the last moment, large enough for every root to be spread out to its fullest extent. Mound up the centre slightly and sit the tree on that.

Get someone to hold the tree for you, keeping it at the right depth with the nursery soil mark in line with ground level and the graft union quite 10 cm (4 in) clear of soil. Oblique cordons should be slanted at 45° with the rootstock underneath at the union.

Fill in the soil gradually working it around and among the roots. No manure need be added and none must ever come in direct contact with roots. A few handfuls of moist peat scattered directly on the roots will aid rapid re-establishment. If you are in doubt about the soil's fertility mix a double handful of sterilized bonemeal with the soil which you will be returning.

Make the soil quite firm, rake tidy and cover with a 5 cm (2 in) deep mulch of rotted manure, garden compost or moist peat, as far as the roots extend, but keep this mulch 10 cm (or a few inches) clear of the stem.

Fasten the tree to its stake, see above, and be ready to adjust after a month or two. Soft fruits, except for cordons, do not need staking. Cane fruits will need horizontal wires.

Plant the soft fruits in a similar manner but blackcurrants should be a little deeper than they were in the nursery. With all strawberries depth of planting is vital: with the crown just level with the soil. They must be firm.

Fruit trees and plants can also be container-grown.

## Fruit thinning

It pays in growing fruit not to be greedy. Overcropping one year can result in no fruit the next. A regular habit of cropping every other year can develop all too easily, particularly with certain varieties of apples, pears and plums. Judicious thinning therefore results in more regular cropping and, in addition, better-sized fruits.

Where the prime object of thinning is to prevent biennial bearing, thinning is most effective if it starts at the blossom stage. When there is a prolific supply of flower buds remove half to three-quarters of the buds. They can easily be rubbed off before they open.

Fruit size can be improved when there is a heavy set by thinning before the natural June drop occurs. Reduce apples to 10–15 cm (4–6 in). Remove the central apple of the cluster first and any diseased, pest-attacked or misshapen specimens.

Thin pears when about 2.5 cm (1 in) long until there is only one, and occasionally two, left on each spur.

Thin peaches and nectarines in two stages, at hazelnut size leaving each fruit enough space to swell, and at walnut size thinning until one fruit is left per 23 cm (9 in) of wood. Apricots are less in need of thinning but when there is a very heavy set thin gradually over a fortnight, reducing the fruitlets to one per cluster.

Thinning is most important with plums. Overcropping frequently causes branch breakage, especially in Victorias, and results in biennial bearing. Thin over several days, after stoning has been completed (test a fruit to see if the stone is present), until the fruits are about 5 cm (2 in) apart, a little less with culinary sorts.

Thinning is unnecessary with most soft fruits but picking unripe gooseberries for early kitchen use is a form of thinning and results in the remaining berries becoming larger.

Grapes for wine need not be thinned. For dessert begin to thin when the berries are only 2.5 mm ($\frac{1}{10}$ in) across and continue at intervals until they are the size of peas and spaced about 2.5 cm (1 in) apart. Use sharp, pointed scissors and a tiny fork-ended stick to hold the grape stalks out so that the bloom on the skin is uninjured.

## Protecting from birds

Birds are probably the most serious pest the garden fruit-grower has to face: they attack all soft-skinned fruits as they ripen and on occasion apples and pears too. In winter they peck out the growth buds, especially from soft fruits.

Ripening tree fruits, such as choice apples and pears, may be protected individually with ventilated bags, which also keep off wasps. This, however, is an expensive and tedious procedure. It is also possible to give individual trees considerable protection where they are sufficiently small to be shrouded with strands of fine rayon web sold specially for the purpose. Do not use nylon thread which can slice off a bird's wing or foot.

The surest protection comes from a complete netting cage erected over the fruit plantation. This is very well worth considering for all soft fruits and top fruits grown as dwarf bushes, pyramids or cordons. It pays to buy a cage high enough for vigorous modern raspberry varieties, preferably 2 m (or 6½ ft) high. There should be a door through which you can wheel your barrow and the roof must be easily removable. This is necessary when snow threatens as the weight might otherwise cause considerable damage.

Wall-trained trees are easily covered individually with lengths of lightweight nylon netting, as are strawberry plots. In whatever you devise, remember the need for easy personal entry at picking time. Strawberries under cloches are at risk when the cloches are opened: a length of netting should be thrown over the top.

## Picking and storing

The picking of soft fruit is mostly a matter of common sense: you pick when they are ripe. Pick currants in complete trusses, using a small pair of scissors if you wish. The ripeness of redcurrants is difficult to judge: try tasting if in doubt for they can appear quite red days before they have acquired maximum sweetness.

Apples and pears are only ready to pick when they will part readily from the tree, complete with stalk, when you lift to the horizontal in the palm of the hand and give a slight twist. No tugging is neces-

Fruit tree shapes. Left to right: pyramid, bush, half-standard and standard. See 'Choice of Shape', p. 54.

sary. Early varieties, usually ready in August, are best eaten straight from the tree. Few early apples keep more than a few days. 'Discovery' is an exception, lasting two or three weeks. Mid-season varieties will keep for a few weeks.

An apple or pear may be ready to pick but not ready to eat. Nurserymen's catalogues give the season when each variety is at its best. Late or keeping varieties of apples for eating from late November and possibly through the winter need to be stored carefully. It is difficult for the amateur to secure the ideal conditions which are: a low temperature of just over 4°C (just under 40°F); darkness; good ventilation but with slightly moist atmosphere; each variety segregated; freedom from air pollution (oil or petrol or onion odours which would impart an unpleasant flavour).

In the home the spare room is too dry, garden shed too variable in temperature and too cold in icy weather, the garage too smelly. If reasonable conditions can be found (cellars are ideal), the apples may be spread out, one layer thick, on shelves or in trays. Wrapping apples individually in special oiled paper wraps or squares of newspaper helps them to keep and isolates any which do not: wrap the paper loosely over and do not attempt to secure a hermetic seal.

Many amateurs have found the best conditions by putting apples in polythene bags, not more than 1.8 kg (4 lb) in each, all the same variety. Fasten the neck round a pencil which you then withdraw to allow ventilation. Also cut a snippet off each bottom corner to let air pass. Store in the dark in conditions that are as cool but frost-free as you can find. There is now a sugar-based 'dip' available to amateurs for the storing of fruit.

Keeping pears should be taken into a warm room for the last few days of ripening. Apples and pears picked too soon or kept too dry in store soon shrivel.

## Fruit garden hygiene

Diseases will cause fewer losses, apples will keep better in winter store and quality will be improved if you always maintain strict hygiene among your fruits.

Always deal with any disease as soon as noticed, dig up virus-ridden specimens and at once burn all suspected material. Never leave fruits attacked by brown rot to mummify on the tree.

When cutting out diseased wood always disinfect the blades of your secateurs or other tools when passing from diseased to hitherto healthy wood. Have a can of disinfectant at hand and a supply of old paper for wiping ready.

## Feeding

The number of possible permutations for fruit feeding programmes is legion. The ordinary gardener must take into account what is available, the character of his particular soil and how his trees or bushes are behaving: then make up his own mind.

The three essential elements are nitrogen (N), phosphorus (P) and potassium (K). In the old 'National Growmore' general fertilizer formula these three were compounded in equal proportions. If you use such a fertilizer, follow the directions on the container.

Dessert apples, sweet cherries, red and white currants, gooseberries and raspberries may need extra potash, so give an extra winter dressing of sulphate of potash, from 35 to 70 g per m² (1 to 2 oz per sq yd).

Many trace elements are vital although required in minute amounts. These are found in natural manures, fish manure and seaweed. They are added to many proprietary preparations. Fertilizers intended for roses are often excellent for fruit.

An annual mulch of farmyard or stable manure, spread without touching the stem and slightly farther than the branches extend, is hard to beat as the basis of a manurial programme.

# Rock Gardening

## Construction of a rock garden

Ideally, a rock garden should be situated in the open, away from any shade and possible drip from overhanging trees, and on a gentle south or south-western slope. Such a site may not always be available, but as long as the situation is open and the drainage good (an essential requirement for alpine plants), other aspects can be used. If possible, however, it is best to avoid an aspect facing to the cold and unsympathetic east.

When planning to build a rock garden, the first consideration is the type of stone to be used. If a local stone is available, it is likely to be cheaper than one brought in from another area, because of high carriage costs, and it will look more in keeping with its surroundings. You should also bear in mind that some types of rock, such as limestones, can be affected by impurities in the air. (Do not choose a limestone if mainly lime-hating plants are to be grown.)

However small the rock garden, use reasonably large rocks—as large as can be comfortably handled. Pieces weighing from 25 to 50 kg ($\frac{1}{2}$ to 1 cwt) can be moved without too much strain, and even larger pieces can be moved using a sack-truck running on planks, and by using a crow-bar to lever them into place.

The rocks should blend together either in outcrops or continuous building. Do not lay them in isolated splendour or put them on their narrowest ends. Rocks should always be placed with a slight backward tilt and they should fit flush together or overlap slightly. The strata of the outcrops should always tilt in one direction. Bury every rock used so that its base cannot be seen.

The amount of work required will depend to some extent upon the building style adopted, but a site measuring say 15 m² (160 sq ft) can be made into an attractive rock garden by using 2–3 tonnes of stone in weights as previously suggested. Additional soil will be required to fill the outcrops as they are constructed. A properly constructed rock garden provides a great many cracks and crevices between the rocks, and these form ideal homes for plants such as sempervivum, saxifraga, small dianthus, gypsophila and sedum. A few of these should be at hand during construction so that they can be put into place at the time of building, as it is not easy to plant in a narrow crevice once building has been completed.

*Compost*  As an approximate guide, 1 m² (1 sq yard) of compost will be needed for each tonne of rock. A good standard compost can be prepared by mixing 2 parts of loam (or good top-spit garden soil), 1 part of fine-grade moss peat (or leafmould), and 1 part of sharp sand or fine grit. When the ingredients are assembled, and before they are mixed, a generous sprinkling of bonemeal (3 kg/m³—5 lb/cu yd) will be a valuable addition. No other fertilizer is needed. This compost will be suitable for the majority of alpine plants.

## Alternatives to a rock garden

Not all gardens or circumstances permit the construction of a rock garden. Rock or alpine plants will flourish, however, in other locations, for example in walls, containers and paved areas.

*Walls*  It is easier to put in the plants as the wall is being built, but old established stone or 'dry' walls can usually be colonized, if not by actual plants, then by mixing the seeds of alpine plants with damp sand and dropping it into the crevices. There will be a considerable mortality, but enough will survive to begin the colonization. In due course there will be self-sown seedlings. Walls can be retaining, built against a bank to hold up differing levels, or free-standing and two-sided, built hollow, with the centre filled with soil. The latter provides a number of aspects, as both the sides, the top and the end of the wall can be used for a diversity of plants. One side may be sunny and the other shaded, which provides the opportunity for an even wider choice. Such dry stone walls house a very wide collection of alpine plants and can be extremely decorative and space-saving.

*Containers*  Using old stone troughs and sinks as homes for alpine plants is now very popular; they can look most attractive standing on patios and paving near the house. Such containers are very scarce and expensive. You can, however, easily 'convert' a glazed sink (*see* p. 46).

One variation on the normal rock garden theme is to cover a stone wall with a selection of alpine plants.

*Paved areas* The cracks between paving stones offer just the conditions most alpine plants appreciate. Their roots will be in cool, moist soil beneath the stones, their heads will be in the light and their stems will be protected from a collar of wet soil. They will also relieve the monotonous flatness of a paved area, making it far more pleasing to the eye. As paving stones are often laid upon sand or some other unsympathetic material, the cracks should be excavated and filled with good compost so that the plants can get a good start. Once established, they will send their roots far and wide in search of nourishment. If the joints between the paving stones have been cemented, it is usually possible to break away a corner here and there to provide an adequate planting position. As not all rock plants will tolerate being trampled on occasionally, it is important to plant suitable kinds (*see* suggestions given below).

*Tufa rock* Tufa is a comparatively soft and very porous material into which holes can easily be bored, and seedlings and small plants can be set. As the plants become established, their roots penetrate the porous rock and they grow into characteristically hard and compact specimens. A sizeable piece of tufa can be bored with a great many such holes and used as an isolated feature of great beauty and interest. It can be stood on paving or, preferably, by removing one paving stone, set a few centimetres into the ground. This encourages the absorption of water by capillary action so that overhead watering is needed less frequently. Small pieces of this useful stone are invaluable for making up the miniature mountain-scapes which make sink and trough gardens so attractive. Even the small pieces can be drilled to contain individual plants, which enlarges the scope in even the smallest miniature garden. Tufa can also be used in an ordinary rock garden, but can be very stark until it weathers.

*Scree* If all else fails, there is no reason why an area in the garden should not be excavated to a depth of 30–45 cm (12–18 in) or larger if drainage material is provided and filled with the rock garden compost described earlier, with extra grit

Gentians provide luscious summer colour.

This campanula grows well in crevices.

to provide a more open compost. A few flat stones partially sunk here and there provide easy access and there are a great many rock plants which will be quite content in such an environment. Dress the surface with grit or stone chippings.

## Winter protection and alpine houses

Many true alpine plants are not altogether happy in the open, especially during unpredictable winters, and the experienced rock gardener will soon feel the need for an 'alpine house'. This enables the less hardy or more difficult varieties to be cultivated. Ideally, an alpine house should be purpose-built, and some greenhouse manufacturers specialize in their construction. The house should have a low 'pitch', to bring the plants as near as possible to the glass and continuous ventilation along both sides of the roof and the sides at staging level. It should preferably run north to south, with the door at the south end.

For the less ambitious gardener, however, an ordinary greenhouse can be adapted and will serve just as well to see the more difficult plants through the winter. Additional ventilators can usually be inserted at no great expense and a steeper pitch is not a serious drawback. The target is to ensure the maximum amount of light and air.

There are two schools of thought regarding heating in an alpine house. Some gardeners like to be able to exclude frost. Others prefer to have no form of artificial heating, an important point

when fuels and energy are so expensive. It is best not to grow alpine plants with other greenhouse plants which require very different conditions.

*Watering* Great care should be taken in the watering of plants in an alpine house. Many plants are killed by injudicious watering. The safest rule to observe when deciding whether to water or not is—'if in doubt, don't'. A plant which has been over-saturated will seldom recover, whereas one which has been kept too dry will usually revive. During the winter months, when many plants are at rest, watering should be minimal, but at any time a mere splash is quite inadequate. Always water thoroughly, ensuring that the moisture reaches down to the bottom of the container where most of the roots will be.

## Some useful alpine plants

Sunny places: acaena, *Alyssum saxatile*, artemisia (dwarf kinds), dianthus (rock type), genista, saxifraga, thymus, veronica

Shady places: andromeda, astilbe, cassiope, cyclamen, helleborus, mimulus, phyllodoce, uvularia

Crevices in paving: achillea, campanula (dwarf kinds), *Festuca rubra* 'Viridis', raoulia, *Thymus serpyllum*

Stone sinks and troughs: campanula (most dwarf kinds, but avoid *C. poscharskyana*, which is too vigorous), *Gentiana verna* 'Angulosa', *Geranium subcaulescens*, primula (dwarf European species and hybrids)

# Cloches and Frames

## Frames

A garden frame is useful in its own right, but as an adjunct to the greenhouse it is invaluable. Without a frame, hardening off bedding plants becomes extremely difficult, and many of the resting plants that can be housed in the frame would otherwise clutter the greenhouse and detract from the more decorative plants. The frame can also be used for housing many greenhouse plants that are not particularly attractive in their early stages, such as primulas and cinerarias.

Frames are also useful for propagating a variety of cuttings, particularly if soil-warming cables are used. If you do not have a greenhouse, a frame also widens your scope for raising plants from seed.

In the kitchen garden there is the possibility of raising earlier crops of vegetables such as turnips, carrots and radishes, and possibly a winter crop of lettuces if a suitable variety is chosen. If you do not have a greenhouse (or do not want to give over the space to them) you can use frames for summer crops such as melons and suitable cucumber varieties.

Aim to have your frames in use the year round. A typical programme might be as follows. Hardening off bedding plants from March to May or June, followed by either a crop of cucumbers or melons, or standing for resting house or greenhouse plants. In August or September these can be moved or cleared and the frame used to root shrub cuttings, and by October pots of bulbs can be plunged until they are ready to take in for flowering. The frame can also be used to overwinter chrysanthemum 'stools' (roots).

*Types of frame* Most of the frames available in kit form sold at garden centres have an aluminium framework with glass sides and top. They are easy to assemble and admit plenty of light. One drawback is the fact that they do not retain the heat as well as a brick or timber-sided frame. If you want to run heating cables round the side, glass is not going to be as convenient as wood or brick.

A timber-sided frame overcomes this problem, but cedarwood frames are not cheap, and although they may be easier to keep warm, are not so light.

Some designs are all plastic—frame and top (but with metal feet for firm anchorage).

Soil-warming cables

The frames with metal sides and glass or PVC tops are more robust, but can act rather like a cold radiator in winter (but you can always line them).

There is one design of frame that needs special mention: the very large barn-shaped frames which are more like giant cloches or mini-greenhouses than frames. They are more expensive than ordinary frames or cloches, but very useful.

*Heating and ventilation* Garden frames have traditionally been called cold-frames, but there is absolutely no reason why they should be 'cold'. In the days when horse manure was plentiful gardeners used to generate enough heat by making a 'hot-bed' beneath the frame, the decomposing manure providing the warmth.

Nowadays it is more straightforward if you are prepared to provide a power supply (you will need special outdoor fittings and cable, so consult a qualified electrician). The choice usually lies between tubular heaters or soil-warming cables (which can be run round the sides of a wooden frame to provide air heating as well). As soil temperature is often more important than air temperature (provided it is not *too* cold), especially with cuttings and for germinating seeds, there is a lot to be said for soil-warming cables, which also have the advantage of being fairly inexpensive to run. Cables are run at mains voltage, and should be connected to a circuit protected by a 30 ma residual current device.

It is usual to excavate about 15 cm (6 in) of soil, line the bottom with heavy-gauge polythene, and lay the cables on 7.5 cm (3 in) of sand, with a 2.5 cm (1 in) layer on top. Cover this with fine-mesh wire-netting. Finally top with a 10 cm (4 in) layer of compost, with a rod thermostat buried in it. Cuttings can be rooted directly into the compost; boxes and pots can be placed on top.

Heat kept in the frame is money kept in your pocket, so it makes sense to insulate. Covering with hessian or sacking on cold nights is advisable, but weight or tie it down to prevent it from blowing away. If the frame has glass or metal sides you may want to consider placing straw bales against the sides.

Although heat can widen the potential of a garden frame, it must not be achieved at the expense of ventilation. Even in winter ventilation can be important, and on warm days you should try to open the 'light' (top) a crack. Do not do this, however, on cold, damp, or foggy days.

From March onwards frames should be ventilated as often as possible, particularly when bedding plants are being hardened off. On mild days it is useful to remove the 'lights' completely and replace them by a wire-netting frame to keep off birds, which will often make a feast of succulent young plants recently moved from the greenhouse.

Some modern frames have sliding tops that make various degrees of ventilation easy, but some of the hinged types may be more difficult to open the right amount. To overcome this you can make yourself some stepped blocks of wood to wedge under the top for a little ventilation.

There is one type of structure that is half-way between a frame and a cloche. These glass and aluminium frames are shaped rather like a large barn cloche, but with the width of a frame. The sides often slide to allow ventilation. Although expensive, these versatile structures are ideal for summer crops such as tomatoes and sweetcorn (you will have to remove the top glass later), as well as all the normal winter crops.

Do not forget that frames can need shading too, as protection from strong bursts of sun in late spring.

# Cloches and Frames

## Cloches

Cloches are usually thought of as having a brief spell of usefulness in spring and early summer, with little use afterwards. Certainly they are usually put away until the next spring.

Naturally their greatest use *is* to protect and hasten the development of vegetable crops, many of which can be enjoyed weeks or months earlier than you would otherwise have them, but it makes sense to get as much mileage as possible out of what can be an expensive item.

In the kitchen garden, cloches are equally useful at the end of the season when they can be used over perhaps late peas or a final sowing of French beans. The lettuce season too can be extended by a combination of cloches and suitable varieties.

Even during the summer months cloches can be used with advantage over tender crops such as aubergines and capsicums (peppers). Obviously you must use the high-sided barn type for this, and the top panes may have to be removed as the crop grows, but the protection offered by the side glass can make a significant difference.

If you plan your cropping carefully you can soon make your cloches pay for themselves.

Do not overlook their role in the flower garden either—they can make autumn-sown annuals a possibility in areas that would otherwise be unsuitable. By using cloches you can also usefully advance and extend the flowering period of anemones.

*Types and materials* There are three main types of cloche—tent, barn and tunnel. Some of the modern designs do not fall neatly into these traditional categories, but their potential uses will be obvious.

*Tent cloches* are those with a profile like an inverted V. These tend to be comparatively inexpensive and are perfectly adequate for warming the soil up and germinating seeds, but there is little headroom for a growing crop, and (apart from things like lettuces and radishes) few crops can be grown to maturity beneath them.

*Tunnel cloches* are long strips of polythene or plastic stretched over wires. They do not look elegant, but can be very useful for crops such as strawberries, provided you ventilate to allow bees in to pollinate the flowers.

*Barn cloches* are undoubtedly the most useful because they have more height and a good width (sometime enough for a couple of rows). The panes of glass are removable, which is useful for tall crops that would still benefit from some protection, and with some designs a bird netting replaces the glass when the crop no longer needs weather protection. Barn cloches are also useful for ripening off outdoor tomatoes at the end of the season (you will have to lay the plants down).

*Using cloches* Never be in too much of a hurry to sow in the spring, as a crop sown a week or two later that grows away without a check will usually overtake one

sown earlier with a check. *Always* put the cloches in position at least two weeks before sowing, as the seeds will germinate more readily if the soil has been warmed first. If the ground is dry, water it thoroughly *before* sowing.

Ventilation should never be overlooked. For some crops it is essential to allow pollinating insects access to the flowers, but it also helps to avoid an undue build up of heat, and encourages the plants to be hardier while still protecting them from the worst of the weather.

With many cloches ventilation is a matter of moving them apart slightly, but with most barn cloches it is also possible to adjust or even remove the top panes. If you move the cloches apart, be sure that the gaps are not large enough for birds to enter. *Never* remove the end pieces for ventilation—it is a sure way to produce an instant wind tunnel, which will damage the plants.

Ventilating polythene tunnel cloches is more difficult; you will have to pull up one side between the tensioning wires, replacing it later and covering the edges with soil to anchor the material. Alternatively you can use a flower pot beneath one edge to lift the polythene.

Surprisingly it is not normally necessary to remove the cloches to water, except perhaps for seedlings. Sufficient should run down the sides to penetrate horizontally beneath the ground, although it obviously makes sense to start with thoroughly moist ground.

Weeding and thinning should never be overlooked, and will probably mean removing the cloches.

1 Tunnel  2 Tent  3 Barn

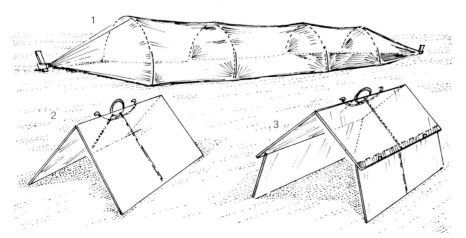

# Greenhouse Gardening

A greenhouse not only makes it possible to extend your gardening activities considerably, it enables you to do it in comfort. It is a wonderful treat at any time of the year, and provides an added dimension to the garden whether you heat it and grow exotic flowers or use it unheated to produce, perhaps, winter lettuce, summer tomatoes, and autumn chrysanthemums. A greenhouse can be as simple or as complex as you wish to make it, and inexpensive or expensive to buy, heat and run, but it will always enable you to grow a much wider range of plants than would otherwise be possible.

If you are to be successful with the things you grow, however, it is important to be clear about what you expect from your greenhouse. If you are uncertain about the temperature you aim to maintain, or the types of plants you want to grow, there is a real risk that half the things you attempt will not succeed and the greenhouse will become an untidy collection of plants in various stages of growth and health.

You do not *have* to heat your greenhouse—certainly not all winter. If you are content to use it like a giant cloche you will be able to harvest a wide variety of crops from tomatoes and capsicums in the summer to lettuces in the winter. It can even be colourful with out-of-season flowers such as anemones, forced bulbs, and pots of hardy annuals. If you can ensure it is frostproof there is obviously the potential of overwintering many plants that are fairly hardy but killed or damaged by frost. Inevitably, however, most of us are going to want to get the most from our greenhouse by providing a little more than frost protection.

## Types of greenhouse

The majority of greenhouses are free-standing, and nowadays are likely to have aluminium alloy frames, although wooden frames are still available. The four main types of greenhouse are the lean-to, the span, the three-quarter span and the dome.

A lean-to is worth considering if you have a suitable south-facing wall, although an easterly or westerly aspect is also suitable provided that it is not shaded too much. Restricted light is the major drawback to a lean-to, but it is often less expensive to heat due to the reduced heat loss through a brick wall, especially against the house. Laying on an electricity and water supply is usually a simple matter and much less expensive than running a supply to a more distant part of the garden.

Span greenhouses often have straight or only slightly sloping sides, but the Dutch style have a more pronounced slope and large panes of glass to the ground. These are the traditional choice for crops such as tomatoes, which are planted in or on the border and need plenty of sunlight.

Three-quarter span greenhouses are a compromise between a lean-to and a span, and they do have improved light penetration, but are not so popular.

The dome-shaped greenhouses are also worth particular consideration for a very exposed, windy site, as they offer less resistance (and wind can also have a profound effect on heat loss).

## Siting and erection

Choose a sunny position for your greenhouse, and try to integrate the house into the over-all garden design. It should be conveniently sited for the provision of water and electricity. The traditional alignment is north to south, but this is by no means essential. Avoid a very exposed site subject to strong winds from the north and east. These will cause a rapid loss of heat and damaging draughts.

The majority of greenhouses are easily erected in a day or two, provided that the ground and any foundations have been prepared, but it is as well to have at least two pairs of hands. In most cases, the framework comes packed flat in a number of boxes. Sometimes the glass will arrive separately later. A screwdriver and spanner are usually the only tools required, and full instructions are invariably provided.

The structure must be square and level, so check the vertical and horizontal levels frequently during erection.

Foundations are essential for a brick base, and even a modern metal greenhouse must be laid on firm, level ground. A perfectly adequate foundation is made by removing a trench 30 cm (1 ft) deep, filling it with hardcore and sand, and then finishing with concrete or paving slabs. Always check with the manufacturer's instructions first—some provide special fixing pegs to set into concrete or drive into the ground.

## Heating and insulation

Being able to maintain a temperature of of even 7°C (45°F) will enormously widen the potential, and such a temperature is easily maintained by most modern paraffin heaters. Naturally it may not be warm enough for propagation, but a propagator can be used to provide adequate temperature for germinating seeds (*see* page 95).

Maintaining about 13°C (55°F) will enable most plants to be overwintered, and provide an adequate temperature for growing on most bedding plants. Unless the greenhouse is small, however, you may need to consider electric, gas or solid fuel heating. Remember that the system you choose should be capable of maintaining your minimum temperature on the *coldest night*. It is no use keeping your greenhouse frost-proof for all but one night of the year.

The cost of heating makes insulation worth serious consideration. If you intend to maintain a higher winter temperature and the greenhouse is devoted mainly to decorative plants, the investment in a fully double-glazed greenhouse can easily be justified (you are likely to recover the cost in three to four years). If you do not want to maintain such high temperatures, and appearance is not so important, then one of the polythene type of liners may be a better proposition—especially the 'bubble' type (double-skinned with sealed air pockets). These are easily fixed to a metal-framed house with special clips.

## Greenhouse management

The actual plants to grow are legion and it is impossible to deal with individual crops or plants in the short space of this chapter. Nevertheless the rules of good greenhouse management are valid for all plants, and if you can overcome the particular problems of greenhouse gardening—such as watering and ventilation—the demands of individual subjects are easily accommodated.

*Watering* This is simplified if you use an automatic system. It is more difficult if

# Greenhouse Gardening

you are inexperienced and have to judge not only *when* to water but also *how much* to apply to each pot by hand.

It would be nice to be able to recommend a rule like half a pint twice a week, but unfortunately life is not as simple as that—size and kind of pot, type of compost, size and vigour of the plant, and of course temperature, all play a part in determining when a plant needs water, and how much.

One of the problems with greenhouse plants is that you are likely to have a lot of them, so you need a quick and simple method. Tapping clay pots with a bobbin on a cane is a traditional method, but you almost need the skills of a piano tuner if you have lots of pots of different sizes and types. If the soil is dry the pot should give a hollow ring; if it is still moist the tone is dull.

With a little experience it is possible to tell by sight whether a loam-based compost is likely to need water, but you will probably have to feel a peat-based compost with your finger if in doubt. As this comes with experience, however, the best way to gain it is by using a moisture meter as a guide until you are able to judge as accurately as the aid. Meters are useful in this context, but as you hardly

want to place probes into dozens (perhaps hundreds) of pots every time you water, there is every incentive to learn quickly!

Always water very sparingly in winter and generously in summer, but never in dribbles—completely fill the space between compost and pot rim. In summer apply more water if none runs out the bottom after about a minute. If water runs straight through, it could be that the soil-ball has become so dry it has shrunken from the sides of the pot.

Seedlings are best watered with a fine rose, although you may find it more convenient to water some pot plants without a rose. To avoid washing away the compost with a forceful gush of water, try tying a rag over the end to break the force.

It is tempting to think that rainwater must be better for plants, yet the water-butt can be a reservoir of diseases. In any case it is most unlikely that rainfall will provide all your needs, so you will still have to use some tap-water. It is probably best to use rainwater for those lime-hating plants that really will benefit from it, and use tap-water for the rest.

Automatic watering systems overcome most of the problems, and save an enormous amount of time. They also make it easier to leave the greenhouse unattended

for a few days during the summer. An automatic system will also save a lot of physical effort. Tomatoes in a growing bag in summer might need 6.8 litres (1½ gallons) of water a day. In an intensively used greenhouse this can represent a lot of carrying and lifting. The steady supply provided by an automatic system also overcomes some physiological problems such as blossom end rot in tomatoes.

There are many systems on the market, but most fall into one of two categories—capillary benches or trickle feeds. Both can be fed from the mains (via a cistern) or from reservoirs filled by hand.

Capillary systems need some kind of solid bench, and are particularly useful for pot plants growing on the flat (if you go in for a tiered display you may need to think about a trickle system, or a combination of the two). Sheets of capillary matting can be bought or a 2.5 cm (1 in) layer of sand used as a base. You can improvise a water feed, but it is sensible to buy a purpose-made system that will keep the water at the right level. Once a capillary system is set up the plants will take up the correct amount of water themselves, but you should not crock the pots (which involves placing broken pots in the base) as it is important to have good contact with the compost when the pots are pressed into the base, and the compost should be thoroughly moist initially. There is much to be said for choosing a black mat, as white can soon look grubby. If algae growth becomes a problem, you can always cover the mat or sand with black polythene and make a slit, folded back, where the pot is to be placed.

You will have to bear in mind that for plants that should be kept fairly dry (perhaps because it is their dormant season) or for those few that like a very moist compost, you may have to make special arrangements.

Trickle irrigation is the other major option. A network of small-bore plastic tubes feed each pot or position in the border individually. It is a more obtrusive system, especially among decorative pot plants, but the flow from each nozzle can usually be adjusted individually, so it is a very flexible system, and is particularly useful for border crops.

Neither system requires an electricity supply, and it is usually possible to introduce a liquid feed.

# Greenhouse Gardening

*Feeding* Feeding is essential for all greenhouse plants at some time. The fertilizer content of many peat-based composts is only likely to be sufficient to sustain the plant in healthy growth for perhaps a month or two, although loam-based composts like John Innes will probably be all right for two or three months. Root growth is one guide to when feeding is necessary—if the compost has become filled with roots, feeding will be essential during the summer months.

If you have just a few plants, fertilizer pellets or sticks that you push into the compost may be satisfactory (you will need to use them less often than most liquid feeds), but if you have a lot of plants you may find liquid feeding more convenient. Do not overlook the soluble powders, which can often be very good value.

During the winter only feed those few plants that grow at that time, otherwise feed *regularly* during the summer, less frequently in spring and autumn.

*Humidity* This is vital for most plants. Water in the air can be almost as important as water at the roots. It is the combination of warmth and high humidity that gives a greenhouse or conservatory that unmistakable 'growing' atmosphere.

The easiest way to create this humidity is to splash water around on a hot day. Spraying it over the floor is usually known as 'damping down'.

Even though this humidity is adequate for most plants, a few need special treatment and should be given a fine misting once or twice a day. Some tillandsias, ferns and selaginellas are in this category.

Although high humidity should be the aim in summer, the opposite is demanded in winter. If the temperature drops, so should the humidity—a combination of low temperatures and dampness is fairly sure to lead to disease troubles. For that reason ventilation can be important even in winter.

*Ventilation* Ventilation is important at all times. Even in winter it is necessary to keep the atmosphere reasonably dry and buoyant, and essential in summer to prevent soaring temperatures from ruining the crops.

Hand ventilators create no problem in winter, when a lot of human judgement is needed and automatic ventilators may not operate anyway. In summer, however, automatic ventilators really come into their own—not only because they enable you to leave the greenhouse unattended for short periods if you also have automatic watering, but also because they can prevent the sudden build-up of temperature early in the morning before many of us get out to open the ventilators.

If you do have to open and close them yourself, at least you have the advantage of being able to open those on the leeward side rather than let a strong wind blow in.

*Light and shading* These are two conflicting demands. Whether you are trying to keep light out or let it in depends on the time of the year. In winter you need to do everything you can to let as much light as possible reach the plants; in summer shading is beneficial for most crops, and essential for some of the more delicate pot-plants.

There is not much you can do about increasing the light in winter, other than keeping the glass clean or installing supplementary lighting (an expensive exercise). Double glazing, especially polythene, may cut down the amount of light slightly, but it is usually worth sacrificing this for increased frost protection.

Most greenhouse plants, except perhaps cacti, benefit from summer shading, and the choice lies between a shading wash or some kind of blind. If applying a summer wash, just give a light sprinkling, do not apply it too thickly—you only need to break the main force of the sun. Do not use a green wash as this will filter out the parts of the spectrum the plants need. Most shading washes are easily rubbed off in autumn.

Blinds can be bought to fit outside or inside the greenhouse, in materials ranging from wooden laths to green PVC sheeting. If you grow your plants on staging, it is not always easy to reach and control inside blinds. What is more, the sun's rays have heated up the air directly inside the glass before they are intercepted. As all blinds are expensive, however, you may want to consider an improvised system (*see* page 185). Even if you use blinds, they are probably best left in the shade position most of the summer, but in spring and autumn being able to roll them up means you can get the most benefit from the duller days of spring and autumn. When arranging blinds, remember that you will need to leave the ventilators clear.

## Greenhouse hygiene

In the protected environment of a greenhouse it is particularly easy for pests and diseases to take hold and reach epidemic proportions. For this reason it is particularly important to take every precaution to try to avoid troubles ever getting a hold.

Besides most of the pests and diseases to be found in the garden (*see* pages 20–25), there are extra ones that are particularly troublesome under glass. Being able to identify these at first sign is part of the way to controlling them.

Although most garden insecticides can be used with safety in the greenhouse, remember that you are working in an enclosed space, so make allowances and

**1 Lean-to   2 Dome   3 Span   4 Bubble insulation   5 Damping down**

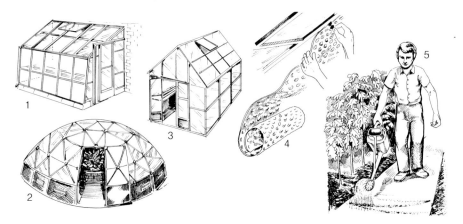

always work from the end to the door, and try to avoid inhaling any sprays.

The greenhouse gardener does have a couple of extra weapons not available to the outdoor gardener. Fumigant smokes are available containing insecticides or fungicides, or both. The less conventional approach is a sort of biological warfare. You can buy parasites that will feed on and kill whitefly (you will need *Encarsia formosa*) and red spider mite (in which case the bug is *Phytoseiulus persimilis*), but for both you will have to maintain favourable greenhouse conditions—not easy in winter.

With the exception of perhaps certain specific crop troubles, such as several tomato problems, most of the diseases are similar to those that affect outdoor crops, with botrytis being particularly troublesome in winter.

You can do much to cut down diseases by removing any dead or dying leaves and making sure that all debris is collected and not left to contaminate floors and benches. Using sterilized compost will also make a big difference not only in getting the plants off to a good start but also in reducing damping-off, which can be a troublesome disease of young seedling, which simply collapse.

If you grow crops in the greenhouse border, there is a particular risk of soil-borne diseases building up, especially if the same crop is grown each season (quite likely with tomatoes). If you do not want the effort of replacing the soil each year, at least sterilize it, using one of the soil sterilizers you can obtain from horticultural sundriesmen. An alternative is to grow the plants in growing bags.

## Bedding plants

If you use many bedding plants, growing your own must be a priority. Not only are bedding plants fairly expensive to buy, but you also gain in being able to choose from a much wider range of types and varieties if you grow your own. Even if you cannot maintain sufficient heat for germination, it is quite possible to use a propagator for this (*see* page 95) or even germinate them in the home. Once they have germinated the seedlings can usually tolerate significantly lower temperatures, although it makes sense to maintain 13°C (55°F) if you can. Even if it means delaying the sowing for a month until the outside temperatures warm up, it may be better as they will grow away with less of a check. March is quite suitable for most bedding plants, and many will still be in bloom in a surprisingly short time from an April sowing.

If you have to maintain a high temperature for other plants anyway, then an early start will mean an earlier display with plants such as antirrhinums and seed-raised pelargoniums (geraniums) that tend to need a long growing period. Remember, however, that bedding plants must be hardened off thoroughly, and until it is safe to put them out into frames the greenhouse is likely to become very congested if you sow a lot of plants early. Mention of bedding plants has to include perennials like geraniums (pelargoniums) and fuchsias. Geraniums are easily raised from seed now, but if you do not have the heat to make a good start with these, then it is still worth overwintering older plants vegetatively. It is most convenient to root cuttings in the autumn and overwinter them in a minimum temperature of about 7°C (45°F), keeping them almost dry until the temperature increases. If grown in individual pots these plants will make a fine display. Fuchsias can be treated in a similar manner, but where they are grown as a standard it obviously pays to retain the old plants.

Some plants, such as antirrhinums and salvias, will make bushier plants if the growing tip is pinched while they are still young, though it delays flowering. You may want to allow for this by sowing earlier.

| Name | Sow | Germination temperature | Germination time |
|---|---|---|---|
| Ageratum | Feb–March | 20°C (68°F) | 3–12 days |
| Alyssum | March–April | 16°C (61°F) | 4–14 days |
| Amaranthus | Feb–March | 20°C (68°F) | 2–10 days |
| Antirrhinum | Jan–March | 15°C (59°F) | 10–25 days |
| Aster | Feb–March | 20°C (68°F) | 4–12 days |
| Begonia, fibrous-rooted | Jan–March | 20°C (68°F) (in light) | 14–21 days |
| Dahlia | Feb–March | 20°C (68°F) | 5–25 days |
| Dianthus | Jan–March | 20°C (68°F) | 3–10 days |
| Heliotrope | Feb–March | 20°C (68°F) | 5–20 days |
| Impatiens | March | 20°C (68°F) | 7–21 days |
| Kochia | March | 20°C (68°F) | 2–10 days |
| Lobelia | Jan–March | 20°C (68°F) | 5–18 days |
| Marigold, African | Feb–March | 20°C (68°F) | 3–10 days |
| Marigold, French | Feb–March | 20°C (68°F) | 3–10 days |
| Mesembryanthemum | Feb–March | 20°C (68°F) | 5–20 days |
| Nemesia | March–April | 13°C (55°F) | 8–20 days |
| Nicotiana | Feb–April | 20°C (68°F) | 5–20 days |
| Pansy | Feb–March | 18°C (65°F) | 7–21 days |
| Pelargonium | Dec–Jan | 20°C (68°F) | 14–28 days |
| Petunia | Jan–March | 20°C (68°F) | 5–20 days |
| *Phlox drummondii* | Feb–April | 13°C (55°F) | 5–15 days |
| Rudbeckia, annual | Feb–March | 20°C (68°F) | 4–14 days |
| *Salvia splendens* | Jan–March | 20°C (68°F) | 5–20 days |
| Stock | March–April | 13°C (55°F) (in light) | 4–14 days |
| Tagetes | Feb–March | 20°C (68°F) | 2–14 days |
| Verbena | Jan–March | 20°C (68°F) | 5–20 days |
| Zinnia | March–April | 20°C (68°F) (in individual pots) | 3–10 days |

# Water Gardening

By thoughtful use of floating, marginal and waterside plants, as well as water lilies, a very pleasant over-all effect can be created, providing a focal point in the garden.

## Position

The pond must be sited in a sunny position, as water lilies thrive on light. It should also be positioned well clear of trees, ideally near an existing path, and not beyond convenient reach of the hose. Do not, however, choose a naturally waterlogged hollow, because of the difficulties of carrying out any form of construction in an excavation partly filled with water.

## Size and shape

The smaller the pond the more likely it is to be plagued with problems. The critical size for an easy-to-manage pond seems to be around 5 m² (50 sq ft) of surface area. It can of course be bigger than this, but any smaller is not to be recommended. This area can be achieved with various shapes—a square with 2.25 m (7 ft) sides,

a rectangle 3.5 × 1.5 m (10 ft × 5 ft), or a circle 2.5 m (8 ft) across. It is a good idea to mark out the proposed shape on the ground with a hose-pipe or clothes line, as this will give a good impression of how the pond will appear seen across the garden. The simplest designs, such as a kidney shape and those described above, are always the best, and the surroundings will usually dictate the most suitable shape to blend in with the rest of the garden.

## Depth

The depth of the pond is determined by several factors—the needs of plants and fish and the possible effect of depth and volume on the pond balance. It is vital to achieve a satisfactory ratio of volume to surface area. Algae, the cause of murky water, thrive on heat and light, and the shallower the pond the lower will be the

volume of water absorbing the sun's effect. The pond 'profile' is also important here: a saucer shape 40 cm (15 in) deep only at one point means an even lower ratio of volume to surface area, and is the worst possible shape for a pond. The maximum ratio would be achieved if the pond had vertical sides and a uniform depth. Vertical sides are not feasible for constructional reasons, but the sides can be steeply sloped at about 20 degrees to the vertical. It is advisable to create a shelf for about a third of the total perimeter 25–30 cm (10–12 in) wide and 20–23 cm (8–9 in) below water level, for the planting of marginal plants. Ideal pond depths are as follows:

| Surface Area | Depth |
| --- | --- |
| 4 m² (40 sq ft) | 40–45 cm (15–18 in) |
| 4–9 m² (40–100 sq ft) | 45–60 cm (18–24 in) |
| Over 9 m² (100 sq ft) | At least 60 cm (24 in) |
| Over 27 m² (300 sq ft) | 75–90 cm (30–36 in) |

## Alternative Construction Methods

The main materials available are concrete, pre-formed ponds and pond liners. It is as well to remember that a spirit level should always be used during construction, whichever method is chosen.

*Concrete* This has great strength, but this strength can be destroyed by its inflexibility, which can lead to cracking. If this happens, there is no way of repairing the pond. The secrets of success with making a concrete pond are careful preparation, speed once the job is started and meticulous attention to detail along the way. Shuttering will be required to prevent the sidewall concrete from slumping to the base before it is set. This aspect will be made easier if the pool is square or rectangular in shape. The hole must be dug 13 cm (5 in) larger all round than the proposed pond size, to allow for the thickness of concrete and rendering, with an additional 13 cm (5 in) below the base to accommodate the hardcore foundation. First complete the base with 5 cm (2 in) of concrete above and below a piece of reinforcing steel mesh or chicken wire. Leave for 30 minutes to an hour before installing the shuttering frame and forming the walls. The rendering coat should be applied as soon as the concrete is firm enough. The pond can then be filled, but the water will need 'curing' before stocking can begin, because free lime, which is very harmful to fish and plants, soaks out of the new concrete. This can be achieved either by emptying and refilling the pond 3 times over a period of 6 weeks, or by coating the concrete with Silglaze, which seals off the harmful lime.

*Pre-formed ponds* In most cases, these are far from ideal. Their shapes are too complicated, and they are very often too shallow, but they can be useful as reserve ponds.

*Pond liners* Polythene was the first sheet plastic used as a pond liner, but it has now been superseded by stronger, more easily repairable materials such as butyl synthetic rubber and laminated PVC. Both are simple and effective in use and offer excellent value. Liner size can be easily calculated, and installation is straightforward. After excavation to the required size and shape, and removal of all sharp objects, the liner is stretched over the hole and the edges are weighted with bricks or stones. Water is then hosed on to the sheet, and gradually this stretches the liner down and moulds it up the walls and over the shelves. The weights are later removed and the liner edge covered with turf or paving. The pond should be left for a week or so before stocking.

## Planting

The temptation to put some fish into the pond straight away must be resisted, as they will prevent some essential plants from becoming established. Oxygenating plants need about 4 weeks' start. In selecting plants, consider both ornamental and practical value. Water lilies possess both these attributes—they produce superb flowers over a long season and their spreading leaves, by cutting off sunlight and shading the water, are a crucial factor in keeping the water clear of green algae. Hardy water lilies will grow almost anywhere and need no winter protection, unlike the tropical varieties. They are happy with a pond depth of 40–60 cm (16–24 in). Oxygenators (often called 'water weeds'), release oxygen into the water during the daytime. They are also valuable because they utilize the same food sources as algae, thus restricting their growth. Floating plants, which also fulfil this function, need no contact with soil and need only be dropped into the water. Marginal plants should be planted on the marginal shelf. All aquatic plants should be planted when they are actively growing.

*Containers* It is advisable to restrict plant roots to containers, so that they do not over-run the pool. Movable containers, such as wooden boxes, plastic tubs and bowls, are preferable to fixed ones. Carrying handles are useful. The ideal soil for aquatics is a heavy rich garden or pasture loam. Perforated sides have some value in a deep container with a small surface area in improving the exchange of dissolved gases between soil and water. Oxygenators will grow happily in gravel.

## Livestock

When the plants are satisfactorily established and the water has become de-chlorinated (usually after about a week), fish can be introduced. Overcrowding must be avoided, and a guide to healthy stocking is 1 fish for every 0.3 m² (3 sq ft) of surface area, regardless of their size. The most suitable fish for garden ponds are goldfish, shubunkins and golden orfe. When introducing fish to the pond, avoid a sharp change in temperature which could kill them. Give the fish 2 or 3 days in which to settle down before feeding them. The best rule for feeding is: feed when the fish are active and give them once a day as much as they will clear up in 5 minutes. Do not feed at all during the cold winter months.

*Natural visitors* Mosquitoes, gnats and midges will arrive to breed in the pond, but the fish will prevent this. Dragonflies and damselflies may be more successful, and their nymphs may feed on fish fry. There are many types of beetle, but only the large ones, such as the great diving beetle (*Dytiscus marginalis*), present a threat to the fish. These should be netted out as they surface for air, and the same treatment should be given to water boatmen. Leeches lay their eggs on the undersides of lily leaves, but they only eat fish if other food supplies are short. Frogs and toads do little harm, and tadpoles in the water are excellent for the pond's ecological balance.

## Green Water

Green water is caused by single-celled free-swimming algae, which depend on light and mineral salts. A newly-filled pond, which has an abundance of both, may become very green very quickly. The use of manure or fertilizer should be avoided, as these encourage the algae. The water will clear as soon as submerged oxygenators and surface-covering plants become established, and it should remain clear except perhaps for a brief outbreak in spring. Algicides are available, but their effect is temporary. Natural control of green water, if this condition persists, can be achieved by removing all the fish and introducing a quantity of *Daphnia*. These are tiny crustaceans sold by many pet shops as fish food, which feed and increase on a diet of free-swimming algae. Once the water is clear the fish can be returned to make a feast of the *Daphnia*.

# Bulbs

Bulbous plants contribute excitingly and significantly to the magical world of flowers. Infinite in colour, form, size, variety and beauty they provide a challenge to creativity yet demand a minimum of effort for a year-round succession of lovely bloom in and around the home.

The word 'bulb' is a generic term describing all bulb-like organs that are sold to the public in a dormant condition. These include true bulbs, corms, tubers and rhizomes. They differ somewhat in structure, shape and size but their function is identical; to tide the bulbous plant over a period of adverse conditions like winter cold and summer drought. All have common factors: food storage; rapid growth under suitable conditions; and the same life cycle, in that during rapid growth and flowering, the following year's flower is formed in miniature, the foliage reaching maturity and dying away, as do the roots in most cases when the plant enters its period of rest.

When you are buying bulbous plants you should never forget that you are investing in bloom for a number of years. Their growth and development varies according to the particular kind of underground storage organ but just as all bloom all also propagate themselves in one way or another—by seeds and by offsets or bulbils or cormlets or stolons—the majority literally producing new stock for the amateur gardener.

Provided that you purchase bulbs of flowering size and treat them with common sense, flowers the first flowering season after planting are virtually guaranteed. Be wary of so-called 'bargains' in bulbs and avoid unidentified varieties. Always buy bulbs from reliable established retailers in ample time for planting. A good bulb is heavy for its size, firm to the touch, plump and free from scars. If you buy the largest bulbs available you cannot go wrong, for generally the size of flower will be in direct proportion to the size of the bulb. In tulips and daffodils, however, some varieties produce bulbs much larger than other varieties and in hyacinths the largest bulbs are essential for indoor cultivation while smaller sizes are adequate for good results in the garden or outdoor containers.

The size of most bulbs has been standardized, narcissi or daffodils being sold as 'single nose' or 'double nose' with the latter producing more blooms per bulb, while the remainder are measured in circumference in centimetres. While universally used in the wholesale trade few retailers relay specific sizing to their customers, using terms like 'top', 'first', 'second' or 'good flowering' size. No bulbs, however, can be exported from Holland without being of flowering size and disease-free.

If you cannot plant your bulbs on purchase do open the bags for ventilation and keep the bulbs cool and dry until you can conveniently plant them.

Bulbs do well in virtually any soil that drains well, in sun or in partial shade, but porous soils with plenty of organic matter will naturally produce superior blooms. Slow-acting fertilizers may be dug into bulb planting sites if desired but fresh manure must never be used with bulbs. Except for greedy bulbs like dahlias, gladioli and lilies it is for their second and subsequent flowering seasons that bulbs will appreciate feeding. Bonemeal or an ordinary 5–10–5 garden fertilizer may be dug into the soil at 100 g per m$^2$ (3 oz per sq yd) when replanting, or applied as a top-dressing to bulbs left *in situ* after flowering. This should be done after clearing away dead foliage and before top growth appears the following season.

Spring-flowering bulbs should be planted from September to mid-November, setting daffodils, hyacinths and tulips 10–15 cm (4–6 in) deep and minor bulbs 5–10 cm (2–4 in) deep. Spacing may vary according to the effect desired but generally spacing equivalent to planting depth is suitable. Closer spacing is, however, more effective in outdoor containers.

Summer-flowering bulbs may be planted from February into June but do ensure the more tender types like begonias, dahlias and freesias are not sited outdoors before the last spring frosts. Stemming primarily from the tropics they vary so much that bulbs of some like begonias and cannas should really be started early in pots indoors. There is no general formula covering the planting depths and spacings. Dwarf dahlias, for example need only half the 10 cm (4 in) covering of soil of the larger varieties and little more than half the 90 cm (3 ft) spacing between plants. Always consult your supplier if the cultivation instructions with the bulb are not specific enough.

Autumn-flowering bulbs are planted from July into August in the same way as the minor spring-flowering bulbs although colchicum varieties will bloom if only placed on a dry saucer on a windowsill.

Many bulbs are planted individually— a trowel being the handiest tool for rockeries, borders and interplanting with other subjects—by setting them at the correct depth, according to their type, in well-dug ground. Many bulbs may also be 'naturalized' in lawns, rough grass or wild gardens. There is a special bulb-planting tool for this or an ordinary spade can be employed to remove a piece of turf with soil. This is replaced when the bulbs have been firmly set in the dug-over soil underneath. A spade is also useful for mass-planting bulbs in one location in beds or borders, when the entire planting area can be simultaneously exposed to the right depth.

When planting different species and varieties together do check stem heights, colour and flowering times to achieve the most effective display. Always water planting sites liberally after planting bulbs and maintain adequate moisture throughout growth, using a hose or watering can when rain is seen to be in-

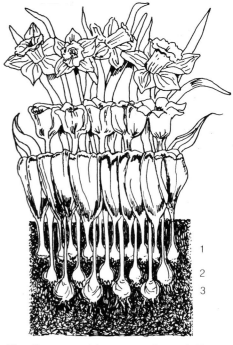

Planting an outdoor container. 1. 5-cm depth: 8–10 bulbs (crocus)   2. 10-cm depth: 5 bulbs (tulip)   3. 13-cm depth: 4 bulbs (narcissus)

sufficient. Good garden hygiene will also reap dividends.

Virtually all spring-flowering bulbs and many summer-flowering bulbs can be left in their garden homes during the winter. When bulbs thrive in spots they like they tend to increase rapidly. After three or four years, however, the growing colonies of bulbs can become congested causing degeneration of flowering. Then it is time to dig up the clumps carefully, divide the bulbs and re-plant the largest bulbs in fresh sites to which bonemeal has been added. Do this during the bulb's dormant period, after the foliage has completely withered away. When lifting bulbs for storage remove all dead foliage and soil and store in a dry, cool but frost-free place until planting time comes round again. Damp is fatal to stored bulbs so do not pile them on top of one another but, rather, store in a single layer with space between each in flat boxes or on open slats to ensure ventilation. Dahlia and begonia tubers are best stored in peat.

Bulbs are as easy to grow indoors as outdoors if you follow a few logical principles. Bulbs contain a tiny flower, leaves and stem as well as a supply of food to produce one or more handsome blooms. Before flowering (in the garden or indoors) most bulbs require a period of 'cold' or winter weather. When planted outdoors the British climate automatically provides this. When planted in indoor containers the home gardener must provide this period of 'cold' by storing the planted containers in a garden 'plunge' or suitable indoors storage place.

It is during this period of 'cold' that the bulb develops its root system, and the process normally takes up to three months. Provided that home gardeners never try to 'force' bulbs into flower until the roots are developed and ensure regular watering from the very beginning success is almost automatic. 'Forcing' means simply the stimulation of the growth cycle by bringing well-rooted bulbs into the warmth and light of the home or greenhouse to produce blooms earlier than their counterparts planted in the garden.

Never hesitate to buy top quality bulbs; the largest size of each type will produce the best floral results. Almost anything that will hold a growing medium is suitable for growing bulbs for indoor bloom. Containers should be clean and at least twice the depth of the bulb to provide room for root growth. New clay pots should be soaked for at least 24 hours before potting.

A loose, light growing medium is best. Use a peat-based potting compost or John Innes No 3 with pots with drainage holes or bulb fibre with bowls without drainage holes. Fertilizers are not necessary. Place a few crocks or flat stones over the drainage holes to prevent clogging and loss of growing medium. Then partly fill the container with compost.

Next place bulbs gently and firmly but without pressure on top of the compost so that their tips are just below the level of the rim. Use the same method with bulb fibre in bowls, first soaking fibre thoroughly and then squeezing it out until it stops dripping. Bulbs should not touch each other or the sides of the container. A 15 cm (6 in) pot will take one hippeastrum, three hyacinths, six tulips or about 15 crocuses.

More compost or fibre should be added and pressed firm with the fingertips to anchor the bulbs, leaving their tips exposed and room for watering. Water planted containers thoroughly and then label them. Bulbs can, of course, be replanted in planned succession to ensure continuous bloom.

For indoor rooting store containers in a cool, frost-free and dark airy cellar, garage, or outdoor shed. Water regularly to prevent the growing medium from drying out. For outdoor rooting place containers on a bed of ashes, sand or peat in a cool, shady place in the garden. Dig a trench round the position and use soil from the trench to cover the containers by 15 cm (6 in), adding peat if the soil is heavy. Water regularly until frosts arrive and then mulch with straw or peat.

Temperature in store should remain within 5–10°C (40–50°F).

Sprouts should be about 5 cm (2 in) high before they are removed from storage into a semi-dark area in the home or greenhouse where the temperature does not exceed 10–13°C (50–55°F). After a week they can be moved into full light. The flowers will bloom a few weeks after the containers are brought indoors. Regular watering is essential and direct heat and draughts should be avoided. Forced bulbs prefer cool conditions.

If you want bulbs in flower for Christmas you must buy 'specially prepared' bulbs of hyacinths, tulips or daffodils. These are bulbs which have been specially treated to advance their normal growing cycle for extra early bloom. Cultivation is the same but timing is different. 'Specially prepared' hyacinth bulbs must be planted before the end of September and brought indoors about December 5. 'Specially prepared' tulip bulbs must be planted before mid-September and brought inside about December 1. 'Specially prepared' daffodil bulbs must be planted during the second week of October and brought indoors about December 1.

Of course, all varieties of hyacinths can be grown in water in hyacinth glasses or specially designed plastic containers.

The emperor of indoor blooms, the hippeastrum, is available both 'specially prepared' and as an ordinary bulb to bloom from the Christmas season into June. It likes bottom heat immediately after planting and restricted water supplies and needs no storage in the dark and cold to stimulate root production. Other summer-flowering bulbs from the tropics, like hymenocallis, sprekelia, vallota and zantedeschia, also bloom without a rooting period in the dark and cold.

1 Crocus   2 Snowdrop   3 Hyacinth   4 Narcissus   5 Royal Lily   6 Tulip
7 Gladiolus   8 Crown Imperial   9 Dahlia

# Shrubs

Shrubs differ from trees in that a tree has a central trunk from which branches radiate, whereas a shrub branches from the ground. So far as gardeners are concerned many plants that are botanically trees are treated as shrubs—the difference is rather one of dimensions and placing. Trees are often planted as isolated specimens, which can be viewed from all angles. Shrubs, on the other hand, are more often grouped in shrubberies or shrub borders and are usually less tall than trees.

The Japanese maples (*Acer palmatum*) are certainly tree-like in structure and a few even reach tree-like dimensions, but they are generally treated as shrubs and provide the best exception to the statement that most shrubs have attractive flowers; they attract by their graceful, often coloured foliage and their delightful habit. One, 'Senkaki', is mainly grown for its coral-coloured young growths, which illuminate the garden in winter.

The technique of planting shrubs differs in no way from that of planting trees. Like trees the shrubs, when they arrive, are comparatively small, and can be expected to grow considerably in height, and, even more important, in width. The temptation is to put in far too many shrubs with the promise that when they become too crowded half the shrubs can be removed. This is fairly fatal. In the first place removing well-grown shrubs requires a great deal of energy and provides some difficulty in the disposal of the unwanted plants; in the second place the choicer shrubs that you are deciding to retain will have distorted shapes, having been hemmed in by the fillers that have now been removed.

Nevertheless, the tiny shrubs will look rather isolated for a few years, until they have grown sufficiently to make the gaps between them less of a yawning gulf than they will show the first two or three years after planting. It is as well to have something to attract the eye, and there are a number of choices open to the gardener. Most spring-flowering bulbs appreciate a certain amount of shade in the summer, as does the autumn-flowering *Cyclamen hederifolium* (*C. neapolitanum*), so these are obvious candidates to give interest to the place where your young shrubs are growing. The cyclamen come readily from seed and in some gardens naturalize them-

The bright spring flowers of forsythia.

selves without the gardener having to do much about it; the same can be said of crocus species, such as *C. tommasinianus*. The foliage of the spring bulbs soon dies down, enabling one to mulch around the shrubs in the summer. The exception is the various daffodils, which retain their leaves until the end of June. Meadow saffron, colchicum has attractive crocus-like flowers in the autumn, but large unsightly leaves in spring and summer, so that the shrubbery is the ideal place to plant them. Bulbs, though undeniably attractive, are not cheap, in which case they could be replaced by herbaceous plants, either biennials, such as foxgloves, which like fairly shady conditions, or perennials which could include such plants as solomon's seal and lily of the valley. If your soil is acid, the various low-growing heathers make a good and attractive ground cover and also provide colour, either in the autumn or in the winter. The spring-flowering heathers such as *Erica arborea* and *E. lusitanica* will grow too tall for your purpose. Apart from the winter-flowering *E. carnea* (which is one of the few heathers to tolerate some lime) some varieties of the ling, *Calluna vulgaris*, turn brilliant colours in the winter. Thus 'Blazeaway' and 'Robert Chapman' turn red, whereas 'Joy Vanstone' and 'Orange Queen' turn orange. All these heathers and lings are,

*Buddleia crispa.*

of course, shrubs in their own right. Another possibility are the shrubby spurges, *Euphorbia characias* and *E. wulfenii*. These have attractive evergreen, rather glaucous, foliage, and heads of green or yellow flowers any time from February to April. They come readily from seed and flower in their second season. They come from southern Europe and could be damaged in an exceptionally severe winter. Another spurge that rambles is *E. robbiae*, which is much shorter, little more than 23 cm (9 in) in height with yellowish flowers in April and May. Finally a good ground cover between shrubs is the newly introduced *Geranium procurrens* from the Himalayas. This spreads by means of runners and covers itself with vivid violet flowers from July.

Unlike trees most shrubs will benefit from pruning (*see* pp. 30–1).

The choice of shrubs for the gardener is very large. A Japanese Maple may not have any burst of colour as the forsythia does, but it will give pleasure for very much longer and the variety 'Osakazuki' may well turn pillar box scarlet in the autumn and even rival the forsythia for brilliance. With an acid soil you can grow rhododendrons, but the commoner hardy hybrids have dull leaves. On the other hand a rhododendron like 'Bo-Peep' not only gives yellow flowers in early spring but a month later produces copper-coloured new growth and has a second season of attractiveness. *R. cinnabarinum* and its hybrids 'Lady Chamberlain' and 'Lady Roseberry' not only have attractive hanging red or salmon flowers but the new leaves keep an attractive blue-green colour throughout the summer. The old yellow azalea, *Rhododendron luteum*, not only has its fragrant yellow flowers in late spring but the leaves turn brilliant colours before falling in the autumn— some of the hybrid azaleas such as 'Corneille' and 'Unique' will do the same. It may happen with the loveliest of all the azaleas, *R. schlippenbachii*, with soft pink flowers in April. Many of the evergreen rhododendrons also have attractive leaves as well as brilliant flowers. *R. yakushimanum* is one of these with its very compact habit and apple-blossom pink flowers. This has been much used recently for hybrids and they too have not unattractive leaves, although usually the flowers are too large for the small compact bushes. The Japanese *R. makinoi* has very narrow leaves and although it produces its pink flowers in late May, the white new growths do not elongate before August, to give interest to a rather sombre scene. If you have room for a large plant, *R. thomsonii* has, in its best forms, superlative blood-red flowers and brilliant blue-green young growth. It does, however, take its time to come into a flowering state. Although most rhododendrons can be pruned, this is not usually done. What is essential is to dead-head them; to remove the heads of dead flowers. The new growths emerge from just below the flower heads, so this must be done carefully and with a large well-flowered plant is tedious and time-consuming. It is, however, essential. Rhododendrons can be had in flower from January when *R. dauricum* and *mucronulatum* cmcrgc until August, when the very large *R. auriculatum* flowers. This is so large, however, that it will only suit a large garden, and for most people the season will end in July with such plants as 'Redcap' and 'Impi' which are nice and compact and have deep red flowers in July.

Ornamental fruits are more rewarding and in many varieties of *Berberis* they may be joined by autumn colour. *B ×rubrostilla* is one of the best and has many good named forms of which 'Barbarossa',

'Buccaneer' and 'Fire King' are all good plants with yellow flowers in June and red fruits and good autumn colour later. The only trouble with the barberries is their extreme prickliness. The South American *B. darwinii* and *B. linearifolia* have the most handsome flowers, but the fruits are dark blue and not very interesting. The callicarpas have lilac-pink flowers, albeit rather small, in July, and dark lilac or violet fruits in the autumn, and the leaves of *C. bodinieri* often turn purple before they fall. This is quite vigorous, whereas *C. japonica* is somewhat more compact. Both are good value. In this class should come the blueberries, although their edible fruit is not particularly conspicuous, the pink flowers in the late spring and the vivid autumn colours make *Vaccinium corymbosum* an excellent plant for acid soils, with blueberry pie as a possible complement.

Most shrubs are planted mainly for their flowers and some shrub can be had in flower in any month of the year. We can start January with the witch hazels. *Hamamelis mollis* and *H. japonica* are usually at their best in this month with their twisted, yellow, fragrant flowers. These shrubs are generally left unpruned. They are slow-growing. Their leaves colour golden in the autumn. Frost may delay the flowers and damage any that are out, but the unopened buds will survive anything. The wintersweet, *Chimonanthus praecox*, is also open during the winter. It is not showy and takes time to come into flower, but a few flowering

*Rhododendron* 'Vuyk's Scarlet'.

twigs will perfume a room. February will see *Mahonia × media* at its best, although it may start to flower as early as November. 'Charity' is the best known, but all are good, with bold handsome spiny leave and masses of yellow flowers. *M. japonica* with paler flowers scented like lily of the valley is also at its best around now, although it can flower any time between November and April.

February and March can show many rhododendrons, although these early flowerers are liable to be damaged by unseasonable frosts. 'Praecox' is an old favourite and both 'Seta' and 'Bo-Peep' are very rewarding. *Stachyrus praecox* and *S. chinensis* both open their catkin-like spikes of primrose coloured flowers in March, as do the other catkin-like flowers of the various corylopsis. There are such a plethora of good shrubs for April, May and June, that they can pass unmentioned and quite a few in July, including escallonias and *Fuchsia magellanica* and 'Riccartonii' which will keep on flowering until October. The graceful and fragrant *Buddleia alternifolia* is another July beauty. August is the month for hydrangeas and for the ceanothus, either the deciduous 'Gloire de Versailles' or the evergreen 'Burkwoodii' and 'Autumnal Blue' which will continue into September. The tamarisks are graceful shrubs and *T. pentandra* flowers in August and September. The September shrub *par excellence* is *Eucryphia glutinosa*, with huge white flowers like roses. Other eucryphias flower even later, but tend to be very large before they flower. *Hoheria sexstylosa* also makes rather a large plant and is said to be delicate, although many plants have weathered bad frosts without damage. October sees the flowering of *Colletia armata*, which looks like a large gorse and is very spiny, but splendid when covered with its white or pink flowers. About this time *Viburnum farreri* (*V. fragrans*) and its hybrid *V. × bodnantense* start to open their flowers, which they will continue to do throughout the winter, as will the cherry *Prunus subhirtella autumnalis*. These with premature mahonias and the winter jasmine will keep us going until the witch hazels start to open again, although the castor oil tree, *Fatsia japonica*, also opens its greenish flowers in the month of November.

# Trees

The placing of trees in a garden is arguably the most important decision the designer can make. In small gardens a tree can be the focal point of the whole design, whereas in larger gardens it is possible to have more than one tree; but even so they will be of paramount significance. It is clear, therefore, that the selection of suitable trees requires some considerable thought. It also requires imagination. When you purchase your tree it will probably be a slender sapling, about 2 m (6 ft) high and with a spread of only about 60 cm (2 ft). It is not easily to be taken as a focal point at that stage. Eventually it may be 20 m (60 ft) or more high with a very wide canopy, and you must envisage this final result before you plant your tree, even though you will have to wait many years before this result is achieved. Once a tree is established it is difficult and very expensive to move it, so it is worthwhile giving much thought before the tree is actually planted. Of course not all trees reach such dimensions and there are a number of smaller trees which are more suitable for the small garden. However, even the smallest tree can obscure light if planted too near the dwelling and it is as well to reckon on a distance of at least 10 m (30 ft) between the dwelling and the nearest tree, and a larger distance is preferable. There are some trees which it is always inadvisable to plant near a house and these include poplars and willows. The roots of these seek avidly after water and are liable to penetrate the smallest crack in the drains. Once in they expand and either crack the drain or fill it with roots and block it. On shrinkable clays such trees will commonly shift foundations of houses.

Once you have decided where you are placing your tree, the next decision you have to make is what type of tree you require. Is it to be large or small; evergreen or deciduous; a conifer or a flowering tree? You have a large choice in almost all these categories, except that moderate-sized conifers are not very numerous. You have, however, a large choice of ones with a columnar habit, so that though they may become tall they will not take up much room laterally.

Other options are open to the tree planter. All trees flower, but with some the flowers are conspicuous, whereas those of others are somewhat drab. Similarly all trees will bear fruits and some of these, such as rowans and hawthorns, are ornamental, while others are unremarkable. Some trees have exceptionally delicate leaves, while others are less attractive. Some trees have forms with coloured leaves or even leaves that are variegated. Many trees, often with the epithet 'Pendula', give a weeping effect which is often very attractive; others, which are naturally fairly widespread, have fastigiate forms, with the branches growing vertically so as to give a columnar effect and so take up less room. The leaves of many trees turn most gorgeous colours in the autumn, but with others it is the new growths that are brightly coloured. Finally many trees have most ornamental bark, ranging from the whiteness of many birches to the polished mahogany of *Prunus serrula* and the stripes of the so-called snakebark maples. There are a great number of ornamental features available to the planter and it is up to him to make his choice.

Whatever tree he selects the preparations for planting are the same. A hole must be excavated which will contain the roots of the tree when fully expanded. It must be deep enough to bury all the parts of the tree which were buried before and at least 15 cm (6 in) below this must be dug and broken up. An extra 30 cm (12 in) is even better, and since you do not plant many trees it is worth taking all the trouble that it entails. Until the tree has made ample fresh roots and is well established it will require staking, and the

A simple tree guard.

stake should be inserted as soon as the tree has been put in position. It should be at least 1.8 m (6 ft) long and if it can be tipped with creosote a year before you plan to use it it will have a longer life. However, any wood preservative is liable to damage the young plant, so if it has not been applied for a long time do not apply it at all. If the young tree has any roots that are cracked or broken, these should be removed before planting takes place. Container-grown plants, such as garden centres offer, have the advantage that the roots will be undamaged, but they are probably somewhat confined and should be spread out, if it is possible to do this without damaging them. With these container-grown plants it is best to make the hole somewhat wider than the soil ball, as the new roots will tend to spread out horizontally. Once the tree and the stake are in position replace the soil, which can with advantage be mixed with some peat to enable the roots to penetrate the soil more easily. Since many trees are planted in late autumn it is perhaps necessary to mention that no planting should be undertaken in frozen or in very wet ground. This applies to all plants, not only trees. When you refill your hole over the roots it is as well to remember that it will subsequently settle somewhat. It is usual to tread it down after planting, but even so the level should be an inch or so above the surrounding soil. It will soon level out. The stake should be attached to the trunk with some rather wide tie. Wire or string is liable to chafe the bark; bits of old car tyres are ideal. With trees from open ground, where there is bound to have been some root damage, it is advisable to prune all growths by about a quarter of their length. A mulch applied in spring should help to prevent the soil drying out in the crucial first season. If any feeding is indulged in, it should wait for the second season, by which time the tree should have developed a good root system, which can take advantage of the added nutrients. Deciduous trees are usually moved at any time between the last week in October and the end of February, but evergreens are best moved in mid-September or in early April.

Selecting your tree is a matter of taste, but it is as well to consider some of the options. In the following lists emphasis is placed on trees that are suitable for small gardens, and noble specimens like cedars or beeches are not given much space. Let us first consider conifers. Most of these are evergreen, but the swamp cypress (*Taxodium distichum*) and the dawn redwood (*Metasequoia glyptostroboides*) are deciduous. Although they have a columnar habit, they are really too large eventually for the small garden. There are other columnar conifers which are more restrained, such as the many forms of Lawson's cypress (*Chamaecyparis lawsoniana*). These vary in colour from the glaucous blue-green of 'Allumii' to the yellow of 'Hillieri' and 'Lutea'. An even more compact plant is *C. obtusa* 'Crippsii' with golden foliage. If a dark green column is wanted you cannot do better than the slow-growing *Libocedrus decurrens*. Apart from these columnar trees there are many dwarf and slow-growing species like *Abies koreana*, which makes a low, bushy pyramid, and even when quite small produces handsome violet-purple cones. It grows very slowly but will not thrive in polluted atmospheres such as may occur in towns or near factories. Nurserymen may carry a selection of more amenable dwarf conifers.

Conifers are not the only evergreen trees and there are a lot of very attractive alternatives if an evergreen is what you crave. The evergreen oak (*Quercus ilex*) is a bit sombre and eventually massive, but the strawberry tree (*Arbutus unedo*) is full of charm with attractive smooth cinnamon bark, white flowers and red fruits in the autumn months and attractive leaves. *A × andrachnoides* is equally delightful. Unlike most ericaceous plants the arbutus seem to have no dislike of alkaline soils.

When we come to deciduous trees the choice of attractions is extensive. Many have decorative flowers, but it is worth remembering that they probably only persist for 3 weeks out of the 52 in the year and may be rather dull for the rest of the time, so if you have not room for many trees it is as well not to rely solely on flowers. Other attractions include attractive bark, coloured young growth, autumn colour, ornamental fruits, graceful habit and attractive leaves. There is one tree that contains many of these qualities, and that is the golden rain tree (*Koelreuteria paniculata*). This is a tree with bright pink young leaves, which later turn bronze and finally green. When mature it produces panicles of yellow flowers in July, which are followed by attractive bladder-like fruits, and the leaves turn golden or red before falling. It is rather slow-growing and does not flower until mature, but it is always attractive and, remarkably, comparatively inexpensive. It sounds too good to be true. Although it eventually becomes rather large the Indian horsechestnut (*Aesculus indica*) has attractive bronze young leaves and heads of typical horsechestnut flowers a month or so later than the ordinary conker. The variety 'Sydney Pearce' is the most handsome. Many of the hawthorns have attractive flowers, fruits and autumn colours and one of the best small trees is the Washington thorn (*Crataegus phaenopyrum*), which does not flower until July, at a time when there are few flowering trees about. Other thorns which have good autumn colour as well as flowers and haws would include *C. crus-galli*, the cockspur thorn, *C. prunifolia*, *C. pedicellata* and *C. pinnatifida major*. In the country birds are liable to clear the fruits of hawthorn and rowans before you have time to enjoy them, so here it is best to go for crab apples. The best of the fruiting crabs are *Malus baccata*, *M. prunifolia* (of which the variety 'Rinki', sometimes met with as *M. ringo*, has the advantage of pink flowers, whereas those of the others are white). The hybrid *M. × robusta* has forms with yellow or red fruits, and *M.* 'John Downie' has larger orange and red fruits which persist for a long time. Other crabs have purple leaves and deep pink flowers, whereas *M. tschonoskii* has silvery young foliage which colours most gorgeously in the autumn, but no beauty of flower or fruit.

The trees with the most ornamental bark are arguably some of the birches, but they have so extensive a root system that they are not ideal for the small garden. The snakebark maples are attractive and *Acer capillipes* has the added bonus of good autumn colour. Other good snakebarks are *A. davidii* and *A. rufinerve*. *A. pensylvanicum* has leaves which turn yellow in the autumn. The bird cherry known as *Prunus maackii* has attractive cinnamon bark, but no other virtues, and the same applies to the polished mahogany trunks of *P. serrula*.

Trees with coloured leaves are sometimes popular, and the false acacia (*Robinia pseudoacacia*) known as 'Frisia' with attractive golden leaves is becoming widespread. It is rather brittle if there are strong winds about, but otherwise no trouble. There is also the variegated box elder (*Acer negundo* 'Variegatum') and a variegated form of the attractively shaped *Cornus controversa*, with its layers of branches.

Weeping trees have an attractive habit, but the weeping willow would probably be too near the drains in a small garden. There is a weeping oak (*Quercus robur* 'Pendula') if it can be obtained, a weeping ash (*Fraxinus angustifolia* 'Pendula') and the weeping wych elm (*Ulmus glabra* 'Pendula').

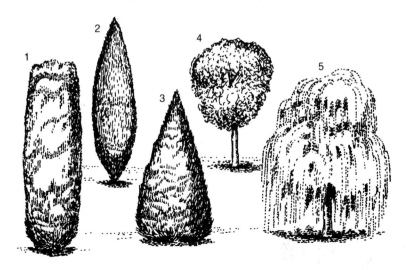

1 Columnar   2 Fastigate   3 Pyramidal   4 Globose   5 Weeping

'Picasso'.

'Grandpa Dickson'.

'Orange Sensation'.

## Preparation of the soil

Nothing is more important, if one wishes to get the best out of roses, than to prepare the soil thoroughly before planting. Double-dig the whole area (see page 14). Deep cultivation has several advantages: it assists drainage, it sweetens by aeration and allows the roots of the trees to penetrate further afield in search of food; and the manure improves its physical condition, and supplements the natural fertility of the soil. Farmyard or horse manure are best if obtainable, but practically anything of vegetable origin can be used—compost, leaves, leafmould, chopped turf and even rags and waste paper. Peat, likewise, is beneficial, though for its moisture-holding capacity only. If you do not have any manure or compost, moss peat is good (but expensive). If you use peat, it is essential to use a good rose fertilizer in the spring and summer. Prepare all rose beds at least three weeks before planting to allow for consolidation.

## Planting

Planting can be carried out in open weather at any time between October and April. Open up a hole in the prepared ground about 45 cm (18 in) square and 30 cm (12 in) deep, and place the roots of the tree in it so that the union of scion and stock is level with the surface of the surrounding soil. Spread the roots over as large an area as possible and then cover with some fine soil, to which some peat and a little bonemeal can be added, and firm it with the hand to avoid air pockets beneath the roots; then cover with more soil and tread lightly. Replace the remainder of the soil and tread firmly. When all is finished the union of scion and stock whether of bush, shrub or climbing rose should be just below the surface. With standards, plant as shallowly as possible: the original soil mark will give the correct depth.

Standard roses are best planted at least 1.4 m (4½ ft) apart, and bush roses 45–60 cm (1½–2 ft). Shrubs according to their vigour but not less than 1.2 m (4 ft), while climbing roses require a minimum of 2.4 m (8 ft) and ramblers 4.5 m (15 ft).

Container-grown bush roses can be planted at any time during the growing season.

## Replacements in old beds

A common mistake resulting in the failure of new rose bushes is filling up gaps in old beds without taking the precaution of renewing the soil. Where an old plant has lived for some years the soil quite naturally is exhausted, and it is essential if one wishes to give the new tree a reasonable chance of survival that this soil should be replaced. Remove a spadeful or so of the old soil, break up the subsoil, manure and refill with fresh topsoil from another part of the garden.

## Feeding

Established beds need a good mulching with organic manure annually in the spring; alternatively a balanced fertilizer can be applied in conjunction with garden compost and peat.

In addition extra feeding in liquid form can be given from the time the buds begin to form until they flower, which is usually in about three weeks. An excellent formula is a mixture of the quick-acting chemicals—nitrate of potash and sulphate of potash at the rate of 14 g (½ oz) of each to 15 l (3 gallons) of water. Apply 5 l (1 gallon) of the liquid to 1 m² (1 sq yd) and repeat the application every five days during the formative period.

There are also many proprietary liquid fertilizers on the market.

No stimulants should be applied during a dry period without first well watering the soil, and the applications are best stopped after the main flowering at the end of July so as not to induce soft lush growth late in the season. They can, however, be given in late July a final dressing of rose fertilizer.

Newly-planted trees would also benefit from the extra feeding as above and they, as well as established trees, will also benefit if kept well watered during a dry period.

## Suckers

Undoubtedly everyone knows that a sucker is a wild growth, but perhaps for beginners it is as well to explain how and why roses are troubled with them. It is because the tree purchased from a grower is a budded plant in practically every instance. In other words, it is made up of two parts, top growth which is a specific cultivated variety and a root system which is of a selected strain of 'wild' rose. The purpose of marrying the cultivated rose with the wild rose by budding is to provide the former more quickly with a vigorous root system. Nevertheless there is the disadvantage that it is impossible to suppress entirely the wild root system and from time to time it sends out growths which, to distinguish them from the cultivated rose, are termed 'suckers'. If they are allowed to grow freely they will quickly outgrow the cultivated variety, therefore it is necessary to cut them away immediately they are spotted. The proper way to do it is to trace back the sucker and cut it away at its base, even though this may involve scraping the soil away from the union or a section of the roots.

Suckers which appear on the stems of standards, as they are prone to do quite freely anywhere below the point of budding, should be removed at their base and a nick should be cut into the stem to ensure the removal of further eyes.

There is an erroneous belief that suckers sometimes develop from the top growth, but that is impossible—they can come only from the wild rose part of the tree which is below the union. They may come from immediately below it or from the roots. A further fallacy is that all growths are suckers which carry more than 5 leaflets to the leaf, but this is a most unreliable method of identification. A rambler rose almost always has 7 leaflets while bush roses, hybrid teas and floribundas have both 5 and 7 leaflets.

The most certain way of identifying a sucker is to confirm that it comes from below the union. It is only those that are so close to the union that they appear to come from it that there should be any doubt about, but comparison of the stem and foliage of the suspect growth with that of the cultivated rose should settle the question.

## Types of rose

Although most roses are still sold under the traditional names of 'hybrid teas' and 'floribundas', these are now officially called 'large flowered bush' and 'cluster-flowered bush' respectively. You are most likely to encounter these descriptions at rose shows, and they do appear in some catalogues. Many of the shrub roses are now technically termed 'polyantha' roses. For the purpose of this section, the traditional names that you are most likely to meet have been used.

*Modern Roses*
*Hybrid Tea*  Suitable for bedding purposes and which in the main produce shapely blooms of good substance.
*Floribunda*  Likewise suitable for bedding, but primarily massed for colour effect and not for the beauty of the individual bloom.
*Floribunda hybrid tea type (Grandiflora in America)*  Varieties in which the characteristics of both parents, the floribunda and hybrid tea, are present, some stems producing clusters of blooms and others fewer blooms of more substance.
*Polyantha Pompon (dwarf polyantha)*  Of dwarf habit bearing clusters of small blooms. One of the parents of the hybrid polyanthas.
*Polyantha compacta*  A new race which, as the name implies, are compact and dwarf. Very free-flowering in clusters and ideal for edging.
*Miniature (Fairy Rose)*  In the main very dainty dwarf growing plants, producing miniature flowers. Suitable for edging. Grown extensively in pots, but quite hardy out-of-doors.
*Climber*  Of upright climbing habit requiring support. Both types of bloom— full petalled, similar to the hybrid tea, and single or semi-double blooms of the floribunda cluster habit—are to be found in this group.
*Rambler*  As the name implies, of rambling habit; the varieties in this group are best suited for covering fences, pergolas, banks and trellis. Summer-flowering only.
*Hybrid Musk*  Shrub roses which are the result of crosses between the species *Rosa moschata* and various modern roses. The blooms, which have a musk fragrance, are freely produced in early summer and intermittently for the rest of the season. In recent years there have been some notable continuous flowering additions to this Group. Excellent for hedging purposes.

*Old Roses*
*Rosa alba*  Erect shrubs, which freely produce flat blooms of good fragrance.

'Elizabeth of Glamis'.

'Elizabeth Harkness'.

'Alec's Red'.

# Roses

A feature is their greyish-green foliage. Summer-flowering.

*Rosa banksiae* A group of climbing roses which are somewhat tender and require a sheltered position. Growth strong with few thorns.

*Rosa bourboniana* The 'Bourbon' rose—most develop into fine shrubs, although within the group are to be found some vigorous pillar and climbing forms. The blooms are variable in shape, though typical specimens resemble camellias. Most are very fragrant.

*Rosa centifolia* (the moss rose) In the main the respective varieties make moderate sized shrubs 1–1.5 m (3–5 ft) in height. Many have 'mossed' flower stems. They are descendants of the Cabbage rose, a very full petalled variety of intense fragrance.

*Rosa chinensis* The Chinese or Bengal rose from which most perpetual flowering varieties have been evolved. The majority make medium bushes of 1–1.2 m (3–4 ft), but climbing forms within the group require a warm wall as they are rather tender. The stems are reddish with few thorns, and the blooms intensely fragrant.

*Rosa damascena* So called because the variety was presumed to have been brought originally from Damascus. The majority in the group develop into tall slender shrubs carrying nodding loose blooms of delicious fragrance.

*Rosa gallica* Also known as The 'French Rose' or 'Rose of Provins'. Shrubs of moderate height—1–1.5 m (3–5 ft)—bearing flat double blooms; fragrant.

*Rosa rugosa* The Japanese rose, the common variety of which is used largely as a root understock. Cultivated varieties within the group contain among them some of the best roses for hedging purposes. Many are perpetual-flowering and very fragrant.

*Rose spinosissima* (the Scotch Rose)

These are dwarf growing compact plants, which being very thorny are suitable for forming thickets. Recent hybrids of the group, however, make tall shrubs carrying attractive single or semi-double flowers in early summer followed by a display of large shapely hips in the autumn.

*White and white flushed cream or pink*

| Hybrid Teas | Floribundas |
|---|---|
| Pascali | Iceberg |
| | Margaret Merril |

*Cream to yellow*

| Hybrid Teas | Floribundas |
|---|---|
| Elizabeth Harkness | Allgold |
| Grandpa Dickson | |
| King's Ransom | |
| Peace | |
| Sutter's Gold | |
| Yellow Pages | |

*Apricot, buff and orange shades*

| Hybrid Teas | Floribundas |
|---|---|
| Just Joey | Orange Sensation |

*Light pink*

Hybrid Teas
Blessings
Silver Jubilee
Stella

*Salmon, salmon pink to vermilion*

| Hybrid Teas | Floribundas |
|---|---|
| Alexander | Elizabeth of Glamis |
| Mischief | Paddy McGredy |
| Super Star | |

*Deep pink*

| Hybrid Teas | Floribundas |
|---|---|
| Wendy Cussons | Dearest |
| | Pink Parfait |
| | Queen Elizabeth |

*Carmine to crimson red*

| Hybrid Teas | Floribundas |
|---|---|
| Alec's Red | Evelyn Fison |
| Fragrant Cloud | Lilli Marlène |
| National Trust | Topsi |

*Dark crimson*

| Hybrid Teas | Floribundas |
|---|---|
| Ernest H. Morse | Europeana |
| | Rob Roy |

*Bicolours, red and yellow and red and silver*

| Hybrid Teas | Floribundas |
|---|---|
| Piccadilly | Masquerade |
| Rose Gaujard | Picasso |

*Climbers and ramblers*

| | |
|---|---|
| Albertine | Mme Edouard Herriott |
| Hugh Dickson | Sweet Sultan |

*Shrubs and hedges*

| | |
|---|---|
| Buff Beauty | Prosperity |
| Fountain | Sarah van Fleet |
| Munster | Queen Elizabeth |
| Joseph's Coat | Roseraie de l'Hay |
| Nymphenburg | Scabrosa |
| Penelope | Schneezwerg |

## Budding

The method of propagation known as budding is really a form of shield grafting. It has, however, developed into a branch of propagation in its own right and is extensively used for the propagation of roses (although many fruit trees are also increased by the method).

Although some roses, particularly those nearest the original species (i.e. *Rosa moschata*, the musk rose), can be raised from cuttings, many modern varieties are not strong enough to perform on their own roots to any satisfaction. To overcome this problem such varieties are budded onto various strong growing rootstocks which, generally speaking, are wild

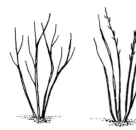

Rose forms. Left to right: climber, rambler, bush, half-standard, standard, weeping standard and miniature.

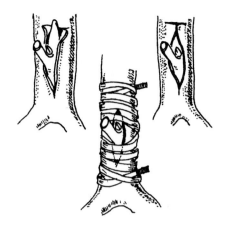

Budding.

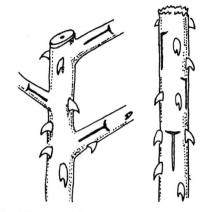

Budding standard roses. Left: *Rosa canina*; right: *Rosa rugosa*.

species of rose or selected strains of wild species. The object of the graft is to transfer a well developed bud from the cultivated variety to the rootstock.

The first essential is to undertake the graft when the plants are in full growth. The sap must be travelling freely within the stem to allow the bark to rise from the wood of the rootstock without damaging the vital cambium layer (the layer of growing tissue between the bark and wood of most plants).

The only tool needed for successful budding is an extremely sharp knife. The shoot selected to supply the bud should be a good one which is carrying a flower near to shedding its petals. The shoot should be cut some 15–20 cm (6–8 in) in length so that it carries several buds or 'eyes'. Once a stem is selected it can be removed from the parent plant, at the same time cutting the leaves off, leaving 2.5 cm (1 in) of leaf stalk attached to the stem to protect the bud and allow for easier handling. Place the stem in a jar of water.

The next stage is to prepare the rootstock. This is done by removing the soil from around its stem as close to the roots as is practicable and wiping the resultant exposed area with a rag to clean it.

A T-shaped cut is then made just below the original ground level. This cut should be no deeper than the bark, with the downstroke of the T-cut being about 2.5 cm (1 in) in length. Once the cut is made the bark is raised carefully from the stem to form two flaps. Press the flaps back against the stem to avoid any drying whilst the bud itself is prepared. This is done by cutting the bud or eye from the prepared stem complete with a shield of

bark. Start the cut about 2.5 cm (1 in) below the chosen bud and gradually cut deeper until the bud is reached whereupon the cut is made shallow again to allow the knife to emerge around 2.5 cm (1 in) above the bud and naturally on the same side of the stem. What is then produced is a shield of bark containing a bud, a leaf stalk, and at the back a thin sliver of wood, which is then removed.

With the bud shield and rootstock now prepared the base of the shield is trimmed with a cross-cut 13 mm ($\frac{1}{2}$ in) below the bud. Once more lifting the bark at the T-cut in the rootstock, the shield is carefully pushed down the cut as far as it will go. For this purpose the leaf-stalk makes a convenient handle and also ensures the eye is facing outwards in its correct position. With another cross-cut the top of the shield is trimmed to fit neatly in place at the top of the cut. The bark is then pressed into place around it.

Finally, the wound is bound firmly yet not tightly with moist raffia, leaving only the bud and leaf-stalk exposed. Alternatively a rubber budding patch can be used. This will eventually perish and fall away, by which time the union should be secure.

*Chip budding* A brief mention may be made here of another method of budding which is said to be easier and just as successful as the traditional method. The operation involves the removal of a chip of stem from the rootstock and the replacement of this by a similar piece from the mother plant containing a bud as with ordinary budding. This is effected by making two cuts across the rootstock 2.5–4 cm (1–1$\frac{1}{2}$ in) apart and removing a

chip of stem from between the cuts with a knife. This is replaced with a chip from the mother plant, the bud being near the centre of the replacement chip. When in place it should be tied securely with raffia as before.

*Rootstocks* The most readily available rootstock for the amateur is probably the wild dog rose, *Rosa canina*. Stock from this species, either from cuttings or seed, is best suited to grow on heavy soils.

For light sandy soils, except those over chalk, it would be best to use *Rosa rugosa* or *Rosa multiflora*, which also does well on shallow sandy soils. For light soils of a calcareous nature *Rosa laxa* is to be recommended.

Bush roses are budded on to two-year-old plants, mainly of *R. canina* or its numerous strains. Standard roses need to have a rootstock with a stem some 1.2–1.5 m (4–5 ft) in height. It is possible to find such stems growing as suckers from hedgerow plants in the wild, but commercially standards are budded on to stems of *R. rugosa* or *R. polyantha simplex*.

With standards, the method of budding is the same as for bush roses except that it is carried out at the top of the stem rather than near the roots. Usually three buds are inserted on either side of the main stem at some convenient height in the case of *R. rugosa*, but on the side branches growing from the three buds left to grow on the original cutting in the case of *R. canina*.

When planting cuttings for rootstocks of either bush rose or standard production it is essential to remove all buds except the top three prior to insertion of the cutting. This will hopefully avoid a mass of sucker and unwanted side-growths on the eventual budded plant.

Rootstocks intended for budding should be planted out in their budding positions the autumn preceding the budding period. In the case of those intended for bush production either seedlings or rooted cuttings are best planted out 30 cm (1 ft) apart in rows 60–75 cm (2–2$\frac{1}{2}$ ft) apart. For standards more space is obviously needed and these rootstocks should be planted out 60 cm (2 ft) apart in rows 90 cm (3 ft) apart. The area chosen for planting out should be in good light and the soil cultivated to a satisfactory growing condition.

# Climbers and Wall Plants

Climbers and wall plants can give an added dimension to any garden, large or small. The imaginative use of these plants on walls and trees provides colour and interest, often at times of year when flowers in the garden are scarce. Some of the loveliest plants available to the gardener fall into this category, and they can be used to enhance the appearance of ugly utilitarian buildings, walls or fences, as well as being a pleasure in their own right.

## Soil Preparation

When preparing the soil for climbers, remember that it is hoped that they will be permanent, so preparations should be thorough. Dig the ground deeply; against house walls you may encounter foundations, and as there is little point in planting in shallow soil you may have to plant a little way away from the wall base. Work in plenty of humus as you dig, preferably cow or farmyard manure with not too much straw. Failing this, well-rotted compost, spent hops or mushroom bed compost will do, but remember that the latter may contain a certain amount of lime. After digging but prior to planting, fork into the top 15 cm (6 in) of soil bonemeal or hoof and horn at 170 g per m$^2$ (5 oz per sq yd).

## Planting

Unless the ground is heavy clay, tread the soil lightly before planting. Climbers, like most shrubs, are best planted in the autumn, October to December; failing this in the spring, March to the end of April.

Planting is a reasonably simple operation. Remove the plant from the container or root-wrap and then dig out a hole sufficiently large to receive the root ball so that when well firmed the mark on the plant collar of the level of the nursery soil is at or only slightly below the soil surface of the border. Make sure the root ball is moist; if in doubt immerse in a bucket of water for a few minutes. Never plant into dry soil. If necessary, thoroughly flood the planting hole, leave it to percolate the surrounding ground and then plant. Always make sure that plants are not allowed to dry out in their early years. Apart from watering this may entail temporary shelter from drying winds.

Protection from frost may also be necessary even though the same plants when older would withstand frost perfectly well. The best protection against frost is dry bracken, leaves, straw or even the dead stems of herbaceous plants loosely spread to about 30 cm (1 ft) thick about the base of the plant and over the immediate soil.

After planting it is often necessary to 'lead' the plant to the wall by means of a stake or cane; this should be set in the planting hole, fixed to the wall and the plant planted to the cane, rather than by thrusting the cane in after planting. When planting climbers that are to ascend trees it is rarely possible to set the plant immediately against the trunk, as there is usually so much existing root present even in the case of a dead tree that successful growth is unlikely. The best method is to drive in a stake some 1.8 m (6 ft) or more from the trunk and attach it to one of the lower branches. Plant the climber against the stake where it will be free from competition from the tree roots and train it up and into the tree.

## Training

A few plants, ivy and Boston ivy (*Parthenocissus tricuspidata*) for example, are self-clinging. The vast majority, however, need support. For walls of plain brick the fixings can be permanent and are best provided by means of screw-eyes driven into the wall in vertical lines 30–45 cm (12–18 in) apart and protruding 5–8 cm (2–3 in) from the wall. For a wall 2.4 m (8 ft) high one will require a top and bottom eye and two 'steadying' eyes in between. Galvanized wire (Gauge 12 or 14) is fixed to the top eye, threaded through the intermediate eyes, pulled tight and fixed to the bottom eye. Strainers are not needed for vertical wires since the downward pull of the foliage keeps the wire taut.

Flexible climbers, such as rambler roses, clematis, passiflora, jasminum etc, can be affixed in such a way as to be lowered, with care, away from the wall when repainting is found to be necessary. This can be achieved by fixing the wires in horizontal lines 45 cm (18 in) apart with hook and eye at one end and strainer at the other; by this means the wires can be slackened and detached, starting with the

The ornamental quince, chaenomeles.

*Hedera colchica* 'Sulphur Heart'.

*Clematis montana.*

Climbing rose 'New Dawn'.

Climbing rose 'Schoolgirl'.

*Abutilon vitifolium.*

top wire, and the whole 'mat' of climber gradually laid down to the ground. An alternative is to use a framework of preservative-proofed wood laths.

## Uses in the Garden

*Walls and House Walls* Pyracantha is frequently used as a wall plant, particularly for north and east walls; it stands clipping, is pleasant in flower and lovely in berry. The wintersweet, *Chimonanthus fragrans*, will grow perfectly well in the open, but its sweetly-scented flowers can perhaps be better appreciated if it is on a house wall. The pink acacia-flowered *Robinia hispida*, a whole range of lovely blue ceanothus, the curious fuchsia-flowered currant, *Ribes speciosum*; the pineapple-scented broom, *Cytisus battandieri*, slightly tender buddleias such as *B. crispa*, and even camellias, all can make first-rate wall plants.

An excellent shrub for north or east walls is *Cotoneaster horizontalis*. Curiously flat, fish-bone style, wall-hugging branches are covered with small pink flowers in May followed in September-October by red berries. For a contrast plant against the wall, some 60 cm (2 ft) to one side of the cotoneaster, *Hedera helix* 'Glacier'; this has leaves of silvery grey and will climb up through the cotoneaster to make a lovely foil for the red berries.

In choosing climbing or wall plants it is necessary to bear the wall colour in mind. That fine dark red climbing rose 'Guinee' planted against a red brick wall can be 'colour lost', becoming just another red rose easily overlooked by the observer. Against a whitewashed wall it is superb, the flowers standing out and the dark red colour seeming almost black. *Osmanthus delavayii* and *Choisya ternata* with their white flowers and ample foliage are ideal against a brick wall.

*Pergolas* A well made pergola can be a delightful feature, but the first lesson to be learnt is not to create the pergola over a main path or route; let it be a secondary path or way that can be ignored or by-passed in inclement weather. Secondly do not plant it with over-vigorous subjects; if they grow well they will thrust upwards and flower primarily on the top, creating only a darkened thoroughfare for the gardener or visitor.

*Arbours and Summerhouses* Plants used for coverage of such places should be summery, fragrant if possible, and sufficiently twining and luxuriant to give shade from the summer sun and even shelter from the passing shower.

A summer spot such as this is the ideal site for climbing roses of character and the summer-flowering *Jasminum officinale*.

*Screening of Buildings or Sheds* For these structures luxurious and rapid growth are vital, and what better than *Polygonum baldschuanicum*, the Russian vine? It is rampant of leaf and with a bonus of foaming white flowers in September. Once established the plant grows rapidly and in summer the long shoots flare out seeking a support to entwine. *Polygonum baldschuanicum* is, however, deciduous, and unsightly buildings do not go away in winter. For evergreen coverage nothing can equal ivy, and few plants are brighter in winter than the variegated Persian ivy, *Hedera colchica* 'Dentata Variegata'.

*Boundary Fence Cladding* A close boarded fence will act host to much the same range of climbers as a brick wall, except that some, ivies for example, are less inclined to cling to boarded fencing than to brick. Wall plants can equally be planted against fences but there must be sufficient height to provide a protective backing. The height of the fence will also dictate the choice of climbers.

Wattle hurdles, hazel or willow, make a pleasant background and have the merit of gaps that facilitate tying and training. They are best stood on a low wall inset at 1.8 m (6 ft) intervals with strong posts of wood or iron to which the hurdles can be fixed with wire. Chain link fencing can be converted into an attractive adornment by thoughtful planting. For this purpose ivies are first rate; they are evergreen, they grow quickly and are amenable to cutting back.

*Tree-supported Climbers* Aged apple or pear trees make excellent vehicles for climbers. Some climbers such as roses and clematis can live very happily with their tree hosts, as their growth is sufficiently thin to enable the tree still to flower and leaf; others, such as *Lonicera japonica*, celastrus and vitis species, are sufficiently vigorous as to smother the tree eventually.

# Houseplants

No plants can be classed as natural indoor plants. The term covers a wide variety of plant types of which a collection may include shrubs, climbers, herbaceous species, bulbs, tubers or even annuals. Nurserymen and florists have had to search out those plants which grow under low light intensity and which are able to tolerate a greater fluctuation of temperature, as well as generally drier air, than they would enjoy in their natural habitats. Conditions in modern homes, however, are becoming increasingly favourable for the cultivation of indoor plants, with more light, warmth and insulation against extremes of temperature.

## Choice of plants

Provided that you do not regard indoor plants as simply part of your furnishings, you will, by careful consideration of the conditions existing in your home, and wise selection, be certain to choose a suitable species. This is better than obtaining your plant first then trying to find a place for it. Indoor plants come in a wide variety of shapes and sizes to suit all requirements. There are erect growing kinds, such as ficus, philodendron and sansevieria, some of which eventually need plenty of head-room. Climbers require the support of trellis, bamboo poles or cords suspended from the ceiling. Trailers, e.g. tradescantia and columnea, need to be placed high up, perhaps on a shelf or in a suspended pot, for their drooping stems to be displayed to advantage. Mixed bowls, in which a selection of plants are accommodated, should be planted so that leaf or flower colours are complementary, growth rate is balanced and the plant's environmental requirements are similar.

Smaller bowls are most effective when placed upon a low table. Living screens of greenery, either light or dense, can be arranged according to needs. An example is ivy, hedera, trained up several cords behind a sunless window, effectively blocking out the unsightly rear of a neighbouring town house. In open plan interiors, room dividers are softened by the careful placing of indoor plants. In these situations, bold-growing specimens can, by breaking the line of vision, themselves become effectual room dividers.

The dark glossy-leaved sorts can tolerate positions offering the least amount of available light. Consequently they are frequently placed in corners where they recede naturally into the background. Brightly-coloured or architecturally interesting kinds have to be positioned with caution for, if too many 'accent plants' are used, they will clamour for visual attention. There is little doubt, however, that, when used with discretion, these magnificent individuals become an important part of a room layout. In a small room, as in a small garden, the temptation is to scale down the size of the plants accordingly. This is a mistake. A better balance is obtained by the bold inclusion of one or two large specimens rather than several small pots. Also, in small rooms, an illusion of space can be created immediately by the use of a mirrored wall to reflect the plants.

## Soil and compost

Do not use ordinary soil from the garden for your houseplants. This soil varies greatly in composition and carries the risk of pests and diseases which may be present in it. It is far better to purchase one of the soilless potting composts, or use a loam-based potting compost such as John Innes. Peat-based composts are perfectly satisfactory for most kinds of houseplant, but you will find that a few plants (such as palms) prefer a loam-based compost. You will also find that John Innes compost will provide a better anchor for large plants that might be too heavy for a light soilless compost, and is more satisfactory if the plants are to be kept much drier in winter (peat-based composts are difficult to re-wet after drying).

## Pots

Clay pots are porous whereas plastic ones are not. This means that evaporation takes place through the sides of clay pots, and plants in these pots need watering more frequently than those in plastic pots. On the other hand, it is easier to over-water a plastic pot.

## Potting and repotting

Regardless of the method used to propagate them, when your young plants are well rooted is the time to pot them up. Naturally enough, the initial pot size depends on the size or vigour of your subject. Under- rather than over-potting (selecting too large a pot) is best, for there is a real danger of surplus compost turning sour before it is utilized by the plant roots, something which invariably happens when the pot is too large. If your pots have been used previously, make certain that they are washed scrupulously clean then sun-dried.

When plants are young, repotting is frequently required annually for, after a full season's growth, the plants' roots will have used up all the space in their container. When an established plant makes more than usual demands for water this is also an almost certain sign that little free compost is left in the pot and that repotting is needed. Confirmation of this can be obtained if a mass of roots is seen when the plant is tapped out of its pot. Additionally, some poor plants that have not established well for some reason or other are frequently improved by potting back. This is the opposite to potting on and, instead of using a larger pot for the move, the compost is reduced and a smaller pot used. It must be understood that not all plants require frequent repotting, even when their pots are filled with roots. Most of the splendid, long-lived palm family fall into this category. These continue for many seasons in a comparatively small container. After potting or repotting, always water the plants gently but thoroughly, placing them in the shade for a day or so. Allow the compost to become dry between each of the first few waterings because some plants become a little lazy at making fresh roots when they are receiving liberal amounts of water without having to search for it.

## Light

If their full individual potential is to be realized, indoor plants must be well-positioned to ensure that they receive their daily light requirement, light being the regulating factor in all plant growth. Compared with a plant growing in the garden, a similar individual placed behind a window receives barely a quarter the amount of light, and mid-way into a normally sun-lit room the proportion is considerably less. Fortunately, many of

Repotting. 1 Pots with only one drainage hole will require a crock.  2 Put a small amount of compost into the bottom of the larger pot and place the plant with moistened soil ball in the centre.  3 Add compost all around the plant.
4 Press down firmly to the depth of 15 mm from the top of the pot, and water gently.

the species which we cultivate indoors are naturally shade-lovers and so are perfectly able to cope with low light conditions. The dark leathery-leaved sorts of houseplants are, generally, the best equipped to thrive in these places. Those with leaf variegation require rather more light, but not direct sun, if they are to retain this feature. Purple-leaved plants normally come into this group too. Most flowering sorts (including temporary pot plants) need the brightest positions. Plants such as cacti and succulents, which require dry soil for much of the year, also favour light positions and many will tolerate sun although few of them dislike being baked alive in their pots.

## Water

This is the second factor vital to plant growth; indeed plants, like most animals, are largely composed of water. Also, without moisture, chemicals remain locked in the soil and are unavailable for the plant's use. Problems associated with watering are unfortunately the single biggest headache for the novice indoor 'gardener'. Generally too much water at the wrong time rather than too little causes the failures. In the cultivation of plants indoors, it is of prime importance to regulate the watering according to individual need. Those species which

develop a weak root system, for example, will require less water than a fibrous-rooted plant in a similar-sized pot.

As mentioned previously, light and water, as well as temperature, must be in direct proportion to one another. During the low light/temperature conditions of winter, many plants become (or attempt to become) semi-dormant. At this time, watering has to be adjusted accordingly. It is far better to err on the dry side than the wet; it is easier to revive a wilting plant with a good soak than salvage something of a plant with a decayed root system. Increased amounts of water may be given when temperatures are higher and light stimulates growth.

Although some plants naturally require more water than others, very few species can tolerate permanently wet compost for very long. The age of the specimen, the size of its container, type of compost—and most importantly the temperature of the room, together with its atmosphere—all have a bearing on the frequency of watering. Pots should be checked by feeling the compost with the fingers or, better still, by weighing the pot in the hand. If similar composts are used, you will very soon become proficient in determining the difference in weight between a dry and a waterlogged one. No pots should be allowed to dry to the extent that the compost actually

shrinks away from the sides of the pot.

Plant roots require air as well as water. When cold and saturated, all the soil air spaces are filled with water so the action of most beneficial bacteria ceases and harmful fungus diseases proliferate, causing the death of root ends, which, more often than not, means the demise of the plant. Experience will also enable you to group your plants mentally according to their needs. Only very few can remain wet—these are naturally lovers of bog conditions. With many, you may be liberal during their active growing season then, at other times, you must keep the compost just moist. Other plants prefer the compost to be partially dry between waterings so that their roots really have to search for moisture, and these are the most susceptible to over-watering during dull weather.

Most pots may be watered with a narrow spout can from above, filling the space between the compost and the pot rim as many times as is needed to allow excess to run from the drainage holes in the base. Always allow the compost to drain through completely before replacing the pots in their saucers or covers. Surplus water which gathers in the saucer must be tipped away. Bowls seldom have drainage holes and here special care is needed to ensure that surplus water is not allowed to stagnate.

81

# Houseplants

A pink-flowered cyclamen.

The painted nettle (coleus).

Crotons have striking leaves.

Some plants, particularly those with hairy leaves, object to being watered over their leaves. Saintpaulias are particularly difficult to water in the conventional way. With these, place the pots up to their middles in a bowl of water instead. Never use icy-cold water direct from the tap for tropical indoor plants as this lowers the soil temperature and is likely to cause a shock to the plant's root system. Ideally, the water should be drawn several hours previously, enabling the temperature to rise naturally. It is, of course, also possible to warm the water by adding a little hot water to it. Normal tap-water additives, such as chlorine and fluoride, can harm certain plants, turning their leaves blotchy and their tips brown. The gas in chlorinated water will disperse if the water is first run into a wide-mouthed container a week or so before use. When fluoride is the cause of noticeable damage you may have to resort to giving your plants rain or pond water instead. Softened water can also be harmful to sensitive plants. Where water is 'hard', a white deposit may be left on leaves.

## Atmosphere

Walk through a forest or into a glasshouse on a warm day and you will quickly detect the humid atmosphere which living plants enjoy. This humidity is lacking in our homes, the air being too dry for the comfort of many plants. Their well-being is assured if the moisture content in the air surrounding them is increased. One way of achieving this in warm weather is to mist over the plants using a hand-held atomizer filled with clean water. A moist micro-climate can also be provided if the pots are plunged into a planter containing moist peat. Instead of peat, some people prefer to stand the pots on a layer of pebbles which receives periodic tricklings of water. Like us, plants require freely circulating air for they too have to breathe. Under normal indoor conditions there is sufficient movement of air caused, for example, by the opening and closing of doors.

On fine days during the autumn, every advantage should be taken to see that your plants have as much air and light as possible. This guarantees sturdy growth with ripened stems—essential for cooler days ahead. Although plants appreciate fresh air, very few indeed can tolerate cold draughts for very long. Where plants are placed on inside window-sills, do check for draughts first. Some subjects, such as maidenhair fern, are damaged irreparably when placed in a cold airstream. Fumes from fires, either coal, gas or oil, can also be damaging to sensitive species. The slightest leak overnight will hinder development.

## Temperature

The ideal average temperature for indoor plants is in the range of 15–21°C (59–70°F) during the day and 7–10°C (45–50°F) at night. Most plants, provided that they are healthy, well ripened and have an established root system, are able to tolerate lower temperatures for short periods during the resting period of their growth cycle. Few tropical plants, when in active growth, can survive temperatures much lower than 5°C (41°F) without damage.

## Feeding

Strange as it may seem, many beginners appear to care for their new charges well by siting them carefully and systematically watering them, but then totally neglect the fact that, after the plants have exhausted the feeding element in the compost, frequent feeding will be required. This is another factor which is linked to prevailing conditions. For example, you do not feed a plant which is dormant or has been recently repotted. Nor do already sickly-looking individuals take kindly to stimulants offered. The modern resin-coated or time-release granules containing a balanced fertilizer are of particular value to the grower of houseplants. These may be incorporated in the compost then, when exhausted (you can determine this either by the time-life of the product or by the empty cases on the compost surface), simply scatter a few more in the pot. Concentrated liquid feeds are also available to the amateur. These should be diluted with a carefully measured amount of tepid water to provide a weak dose at intervals during the active growing season.

There are also foliar feeds which are

The tropical dragon lily (dracaena).

A show featuring a poinsettia.

A maidenhair fern (adiantum).

very efficient when misted over and under the leaves. Foliar feeds are quick-acting on healthy plants. They may also be used successfully on poor plants whose intake of normal water has been reduced for a while. When applying any kind of fertilizer, make certain that the compost is already moist. Bear in mind that there is a real danger of scorching tender roots when dry fertilizer is added to dry compost and then watered in. Always resist the temptation when feeding plants to hurry growth along by applying stronger solutions or more frequent applications than recommended.

## Cleaning leaves

Leaves are the main centre of photosynthesis in a plant. Photosynthesis is a process whereby, under the influence of light, the chlorophyll contained in the leaves converts water and carbon dioxide gas, present in the atmosphere, into carbohydrates and oxygen. Although the primary intake of water is through the roots, considerable amounts of water vapour are also both absorbed and exhaled, together with the gases mentioned, through the stomata, or pores, of the underleaf. Because of the importance of this function, quite apart from the appearance of the plant, regular weekly sponging to remove clogging dust is essential. Both upper as well as lower leaf surfaces of smooth-leaved kinds can be washed with water to which a few drops of a proprietary leaf-shine liquid have

been added. Some people prefer to use a 50/50 mixture of milk and water instead. Resist the temptation to wipe the leaves with olive oil for, although they gleam at first, this can have a detrimental effect on them. Most hairy-leaved plants dislike water on their leaves. Use a soft brush to clean them gently instead.

## Top-dressing

An annual top-dressing with fresh compost is normally sufficient for established plants in large pots. Before carrying out the top-dressing remove about 5 cm (2 in) or more of old soil and roots from the top of the pot. Whenever possible, all potting operations carried out at home should be done in the early spring when the roots are most active.

## Pruning and shaping

Except when it interferes with their flowering, indoor plants, particularly climbers, require attention in late autumn or early spring which is the time to thin out or cut back straggly growths. Depending on their style of growth, some rampant growers may also require attention during the season to keep them in check. Frequent nipping-out of the tips of new growths encourages many plants to 'break' so that they develop into bushy specimens. Left to their own devices, they could become too large and consequently worthless for their position. The style of support must be decided upon

early in the life of the specimen. For some a simple wire loop may be all that is needed, others can be trained to cover a large area of wall. Plants such as some ficus, monstera and philodendron will become lanky or top-heavy, eventually out-growing their position. These may be pruned back fairly hard during the spring. New growth will emerge which, before very long, develops into a useful bushy plant once more. In all staking, arrange to have the supports as unobtrusive as possible. Even the ties should not be seen; for these choose neutral colours which merge with the foliage. When pruning, care must be exercised when dealing with species which flower on their old wood, many of these require little attention. Any kinds which produce flowers on the current season's wood may be cut back after their blooms fade or very early the following season.

## Hydroponics

Hydroponics is a technique whereby plants are grown in water to which fertilizer is added at regular intervals. This method is particularly useful for plants in offices or shop displays, where the plants may receive little attention for fairly lengthy periods. A popular method is to place the plant in a container of pebble-sized clay granules for support, together with a fertilizer and water input tube and a water level indicator gauge. You must use fertilizers specially made for hydroponic culture.

PART TWO

# The Garden
# Week by Week

# Week 1

## THE KITCHEN GARDEN

**Celery** may need extra protection if the weather is severe. A temporary covering of straw or bracken heaped over a wire-netting arch can be used for a day or two, but must be removed when the weather improves.

**Cut winter cabbages and savoys** as required.

**Gather spinach and Brussels sprouts.**

**Lift a few celery plants** and stack them close together in deep boxes of moist peat or sand, but do not allow the blanched stems to be exposed to light.

**Order seed potatoes** in plenty of time. The tubers are likely to be in better condition if you order early, and they need to be 'chitted' (put into a cool but frost-free, light place to sprout) before you need to plant them.

**Seakale** can be forced in a similar way to rhubarb.

**Start to force rhubarb** by covering a mature root with a bucket or lightproof box, preferably packed with straw.

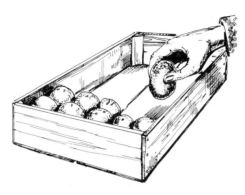

You should be able to pull a few sticks by early March, but this can be advanced by a couple of weeks if you can pack fresh horse manure round the outside of the container.

**Witloof chicory** can be potted up and forced indoors.

### FRUIT

**Collect and burn fallen leaves** around fruit trees, otherwise they may harbour diseases.

**Inspect apples and pears in store**, and remove any showing signs of rot.

**Rabbits** can easily damage young fruit trees by gnawing the bark. Make sure you have protected them with proprietary plastic tree guards or wire-netting.

## THE FLOWER GARDEN

**Roses** can be planted any time this month if the soil is not frozen or waterlogged. If the ground is not suitable for planting, or new rose beds have not yet been prepared, heel the plants into a trench in a sheltered part of the garden until the soil is workable and the bed prepared. Do not leave the roots exposed.

**Seed labels**, boxes and pots can all be prepared for the season ahead. Clean plastic boxes and pots with soapy water to remove any of the old soil.

**Check wooden boxes** to ensure the corners are secure and strong enough to support the pressure of compost.

**Seed orders** that arrive early are best stored in a cool, dry place. Old, clean biscuit tins with well-fitting lids make excellent storage containers if placed in a cool cupboard. If you have not already ordered your seeds, do so now.

**Spring bulbs** will be appearing in mild districts. Check to make sure that border rubbish that has not yet been dug in has not blown against them. Wet leaves will encourage pests and diseases.

### THE WATER GARDEN

**Garden pools** need very little attention during the winter, but make sure that the pool is kept topped up with water if necessary. If it becomes too low and the water freezes, plants at the bottom may be damaged and the fish killed.

### LAWNS

**Established lawns** that did not receive a top-dressing in the autumn can be given one now, but wait until the grass is dry.

**Lawn edges** can be trimmed up and straightened. Use a half-moon edging-iron and a sharp pair of edging shears.

## THE GREENHOUSE

**Bulbs** that have been outside in a plunge bed of moist peat or ashes can probably be brought into the greenhouse to flower. Try to avoid moving them into a high temperature initially. It is always best to increase the heat gradually.

**Clean pots and seedboxes.** If you leave it until later you will probably be too busy sowing and pricking off.

**Cold greenhouses** that are empty for the winter can be scrubbed clean with a disinfectant. Clean all the glass, frames, and staging. If the greenhouse border is used for plants in the summer, sterilize the soil with a soil sterilizer used as the manufacturer recommends.

**Composts** for seed sowing and for cuttings will be needed during the next few months. If you prefer to mix your own, do so now and make up enough to last you through to early spring.

Tip off excess peat or ashes when bringing bulbs inside.

Alternatively you can buy prepared composts; but again it is sensible to buy one large bag rather than a number of small ones over the next month or two. Do not, however, buy more than you use fairly soon, as composts do not store in good condition indefinitely. The fertilizers in John Innes compost can cause chemical reactions in store that can actually inhibit growth. There is little to choose between a loam-based or a soilless compost for seed sowing.

**Daffodils** brought into flower may need support from split canes and unobtrusive ties.

**Houseplants** indoors that are not doing too well can be given a 'holiday' in the greenhouse, where they will benefit from the better light and conditions more conducive to growth.

**Remove dead flowers** from cyclamen and other winter-flowering plants. If left on they look unsightly and allow various rots to get a hold on the plant.

**Water** plants such as cyclamen, cinerarias and calceolarias carefully. The compost should not be allowed to dry out, but it should never remain saturated either.

**WEEKEND PROJECTS**

### Make a trellis

It is very easy to make a trellis, like the one shown clothed with climbing rose 'Pompon de Paris'. Ideally make the trellis from Western red cedar wood, although larch, as used for fencing, and even sawn softwood are suitable. Hardwood, like oak, is very durable, but this wood may warp in use.

In the example shown, the first stage is to fix 50 × 50 mm (2 × 2 in) vertical supports to the wall at intervals of about 1.5 m (5 ft). To make a secure fixing, first drill the uprights and then mark the wall and drill out holes with a masonry drill bit so that plastic wall plugs can be inserted. Use gauge 10 zinc-plated woodscrews to make the fixings. A spirit level will ensure that the uprights are exactly vertical.

It is best to make the actual trellis part on flat ground and then lift it into position when assembled. In the example shown the horizontals and uprights are placed 60 cm (2 ft) apart. Lay out the horizontals and then position the vertical pieces. Where the pieces intersect, fix them with galvanized nails. Before completing the assembly, measure the diagonals and check that they are equal, in which case the trellis will be square.

Before fixing the trellis panel to the wall, treat it and the wall supports with wood preservative. Red cedar preservative will give most wood the appearance of Western red cedar, or ordinary brown preservatives can be used. It is best not to use creosote.

Fix the completed trellis to the wall supports using zinc-plated woodscrews.

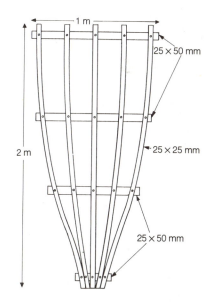

To make a fan-shaped trellis, take five pieces of 25 mm (1 in) square timber about 2 m (6 ft) long. Lay them side by side and tie one end together. Splay out the other ends and screw them at equal distances to a 50 × 25 mm (2 × 1 in) cross piece about 1 m (3 ft) long. Fix other intermediate cross pieces until the trellis is shaped as required.

## THE KITCHEN GARDEN

**Lift celery, parsnips and Jerusalem artichokes** as required. If there is a mild spell lift sufficient to see you through a period when the ground might be frozen.

**Test your soil.** Although it is best to apply fertilizers nearer to sowing or planting time, you need to think about applying lime now if the pH indicates this is necessary.

### FRAMES AND CLOCHES

**Cloches** should be put in position several weeks before sowing, and it is not too early to do this now for early February sowings.

**Hot-beds** (*see* page 60) are not used much now, but if you are going to prepare one then now is the time to make a start.

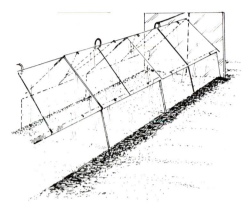

**Soil-warming cables** in frames should be put in position in plenty of time. You should switch them on for a few days before sowing to warm up the soil.

## FRUIT

**Check tree ties** and adjust any that are beginning to bite into the wood.

**Firm strawberries** planted in the autumn if ground frosts have loosened them.

**Grease bands** should be checked to see that dead leaves and other material has not become stuck to them, forming a bridge for the pests.

**Twiggy branches** on bushes and trees that need to be cut out anyway should be removed and stored under cover as plant supports.

## THE FLOWER GARDEN

**Border carnations and pinks** may be attacked by slugs in damp weather. If they are troublesome, put down slug pellets.

**Brush off snow** that has fallen on choice shrubs and trees. If left on, the weight may break or damage the branches.

**Clean up the herbaceous border**, removing dead stalks and leaves, and hoe off any weeds.

**Garden chrysanthemums**, which will be planted out from late April to early May (depending on the area), should have the ground prepared in plenty of time. Dig the border now if it was not prepared in the autumn. Dig the soil thoroughly, removing all perennial weed roots, and mix in well-rotted manure or garden compost.

**Order flower seeds** if you have not already done so. If you delay much longer there is an increased chance that some of the varieties you want will be sold out.

**Stakes and ties** on ornamental trees need to be checked occasionally, especially during winter months when gales are likely to loosen them. Make sure tight ties are not restricting growth.

## THE ROCK GARDEN

**This is a good time** to make a new rock garden or improve an old one. It is too early to fill it with plants yet, but the construction work can be done now. A good builders' merchant specializing in garden construction materials should have a range of rocks and will be able to advise you on costs, and how much you are likely to need.

## LAWNS

**Broken lawn edges** can be repaired now. Use a sharp spade or a half-moon edging-iron to cut the turf so that the broken edge can be turned into the lawn and a fresh, new edge left at the outside. Use sieved soil to fill up the hole where the turf was broken.

**Send mowers for serving** and sharpening if this has not already been done.

## THE GREENHOUSE

**Cacti** are usually happy in a winter temperature of 7°C (45°F), but a few South African succulents prefer a higher temperature and it may be worth taking these indoors for the coldest months, keeping the others cooler. Keep them all in good light.

**Clean up** the outside area. If it is just trodden earth, it is well worth excavating a shallow trench and filling it with gravel. If you prefer a harder surface, paving slabs laid on a sand base will be perfectly adequate and easy to keep clean.

**Clean watering-cans** thoroughly. This is also a useful time to clean out the water butt, which can become an unhealthy reservoir of dirt and disease if left exposed and unattended.

**Cyclamen** are best sown in the autumn, but you can still sow now if you can provide a temperature of 15°C (60°F) for germination.

**Electricity cables** should be checked every year to ensure they have not perished in the high humidity. A competent electrician is the best person to advise you if you are in doubt.

**Hippeastrums** can be started into growth, repotting if necessary. They

Potting up chrysanthemum cuttings with a dibber.

will normally only need repotting every two or three years.

**Paraffin heaters** not already in use should be cleaned ready for when you want to provide a little warmth. Pay particular attention to the burners, which can smoke if they are too dirty, and trim or replace wicks.

**Pot up cyclamen seedlings** sown in the autumn into small pots of John Innes potting compost.

**Prune fuchsias** into shape.

**Prune** *Plumbago capensis* and passion flowers. Cut back last year's growth on plumbago to within about 23 cm (9 in) of the previous year's growth (unless you have a young specimen you want to fill out the space). Prune the passion flower by taking last year's growth back to about two buds, cutting out weak shoots completely.

**Take carnation cuttings.** Perpetual-flowering carnations are best propagated from sideshoots about 7.5 cm (3 in) long. Pull them off and trim off any of the main stem that tears off with them, and root in a propagator at about 10°C (50°F).

**Take late-flowering chrysanthemum cuttings,** preferably selecting the new shoots that arise directly from the roots. Trim off the lower leaves at the base and cut cleanly below a joint, then insert in pots or boxes.

**Water** can be piped to the greenhouse with plastic piping, and this will save a lot of carrying. The pipe is usually laid in a trench about 30–45 cm (1–1½ ft) deep, but check with your local water authority first to make sure you are not breaking any regulations, and use the fittings they recommend.

## WEEKEND PROJECTS

### Fixing trellis

Trellis should not be fixed flat to a wall. Space is needed behind it to allow climbers to develop. Allow a gap of 2.5–5 cm (1–2 in) between the trellis and the wall.

To do this, you can drill a hole through the centre of some small blocks of wood and position these behind the trellis to act as spacers. The fixing screws pass through the trellis, through the holes in the wood and into the wall. Cotton reels make handy spacers as they have a hole ready-made through them.

To fix screws in the wall you need an electric drill which incorporates a hammer action; also needed is a carbide tungsten tipped masonry drill bit. Finally you will need some wallplugs and non-rusting galvanized screws. Use number 8 screws, about 7.5–10 cm (3–4 in) long—these will be long enough to

ensure that the threaded part of the screw is buried completely in the brickwork.

It is a good idea to smear grease on the screw threads; not only does this

make them easier to drive in but also makes them much easier to remove later should you want to paint or repair broken trellis.

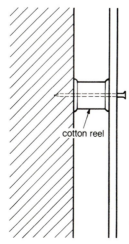

cotton reel

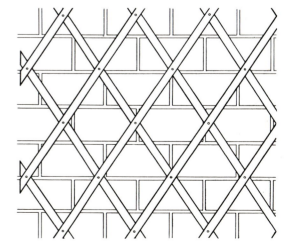

## THE KITCHEN GARDEN

**Continue winter digging** whenever the weather is suitable, but keep off the soil if it is wet or frozen.

**Order seed potatoes.** If you leave it too late the quality may not be so good, and some varieties tend to sell out quickly.

**Plan this year's vegetable plot** in detail and order the seeds, if you have not already done so.

## FRAMES AND CLOCHES

**Sow broad beans** under cloches in mild areas, for June picking, but choose a dwarf variety.

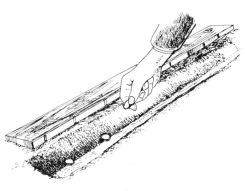

**Spring cabbages** can be advanced if you cover them with cloches now. You should be able to pick spring greens in late February or early March.

## FRUIT

**Apply a tar oil winter wash** to fruit trees, if you have not already done so. This will kill insects and their eggs lurking in crevices in the bark.

**Check labels**, and if they have become illegible renew them. This job is always easier now than when the plants are in full leaf.

## THE FLOWER GARDEN

**Azaleas** that have flowered indoors over Christmas can be stood outdoors in a sheltered spot once the flowers finish. Less water will be needed, but never let the compost dry out.

**Bulbs** for flowering indoors should be brought in from the plunge bed (where they have been covered with sand or peat) when they have developed sufficiently. Bowls of bulbs that have finished flowering should be planted out in the garden in a sheltered position.

**Evergreens** planted in the autumn may benefit from some protection if the site is very exposed. Polythene, sacking, or even fine-mesh netting, wrapped round a framework of canes, is adequate.

**Plan the annual border** and bedding schemes if the weather is too severe to get out into the garden. If you have not already placed your seed order, do so now to avoid the disappointment of choice varieties being sold out.

**Roses** should be planted as soon as possible, provided that the soil is not frozen or too wet.

**Trees planted in the autumn** may have had their roots loosened by frost. Refirm the soil, but choose a dry day as wet soil will become too compacted.

## THE WATER GARDEN

**Severe frost** may freeze water in the pool. To prevent the entire pool freezing over, leave a rubber ball on the surface. If the pond does freeze over, the ball can be removed by pouring boiling water around it. By removing a few centimetres of water and covering the hole with thick sacking, you should reduce the chances of the surface freezing again. Never use a hammer to break the ice, as shock waves may kill or severely injure the fish.

## FRAMES AND CLOCHES

**Autumn-sown seedlings** in frames and cloches will benefit from a little ventilation on mild days.

**Sweet peas** in particular should be given plenty of ventilation unless it is actually frosty. If the growing tips have not already been pinched out, do this now to encourage bushiness.

## THE GREENHOUSE

**Antirrhinums** benefit from a long growing season and are hardy enough to plant out early, so it is worth sowing them now if you can provide a germination temperature of 10°C (50°F).

**Check chrysanthemum cuttings** to ensure that the compost has not dried out, and remove any leaves that have started to decay.

**Chrysanthemum cuttings** of late-flowering varieties can be taken, as sufficiently long shoots are produced from the 'stools' (roots of last year's plants).

**Dwarf French beans** can be sown in small pots of John Innes seed compost. Plant the seeds 2.5 cm (1 in) deep, and try to maintain 15°C (60°F) for germination, then a temperature of 13°C (55°F) by day, at least 5°C (41°F) at night. Later they can be hardened off in a garden frame if you want to plant them outdoors under cloches for an early crop (or you can continue to grow them in pots in the greenhouse).

**Heliotrope cuttings** can be taken now if you have a heated propagator.

**Onions** can be sown now if you want large plants in the autumn. The plants will be more advanced than those from seed sown outdoors in spring.

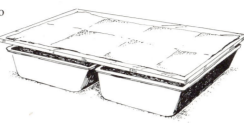

Sow annuals in seed trays and cover with glass and paper.

**Prune fuchsias.** Cut back side growths on standards to within 13 mm ($\frac{1}{2}$ in) of the main stem. Bush specimens will also need fairly hard pruning.

**Schizanthus** can be potted into 15 or or 20 cm (6 or 8 in) pots if the weather is mild and the greenhouse warm.

**Soil** known to be infected by pests or diseases is best dug out of the border and replaced by fresh soil from other parts of the garden. This may be more convenient than sterilizing it if you still have a lot of plants in the greenhouse.

**Sow** *Begonia semperflorens* and gloxinias in a minimum temperature of 15°C (60°F)—use an electric propagator if this is too high for the main greenhouse. If you live in a cold area, delay sowing for a few weeks.

**Sow bedding pelargoniums** (geraniums) in a temperature of 20°C (68°F). They can be sown a few weeks later, but flowering will be delayed.

**Sow cauliflowers** for making heads in the summer. They should be ready for planting out in April after hardening off in frames.

**Sow leeks** in boxes if you want large stems. It is only worth doing this if you want exhibition rather than table quality leeks.

**Pot-grown strawberry plants** that have been kept in a frame can be brought into the greenhouse for an early crop. Scrape soil away from the surface of the pots, and replace with fresh compost such as John Innes potting compost No. 2 or 3. Keep the plants moist once they are in the greenhouse, but be careful not to overwater.

**Tomatoes** can be sown in mild areas where the greenhouse can be maintained at a minimum of 15°C (60°F). In cold areas it is better to wait for a few weeks. Do not sow tomatoes for an outdoor crop yet, and if growing a greenhouse crop remember that the plants will be quite large when you have still got bedding plants to find room for.

---

**WEEKEND PROJECTS**

## Simple plant stand

This small plant table can be made from 19 mm ($\frac{3}{4}$ in) thick, veneered chipboard, plywood or blockboard. The height of the table is optional but it is vital that the two legs are exactly the same height and interlock firmly.

The best way to make the legs and ensure accuracy is first to make a template for one leg and satisfy yourself that it is the right shape and size needed. Mark the outline of the template on to a sheet of chipboard and cut out the shape using a coping saw or powered jig saw. Next, place the first leg onto a second sheet of chipboard, and mark in pencil carefully around its outline as a guide to cutting the second leg.

If you have the facilities such as clamps, then the two legs can be cut out together by securing the two sheets of chipboard firmly together.

The slot in each leg should be about 19–25 mm ($\frac{3}{4}$–1 in) wide. When the two legs are interlocked they should stand firmly on the ground.

The top can be square, round or shaped. Fix it to the legs with plastic joint blocks or L-shaped steel brackets.

If veneered chipboard is used then all sawn edges can be faced with matching iron-on edging veneer.

If plywood or blockboard is used, then sand down all sawn edges using glasspaper before painting.

## THE KITCHEN GARDEN

**Early crops** will benefit from improvised protection from biting winds. You can tie polythene sheeting or hessian to stout stakes, or buy a special plastic windbreak. These do not look attractive, but in the kitchen garden this may be a price you are prepared to pay.

Always position windbreaks on the predominantly windward side of the plants.

**Pinch out the tips of curly kale** to stimulate leafy shoots to develop.

**Rhubarb** for planting in spring should have well-prepared ground. Double-dig the planting site now, and incorporate as much manure or compost as you can spare.

A leatherjacket.

**Seeds** should be kept in a cool, dry place until required.

## FRAMES AND CLOCHES

**Sow suitable varieties of lettuces** in frames for transplanting to open ground later.

### FRUIT

**Apply a tar oil winter wash** to fruit trees if you have not already done so. This will help to control pests during the coming season by killing off overwintering adults and eggs lurking in the bark. Apply it on a mild, still day when it is not raining.

**Grease-bands** should be inspected and the grease renewed if necessary.

**Plant top and even soft fruit** (other than strawberries) at any time that conditions are suitable. Do not plant if the soil is frozen or waterlogged.

**Pruning of fruit trees** should have been completed before Christmas, but if it was delayed complete it now without delay.

## THE FLOWER GARDEN

**Check dahlia tubers** in store to make sure they have not become too dry and started to shrivel. If they have, syringe with water. Any damaged parts can be cut out, but dust the cuts with flowers of sulphur.

**Cut back branches** from trees if they have become dangerous or are casting too much shadow. To prevent the bark being torn as the branch falls, first cut under the branch and then saw from above.

In mild areas rose pruning can be started. Always make clean cuts just above an outward-facing bud. Hybrid teas can be shortened to just below knee height; floribundas to just above. Shrub roses should be thinned out rather than cut hard back.

**Severe weather** may confine you to the garden shed, so use the time usefully and give it a tidy-up. If you do not already have them, it is worth fixing hooks to the wall to hang garden tools

on. This will create much more space for other things and the tools are less likely to be damaged.

**Tulips** that were potted up for spring-flowering about 14 to 16 weeks ago can now be brought inside as soon as the tips of the shoots are 2.5–5 cm (1–2 in) above the compost. Place them on a cool window-ledge in a temperature of 7–10°C (45–50°F).

### THE WATER GARDEN

**Continue to protect pools** from ice (*see* page 90) and feed the fish with *Daphnia* in a mild spell.

### FRAMES AND CLOCHES

**Root cuttings** are a useful way to propagate Oriental poppies, anchusas, border phlox gaillardias, and *Romneya coulteri*. Choose pieces of root about the thickness of a pencil (this is not always possible as some—such as phlox—have thin roots) and cut into pieces about 2.5–5 cm (1–2 in) long. Phlox, gaillardia and romneya cuttings should be laid horizontally and covered with 6 mm ($\frac{1}{4}$ in) of soil. The others should be pushed into the soil vertically, with the top level with the surface. It is a good idea to cut the top end of each cutting straight across, the bottom end at a slant, so that you know which way up to insert them. If placed in a frame they should root by late spring.

# Week 4

## THE GREENHOUSE

**Achimenes** can be started into growth. Place the tubers in a box of peat-based compost, just covering them, and provide a temperature of 15°C (60°F). When the shoots are 3–5 cm (an inch or two) high, the plants can be potted up, about five in a 12.5 cm (5 in). pot.

**Aphids (greenfly)** can be active even at this time of year, and can be particularly troublesome on some of the spring-flowering pot plants. Spray or fumigate as soon as they are noticed, and before they have a chance to build up in numbers.

**Bring more bulbs in** as they become ready.

**Broad beans** grown for an early crop in cold districts can be sown in pots in the greenhouse, one seed to an 8 cm (3 in) pot. They will eventually be planted out after hardening off in a garden frame.

**Clean the glass**, inside and out. Plants need all the light they can get at this time of year.

**Coleus cuttings** can be rooted now in a warm propagator.

**Continue to take cuttings of carnations and chrysanthemums** as suitable shoots become available.

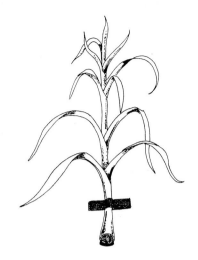

A carnation cutting.

**Feed primulas**, but continue to water carefully.

**Ferns** can be divided and repotted—but do not disturb them unless the roots have filled the old pot.

**Grape vines** can be started into growth any time between now and March. Close the ventilators so that the night temperature rises to at least 10°C (50°F), and give the roots more water. The particular requirements of the vine often make it difficult to grow in a mixed greenhouse.

**Half-hardy annuals**, and perennials usually treated as annuals, such as antirrhinums, petunias and lobelia, can be sown now.

**Peas** can be sown in 7.5 cm (3 in) pots for planting out later. Place three or four seeds in each pot, and do not let the compost become dry.

**Pelargoniums** now starting into growth can be potted on into larger pots, using John Innes potting compost No 2. Give them more water as they start to grow again.

**A few polyanthus** can be potted up and brought into the greenhouse to provide an early spring display.

**Pot-on calceolarias.** They should be ready for 15 cm (6 in) pots.

**Remove faded flowers regularly** from cyclamen and primulas, together with any discoloured leaves.

**Schizanthus** will make bushier plants if you pinch out the growing tips.

**Sow asparagus 'ferns'.** These are easy foliage plants to grow from seed.

**Sow sweet peas** in individual peat pots if you did not sow in the autumn.

## WEEKEND PROJECTS

### Make a tool rack

Somewhere to hang all that paraphernalia like trowels, secateurs, gloves and so on can be made simply and quickly using welded wire mesh which is available at builders' merchants and garden centres. Remember that space should be allowed not only for present needs but also for items acquired in the future. Clear as much wall space in the shed or garage as possible and cut out a piece of mesh to fit the space exactly.

Secure the mesh to the wall using strong screws or suitable brackets.

There are various ways in which items can be hung on the mesh. For example, you can cut the wire here and there and turn it up to form hooks where needed. Clothes pegs, wire ties and so on make useful fasteners.

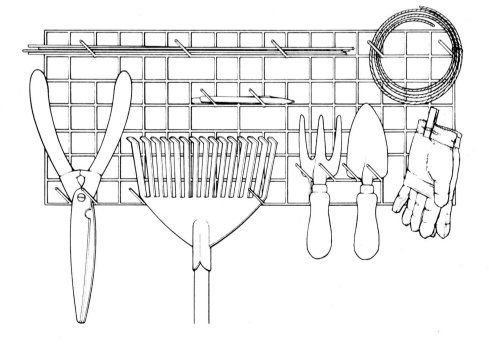

# Week 5

## THE KITCHEN GARDEN

**Autumn-sown onions** must be kept free of weed competition so take the opportunity to use the hoe between rows whenever the weather is suitable.
**Brussels sprouts**, kale, and spinach beet will need continuous harvesting.
**Complete winter digging** if you can. If the ground is frozen take the opportunity to get the wheelbarrow over the ground to position manure or garden compost in a convenient position for digging it in when the weather improves.
**Force rhubarb** outdoors. It does not matter much what you cover the crowns with, provided that they are in complete darkness, and in a fairly even temperature. Straw or dead leaves packed around the plants will encourage growth.

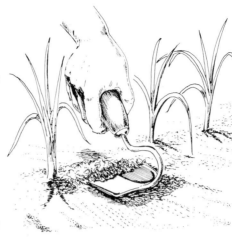

**Plant Jerusalem artichokes** during the next few weeks, provided that the ground is not frozen.

### FRAMES AND CLOCHES

**Grey mould** (botrytis) can be a problem with lettuces in frames. Keep picking off dead or decaying leaves to discourage disease.
**Lettuces** in frames are also attractive to slugs, leatherjackets and cutworms. Use slug pellets and a soil insecticide as necessary.
**Peas and broad beans** can be sown under cloches within the next few weeks. In mild districts you could also sow a few Brussels sprouts or cauliflower seeds beneath the same cloche to transplant in late spring.
**Sow cabbages and carrots** in frames or under cloches, but choose early varieties. The cabbages will have to be transplanted to open ground in the second half of May.

## THE FLOWER GARDEN

**Containers** such as hanging baskets, window-boxes, tubs and troughs will need cleaning and renovating, and this is a good time to tackle the job. Clean off all the old soil and wash them thoroughly to ensure cracks and corners are not harbouring pests. Allow the wood to dry thoroughly before painting it. Window-boxes may need special attention for safety reasons. It is always worth checking any securing anchors.
**Order gladiolus** corms from a specialist supplier if you want a wide range of varieties and quality stock.
**Order herbaceous plants** if this has not already been done. You can usually buy plants easily from garden centres later, but if you want a particular variety or an unusual plant, then it is best to order from a specialist nursery.
**Plant deciduous hedges** if the weather is mild. If the ground is frozen they can

be kept in a frost-free shed for a few days with straw packed around the roots. Plant as soon as the ground thaws sufficiently.
**Prune wisteria** by shortening sideshoots from the main branches back to about three buds.

**Rose beds** should be prepared for spring planting. Prepare the ground thoroughly by double-digging and incorporating plenty of manure or compost.
**Sink gardens** may be looking a bit tatty. Tidy them up, taking the opportunity to remove some of the compost where it can be dug out without disturbing the plants too much, and replace with fresh. Dress the surface with stone chippings to give it a clean finish.

### LAWNS

**Bare patches** can be reseeded later, but if the area is in a position where it receives a lot of regular wear during the summer it may be best to patch in with turf. This is a good time to do this job, provided that the weather is fine.

## THE GREENHOUSE

**Dahlia tubers** can be boxed up in moist peat and placed in a warm greenhouse to produce shoots for cuttings. Make sure that the tubers are clearly labelled to avoid confusion when the cuttings are taken.

**Electric propagators** are an invaluable aid for germinating seeds and rooting cuttings. If you are considering buying one, do so now that you can get the maximum benefit from it during the next few months.

**Fuchsias** that were pruned back a few weeks ago will benefit from a daily misting with clean water. This, combined with a higher temperature, should encourage the plants to produce shoots more readily.

**Grevilleas** make nice foliage pot plants, and can be sown now.

**Insulate** your greenhouse for the bedding plant season if it is not already insulated. Even plastic 'bubble'

insulation can be very effective and it will either enable you to reduce the fuel bill or maintain a higher temperature.

**Look for pests and diseases** on your plants. It pays to find attacks before they become so established that they are obvious. Spray or fumigate promptly to reduce the chance of a bigger problem later.

**Salvias** can be sown now. These plants are often more successful grown in pots, although they will be perfectly satisfactory if pricked off into boxes.

**Tomatoes** for a greenhouse crop can be sown if you can provide a minimum night temperature of 15°C (60°F).

**Trickle watering systems**, which deliver water to plants in growing bags and pots through a network of small tubes, can be useful, and it is worth installing one in advance of the main watering season. It will cut down the work significantly in spring and summer.

**Ventilate** whenever you can on warm afternoons. Automatic ventilators are very useful if the greenhouse has to be left unattended during the day.

**Water** carefully at this time of year. Too much water is likely to lead to root rots. Give sufficient, however, to meet the growing demands of many plants.

## WEEKEND PROJECTS

### Stepping stones

Stepping stones do not have to cross water. In fact, in a garden they look most attractive as a pathway meandering across a lawn, beside a flower border, and through a shrub border. Stepping stones are ideal for places that could be trampled by heavy wear, yet they are economical in materials and do not have the hard appearance of a conventional pathway.

Ordinary pressed concrete paving slabs are ideal for stepping stones and purpose-made circular slabs are also available. For anyone living near a quarry, stone is a perfect material of course, and if you have access to large trees, such as old elms, the logs can be sliced with a chainsaw to make timber slabs which tone very well with shrub borders. Remember, however, that logs are slippery in wet weather. Soak the timber in wood preservative before laying the slabs.

To make a stepping stone path in a shrub border, set the slabs a comfortable short pace apart. Simply compact the soil at each slab position and rest the slab on the soil surface. Add or remove soil as necessary until the slab rests perfectly level and then lightly tap down each slab with a hammer, using a block of wood to protect the surface until it is firmly bedded. Keeping the surfaces of the slabs above soil level will help to keep them clean and non-slippery.

However, when making a stepping

stone path in a lawn it is important to set the slabs fractionally below the grass surface so that the lawnmower can be run over the slabs without damage. Lay out the slabs on the grass surface until they are arranged as you want them. With a spade or lawn edging iron, cut down around the perimeter of each slab to a depth of about 75 mm (3 in). Lift the turf and soil within each area to a depth of about 75 mm. Scatter some sharp sand or fine soil in each hole, lower a slab in place, and tap it down so that it is firm and level, with the surface just below the grass surface.

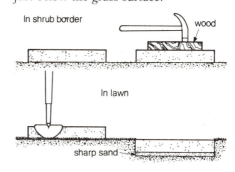

In shrub border    wood

In lawn

sharp sand

## THE KITCHEN GARDEN

**Break up exposed soil** by forking and treading, but do not attempt to produce a fine tilth at this stage unless you expect to sow early crops.

**Cabbages** overwintered in frames can be planted out now in a sheltered position.

**Check potatoes** in store for eating, and rub off any sprouts that are developing.

**Continue to cut winter cabbages** and savoys as required.

**Jerusalem artichokes** can be planted, as they are perfectly hardy; but remember that they make a lot of tall, bushy top-growth, so plant them where this does not matter.

**Lift** a few roots of chicory if they are still in the ground. Shorten the roots and force indoors or in the greenhouse to produce blanched chicons.

**Potatoes** should be placed in trays in a frost-free place to 'chit'. Keep in a light place to encourage sturdy shoots. They must not be exposed to frost.

### FRAMES AND CLOCHES

**In frames** sow Brussels sprouts, summer cabbages and cauliflowers, for planting out in April.

**Under cloches** sow peas and broad beans, and in mild areas early varieties of carrots.

### FRUIT

**Apricots** may soon start trying to flower in mild districts, and the blossom will have to be protected from hard frosts. If you hang hessian or polythene sheeting over the trees during frosty weather you must be prepared to remove it as soon as the frost has gone. It is vital that pollinating insects are allowed to do their work.

**Check stakes** to see that wind-rock has not caused stakes or ties to work loose.

**Newly-purchased fruit trees** are easier to spray (perhaps with a tar oil winter wash) while they are still in a bundle and before they are planted.

**Prune autumn-fruiting raspberries** by cutting back to within 15 cm (6 in) of the ground.

## THE FLOWER GARDEN

**Bring pots of bulbs into the house** as they are ready.

**Check shrub borders** to see if any plants need replacing.

**Old shrubs** that have become overgrown and unattractive are best replaced. Choose subjects that have a long flowering period, such as potentillas, or that have attractive foliage. Those with gold or variegated leaves can be particularly effective against dark-leaved types in the background.

**Delphiniums** will soon be sending up new shoots, which make an ideal meal for slugs. As a precaution, sprinkle slug bait round the plants.

**Examine dahlia tubers** in store. Cut away any portions that have rotted, and dust with flowers of sulphur.

**Lilium regale** can be planted now. The shoots of established bulbs will soon be appearing through the soil and

a covering of bracken or straw will give them some useful extra protection from severe frosts.

**Paths and walls** covered with moss or lichen can be cleaned up during the winter by spraying them with a weak solution of tar oil winter wash. It is particularly worth treating paths, which might otherwise become slippery and unsafe.

**Tidy up the herbaceous border** if it has not already been done. Cut off dead stems and generally tidy the bed.

**Sweet pea trenches** should be prepared by now. If the ground has already been dug, break the soil down for a finer tilth.

**Winter-flowering heathers** can be trimmed back as soon as the flowers fade, using a sharp pair of shears to clip off the flower heads. This will prevent the plants becoming straggly.

### FRAMES AND CLOCHES

Cut flowers are especially welcome early in the season, and it is well worth sowing some hardy annuals early under cloches. These will provide flowers for cutting in early summer. Place the cloches in position now to warm up the soil.

## THE GREENHOUSE

**Bring potted strawberries** in from the garden frame if you have not already done so. It is a good idea to replace the top few centimetres of soil with fresh John Innes potting compost No 3. Keep the plants in good light.

**Clean the glass** if this has not been done recently, and attend to any panes loosened during the winter (you can try sealing them with a strong adhesive tape as a temporary measure).

**Houseplants** often benefit from a few weeks in a warm greenhouse, especially at this time of year when the light indoors is still poor.

**Mice** can be troublesome in the greenhouse. Use traps or bait. If bait is used, place it in a drainpipe laid on its side so that pets cannot get at it.

**Schizanthus** plants that are well established in their final pots can be fed every two weeks with a liquid fertilizer.

**Sow dwarf French beans** in pots for an early crop in the greenhouse or for planting out under cloches later. Plant the seeds 2.5 cm (1 in) deep and germinate at 15°C (60°F), then maintain 13°C (55°F) by day, 5°C (41°F) by night.

**Sow melons** 13 mm ($\frac{1}{2}$ in) deep in 9 cm ($3\frac{1}{2}$ in) pots of John Innes seed compost, and germinate them in a temperature of 18°C (64°F). They will tolerate a few degrees lower once they have germinated.

**Sow** *Primula obconica* if you can provide a germination temperature of 15°C (60°F). Just sprinkle the seeds on the surface of a seedpan containing John Innes seed compost and leave uncovered. Keep the compost moist.

**Start fuchsias into growth** if not already done. Trim them into shape, bring them into good light, water regularly and mist with water daily.

**Sweet peas** can be sown in pots. These will flower later than autumn-sown plants, but earlier than seed sown outside this spring.

**Take cuttings of coleus** from overwintered plants, providing a temperature of 10°C (50°F) for rooting.

## WEEKEND PROJECTS

### Fence repairs

Timber posts are the most vulnerable parts of a fence. Often these rot at ground level. The old post can be dug out and a new one inserted (*see* erecting a fence, page 181). If this is done, the fence on either side of the post should be supported temporarily with struts. Alternatively fit a concrete spur to support the existing post. The spur will be pre-drilled to receive two bolts. Buy bolts which are long enough to go through the spur and the post. Dig a 45–60 cm ($1\frac{1}{2}$–2 ft) hole beside the post and put the spur in it. Mark off and drill the two holes through the post using a brace and bit; then insert the bolts keeping the nuts on the spur side. Pull the post up vertical and support it with struts. Pour a dryish concrete mix (one part cement to five parts ballast)

into the hole and compact it thoroughly. Allow the concrete to set before using a hacksaw to take off the tails of the bolts.

*Gravel board* Nail a new gravel board to small battens screwed to the bottom timber posts. With concrete posts, the battens will have to be driven down into the ground beside the post to provide fixing points.

*Arris rail* Special galvanized steel brackets can be used to strengthen a split in an arris rail. If the damage occurs where the rail enters the post a different type of bracket is required. New arris rails or cant rails can be bought and shaped to fit into the mortise slot in the post. The other end can be square sawn and fixed with a galvanized bracket.

*Feather-edged boards* For economy, old feather-edged boards can be refixed upside down and their rotting ends trimmed off. New boards should be overlapped by 13 mm ($\frac{1}{2}$ in) and nailed to the arris rail with galvanized nails. The nails should pass through the thick edge of one board into the thin edge of the board it overlaps. Keep the boards vertical and use a small block of wood to ensure a uniform overlap.

Arris rail

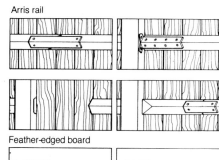

Feather-edged board

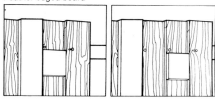

Concrete spur

Gravel board

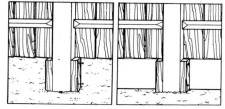

# Week 7

## THE KITCHEN GARDEN

**Chit seed potatoes** by placing them in shallow trays in a light but frost-proof place.

**Lift celery, leeks, parsnips and Jerusalem artichokes** as required, taking advantage of any mild spells to lift enough to see you through periods when the ground will be frozen.

**Sow parsnips** on deeply dug and well-prepared ground provided that the soil is not too wet. If you want exhibition parsnips it is worth making holes with a crowbar and filling the hole with potting compost. If you do this it is necessary to sow two or three seeds at each position, thinning to one later. This is a good idea anyway.

**Spring cabbages** sown last July or August are normally planted in the final positions in the autumn, but if you still

have some seedlings left in the seedbed because there was not room to transplant them all then, you can try moving a few now if the weather is fine.

### FRAMES AND CLOCHES

**Carrots** can be sown in frames from now on in mild areas. In colder districts it may be best to wait another week or two, but you can prepare the frame by forking over the soil and raking in a balanced fertilizer if crops are to be sown directly into the soil.

**Lettuces** for succession should be sown in frames for planting out later.

### FRUIT

**Raspberry canes** that are becoming too long and whippy can be tipped back slightly, but do not cut too far back otherwise you will remove cropping wood.

**Spray peaches** with a fungicide to control peach leaf curl in the coming summer.

## THE FLOWER GARDEN

**Acid-loving plants** are often difficult or impossible to grow in limy soil. If you are keen to grow a rhododendron or an acid-loving heather, it is worth preparing the ground now by digging a hole about 75 cm (2½ ft) deep, and replacing the old soil with a mixture of peat and lime-free soil.

If the surrounding soil is very chalky, you can build a raised peat bed 45 cm (1½ ft) or so high. Excavate a 30-cm (1-ft) deep hole first; line it with polythene and fill it with fresh, acid soil. Build up the perimeter of the area with peat blocks to a height of 30 or 40 cm (1–1½ ft) and fill this with more acid soil. Collect rainwater for irrigation purposes.

**Apply a general fertilizer** to flower beds and shrub borders during the next few weeks.

**Hoe** the borders if weed seedlings start to germinate.

**Plant anemone and ranunculus tubers** during the next month. It is best to soak the tubers first, and plant the ranunculus tubers 'claws' down.

**Plant deciduous hedges** as the weather permits. The plants should be all right in a frost-free shed for a few days if the roots are covered—but try to plant them as soon as the soil can be worked.

**Spring bedding plants** not moved to their flowering positions last autumn can be transplanted now if the weather is fine. Wallflowers, polyanthus, forget-me-nots and pansies are all useful spring bedders. Pansies can often be bought at garden centres at this time, if you have not grown a supply of your own.

### FRAMES AND CLOCHES

**Sow hardy annuals** under cloches. Those suitable for early cut flowers include clarkia, helichrysum, and larkspur.

### THE ROCK GARDEN

**Firm plants loosened by frost**, and take the opportunity to check the labels. Write fresh ones before the old names become totally illegible.

**Protect early-flowering irises** in the rock garden with sheets of glass.

**Stone chippings** often give the finishing touch to a rock garden and set off the plants. This is a good time to spread new chippings or 'top up' bare patches of existing chippings.

### LAWNS

**Lay turf** as soon as possible if you are making a new lawn. If you are planning to sow seed, wait for another month or so—although you can prepare the ground now.

## THE GREENHOUSE

**Broad beans** can be started in boxes or pots for planting out later. Space the seeds 5 cm (2 in) apart, covering with about 19 mm ($\frac{3}{4}$ in) of compost. This method is particularly useful for an early crop in areas where outdoor autumn-sown broad beans are not successful.

**Cucumbers and melons** will need canes and horizontal wires for support later. If these are already present, check that they are sound enough to support the crop for another year. If you have to fix new wires along the roof, it is worth doing it now before the greenhouse activities increase during the next few months.

**Paint brickwork white** in greenhouses and conservatories with brick walls. This will help to reflect light, and is especially valuable for lean-to structures.

**Prune acalyphas**, just trimming them to shape.

**Replace or sterilize border soil** if this has not been done yet and you want to

Plants without hairy leaves can be watered from above or below.

grow tomatoes or cucumbers in the soil. If this is inconvenient, it is worth considering the use of growing bags, which overcome the problems of soil-borne diseases.

**Start achimenes** if you have not already done so. The tubers are best started off in a box of peaty compost in a temperature of 15°C (60°F). Pot them

up once they have started into growth.

**Solanum capsicastrum** (the winter cherry) is a popular plant in the home and in the greenhouse during the winter months. You can sow seed now in a temperature of about 13°C (55°F). You can also try to save old plants by cutting back the shoots to about 15 cm (6 in) long, then repotting.

**Sow lettuces, peas, and cauliflowers** for an early crop outdoors. Sow and prick off into boxes (or sow in peat blocks in the case of lettuces). They will eventually be planted out after hardening off in frames. 13°C (55°F) is adequate for germination.

**The shrimp plant (Beloperone guttata)** should be kept tidy by trimming it back to a neat shape. It will soon bush out again, and if pruning is neglected it is likely to become straggly.

**Water greenhouse plants more freely** now, but still be careful not to overwater. Try to keep the humidity fairly low, otherwise various fungus diseases can be troublesome at this time of year.

## WEEKEND PROJECTS

### Laying 'flexible paving'

Concrete block paving or clay paviors laid on sand makes a hard-wearing and unusual path or drive. Rectangular blocks each measure $20 \times 10 \times 6.5$ cm. Shaped blocks are also available.

Grey and red are the most popularly used colours.

A drive requires a sub-base of well-compacted hoggin or hardcore. Check that the finished level of a drive or path, if joining a house, will be 15 cm (6 in) below air bricks and damp-proof course level. When setting out the site, allow for a fall of about 5 cm (2 in) in 2 m (6 ft). Inspection covers and drain gratings should be boxed in with timber battens. Blocks can be laid right up to pre-cast inspection covers.

The paved area must be surrounded by a soil edge. Walls serve as supports but elsewhere $12.5 \times 5$ cm ($5 \times 2$ in) pre-cast concrete kerb edging is needed. Curved kerbing is also available. Set the

kerbs in concrete and allow 24 hours for them to set.

Spread a 6 cm ($2\frac{1}{2}$ in) layer of sand over one or two metres between the kerbs. Level off the sand with a screeding board then make sure it is not disturbed.

Start laying the blocks at a fixed edge. Butt up the blocks closely and ensure that the correct pattern is being made. A stringline should be used to check that each course is being laid correctly. Spacer lugs on the blocks maintain a uniform 1.5 mm ($\frac{1}{20}$ in) gap between blocks. Kneel on a plank when working on newly laid blocks.

When the screeded area has been covered with full blocks, use a bolster chisel and club hammer to cut part blocks to fill edge spaces. Lay another couple of metres of blocks and continue until a reasonably large area is complete. At this stage you will need to

hire a machine called a 'rubber bedded plate vibrator'. This is passed over the newly laid blocks to compress the sand below and force it up between the joints to lock the blocks together. When the whole area is paved, spread more sand on the surface and use the vibrator to force it down to fill the joints. The area is then ready for use.

# Week 8

## THE KITCHEN GARDEN

**Autumn-sown onions**, and spring cabbages, will benefit from a light dressing of a nitrogenous fertilizer lightly hoed in between the rows. In cold districts it is probably best to delay this for a week or two if the weather is bad.

**Break down lumpy soil** with a fork, but do not try to work the soil if it is too wet or cold.

**Lift parsnips** still left in the ground from last year, to prevent them starting into growth. Store in damp peat or sand in a cold place.

**Lime** any areas still to be done—but only if the soil needs it. If you did not test your soil earlier in the winter, do it now.

**Onion seed** can be sown outdoors any time the soil is in a suitable condition. In most areas cloche protection will get them off to a better start.

### FRAMES AND CLOCHES

**Strawberries** respond well to cloche protection. Cover with barn cloches or plastic tunnel cloches any time within the next few weeks.

### FRUIT

**Check fruit in store.** Remove any apples or pears that show the least sign of rotting.

**Continue planting fruit trees**, but only if the weather and soil are suitable. Delay planting if soil conditions are not right.

**Feed blackcurrants** with a nitrogenous fertilizer to give them a boost once they start into growth.

**Firm recently planted trees** or bushes loosened by frost.

**Raspberry canes** that reach above the top wire should be cut off level with it.

**Root-prune trees** that are too vigorous, by digging out a trench 60–120 cm (2–4 ft) from the trunk and cutting through the roots. Only treat one half of the tree in a year.

## THE FLOWER GARDEN

**Caryopteris clandonensis** (blue spiraea) can be pruned in late February or March. Cut back the shoots that have flowered during the previous season to within 5 cm (2 in) of the old wood.

**Dogwoods** (*Cornus* spp) and the red- and yellow-twigged willows (*Salix* spp) can be cut back now to encourage the development of young, well-coloured shoots. Prunings from the dogwoods can be used as hardwood cuttings; just insert them in the ground in a sheltered part of the garden.

**Hardy fuchsias**, such as *F. magellanica*, are best pruned back almost to soil level in February or March to encourage new growth to develop from ground level, which will carry this season's flowers.

**Hydrangea paniculata** can be pruned now to encourage the development of good-sized flowers in late summer.

Cut back the shoots that flowered last year to within two or three buds of the old wood. Large bushes of this shrub can be left unpruned to produce a mass of smaller-sized flower heads.

**Montbretias** deteriorate in flower quality and size if left to form very large clumps. Now is the time to lift and divide the plants. Replant with the younger pieces from the outside of the clump.

**Plant lilies of the valley** before the crowns start into growth. Spread out the roots and cover with 3.5–5 cm (1½–2 in) of soil. Plant in clumps for the best effect.

**Plant new roses** as soon as possible, especially in mild areas where they are likely to start into growth early.

**Sprayers** put away at the end of last season should be checked now. Replace any washers that show signs of perishing.

**Wallflower beds** that have gaps where plants have succumbed during the winter can be filled up with spare plants that were planted at the edge of the bed or on a spare piece of ground. Firm them in well.

## THE GREENHOUSE

**Check the heating system,** including thermostats and thermometers. Clean paraffin heaters and renew wicks if necessary.

**Check your plants** for signs of pests or diseases, and spray or fumigate promptly if you find any. Keep yellowing leaves and dead or dying flowers picked off pot-plants. Remove any decaying leaves from cuttings. Greenhouse hygiene is particularly important at this time when temperatures are often low and ventilation poor.

**Ferns** can be repotted now, but only do it if the plants have filled their pots with roots. Ferns can also be divided now. Use a peat-based compost, place the more tender kinds in a warm part of the greenhouse, and mist with water daily.

**Gloxinias and tuberous begonias** can be started into growth. Place the tubers in a peaty compost without covering

Hairy-leaved plants such as this gloxinia must be watered from below.

their tops. They can be spaced 2.5–5 cm (1–2 in) apart in boxes, and potted up individually once they have started to grow again. Onion seedlings sown earlier can be pricked off into boxes, 3.5–5 cm (1½–2 in) apart each way.

**Perpetual-flowering carnations** can be potted on as soon as the roots fill the pots. Stand repotted plants in a cool, well-ventilated position, and keep the compost just moist.

**Sow greenhouse plants** such as cannas, coleus, begonias, celosias and streptocarpus. These will all germinate in a temperature of about 15°C (60°F), which is probably best provided by a propagator. They can all be grown on a little cooler once they have germinated. Sow more schizanthus to provide continuity of bloom from these invaluable pot-plants.

**Tomatoes** for growing on in a cool greenhouse later can be sown any time during the next month. They should germinate readily in John Innes seed compost in a temperature of 15°C (60°F).

**Ventilate** the greenhouse whenever the weather is suitable.

WEEKEND PROJECTS

## Labels, seed trays, dibbers and pressing boards to make

Labels take on extra usefulness if crucial cultural details are put on the reverse side. For example, in the case of shrubby plants and climbers, like clematis, the name and planting date can be on one side, and brief pruning details on the other side. Use a Dymo-type printer for long-lasting legibility, and wire the labels on to the training wires of a climber so they are not inadvertently lost.

Make long-lasting labels by cutting open old washing-up liquid containers. Rub the surface with abrasive paper to prevent the writing from being wiped off, and use a Chinagraph pencil.

Seed trays are easily made by washing out and punching holes in the base of metal foil or plastic food trays, but it is important that the trays are about 6 cm (2½ in) deep. If they are deeper than this soil may become waterlogged and stale; if they are too shallow there will be insufficient compost for the seedlings and it will tend to dry out rapidly.

Conventional wooden seed trays can be made by re-using timber from old fruit and vegetable boxes. The side and end pieces should be about 6 cm (2½ in) deep, and small gaps should be left between the base pieces for easy drainage. The usual size for a seed tray is about 33 × 20 cm (13 × 8 in). Treat each tray with green timber preservative.

Compost should be evenly firmed in seedtrays and pots, and you can make pressing boards for this job from 13 mm (½ in) thick pieces of flat wood cut about 6 mm (¼ in) smaller all round than the box or pot in which they should fit. Screw a drawer handle to the upper surface of each board so it can be handled easily.

A small dibber for transplanting seedlings and planting larger seeds in boxes can be simply made by tapering one end of a 10 cm (4 in) long piece of 9 mm (⅜ in) dowel.

Make a full size dibber, for potato planting and so on, by cutting an old or replacement fork or spade handle down to about 45 cm (1½ ft) long and then taper the end to a gradual point.

## THE KITCHEN GARDEN

**Apply a balanced fertilizer**, raking or hoeing it in, where seeds are to be sown within the next three weeks.

**Broad beans** can be planted in most areas, provided the ground is not frozen or wet.

**Brussels sprouts** must be picked regularly at this time, otherwise the plants will deteriorate.

**Garlic** can be planted now but it needs light, rich ground. Remove the papery skin to separate into small bulbs for planting.

**Peas** of the round-seeded type can be sown from now on if the soil is suitable. Although not essential, cloche protection will help and give an earlier crop.

**Plant Jerusalem artichokes** if this has not already been done.

**Prepare the runner bean trench** during the next few weeks. You can probably get a crop of radishes from the area before you plant the beans.

**Shallots** are traditionally planted on the shortest day, but any time now is suitable provided the soil is not frozen.

## FRAMES AND CLOCHES

**In cold frames** you can sow cabbages and cauliflowers to plant out in April or May.

**Under cloches** or in frames, sow lettuces and radishes. You can also try a short row of parsley; it will give you a supply in early summer before the main sowing is ready.

## FRUIT

**Apple trees** that did not have a tar oil winter wash should be sprayed now with a suitable insecticide to control red spider mites and aphids.

**Spray peaches** with a fungicide against peach leaf curl, to follow up the first spray (*see* Week 7).

## THE FLOWER GARDEN

**New herbaceous borders**, ideally dug last autumn, can now be prepared for planting. Use a rake or the back of a garden fork to break down large lumps of soil, and rake in a dressing of a general fertilizer.

**Plant trees and shrubs** whenever the soil is suitable for working.

**Prepare for hardy annuals** by forking over the area they will occupy (unless spring bedding plants are still growing). If the ground was dug roughly earlier in the winter it should be enough to rake the soil and to hoe out any weed seedlings.

**Prune roses** any time between now and the end of March. Use sharp secateurs and always cut just above an outward-pointing bud. Cutting too close to a bud may cause damage.

**Roses** attacked by black spot last year should be tidied up and sprayed with a fungicide. Remove all fallen leaves from around the bushes.

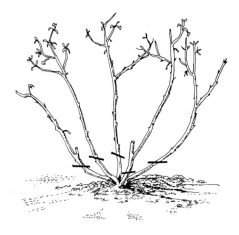

**Salix alba 'Vitellina'** (the golden willow) is best cut back hard in spring to encourage more of the attractive golden-yellow stems.

**Shrub cuttings** inserted in the open ground last autumn might need refirming in the ground. The action of winter frosts sometimes loosens the soil around them and makes rooting more difficult.

**Shrubs and trees** planted in the autumn may need their roots refirming in the soil.

**Snowdrops** can be lifted and divided as soon as the flowers have faded. Do this every three or four years if you want to increase your stock.

**Sweet peas** sown last autumn and overwintered in pots in a garden frame should be hardened off steadily. If you were unable to sow last autumn, now is the time to sow the seed outdoors where the plants are to flower. Wait another couple of weeks in cold districts.

## LAWNS

**Scatter wormcasts** by brushing them on a dry day. Brush off any leaves that have been blown onto the lawn.

## THE GREENHOUSE

**Badly-fitting ventilators** will let out a lot of warm air, which represents wasted money. Check that they are a good fit, and adjust if necessary. Nevertheless, take the opportunity to open ventilators whenever the weather is mild enough.

**Dahlia cuttings** can be taken any time within the next month. If old tubers have not already been boxed up in damp peat, do this without delay to produce shoots for cuttings. Mist the tubers with water to encourage them to break into growth.

**Freesias** that have finished flowering can be rested. Gradually withhold water, then lay the pots on their sides beneath the staging.

**Melons** to be grown in a heated greenhouse can be sown now. Sow in individual peat pots and place in a temperature of 15°C (60°F) for germination.

**Prepare labels** that will be needed when bedding plants have to be pricked out and various cuttings taken or potted up. The next month is a very busy one in the greenhouse, and any routine jobs that can be done in advance will make the jobs easier when the time comes.

**Prick off seedlings** sown last month and the beginning of this. It is best to prick them out as soon as they can be handled even though they are small. Most seedlings will do equally well in John Innes or a peat-based compost.

**Regal pelargoniums** should be potted on during the next few weeks.

**Sow bedding plants** that need to be started early, such as ageratum, amaranthus, antirrhinums, asters, fibrous-rooted begonias, bedding dahlias, dianthus (including carnations), heliotrope, lobelia, African marigolds, mesembryanthemums, nicotiana, pansies, petunias, *Phlox drummondii*, rudbeckias, salvias, tagetes and verbena.

**Sow cucumbers**, one seed to a 7.5 cm (3 in) pot. Use John Innes seed compost and provide a temperature of 18°C (64°F) for germination. If you find cucumbers difficult to germinate, you could consider buying chitted (ready-sprouted) seeds. These are offered by several mail-order seedsmen.

WEEKEND PROJECTS

## Lay paving slabs

Paving slabs are available in various sizes, shapes and colours. The pattern chosen is optional, though a lot of work in cutting slabs can be avoided by working to an exact area and shape to be covered by full size slabs.

There are two types of slab. Cast slabs, 50 mm (2 in) thick, are suitable for paths and patios. Hydraulically-pressed slabs are usually about 38 mm (1½ in) thick. These are lighter in weight but strong enough to withstand a car.

A patio or drive should slope away from any building to ensure that rainwater drains away safely; a fall of 2.5 cm in 3 m (1 in in 10 ft) is suitable. The surface should be at least 15 cm (6 in) below the house damp-proof course or any airbricks. If necessary the ground will have to be excavated.

Slabs can be laid on an existing sound concrete base, bedding down the slabs on 5 blobs of mortar (one in each corner and one in the middle) or on a 19 to 25 mm (¾–1 in) thick bed of moist sand. If the slabs are to be laid where there is soil or grass, dig down 10–15 cm (4–6 in) and compact well. Lay 7.5–12.5 cm (3–5 in) of well compacted hardcore and level the surface by rolling over a covering of sand or ballast.

Set up string lines across the house wall and down one side of the site to ensure that levels and falls are followed correctly.

Laying on a sand base is a speedy way to form a patio or path that will only have to withstand foot traffic. However, there is a risk of long-term settlement problems. Also, while laying the slabs, levelling can become tricky. This is not a problem where the five blobs of mortar method is used.

A solid 2.5 cm (1 in) mortar bed is essential where a car is to be used.

The mortar for the slabs should be 1 part cement to 5 parts sharp sand and should be fairly dry. Lay the first slab at the high point of the site. Tap down the slab with the shaft of a club hammer or trowel until its top face is in line with the string line.

It is useful practice then to lay a slab at the lowest point of the site to check that the correct fall will be made. If you have a long, straight-edged timber this can be laid across both slabs with a spirit level laid on top to check the fall. When these slabs are laid it is far easier to align intermediate slabs as work progresses.

Lay all the remaining slabs in the same way, constantly checking for levels in both directions. Leave a gap of about 1 cm (⅜ in) between slabs and fill these later. Dry sand can be used to fill the joints with the sand bed method. With a mortar bed, fill the joints with a dryish, crumbly mortar.

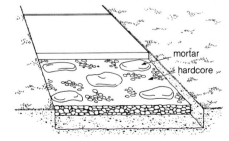

mortar
hardcore

# Week 10

## THE KITCHEN GARDEN

**Brussels sprouts** and spring greens will need regular picking.

**Leeks** can be sown any time during the next few weeks, on a prepared seedbed. Delay sowing if the ground is still wet and cold.

**Lettuces** can be sown in open ground now in favourable areas. Sow just a small quantity, but sow ordinary varieties regularly at fortnightly intervals from now until mid-July.

**Lift leeks** still remaining in the ground and heel them in where they will not be in the way—preferably in a shady spot.

**Parsnips** benefit from a long growing season and should be sown as soon as possible. Sow the seeds in groups of three in the final positions, and thin to one seedling later. Use fresh seeds as parsnip seeds do not store well.

**Potato tubers** bought late will still benefit from 'chitting'. Place in shallow boxes in a cool but frost-free place in good light.

**Radishes** are a useful early crop and the first outdoor sowings should be possible now. Sow only a short row and space thinly. Successional sowings can be

made at fortnightly intervals until the end of May (after that they may be less succulent).

**Rhubarb and globe artichokes** can still be planted.

**Sow onions** if the weather is favourable. The use of cloches will get them off to a good start and probably produce a better yield.

**Spinach** can be sown every two or three weeks from now until the end of May.

**Thin autumn-sown onions** to final spacings.

## FRAMES AND CLOCHES

**Cover frames** on frosty nights, using mats or sacking. Tie them down and always remove them the next morning.

**Lettuces** raised in the greenhouse will probably be ready for hardening off in the frame.

**Sow French beans** and beetroot in heated frames, or those on a hot-bed.

**Unheated frames** can be used to sow early carrots in cold areas. You can also usefully make a further sowing of these and Brussels sprouts in warmer districts.

## FRUIT

**Peaches and nectarines** may soon be showing pink buds. To protect the blossom from frost, you should drape sacks or some other material over wall-trained trees. Remember, however, to remove the protection when there is no frost.

**Strawberries** are best planted in August and September, but if you missed the opportunity you can still plant now—but do not attempt to take a crop this year.

## THE FLOWER GARDEN

**Annual flower beds** dug in the autumn can now be prepared for seed sowing. Use a rake to break down large lumps of soil, then tread evenly over the surface to firm it. Give a further light raking to level the surface.

**Apply weedkillers to paths** to keep them clear throughout the summer.

**Herbaceous plants** are best divided in the spring, especially if an established bed is being replanted. At this stage, the new growth can be seen easily. Use a sharp knife to cut through woody roots after lifting, otherwise gently pull the plants apart with your hands or use two garden forks thrust into the clump back-to-back and lever apart. Order or buy summer-flowering bulbs if this has not already been done.

**Plant clematis**, which are versatile climbers and easy to grow.

**Plant deciduous trees and shrubs** as soon as possible.

**Sweet peas** can be sown outdoors.

**Transplant snowdrops** that have finished flowering but are still in leaf. They divide and transplant more successfully in leaf than dry.

## THE ROCK GARDEN

**Plant alpines** as soon as possible, if not already done.

**Thymes** can be divided this month. These useful carpeters appreciate a sandy soil in full sun.

## LAWNS

**Moss** may become a problem during the next couple of months, especially on badly drained land. Aerating and scarifying the lawn now will discourage it and make treatment with a mosskiller more effective.

**Rake out old grass** using a wire-tined rake to remove any old grass left on the surface.

## THE GREENHOUSE

**Aubergines** can be sown directly into small pots. Germinate them in a propagator at 18°C (64°F).

**Celery** can be sown, in a temperature of about 18°C (64°F).

**Dahlia tubers** in store can now be placed in boxes of equal parts sand and peat and started into growth for cuttings if this has not been done. Ensure that the crowns are not above the surface of the compost. Keep the compost moist. Protect from frost.

**Fuchsias** pruned earlier and syringed frequently will now be making growth. To produce bushy plants, or large heads on standards, pinch out the top of each shoot that has produced five or six pairs of leaves.

**Hoya carnosa** can be increased from cuttings taken now or during the next few months.

**Melons** can still be sown. Set the seeds

13 mm (½ in) deep in 9 cm (3½ in) pots. Germination needs a temperature of about 18°C (64°F), reducing it by a couple of degrees afterwards.

**Morning Glory** (*Ipomoea rubro-caerulea*) can be sown in well-drained pots of John Innes seed compost. When large enough, pot first into 7.5 cm (3 in) pots, then into 12.5 cm (5 in) pots.

**Prune** *Plumbago capensis*, shortening the sideshoots to three or four buds.

**Outdoor (early) chrysanthemums** can be raised from cuttings taken now, in exactly the same way as the indoor-flowering (late) type. Take shoots about 6 cm (2½ in) long, arising from the base of the old plant. Trim the two bottom leaves off and cut the end straight with a sharp knife.

**Primula obconica and Primula malacoides** can be sown in a temperature of about 18°C (64°F).

**Schizanthus** may need stopping again to make bushier plants. Simply nip out the main growing tips.

**WEEKEND PROJECTS**

## Make yourself a propagator

By providing gentle heat from below, a propagator considerably hastens the germination of seeds and the rooting of cuttings. Small heated bases can be bought quite cheaply and are large enough to heat a standard-sized seed tray.

To make a larger propagator, a box is required with specially manufactured electric soil-warming cables to provide bottom heat. You can make the box any size you like; just remember to choose a cable to give between 9 and 12 watts per 0.1 m² (1 sq ft) (which will raise the soil temperature by between 15°F and 20°F). Therefore a 600 cm (20 ft) cable rated at 75 watts will be suitable for an area of 0.5–0.7 m² (6–8 ft).

For more precise heat control, the warming cable should be fitted with a thermostat. In this case choose a cable to give about 15 watts per 0.1 m² (1 sq ft) which will raise the soil temperature about 25°C above air temperature. If you want a large propagator which can be used to overwinter tender plants in an otherwise unheated greenhouse, then

another set of warming cables can be fixed around the sides of the box to give air warming. This cable can also be thermostatically controlled and should be rated as a thermostatically controlled cable for soil warming.

Make the propagator from preservative treated tongued and grooved matchboarding. Line the base

with polythene and cover this with a 2.5 cm (1 in) thick layer of sharp sand. Lay out the warming cable serpentine fashion and bury it in a further 2.5 cm layer of sand. Pots and seed trays can be stood on the sand surrounded by a 5 cm (2 in) deep layer of moist peat. Cover the top of the propagator with sheets of glass.

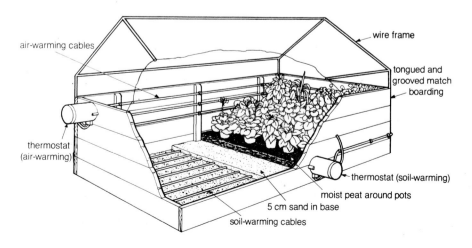

air-warming cables

thermostat (air-warming)

wire frame

tongued and grooved match boarding

thermostat (soil-warming)

moist peat around pots

5 cm sand in base

soil-warming cables

## THE KITCHEN GARDEN

**Asparagus crowns** should never be allowed to dry out, even while planting. If you plan to buy crowns, prepare your bed now in readiness.

Established asparagus beds can have a simazine-based weedkiller applied (check the label carefully for application rates). It must be applied before the spears appear. Remove weed growth first.

**Brussels sprouts** can be sown any time during the next month. An early sowing of a suitable variety is essential for early autumn use.

**Brussels sprout** tops can be used as 'greens'.

**Break down soil** still to be sown or planted up, and rake it to produce a fine, level tilth.

**Broad beans** should be sown if this has not already been done, although successional sowings can be made until early April.

**Early potatoes** can be planted in favourable areas from now on, planting

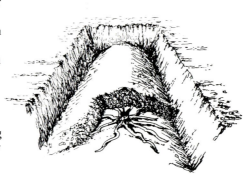

30 cm (1 ft) apart in rows 60 cm (2 ft) apart.

**Lettuces** raised in frames can be planted out.

**Plant mint**—preferably in a bucket sunk into the ground to contain its roots and avoid an invasion.

**Spring cabbages and spinach** will benefit from a dressing of nitrate of soda or sulphate of ammonia, if not already applied. Hoe it in thoroughly.

**Spring greens** may be ready for cutting in some mild districts. Cut alternate plants, leaving those between them to heart in late May or early June.

### FRAMES AND CLOCHES

**In frames** sow cauliflowers for use in July.

**Under cloches** sow early varieties of carrots.

### FRUIT

**Fan-trained** early-flowering fruit, such as peaches, nectarines, apricots and plums, must have any frost-protection coverings removed after the frost has gone in the mornings. Pollination depends on the insects having access.

**Prune currants and gooseberries** if this has not already been done.

## THE FLOWER GARDEN

**Hardy annuals** can be sown any time between now and May. Those sown during March and April will flower from July to September, while May-sown annuals usually bloom from August to October.

**Herbaceous plants** are best planted between now and the end of April. Use a trowel to take out the soil, and try to set the plants in clumps of three or five to form a substantial group. Plant firmly and if the soil is dry water thoroughly.

**Lonicera nitida**, the well-known small-leaved hedging plant, can be increased from hardwood cuttings taken now. Insert them in pots of sandy compost and place in a garden frame.

### THE ROCK GARDEN

**Plant rock plants** as soon as you can. Be prepared to water them in until they become established.

Plant herbaceous subjects now, setting them out in groups to achieve a good show.

**Divide thrift (Armeria maritima)** and sedums. The thrift prefers well-drained soil in full sun. Sedums will tolerate a little shade.

*Polygonum vacciniifolium* can be divided now. Established plants can be split up and given a moist, lime-free soil, preferably in partial shade.

### LAWNS

**Lightly roll** the lawn. On no account, however, use a very heavy roller, and do not do it if the soil is very wet.

**Prepare the ground for a new lawn** if you plan to sow next month. If already roughly prepared earlier, hoe off annual weeds and dig up any perennials that have survived the earlier preparation.

## THE GREENHOUSE

**Abutilons** can be sown now as a greenhouse plant.

**Celery** can be sown in a temperature of 15–18°C (60–64°F).

**Chrysanthemum cuttings** rooted in January and February now already in small pots should be potted on into 10–12.5 cm (4–5 in) pots as soon as they are large enough.

**Coleus, heliotrope and verbena** cuttings can still be taken. They root very quickly in a sandy compost in a propagator.

**Cyclamen seedlings** sown earlier will need to be pricked out into pots or boxes. Set the seedlings with the corms sitting almost on the surface of the soil.

**Exacum** is a charming greenhouse annual easily raised from seed sown now.

**Feed hydrangeas,** and continue to do so every two weeks during the next few months. Make sure the compost never dries out.

**Harden off onions** raised in boxes. Put them into a garden frame during the next couple of weeks.

**Greenfly** (aphids) can be a problem at this time, with so many young plants and cuttings in the greenhouse. Spray or fumigate as soon as you notice them.

**Lettuce** plants can be put into garden frames to harden off thoroughly before planting out.

**Peas and broad beans** raised in the greenhouse should be hardened off slowly. If you have to keep the greenhouse warm for other plants, move the vegetables to a garden frame.

**Propagate passion flowers** (*Passiflora caerulea*) by taking 7.5 cm (3 in) cuttings. Root them in a propagator.

**Sow bedding plants.** A wide range can be sown now, including ageratum, alyssum, amaranthus, antirrhinums, asters, bedding dahlias, dianthus, heliotrope, impatiens, kochia, lobelia, marigolds, mesembryanthemums, nemesia, nicotiana, pansies, petunias, *Phlox drummondii*, rudbeckia, salvias, stocks, tagetes, verbena and zinnia.

**Take more dahlia cuttings.**

**Sow capsicums** (sweet peppers) if you can provide a germination temperature of 20°C (68°F). Sow several seeds in each pot, thinning to one seedling later.

**Sweet pea** plants raised in the greenhouse should be hardened off gradually. Garden frames are ideal for this.

---

WEEKEND PROJECTS

## Ideas for unusual plant containers

Almost any rot-resistant container that will hold at least a bucketful of soil can be planted with flowers. The only essential is to ensure that there are a number of 10 mm holes in the base to allow the compost in the container to drain.

Before use, a wooden container should be painted inside and out with a green wood preservative, which is harmless to plants. When this has dried, the container can be painted if desired. To improve drainage spread a layer of broken bricks or washed pebbles over the base of the container before adding potting compost (ordinary garden soil is not suitable for filling a container because it turns muddy when wet). To reduce the amount of potting compost required, fill the container with bricks or pebbles to within 30–45 cm (1–1½ ft) of the rim, then top up with compost. If you are going to plant a tree in the container, a greater depth of compost will be required. As long as you do not mind a few weeds, a home-made potting compost can be mixed from 7 parts of

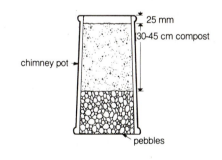

chimney pot — 25 mm / 30–45 cm compost / pebbles

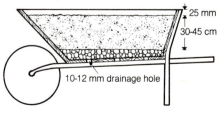

25 mm / 30–45 cm / 10–12 mm drainage hole

good soil, 3 parts moss peat or shredded bark, and 2 parts of washed sharp sand plus a good dusting of general fertilizer.

## THE KITCHEN GARDEN

**Carrots** can be sown, but it is best to choose a small variety for the first sowing, leaving the maincrop varieties with large roots until later.

**Hoe** frequently between growing crops. Weed competition is most serious while the crop plants are still young.

**Lettuces and radishes** should be sown for succession.

**Peas** should be sown now if it has not already been done.

**Sow leeks** if not already sown.

**Sow parsley** any time between now and July.

## FRAMES AND CLOCHES

**Lettuce** sown in the greenhouse in January can be planted out under cloches if they have been hardened off in frames first.

**Frames** should be used to house

vegetable seedlings started off in the greenhouse, such as onions, leeks, cauliflowers, peas and lettuces. Ventilate the frame cautiously at first, but harden off steadily.

## FRUIT

**Apples** will benefit from an insecticidal spray as the buds burst to expose a cluster of folded green leaves.

**Apples and pears** should be sprayed with a fungicide to control scab.

**Apply a general fertilizer** round all top and soft fruit trees and bushes.

**Birds** can damage the flower buds on fruit such as plums. 'Scaraweb' is an effective deterrent.

**Grass around fruit trees** should be mown as soon as it is dry enough. Keep it short.

**Spray raspberries and loganberries** with a fungicide to control cane-spot.

**Spray strawberries** with a suitable insecticide if they show signs of greenfly or red spider mites.

## THE FLOWER GARDEN

**Gladiolus** corms can be planted between now and mid-April, setting them 10 cm (4 in) deep in heavy soil, 15 cm (6 in) deep in light soil. Plant in groups, with each corm 10–15 cm (4–6 in) apart. To improve drainage, sprinkle sand in the hole before planting.

**Layer magnolias.** Choose a young, low-hanging branch, cut the bark away and peg down into loose soil. Roots may take up two or three years to form, but it is satisfying when they do root.

**Plant pansies and violas**, which you can usually buy in flower at this time. These will make an attractive display early.

**Potentillas** need to have all dead wood removed in spring, cutting the shoots back to soil-level. At the same time, cut out weak shoots. This applies to shrubby potentillas, of course, not the herbaceous kind.

**Prune buddleias** by cutting out shoots that have flowered the previous year. It may be best to delay the job for a few

weeks in very cold areas.

**Roses** not sprayed with a fungicide against black spot directly after pruning should be treated now. They will also from a dressing of rose fertilizer.

**Sow hardy annuals** in mild districts, but it is worth waiting another few weeks elsewhere.

**Tidy up herbaceous and shrub**

**borders** if this has not already been done. Large clumps of herbaceous plants can be divided or split up, replanting the small outside pieces.

## THE ROCK GARDEN

**Remove pieces of glass** placed over choice and tender alpines at the end of last year.

## LAWNS

**Start cutting the lawn** if you have not already done so. Choose a day when the surface is dry enough, and set the blades high for the first cut.

**Neaten edges** with a half-moon edger if this has not been done during the winter, but do not cut back too much otherwise the lawn will steadily get smaller and the beds bigger. If just part is damaged, it may be better to cut out a rectangle of turf at that point and reverse it so that the damaged part is on the inside. You can simply fill up the gap with sieved soil.

## THE GREENHOUSE

**Begonia and gloxinia tubers** can still be started into growth.

**Check for pests and diseases.** Often pests will be under leaves. Treat affected plants as soon as possible.

**Christmas cacti** can be repotted now, but only disturb plants that are too large for the pot. Do not repot until the flowers have been finished for a few weeks.

**Chrysanthemum cuttings** of early varieties can still be taken.

**Cinerarias** should be making a bold display. Keep them shaded from strong sun, and do not let the compost become dry at any time. Keep a particular watch for greenfly, which are attracted to these plants.

**Clean glass** with soapy water to ensure that maximum light reaches the plants.

**Cobaea scandens**, the cup-and-saucer vine, is easy to raise from seed sown now.

**Continue to sow bedding plants.**

**Cucumber** plants that have produced three pairs of leaves can be potted singly into 12.5 cm (5 in) pots.

**Dahlia tubers** placed in peat and sand a couple of weeks ago will now have produced eyes on the crowns. You can

let them grow to provide late cuttings, or divide the tubers instead. Use a sharp knife to divide them, making sure each piece has at least one healthy swollen eye that looks as if it is about to grow. Dust all cuts with flowers of sulphur. The individual pieces can be planted out in the garden in early April, covering with 10–15 cm (4–6 in) of soil.

**Freesias** are quite easy to grow from seed sown now.

**Gloriosas** (climbing lilies) can now be started into growth. Set several tubers in a 20 cm (8 in) pot. Place the pots in a warm part of the greenhouse and water well.

**Outdoor tomatoes** must not be sown too early otherwise they will be too advanced before you can plant them out safely, but you should be able to start the seeds off now in a heated greenhouse during the next few weeks.

**Pot melons** on into larger pots.

**Pot on tomato seedlings** as their roots fill existing pots. Early sowings will now need 12.5 cm (5 in) pots.

**Prick off bedding plant seedlings** sown earlier. Do this as soon as possible, even though they can be difficult to handle when small.

**Pteris cretica** is an attractive fern, easily divided at this time. You can also repot now if necessary.

**Sow cucumbers** for growing in a cold greenhouse.

**Sow kalanchoes** to provide bright winter-flowering plants for the home and greenhouse.

**Sow New Zealand spinach** to provide seedlings for transplanting outdoors when there is no chance of frost.

**Watch for damping-off** among seedlings—a disease that causes them to collapse where the stem has rotted at the base. Water with Cheshunt compound.

**WEEKEND PROJECTS**

### Make a bird-table and nestbox

Bird-tables and nesting boxes can be made from any offcuts of wood. There are a few important things to remember regarding the construction and location of tables and boxes.

A bird-table should be at least 1.4 m (4 ft 6 in) above ground and must not be accessible to cats, squirrels or rodents. An open-top table allows every size of bird to profit, so if you want to ensure that smaller birds only are fed put a roof on the table. This also helps keep those tit-bits dry.

A nesting box has even more rules associated with it. The inside of the box must be free from splinters or other protrusions. It is important that the box is waterproofed and that it is not placed in direct sun; the entrance hole should face north-east or north-west. Do not

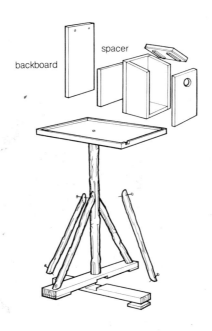

backboard  spacer

make a perch around the box—birds like to fly straight in. The size of the entrance hole should be geared to the species of bird you intend to use the box: 28 mm ($1\frac{1}{8}$ in) diameter for blue tits, 32 mm ($1\frac{1}{4}$ in) for great tits, 50 mm (2 in) for starlings. The size is critical; if the hole is too small the birds will not enter. The box should be set about 2.4 m above ground level and can be fixed to the house wall or tree. The outside of the box can be coated with preservative, but do not coat the inside. Finally the box should be warm at night but not too hot during the day, so use 25 mm (1 in) thick timber or plywood. The entrance hole should be about 15 cm (6 in) above the floor. The interior of the box should measure about 13 × 13 × 20 cm (5 × 5 × 8 in).

# Week 13

## THE KITCHEN GARDEN

**Apply a balanced fertilizer** if this has not already been done.

**Asparagus crowns** are likely to be ready for planting now. Do not allow them to dry out at all, and plant with the minimum of delay.

**Chives** are most readily propagated by dividing established clumps, but if you do not have any they are easily raised from seed sown now.

**Jerusalem artichokes**, globe artichokes and rhubarb should be planted without delay if not already done.

**Maincrop carrots** can be sown from now onwards.

**Sow broad beans and peas**, which should do well now in all areas.

**Sow lettuces.** It should be possible to sow summer lettuces in most areas now without any need for protection.

**Sow scorzonera and salsify** (popularly known as the vegetable oyster) any time within the next month.
**Spinach** should be sown for succession.

### FRAMES AND CLOCHES

**Onions and leeks** raised in the greenhouse should be placed in frames to harden off before planting out in mid-April.

**Sow celery and celeriac** in frames —directly into the soil or into boxes. Some form of heating will be beneficial.

**Spring cabbages** under cloches should be ready for eating. You can leave alternative plants to form a head.

**Ventilate frames** whenever possible.

### FRUIT

**Spray raspberries** with a fungicide to control cane-spot if this has not already been done.

## THE FLOWER GARDEN

**Cut out frost-damaged shoots** from winter-flowering shrubs such as **Chimonanthus praecox** (wintersweet).

**Chaenomeles** must be pruned as soon as it has finished flowering. Grown as a bush it needs very little attention, but grown as a wall shrub it needs to be pruned to retain shape and to keep the plant within the allotted space.

**Dead flower heads** on hydrangeas can be cut off.

**Hebe 'Autumn Glory'** is best pruned now by cutting out all dead and frost-damaged shoots.

**Hypericums** can be trimmed back, shaping up the plants and cutting out dead shoots.

**Montbretia** corms can be planted in March. Set them 10 cm (4 in) deep in a warm, sunny border.

**Roses** will benefit from a mulch of well-rotted compost. They will also need a dressing of a general balanced fertilizer if this has not already been given. The

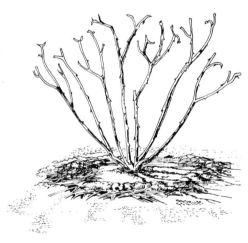

mulch will help to conserve moisture in the soil and the fertilizer will stimulate growth.

### THE WATER GARDEN

**Fish** will need more food now that spring has arrived, but take care not to give them more than they can eat within about 20 minutes.

**The variegated sweet flag** (*Iris pseudacorus* 'Variegata') can be divided now. Cut the rhizome into several large pieces, and replant each individually.

### LAWNS

**Prepare the ground** for new lawns. After digging, break down large lumps of soil and fork in a balanced fertilizer at 70 g per m² (2 oz per sq yd). If wireworms and leatherjackets are a problem, rake in an insecticidal dust at the same time. To finish, systematically tread over the area, and rake it level.

**Wormcasts** can be a problem at this time. If they are not particularly troublesome, just disperse them with a broom; if they are spoiling the lawn, use a wormkiller.

## THE GREENHOUSE

**Acalyphas** can be propagated from cuttings rooted now in sandy compost, in a temperature of about 25°C (77°F). Placed in a humid propagator, they should root within a few weeks.

**Asparagus 'ferns'** can be repotted any time now.

**Aubergines** that have germinated and produced two proper leaves can be transplanted into 7.5 cm (3 in) pots.

**Bedding plants** such as African and French marigolds, annual phlox, ten-week stocks, alyssum, asters, and zinnias, can be sown if not already done.

**Beloperone guttata,** the shrimp plant, can be increased from stem cuttings taken any time between now and mid-summer. They will root most readily in a propagator in sandy compost.

**Chrysanthemum cuttings** should be potted into 7.5 cm (3 in) pots as they become ready. Those rooted and potted earlier can be moved on to large pots if necessary.

**Citrus plants,** including the Calamondin orange (*Citrus mitis*), can

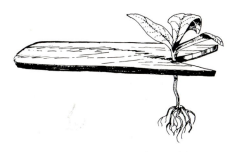

A forked stick is useful for picking up delicate seedlings.

be pruned back. Remove all straggly growth and give the plants a regular misting with clean water. Repot if necessary, but use an acid compost.

**Cucumber** beds can be prepared now. This is a job best done about two weeks before you are ready to plant.

**Pelargonium (geranium) cuttings** taken last month may be ready for potting into 7.5 or 10 cm (3 or 4 in) pots. Young plants from cuttings already potted can be encouraged to make bushy plants by pinching out the top.

**Prick out seedlings** as soon as they can be handled. Some bedding plants, such as zinnias and salvias, transplant better later if you prick them off into pots. Even though this can be more troublesome and take up more space, it is worth it for the better plants later. The vast majority, however, will transplant perfectly well from boxes. The packet will usually advise.

**Repot tradescantias.** If the plants have become too large or straggly, raise new plants from cuttings. These will root easily in a peat-based compost or a sandy compost.

**The coffee plant** (*Coffea arabica*) is an interesting plant to try from seed. The seeds need a high temperature—about 27°C (80°F)—to germinate, so you will will need to use a propagator. You may get some coffee beans, but even if you do not the foliage adds interest to a house or greenhouse display.

**Ventilate** the greenhouse whenever the temperature rises appreciably, which it can do rapidly on a mild spring day.

### Make a window box

A simple and cheap window box can be made from a soaking trough intended for ready pasted wallpaper and available from do-it-yourself shops. These inexpensive plastic troughs need only a series of holes punched in the base and they are ready for use.

If you want a window box to fit exactly on a sill it will be necessary to make one to measure. Ideally use 6 mm (¼ in) thick marine or exterior quality plywood for this job, although both are expensive materials and it is much cheaper to use ordinary 19 mm (¾ in) thick softwood, or secondhand floorboards. The length of the box will obviously be to suit the window opening, and the width and depth should be a minimum of 15 cm (6 in). Two rows of 13 mm (½ in) diameter holes in the base, running the length of the box, are required for drainage. So that the holes do not become blocked, screw 13 mm (½ in) thick blocks to the base running across the width of the box to hold it clear of the sill. Because it is almost certain that the sill slopes away from the window, taper the feet so they are almost like wedges and hold the window box level.

A marine plywood window box does not need to be treated with a wood preservative, although its appearance is enhanced with a coat of paint or varnish. All other types of plywood and timber should be treated inside and out with green wood preservative which can be painted over when dry. The box can look better if moulded plastic decorations intended for whitewood furniture are glued to the outside.

Boxes for upper storey windows should be secured with wires or hooks and screw eyes.

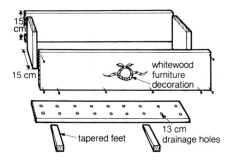

15 cm

15 cm

whitewood furniture decoration

tapered feet

13 cm drainage holes

## THE KITCHEN GARDEN

**Brassica seedlings** (cabbages and related plants) are liable to attack from flea beetles at this time. At the first sign of small holes appearing in the leaves dust the rows with an insecticidal dust.
**Broad beans** for succession should be sown by now.
**Cabbages** for summer and autumn use can be sown in a prepared seedbed.
**Early potato** varieties should be planted within the next two weeks if not already done.
**Hoe** regularly to keep down weeds during the seedling stage.
**Lettuces and radishes** should be sown for succession.
**Lettuce seedlings** raised under glass can be planted out if they have been hardened off.
**Onion sets**, which are the answer if you find growing from seed difficult, can be planted now. They are especially useful in cold areas.

**Plant globe artichokes** by taking rooted offsets or suckers from established plants.
**Turnips** can be sown at three-weekly intervals from now until the end of July.

### FRAMES AND CLOCHES

**Cucumbers** can be sown in frames or under cloches in mild areas. Use ridge or Japanese types, not greenhouse varieties.
**Frames** should be ventilated whenever the weather is mild, as some vegetable seedlings will have to be planted out within the next month. If vegetables are sharing a frame with some of the more tender bedding plants, however, you may have to be more cautious about ventilation.

### FRUIT

**Protect blossom** of early-flowering fruit such as peaches, nectarines, redcurrants and gooseberries if frost threatens them. Hessian or a plastic material will be suitable.
**Strawberries** should have the beds cleaned up and have a high-potash general fertilizer hoed in.

## THE FLOWER GARDEN

**Ceratostigma willmottianum** (hardy plumbago) should be cut down to soil level within the next few weeks. The fresh, new shoots produced will flower later in the year.
**Cistus (rock rose)** need to have all dead wood cut out. No other pruning is necessary.
**Hibiscus syriacus (tree hollyhock)** is best pruned now. Cut out all shoots that flowered the previous year.
**Privet hedges** can be clipped from now through to the end of autumn. Place a sheet of plastic or an old ground sheet at the base of the hedge so that the clippings can be picked up easily.

### THE ROCK GARDEN

**Campanula carpatica** can be divided this month. Alternatively, you can take cuttings.
**Iberis sempervirens** can be increased from heel cuttings taken now.

When preparing a seed bed for annuals a fine tilth should be achieved.

### THE WATER GARDEN

**Rushes and reeds,** *Hydrocleys commersonii* (water poppy) and *Pontederia cordata* (pickerel weed), that have become overcrowded will benefit from being lifted and the roots divided.
**Tender water plants** that were overwintered in a frost-proof greenhouse can now be placed back into the pool as soon as the weather improves. Place the containers on bricks in the pool, and slowly accustom the plants to deeper water by removing a brick periodically.

### LAWNS

**Moss** can ruin an ornamental lawn, but it should be easy to treat with a mosskiller. In order to deter it in the future, make sure the lawn is adequately aerated and the grass well fed.
**New lawns** can be made now from seed or turfs.

## THE GREENHOUSE

**Chrysanthemum cuttings** can be put into a garden frame to harden off, although in cold areas it may be best to wait another few weeks.

**Continued to pot up late-flowering chrysanthemum** cuttings to be grown on in large pots.

**Dahlia cuttings** can still be taken, but do not delay.

**Fuchsias** can be potted on.

**Growing bags** are excellent for plants such as capsicums, cucumbers and tomatoes, particularly if you have automatic watering to ensure that the bags do not dry out. Buy the bags now.

**Half-hardy annuals** can still be sown with the exception of those that need a long growing season to flower—such as geraniums.

**Harden off onions** sown in January, moving them into a garden frame.

**Hibiscus rosa-sinensis** can be repotted. Take the opportunity to trim back the plants to keep them tidy.

**Jasmine** is a useful greenhouse or conservatory climber that can be propagated from cuttings taken now.

**Mimosa pudica**, the sensitive plant, is an interesting if not particularly beautiful

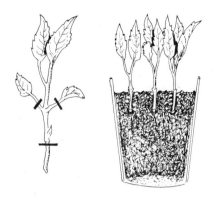

plant, easily raised from seed sown now. The leaves fold up when touched.

**Repot** plants as necessary. Most plants can be potted on during the next few weeks if their roots have filled the pot, but avoid over-potting.

**Outdoor tomatoes** for planting in the open in June can be sown now in a minimum temperature of 15°C (60°F). Prick out seedlings sown earlier as soon as they can be handled. Space according to the habit of the plant, but 40 plants to a standard seedbox is about right, though you can get up to 60 with closer spacing.

**Ring-culture** beds for tomatoes can be prepared now. Ring-culture is a good method to try if you have previously had difficulty with growing tomatoes in the greenhouse border, and do not want to use growing bags. Prepare the bed now by laying a 15 cm (6 in) bed of gravel or expanded clay aggregate. Stand the 23 cm (9 in) bottomless pots or rings on the aggregate and fill with John Innes No. 3 compost. Once established, the plants will be watered through the aggregate and fed regularly through the pots or rings.

**Sow celery and celeriac** for planting out in June.

**Sow cucumbers** for growing in frames or cloches. Sow the seeds singly in individual pots.

**Take cuttings.** You can take cuttings of many greenhouse plants during the next month. They should root readily with a little warmth, and have the whole summer in which to make more substantial plants.

**Water more freely** from now on. As the days lengthen and the temperature increases greenhouse plants will need watering regularly.

WEEKEND PROJECTS

### Bird and cat protection for vegetables

To protect vegetables from birds of all types, and from cats, you need a covering to enclose them completely. Apart from the expense this incurs, complete bird and cat protection will also interfere with normal cultivations, like weeding, so it is an idea to start first with simpler methods of bird and cat control. For example, cabbages and other greens are vulnerable to pigeon attack. These birds swoop down to the feeding area, so it is possible to deter them by making the landing area unsuitable. Simply by draping large mesh anti-pigeon net over the plants will make the landing site unstable. However, in times of food shortage the

birds will investigate and may walk under the netting unless it is fixed flush with the ground at the edges. With cabbage seedlings, by erecting a simple garden net fence around the seed bed you will create a pen into which pigeons might be reluctant to fly, and yet this will not hinder cultivation.

Sparrows and other small birds can play havoc with seedlings, like lettuce, and cats are also a problem because they scratch up seedbeds. A good solution is to cover the seed rows either with polythene tunnel cloches or with bird-proof plastic garden nets stretched over hoops made from old wire coat hangers, flexible split bamboo canes, or

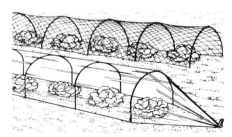

lightweight plastic tubing such as the type used for electrical conduit.

To protect a seedbed completely, hammer 60 cm (2 ft) stakes into the ground around the perimeter, stretch wires between the tops of the stakes and then cover the entire structure with small mesh garden netting.

# Week 15

## THE KITCHEN GARDEN

**Asparagus crowns** should be planted without delay.

**Brussels sprouts** should be sown on a prepared seedbed within the next week if this has not already been done.

**Cabbages** sown last July and August and transplanted in September will be ready for cutting during the next month.

**Leeks** ought to be sown by now if you have not already done so. They should be sown on a prepared seedbed for transplanting later.

**Pea sticks** should be inserted before the plants become too tall.

**Plant out onion and cauliflower seedlings** raised under glass.

**Second early potatoes** should be planted in mild districts, setting them 38 cm (15 in) apart in 75 cm (2½ ft) rows.

### FRAMES AND CLOCHES

**Thin** crops growing under cloches before they become overcrowded.

**Thin carrots** in frames as necessary; you can probably use the thinnings to eat.

**Ventilate cloches** on favourable days, even where they cover tender vegetables such as runner beans and sweetcorn. Remember to secure them at night.

### FRUIT

**Apple mildew** is difficult to control with chemicals alone, and it is a good idea to cut out any severely affected shoots when they are seen.

**Gooseberries** can also suffer badly from mildew but a suitable systemic fungicide applied as the first flowers open and repeated three weeks later should help control it.

**Mulch soft fruit** (except strawberries) with well-rotted garden compost.

## THE FLOWER GARDEN

**Dahlia tubers** that have not yet produced shoots can be planted out in the garden during the next couple of weeks. Set them at least 10 cm (4 in) deep, inserting the stakes now so that the tuber will not be damaged later. Do not forget the label.

**Feed and mulch roses** if you have not already done so.

**Herbaceous plants** should be planted as soon as possible. If you have seedlings growing in a nursery bed from last year, transplant them to the border now.

**Pansies and violas** can be sown outdoors in a nursery bed for flowering during late summer this year and early next year.

**Plant evergreen shrubs and trees**, but choose 'balled' plants (whose roots are wrapped in plastic or sacking) if they are not container-grown.

**Prepare the summer quarters** for late-flowering chrysanthemums. The pots should stand on a firm surface in a sunny position sheltered from strong winds.

**Sow hardy annuals** whenever the ground is in a suitable condition. Sow in rows for cutting; in drifts for display.

**Tulip fire** is a serious disease of tulips, causing small, sunken and grey spots on the leaves. The spots turn brown and then black, and the leaves tend to look as if they have been scorched. Flower buds tend not to open. Infected plants are best pulled up and burned.

### FRAMES

**Bedding plants** will probably be filling the frames during the next few weeks. Harden them off gradually. Take advantage of mild days to ventilate freely, but close the frames at night.

### THE ROCK GARDEN

**Plant rock plants.** There is usually a wide range of pot-grown plants on offer at garden centres at this time.

### THE WATER GARDEN

**Renovate the pool** now if it needs it. Take the opportunity to repair leaks and divide plants. Drain the pool slowly, removing the fish to a large container and placing the plants in buckets to keep their roots moist. Scrub the sides of the pool to remove algae, and clear out loose soil and decomposed leaves from the bottom of the pool. Many pool liners can be repaired with a kit similar to a puncture outfit if they leak.

### LAWNS

**Apply spring fertilizer.** Use a proprietary lawn fertilizer at the rate recommended by the manufacturer.

**Mow regularly** from now on. The grass is much easier to cut—especially with a hand mower—if it is not allowed to become too long between cuts. For the rest of this month, however, it is wise not to cut closer than 19 mm (¾ in).

## THE GREENHOUSE

**Aspidistras** look better and grow more healthily if you clean the leaves with a damp cloth.

**Begonia rex** is an attractive foliage plant, and leaf blade cuttings are an interesting way to propagate it. If you do this now the plants should be large enough to make good growth during the summer.

**Cacti** can be raised from seed quite easily, although most seedsmen only offer mixed packets. Sow them now in pots of John Innes seed compost. Sow thinly, and if they are large use the top of a pencil or sharp stick to space them apart. Lightly cover with sand. Germination may be erratic.

**Chrysanthemums** may need 'stopping' (the growing tip removed), but consult a specialist chrysanthemum catalogue or book to see whether this applies to your varieties—and only stop well-rooted plants.

**Cucumber** plants that are well

established in their pots can be planted in the greenhouse border or growing bags.

**Cucumbers** sown in March can be planted in the border or growing bags now in a heated greenhouse. This will probably be difficult where bedding

plants are being grown and you may have to wait until there is more space.

**Grape vines** in an unheated greenhouse will need the rods tying to their supporting wires.

**Mist ferns** with water regularly from now on as the temperature and need for humidity increase.

**Monstera deliciosa**, the swiss cheese plant, can be repotted now. Take the opportunity to use a damp cloth, or a proprietary leaf-shine, on the leaves.

**Pot on greenhouse chrysanthemums** into larger pots. Do not overpot, even if it means moving them on several times.

**Pot up seedlings** that are large enough to be handled safely.

**Sow melons**, two seeds to a 7.5 cm (3 in) pot. Once they have germinated, thin to the strongest seedling in each pot.

**Sow outdoor tomatoes** if you have not already done so.

## Make a crazy paving path

Crazy paving is available from garden centres, builders' merchants and some local councils. It is sold by the tonne which is sufficient to cover 9 m² (9 sq yd; sometimes a cost per m² or sq yd will be quoted.

It is easier to make curved or informal shapes with crazy paving than it is with formal slabs. Ideally you should order an assortment of large and other size pieces.

Use string lines to mark out the path. Remembering that the path should finish level with the ground, dig down sufficiently to allow for a layer of concrete of about 25–40 mm (1–1½ in), a 13-mm (½-in) bed of mortar, plus the thickness of the paving. If the subsoil is soft, dig down another centimetre or two and fill the base with well compacted hardcore.

Although a far more solid job results when using a concrete base, paths which only have to take foot traffic or wheelbarrows can be laid on a 40–50 mm

(1½–2 in) thick sand bed. There is, however, a danger that the sand could be washed away slowly, so a concrete 'kerb' either side would be advisable.

Plan to lay the path to give a slight fall to one side to shed rainwater. This is not necessary if the path slopes away from the house and the ground at the end of the path drains readily.

Use a mix of one part cement to five parts coarse aggregate for the concrete and use formwork to get it level. When it has set the slabs can be laid on mortar of one part cement to five parts of sharp sand. Use a straight-edged batten and spirit level to check that the slabs are level. Joints between the slabs will vary in size and should be about 13–25 mm (½–1 in) wide maximum. When the bedding mortar has dried, fill the joints with a wetter mortar mix. To ensure that the mortar remains a uniform colour make each batch with exactly the same proportions of ingredients.

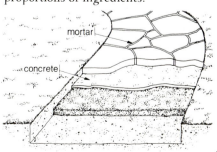

## THE KITCHEN GARDEN

**Cabbages** for summer and autumn use should be sown in a prepared seedbed if this has not already been done.

**Cabbage root fly** maggots can devastate brassicas (cabbages and related crops). A soil insecticide can help to reduce the pest. If the whole area is not treated, dust round each plant within four days of planting.

**Cabbage and Brussels sprout** stumps should be lifted, dried off and burnt to reduce the risk of pests and diseases being encouraged.

**Kale** (borecole) can be sown about this time.

**Peas** for succession can still be sown.

**Plant out vegetable seedlings** that have been hardening off in the garden frame; but if the weather is very cold or windy delay for another week or two.

**Pull radishes** while they are still young and before they become tough and woody.

**Sow kohl-rabi** any time during the next few weeks.

**Sow parsley** if this has not already been done.

**Spinach, lettuces and radishes** should be sown again to provide succession throughout the summer.

### FRUIT

**Apples** often benefit from a light dressing of sulphate of ammonia now.

**Apples and pears** attacked by scab disease last year should be sprayed with a suitable fungicide as a precaution this year.

**Gooseberry sawfly** caterpillars can be a problem on these bushes. Spray or dust with a suitable insecticide at first sign.

**Hoe** around raspberries to keep down weeds. Remove any suckers further than 15 cm (6 in) of the centre of the plant.

## THE FLOWER GARDEN

**Alstroemerias** (Peruvian lilies) can be divided. Replant them as soon as possible.

**Asters** are usually treated as half-hardy annuals, but can also be sown outdoors from mid-April to June in mild areas.

**Coniferous hedges** are best planted about now, when the soil is warming up and the plants have a long season in which to become established before the winter comes.

**Established astilbe clumps** can be divided now. Replant with the younger parts of the plant from around the outside of the clump.

**Evergreen shrubs and trees** are best trimmed to shape this month. However, spring-flowering evergreen shrubs are best pruned after the flowers have faded and dropped off.

**Herbaceous plants** can still be divided, but be prepared to water the plants well afterwards if the weather is dry.

**Sow hardy annuals** if this has not already been done. They will probably germinate more readily now than earlier sowings, especially on cold or heavy soil.

### FRAMES

**Bedding plants** should be moved into the frame as soon as they are ready for hardening off. Ventilate the frames whenever the weather is suitable.

### THE ROCK GARDEN

**Pot-grown rock plants** can be planted at any time when the soil is not frozen or too wet, but April is particularly good as it gives the plants a whole season to become established before winter arrives. Remove the plants from their pots and plant firmly.

**Propagate sempervivums** by removing some of the offsets. The offsets will need a dry, sandy soil.

### THE WATER GARDEN

**Feed established water lilies** by mixing bonemeal with a lump of soft clay. Mix equal parts and make into a tennis-ball sized lump and push it into the soil by the roots.

**Plant water lilies.** It is best to use planting baskets designed for the job.

**Water hawthorn** can be divided any time during the next two months.

### LAWNS

**Stepping stones** are always attractive and spring is a good time to lay them once the ground begins to dry out after the winter. Mow the grass then just lay the stones in position first. Check that they are the right distance apart for easy walking. Then cut around them and take out a hole a little deeper than the stones. Bed the stones in a little sand, leaving them set a little lower than the lawn so that the blades of cylinder lawn mowers clear them.

## THE GREENHOUSE

**Achimenes** can still be started. Even if you planted some in Week 4, it is worth starting off a few more tubers now to have a succession of flowers.

**Arum lilies** that have finished flowering should be dried off gradually.

**Aubergines and capsicums** sown earlier should be ready for potting into 7.5 cm (3 in) pots, if not already done.

**Bedding plants** that can still be sown include alyssum, nemesia, nicotiana, *Phlox drummondii*, and zinnias. Do not delay, otherwise they will flower late.

**Dry off cyclamen** gradually as they finish blooming.

**Fuchsias** will be making a lot of growth, and it may be worth 'stopping' them (pinching out the growing tips) if this has not been done recently to encourage them to make bushy plants.

**Gloxinias and tuberous begonias** can

still be potted up or started off in boxes of peaty compost.

**Greenhouse tomatoes** may require sideshoots removing. Break off any growths coming from the junction between main stem and a leaf.

**Hanging baskets** are best started off early in the greenhouse. Cascading geraniums and fuchsias are ideal subjects whether in mixed baskets or alone. It is always worth filling a few baskets for summer display in the greenhouse as well as those for hanging outside. In a decorative greenhouse, hanging baskets can do much to improve the overall display.

**Prick out** *Primula obconica* seedlings before they become overcrowded. They are best pricked out into small pots.

**Salvias** can be made to bush out more freely earlier by pinching out the growing tips when the plants are about 10 cm (4 in) high.

**Watch for pests** (especially greenfly) which can multiply rapidly at this time. Spray or fumigate as soon as they are noticed.

## WEEKEND PROJECTS

### Installing an outside tap

An outside water supply is important for the keen gardener. The ideal place to situate a tap is on an outside wall where the rising main leads to the cold water tap over the kitchen sink.

Assuming that the rising main is a 15 mm ($\frac{5}{8}$ in) copper tube, then the materials required will be one 15 mm type A compression T-junction with all ends equal; a screwdown 15 mm stopcock with type A compression inlet and outlet (this is optional); two 15 mm elbows and one 15 mm wallplate elbow, all with type A compression connections; one bib-tap with hose connector and sufficient 15 mm copper tube (usually in the situation above about 60–90 cm—2–3 ft—is adequate).

Few tools are required: an adjustable spanner, plus a spanner to suit the cap nuts of the compression fittings, a hacksaw and a small file. You will also need an electric drill with a long masonry drill which will allow a 15 mm ($\frac{5}{8}$ in) diameter hole to be drilled in the wall to feed the copper pipe through.

First, shut down the house stopcock to cut off the water supply to the rising

main. If there is a draincock above the stopcock then the rising main can be drained completely.

Then, cut the rising main to insert the T-branch. The handiest point is usually about 60 cm (2 ft) above a floor level. Make two cuts in the pipe about 19 mm ($\frac{3}{4}$ in) apart. Cut square then remove internal and external burr with the file. Smear some waterproofing compound, such as Boss White, onto the pipe ends. The T-branch is then fitted and the cap nuts tightened. Hand-tighten these, then hold the T firmly and, with a spanner, turn each nut another 1 to $1\frac{1}{4}$ turns.

If a stopcock is being used fit a 15 cm (6 in) length of tube into the branch outlet of the T-junction and tighten up. Fit the new stopcock with the arrow engraved on it pointing in the direction of the water flow to the outside tap.

Next drill the hole through the outside wall. Then cut a 33 cm (13 in) length of copper tube and fit a 15 mm ($\frac{5}{8}$ in) compression elbow. Push the tube through the hole and then cut and fit a length of tube between the compression elbow and the stopcock. Outside, trim

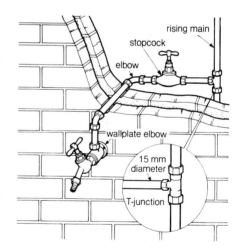

the tube to leave 25 mm (1 in) projecting. Fit a compression elbow (pointing downwards) and then a 75 mm (3 in) length of tube. To this tube fit the compression inlet of the wallplate elbow. Screw the wallplate elbow to the wall. Finally, bind the plastic thread sealing tape to the bib-tap thread before screwing it home.

## THE KITCHEN GARDEN

**Asparagus** should be ready for cutting in the south. Take care when cutting the shoots beneath the ground that you do not damage other spears.

**Broad beans** sown in the autumn will be getting tall and may need supporting to avoid wind damage.

**Cauliflowers** of the 'Australian' kind can be sown any time during the next few weeks.

**Continue to hoe** to keep down weeds. This is especially important while the crop plants are still young.

**Endive** makes a change from lettuce in summer salads. You can sow it now.

**Maincrop carrots** can safely be sown in all areas, following on earlier sowings for succession if required.

**Maincrop potatoes** can also be planted from now on, at the same spacings.

**Onion sets** must be planted without delay if you have not already done so.

**Prepare the celery trench**—one wide enough for a double row is normal.

**Salsify and scorzonera** can still be sown.

**Second early potatoes** ought to be planted by now, if they are not already in.

**Sow onion seed** to provide pickling or salad onions.

**Sow sprouting broccoli** for cutting next spring.

**Thin spinach.**

**Turnips** will need sowing again for a succession of tender young roots.

### FRAMES AND CLOCHES

**Sow French beans and sweetcorn** in frames or cloches.

**Strawberries** under cloches should not be allowed to go short of water.

**Vegetable marrows** can be planted in a cold-frame provided that it is in a sheltered position. If you do not have plants, sow seed directly into the ground and keep the frame closed until germination.

### FRUIT

**Remove grease-bands** as they have now served their purpose.

**Spray gooseberries** after flowering if there are signs of red spider mites.

**Spray strawberries** with an insecticide if there are signs of greenfly.

**Thin peaches** on fan-trained fruit trees by removing the poorest fruitlets. Eventually they should be spaced about 10 cm (4 in) apart.

## THE FLOWER GARDEN

**Bellis perennis** to flower next spring can be sown outdoors now in a seedbed.

**Canterbury bells** can also be sown outdoors now for transplanting later.

**Daffodils** that have finished flowering will need to have their old flower heads removed. This will tidy up the bed and prevent the bulbs putting their energies into making seed instead of making good bulbs for next year.

**Delphiniums, lupins, and** *Scabiosa caucasica* can be increased from 7.5–12.5 cm (3–5 in) long cuttings of young shoots. Cut them from low down on the plants, and trim to below a leaf-joint. Insert them in a sandy compost in a garden frame.

**Hardy annuals** sown in March and early April will need thinning to ensure the seedlings do not overcrowd each other. Thin small types to 10–15 cm (4–6 in) apart, medium types to 20–30 cm (8–12 in), and tall-growing ones to 45 cm (1½ ft) or more.

**Hyacinth bulbs** that have flowered in the garden can be lifted with a fork and placed in a trench. In light soils they can be left in the ground, but they tend to get in the way if you want to plant summer bedding.

**Penstemons** overwintered in a garden frame can now be planted out.

Hand tools can be used to divide smaller plants.

**Plant clematis.** They dislike root disturbances so buy pot-grown plants.

**Plant chincherinchees** (*Ornithogalum thyrsoides*). Select a sunny, sheltered place and set the bulbs 10–15 cm (4–5 in) deep and 5–7.5 cm (2–3 in) apart. These plants produce excellent cut-flowers.

**Thin hardy annuals** before they become too crowded. Never thin to the final spacings immediately; it is always best to thin in stages to allow for plants succumbing to pests or accidentally to the hoe.

### LAWNS

**Kill plantain** by using a daisy grubber to remove them, or use a stick-type spot weedkiller.

**Lawns** from seed sown two or three weeks ago should have germinated. If the weather turns dry give the surface a thorough soaking from a sprinkler. Do not walk on the lawn unnecessarily.

## THE GREENHOUSE

**Aubergines and capsicums** that have filled their 7.5 cm (3 in) pots with roots can be potted on into 20 cm (8 in) pots.
**Bedding plants** that were sown early should be ready to move into garden frames for hardening-off.
**Chlorophytum**, the spider plant, tends to push itself out of the pot as the fleshy roots swell. As soon as this happens, repot into a larger pot, using John Innes potting compost.
**Cissus antartica**, the kangaroo vine, is easily increased from cuttings taken now.
**Cucumbers** may need staking and tying now. If not already done, erect a framework of wires and canes, so that the main stem of each plant can be tied to the cane, and the laterals secured to the horizontal wires, which should be spaced about 15 cm (6 in) apart.
**Grape vines.** Pinch back the young growth to two leaves beyond the fruit trusses. At the same time, thin out the trusses to one on each lateral shoot.

Provide a humid atmosphere for kangaroo vine cuttings with a polythene bag supported on thin sticks.

**Indoor chrysanthemums** can be moved into their final pots.
**Prick out half-hardy annuals** as later sowings become ready. Salvias and zinnias often make better plants if pricked out into pots, and this can be particularly useful with late sowings.
**Primula obconica** can still be sown to flower next winter and spring.
**Runner beans** for planting out at the end of May or in June can be started off in a warm greenhouse. Sow one seed to a 7.5 cm (3 in) pot. As soon as they have germinated and the shoots are 5–7.5 cm (2–3 in) high, move them to a frost-free garden frame to harden off.
**Shade** plants such as gloxinias and begonias on very warm days.
**Ventilate** the greenhouse well whenever the weather is favourable. It is better to keep the plants toughened up at this stage—especially if there are bedding plants that are almost ready for hardening-off.

## WEEKEND PROJECTS

### Make a wheel herb garden

Herbs grown in an orderly formation make an attractive focal point in the garden. A herb wheel is a traditional favourite method, and this can be laid out using bricks or planks of wood, with perhaps an attractive plant or ornament as the centrepiece. The 'spokes' of the wheel serve two purposes: apart from separating each type, they provide useful walkways when collecting the herbs.

Each 'compartment' should have an area equal to at least 0.1 m² (1 sq ft) though 1 m² (1 sq yd) makes a really useful area for the enthusiast.

Drive a stake into the ground at the intended centre of the wheel and tie to it a length of string which, when pulled taut, reaches to the perimeter of the wheel. The string line is then used like a compass to mark out the circle. Use battens to indicate the positions of the spokes.

Each batten, in turn, can be replaced by permanent planks of wood or bricks. The bricks can be loose-laid on the surface or be part buried in the ground leaving about 5 cm (2 in) protruding. For a more permanent wheel, bed down the bricks or mortar and fill the joints between.

Mint is one herb which, left unchecked, will invade neighbouring compartments. To inhibit this, dig down about 30–45 cm (1–1½ ft) and line the spokes in the mint compartment using plastic sheet.

# Week 18

## THE KITCHEN GARDEN

**Beetroot** can be sown without protection from now on. Soak the seed for an hour or two first to remove a germination inhibitor.

**Cabbages** for winter use and kale for next spring should be sown now on a prepared seedbed.

**Carrots** should be thinned while still small, but it is best done in damp weather, and doing it in late afternoon or early evening is supposed to reduce the chance of carrot fly becoming a problem.

**Harvest spinach**, sprouting broccoli, cabbages and lettuces, as well as radishes and onions for salads.

**Leeks** should be thinned but firm the ground around the remaining plants.

**Lettuces and radishes** should be sown for succession.

**Pull radishes** before they become too large and tough.

**Slugs** are likely to be very active around seedling vegetables. Use slug pellets as a routine precaution around lettuces, and whenever there are signs of damage to other crops.

### FRUIT

**Mulch fruit trees** with stable manure or well-rotted compost if this has not already been done. Raspberries particularly appreciate a mulch.

**Spray gooseberries** with a fungicide against mildew.

**Thin peaches**, nectarines and apricots in stages. Apricots do not need as much thinning as peaches and nectarines.

**Woolly aphids** (those insects that hide themselves in a mass of cotton-wool-like material) should be sprayed whenever they are seen. Systemic insecticides can be useful for this pest.

## THE FLOWER GARDEN

**Bamboos** are best planted now. If planted too early, the soil may be cold and cause the shoots to die back or be checked.

**Divide overcrowded hypericums** (rose of sharon). Replant the young outer pieces of each clump.

**Feed sweet peas** being grown for exhibition. However, do not use one with a higher nitrogen fertilizer as it may encourage buds to drop.

**Herbaceous borders** will benefit from a dressing of a general fertilizer hoed into the soil. Water it in if the weather is dry.

**Herbaceous plants** can be raised from seed quite easily, although they are likely to be more variable than those propagated vegetatively. If you sow now seedlings can spend the summer in a nursery bed.

**Plant outdoor chrysanthemums** in mild areas, or wait until early May in northerly areas. Plant them firmly but shallowly, 30–45 cm (1–1½ ft) apart. Insert canes next to each plant, and tie the stems to the canes with soft string. Water well to settle the soil around the roots.

**Plant out sweet peas** raised under glass this year, provided they have been hardened off properly.

**Prune camellias** after flowering. Cut out thin and straggly shoots.

**Prune flowering currants** (ribes) that have finished flowering. Cut out some of the old wood, and remove weak shoots.

**Tie in rambler roses** to their supports. Stray shoots from the base must be tied securely.

### THE WATER GARDEN

**Water lilies** that have become crowded can be lifted and divided. Use a strong, sharp knife to cut up the thick roots. The individual pieces can be placed in planting baskets containing fertile, loamy soil.

### LAWNS

**Cut established lawns** regularly during the summer—twice a week if necessary. Do not set the blades lower than 6 mm (¼ in) above the surface—about 19–25 mm (¾–1 in) is about right for most lawns.

# Week 18

## THE GREENHOUSE

**Dampen** the path in the afternoon whenever it is sunny. The plants will be able to benefit from increased humidity now.

**Greenfly** will almost inevitably make an appearance soon. Make a habit of looking at suspicious plants, such as fuchsias, daily so that you can nip trouble in the bud.

**Harden off bedding plants** by reducing the temperature and moving the plants to a garden frame. Be careful not to allow the plants to become dry.

**Perpetual-flowering carnations** should be 'stopped' (growing tips pinched out) when sideshoots start to develop in the leaf axils (where the leaf joins the stem).

**Red spider mites** may become troublesome with the increasing warmth. This pest is not easy to control, so use one of the treatments recommended on page 21 at first sign. Keeping the

atmosphere humid will help to deter them.

**Runner beans** germinated in the greenhouse should be moved into a frost-free garden frame in mild areas. In cold districts, it is worth sowing seed now to provide plants for planting out in early June.

**Saintpaulias** (African violets) can be increased from leaf cuttings. They will root easily if taken any time during the next few months.

**Saxifraga stolonifera** (mother of Thousands) produces small plantlets at the end of the numerous runners. If you want to propagate the plant, simply place the parent plant in the centre of a seed tray, and push the plantlets on the runners into small pots of an open compost clustered around the main pot.

**Shading** is not usually required this early in the season, but if the weather does turn exceptionally bright be prepared to use temporary shading (not a problem if you have roller blinds), but do not apply a summer shading wash yet.

**Tall rubber plants** (*Ficus elastica*) can be air layered now if they are tall and the bottom leaves have dropped.

WEEKEND PROJECTS

## Make a bottle garden

Traditionally a bottle garden consists of houseplants in a large glass carboy, but you can make a bottle garden using any large glass bottle. If the bottle has a stopper the plants will hardly ever need watering because the water given off by the plants collects on the sides of the bottle and runs down to the compost again, making the garden virtually self-supporting. If the bottle has an open top, even then watering will be needed only rarely and the plants will still benefit from the humid atmosphere within the bottle.

Apart from industrial carboys, cider flagons, goldfish bowls and large sweet jars are all suitable containers for a bottle garden. If the bottle has a narrow neck it will be necessary to make some special long-handled tools to aid planting.

The first stage is to put a layer of charcoal lumps into the bottom of the jar. Because the bottle is not drained, this layer prevents the compost from turning sour. Next add 5–7.5 cm (2–3

in) of a peat- or soil-based seed compost (potting compost has too much fertilizer). A funnel and a long cardboard tube will help the filling of a narrow-necked jar and will keep the sides clean.

Next, small plants can be introduced. Choose slow-growing, humid-loving houseplants such as peperomias, pileas, selaginellas, fittonias and small bromeliads. With the aid of a table fork

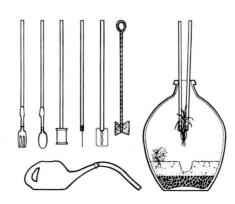

or a tablespoon taped to canes, make the planting holes, then lower each plant into the jar, roots first. Start by setting plants around the edges and finish off with the central plant. Manoeuvre each plant into position, cover the roots with compost and then firm it down. A cotton reel on a cane is ideal here.

After planting, carefully water the plants down the inside of the glass, but remember that excess water cannot escape. If any leaves have been damaged in the planting process remove them with a razor blade wedged into the end of a split cane. Lift out debris with a large upholstery needle taped to a cane. If the sides of the bottle are splashed with compost, wash them when watering. Keep the bottle garden in a well-lit but not sunny place in a warm room. In bright sunlight condensation may be a problem. Move the container to a slightly shadier spot if this occurs and leave the stopper out until the glass clears.

## THE KITCHEN GARDEN

**Blackfly** on broad beans can be a major headache, so keep a close watch on them. Spray at first sign of attack. Prevent by pinching out the shoot tip after four flower trusses have formed.
**Blanch leeks** planted in trenches. It is a good idea to use cardboard tubes 15 cm (6 in) long and 7.5 cm (3 in) in diameter, and slip these over the plants before drawing a little earth round them.
**Chicory** can be sown now.
**Dig** ground cleared of late green crops.
**Maincrop potatoes** ought to be planted by now. Space them 38 cm (15 in) apart in 75 cm (2½ ft) rows.
**Parsley** can still be sown.
**Peas and spinach** can be sown for successional cropping.
**Rhubarb** sometimes sends up flower shoots. Cut them off with a knife as soon as they are seen. Rhubarb that has been pulled heavily during the season will benefit from a nitrogenous fertilizer now.

**Sow kohl-rabi** for a succession.
**Sow New Zealand spinach**, allowing plenty of room for its creeping habit.
**Thin** beetroot, carrots, lettuces, onions (from seed), parsnips, and turnips.
**Turnip flea beetles** can be a problem, so dust with a suitable insecticide as soon as the tell-tale holes appear in the leaves.
**Vegetable marrows** can be sown outdoors in the south. Sow a couple of seeds at each position and thin to one later if both germinate. It is best to cover with a jam-jar or cloche.

## FRUIT

**Apple scab** can spread rapidly, especially in warm, humid weather. Apply a second dose of a suitable fungicide. You may be able to combine it with an insecticide if aphids are also a problem.
**Place straw beneath strawberries.** Be generous with the amount. It is also well worth sprinkling slug pellets at the same time.
**Plant container-grown fruit** if you still have space to fill.
**Spray strawberries** with a fungicide to control grey mould if it is a damp season.
**Strawberries** will be flowering about now, but the early flowers can be damaged by frost—the centres will blacken and there will not be any fruit. If you cannot provide cloche protection, just covering them with hessian or even newspapers when frost threatens may be sufficient.

## THE FLOWER GARDEN

**Ageratums** sown under glass from February to April can now be planted out in their flowering positions after first being hardened off.
**Cockchafer** grubs become active about now. The grubs feed on the roots of many ornamental trees and shrubs, the adult beetles feed on the leaves. If you see the beetles, spray with an insecticide, if you suspect the grubs hoe a soil insecticide around the plants.
**Dead-head tulips** as soon as they have finished flowering. If the space is required for summer bedding later, you can fork up the bulbs and set them in a trench in a sheltered part of the garden. Cover the bulbs with a few centimetres of soil.
**Hardy annuals** sown early will need

twiggy sticks inserted around them for support. The plants should grow through the supports and eventually cover them entirely.
**Hydrangeas** can be increased during the next couple of months. Insert 7.5 cm (3 in) long cuttings, severed just below a leaf-joint, in a propagator.
**Newly-planted trees and shrubs** need a thorough soaking if the weather is dry.
**Sow wallflowers** during the next month on a prepared seedbed.
**Stake gladioli** well, especially on light soils.
**Violets** can be increased by lifting the plants and dividing them.

## LAWNS

**Lawns sown earlier** in the year can be cut when the grass is 4–5 cm (1½–2 in) high, with the blades of the mower set high. Make sure the blades are very sharp so that the grass seedlings are not torn out from the soil.

## THE GREENHOUSE

**Cinerarias** can be sown now in a temperature of 10–15°C (50–60°F) to flower between December and April.

**Cucumbers** that have reached sufficient height should be 'stopped' by nipping out the growing tip to encourage the development of lateral shoots. It is these that will bear the fruit.

**French beans** started off in pots in the greenhouse can be planted out in a garden frame during the next few weeks.

**Harden off bedding plants** by moving them into a garden frame as they become ready. Be prepared, however, to protect them if frost threatens.

**Keep a sharp lookout for pests.** If just a few plants are affected they should be easy to control with a suitable spray, but if they have become established it may be best to fumigate.

**Melons** can still be sown, but do not leave it any later. On windy days open the ventilators on the sheltered side. Always make sure ventilators are closed

at night as temperatures can still fall sharply.

**Pot on annuals** to be flowered in the greenhouse, such as celosias and double petunias.

**Propagate ivies.** Cuttings will root easily in a mixture of sand and peat or a seed compost.

**Repot azaleas** if necessary.

**Shade seedlings** from strong sunshine.

**Take cuttings of azaleas** if you have a propagator.

**Ventilate** the greenhouse more freely now that temperatures are increasing, but close the ventilators during cold nights. Do not leave frost-susceptible plants near the glass unless you can provide adequate background heat on cold nights.

**Watering** can become a major task during the coming months. If you do not have an automatic watering system, it is worth spreading a layer of shingle or sand over a sheet of polythene on the staging. If your sand or shingle is damp it will provide a humid atmosphere around the plants, and the pots will be able to draw up some of the moisture. But this is not a proper capillary system, so continue to water through the pots normally—it only acts as a 'buffer' against erratic watering.

## WEEKEND PROJECTS

### Plant a hanging basket

Many modern hanging baskets consist of a solid plastic bowl with a built-in drip tray underneath. However, traditional hanging baskets are larger and are made with galvanized or plastic coated wires as shown in the photographs. In this case the first stage is to line the basket to prevent the compost from falling through. Stand the basket on a large flower pot or bucket to keep it steady and level. A lining of sphagnum moss (which is available from florists) can be used.

A better and more modern alternative is to line the basket with foam plastic sheet, as used for upholstery, car soundproofing, carpet underlays, and so on. This material is porous, allowing the roots of the plants to breathe easily, but it also retains moisture better than moss so that less frequent watering is required. Remember, however, that all hanging baskets dry out rapidly, particularly those in a sunny spot.

To minimize the weight of the basket, fill it with an all-peat potting compost. The appearance of a wire type basket can be considerably improved if three or four plants are inserted through the sides and bottom of the basket through slits made in the foam lining.

Choose a large plant for the central position and stand it in place after removing its pot. The top of the root ball must be just below the level of the rim of the basket. Next place more

plants around the central one, with trailing plants around the edge so that their stems fall over the sides of the basket. All the plants are removed from their containers, and when they are in a suitable arrangement the spaces between the root balls are filled with more compost which is carefully pushed into all the crevices to avoid air pockets. Thoroughly water the basket before lifting it into position on a secure bracket.

## THE KITCHEN GARDEN

**Beetroot** should continue to be sown for succession—soak the seeds first.

**Carrots** are susceptible to attention from carrot fly from now on, so dust along the rows with a soil insecticide.

**Dwarf French beans** should be sown now—although you should be prepared to use cloches if necessary in cold districts.

**Early potatoes** may need earthing up a little, which will offer some frost protection.

**Savoy cabbages, kale** and suitable varieties of cauliflower should be sown on a prepared seedbed.

**'Australian' cauliflowers** should be sown without delay, but the 'giant' type for spring planting can be sown any time during the next few weeks.

**Stake peas** if this has not already been done. Provide support for runner beans.

**Turnips, lettuces, and radishes** can be sown for a successional crop.

**Winter cauliflower** should also be sown on a prepared seedbed if this has not been done already.

### FRAMES AND CLOCHES

**In frames** early carrots should be ready for lifting.

**Runner beans** for an early crop are best sown now with the protection of cloches.

**Strawberries** under cloches may be bearing fruit, so give them plenty of water, and make sure the berries are raised off the soil on straw or on supports.

### FRUIT

**Birds** can be a menace when the strawberry fruits ripen, and it is well worth covering the plants with a small-mesh net. Do this in plenty of time, using jam-jars on canes to support the net if you do not have a proper fruit cage.

**Keep the grass cut around fruit trees.**

**Peach leaf curl** is a disfiguring disease —the leaves becoming distorted around ugly red 'blisters'. Pick off any affected leaves and burn them. A fungicide applied now might check the disease, but for better control preventive doses should have been given before the leaves began to break.

**Spray raspberries** with a suitable fungicide if cane-spot or spur blight has been a problem in the past.

**Thin** apple varieties that mature early, leaving the fruits about 15 cm (6 in) apart. Other varieties can be left until later.

## THE FLOWER GARDEN

**Asters** sown earlier under glass can be planted out where they are to flower.

**Azaleas** can be increased by layering low-growing shoots. From now until the end of June these shoots can be pegged into the soil and covered with a mixture of peat and soil. Insert a small cane where the shoot enters the soil, and tie the shoot to it.

**Daffodils** that have finished flowering can be tidied up by removing the seed heads. If the bulbs are in a bed needed for summer bedding plants, lift and replant in a trench in a cool part of the garden. Once the foliage has died down the bulbs can be lifted and stored in a cool place until the autumn, when they can be replanted.

**Half-hardy annuals** can be planted out in sheltered sites, but in cold and northerly areas wait until the second week in June, when all risk of frost will have passed. Some of the tougher plants,

such as antirrhinums and alyssum, can planted anywhere now, but it is usually more convenient to plant a mixed bed at the same time.

**Herbaceous plants** will need firm staking. Small types are best given twiggy pea sticks to clamber around, while taller types such as delphiniums will need bamboo canes and strong twine.

**Prune forsythias** after they have flowered. Cut out flowered shoots and dead and crossing branches.

**Sow hardy annuals** if this has not already been done.

### LAWNS

**Weedkillers** can be used when the grass is growing strongly, preferably a few weeks after a spring fertilizer dressing has been applied (do not use a combined weed-and-feed preparation if you have already just fertilized the lawn). Do not use a weedkiller if the weather is very dry, and do not cut the lawn for at least four days after applying it. Never apply a weedkiller to a newly sown lawn. Do not put clippings from a recently treated lawn on the compost heap or around plants—burn them or use a separate heap to decompose for eight months to allow all traces of the weedkiller to disappear.

## THE GREENHOUSE

**Cactus seedlings** can be potted into small pots of John Innes potting compost No. 1. Shade them for a few weeks to give them a chance to become established.

**Carnations** will need to be supported with canes and tied in. The stems are not very strong and are easily damaged or broken off.

**Cucumbers** should have all the male flowers removed regularly (these lack the 'miniature cucumber' swelling behind the flower). Some of the newer varieties are 'all female' and this job is not normally necessary, although some male flowers may be produced if the

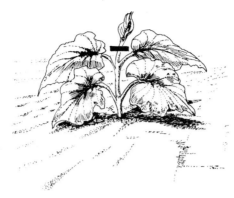

plants are subjected to stress; these should be removed.

**Feed gloxinias** and tuberous-rooted begonias as soon as the pots are full of roots.

**Greenhouse chrysanthemums** can be moved into their final pots, using John Innes potting compost No. 3.

**Melons** that have produced five leaves can be transplanted into the greenhouse border. The plants will need canes and wires in exactly the same way as cucumbers. Train the main stem up the cane and tie lateral shoots to the horizontal wires, which should be spaced about 15 cm (6 in) apart.

**Remove sideshoots from tomatoes** at least once a week. Allowing them to grow only diverts energy from the fruit.

---

**WEEKEND PROJECTS**

### Fixing a hanging basket

A hanging basket filled with soil is heavy, so it must be fixed securely to the wall or ceiling. For wall fixing the simplest method is to buy one of the special ornamental brackets that are readily available. These are usually supplied with one or more pre-drilled fixing holes in the back arm. Hold the bracket to the wall and mark off the position of the holes on the wall in pencil.

The strength of the bracket depends on the screw or screws used to fix it, so choose number 8 or number 10 screws and of a length that is sufficient to ensure that the threaded part of the screw is buried in the brickwork of the wall. A minimum length would be 5 cm (2 in), though 6–7.5 cm (2½–3 in) long is better for a really firm fixing. Drill the hole in the wall, insert a wallplug of the correct size for the screw and push this into the hole. Position the bracket over the hole and drive in the screw. Smearing grease on the screw thread makes it easier to drive in the screw and remove it later if necessary.

For ceiling fixings indoors, a strong cup hook is needed. This should have a thread at least 4–5 cm (1½–2 in) long. It must be fixed in the middle of a joist

above the ceiling. To find a joist, take up a couple of floorboards in the room above and drill a hole down through the ceiling on either side of the joist. From below the two holes will indicate where the cup hook should be inserted. Drill a pilot hole for the cup hook then screw it firmly into the joist.

Watering ceiling hung baskets can be made easier for anyone who dislikes

climbing stepladders, by using a pulley wheel. Fix the pulley wheel to the ceiling as described for a cup hook. Thread strong cord through the pulley and attach one end to the basket. The other end of the cord should be fastened to a special cleat fixed in a convenient position on the wall. At watering time the basket can be lowered and raised by the cord.

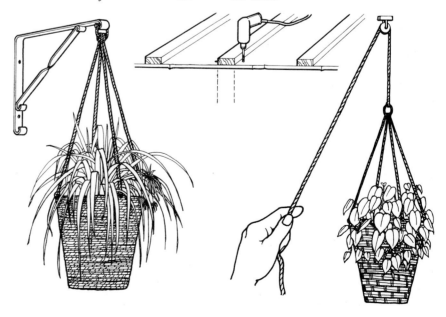

## THE KITCHEN GARDEN

**Apply a nitrogenous fertilizer** such as nitrate of soda or sulphate of ammonia to spinach and early cauliflowers if they look as though they need a boost.

**Brussels sprouts** should be transplanted to their final positions during the next few weeks. Water the bed thoroughly the day before lifting the plants if the ground is at all dry.

**Cabbage root fly** can devastate any members of the cabbage family—the signs of attack include poor growth, wilting and a blue tinge to the leaves. When pulled up the plants will be found to be almost rootless; white maggots may be visible. Burn affected plants and be sure to use a soil insecticide around the other plants and in the planting hole when transplanting if the pest is active.

**Carrots** can still be sown.

**Celeriac** can be planted now, and will benefit from a mulch of well-rotted compost or manure.

**Lettuces** will tend to run to seed in dry weather, so keep well watered.

**Plant tomatoes** in mild areas if you are prepared to face the risk of possible

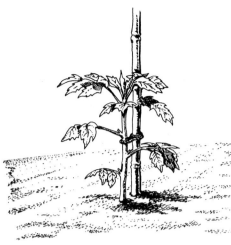

Tie tomato plants to stakes after planting.

frost damage, or can provide tall cloche protection for a few weeks.

**Sage** plants that have become leggy are best replaced by fresh ones. Cuttings of sideshoots with a heel will root easily.

**Sow ridge cucumbers and vegetable marrows** in warm areas, covering the cucumbers with a jam-jar or cloche.

**Sow runner beans outdoors** if you are willing to take a small risk of losses from late frosts, or can provide protection if necessary.

**Swedes** should be sown now in cold areas, choosing a resistant variety if the land is affected by club-root.

**Sweetcorn** can be sown now in favourable districts, but really benefits from cloche protection.

**Water** salad crops and carrots generously if the weather is dry.

### FRAMES AND CLOCHES

**Melons and cucumbers** can be planted in frames.

**Tomatoes** can be planted under cloches. Large barn cloches will give protection for the crucial period, but you can buy tall 'tomato cloches' in which they can be grown for the summer.

### FRUIT

**Gooseberries** will be enlarging now and it may be possible to take a first picking of green fruit for cooking. Treat this as a thinning process, leaving most of the berries to mature.

**Spray gooseberries** if there is evidence of mildew on shoots or there are caterpillars of gooseberry sawflies or magpie moths.

**Water** generously trees and bushes planted this year if the soil is at all dry.

## THE FLOWER GARDEN

**Cutworms**, the larvae of several different moths, are laid as eggs during June. They hatch 10–14 days later and the caterpillars first feed on the lower leaves and on the stems and roots, causing the plants to wilt and topple over. Use a suitable soil insecticide as soon as you suspect this pest. Keep the soil well hoed and pull up all weeds which might act as host plants to the cutworms.

**Cytisus** (broom) is easily increased by pegging low-growing shoots into the soil. Within a year they will have rooted and can be cut from the parent plant.

**Dahlia borders** should be prepared for planting during the next few weeks. Break down the soil with a fork and rake in a dressing of bonemeal at 140 g per m² (4 oz per sq yd).

**Dead-head bulbs** that have finished

flowering, so that the plants put all their endeavours into forming strong bulbs for next year.

**Dead-head rhododendrons** as soon as the flowers have started to fall. Cut off the flower stems completely with a sharp pair of secateurs. It is usually only practical to do this to the large-flowered types.

**Polyanthus seedlings** can be pricked out now into a sheltered and shady seed-bed.

**Roses** will need regular spraying throughout the summer to control sawflies and caterpillars.

**Spray roses** if there are any signs of greenfly or other aphids. If black-spot is a problem, save time and effort by using combined spray. Do not, however, mix insecticides and fungicides yourself unless the manufacturer advises it.

**Sprouted dahlia tubers** can be set out in the garden in *mild* areas with light, dry soil, but in very wet or cold areas wait for a further few weeks.

## THE GREENHOUSE

**Cinerarias and calceolarias** can be sown now to provide flowers next winter and spring.

**Cyclamen** can also be sown now, spacing the seeds about 2.5 cm (1 in) apart and covering with about 3 mm ($\frac{1}{8}$ in) of compost. They will probably take three or four weeks to germinate at 15°C (60°F).

**Cyclamen that have finished flowering** should be rested by gradually withholding water.

**Freesias and lachenalias** that have finished flowering should be dried off. When the garden frames are clear of bedding plants the pots can stand in the frames for the summer.

**Grape vines** should have lateral shoots pinched back two leaves beyond the first trusses. Tie in fruiting shoots to the wires and prevent the fruit actually touching the glass.

A variegated sansevieria, commonly known as mother-in-law's tongue.

**Hydrangea cuttings** can still be taken. Use a hormone rooting powder and insert them in a sandy compost. They are likely to root within about three weeks. Keep ring culture aggregate damp at all times.

**Plant tomatoes** in an unheated greenhouse unless the weather is very cold.

**Rhoicissus cuttings** will root easily if taken now.

**Scindapsus** can be repotted now, using a peat-based compost. If the plants are too large, divide them and remove unwanted basal shoots to use as cuttings.

**Variegated sansevierias** can be divided if the plants are large. The leaf cuttings usually taken will produce plain-leaved plants without the variegation.

**Water hanging baskets** regularly— twice a day if necessary. Their exposed position means that they will dry out rapidly on a warm day. There is also little reserve of soil for the number of plants usually grown in a basket.

## WEEKEND PROJECTS

### Make a peat garden

By conventional means it is almost impossible to grow acid soil-loving plants, like rhododendrons, azaleas and heathers, on chalky, heavy clay and other types of alkaline soils. An area of acid soil is required and a solution to the problem is to make a raised bed peat garden using peat blocks to form a retaining wall to hold the lime-free soil in place. Because the peat garden is above the surrounding ground, the soil in the raised bed will tend to remain acid for a long period.

Site the garden in a sheltered and shady spot, but away from surface rooting trees, like birches, which can rob the garden of moisture. A corner position is often ideal because it is economical in blocks if the backing walls are suitable for supporting the back of a raised bed.

Dig the area where the raised bed will grow and remove all traces of weed roots at the same time. Soak the peat blocks in water before laying them in the manner of a conventional dry stone retaining wall. Lay the largest blocks first, setting them into the ground and sloping them back slightly to give the wall an inward tilt for strength. Subsequent blocks are laid in brickwork fashion, set back slightly from the previously laid blocks. There is no need to put soil between the blocks. If necessary the blocks can be cut to shape at corners and so on using a wood saw.

As each two or three courses of blocks are laid, lime-free soil mixed with at least its own volume of peat, leafmould, shredded bark and sharp sand should be filled in behind them. If lime-free soil is not available, it is

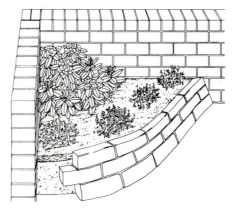

possible to acidify alkaline soil by sprinkling it sparingly with flowers of sulphur. After each treatment, test the acidity with a soil pH test kit. (This treatment will only have a temporary effect.) Tread the soil firm as it is filled in. The finished bed should be about 30 cm (12 in) deep and topped with a 5 cm (2 in) thick layer of pure peat or shredded bark. After planting acid-loving plants, water them thoroughly, and make sure the bed is always kept well-watered.

## THE KITCHEN GARDEN

**Celery** can be planted out in favourable areas, but wait a couple of weeks in colder districts. Buy plants if you did not sow your own in the greenhouse.

**Leeks** sown earlier in seedbeds can be transplanted to their final positions any time during the next few weeks. Use a dibber to make the 15 cm (6 in) deep holes to drop the plant into. Do not refill with soil, just water in to settle the soil around the roots.

**Lettuces** can be successionally sown.

**Onion fly and carrot fly** can be active at this time. Use a soil insecticide after thinning or if there is any evidence of these pests.

**Peas and spinach** can still be sown for a late crop.

**Potatoes** should be earthed up regularly, using a draw-hoe to pull soil up around the stems.

**Radishes** sown in the summer tend to bolt (run to seed) and are often unsuccessful, but you should still be able to make a sowing now without difficulty.

**Sweetcorn** can be planted out now.

**Thin maincrop carrots**, dusting the row with a soil insecticide afterwards as a precaution against carrot fly.

**Turnips and kohl-rabi** can still be sown.

### FRAMES AND CLOCHES

**Cloched strawberries** should be ventilated on warm days, but do not let birds get in otherwise they may strip many of the berries.

**Melons** in frames may need hand pollinating if they do not set fruit on their own. Pinch off a male flower and tap the pollen over the female flower (this will have a swelling at the back).

**Peppers** (capsicums) can be planted out beneath cloches or in frames in all but cold areas.

**Tomatoes** can be planted out under cloches if not already done.

### FRUIT

**Apple mildew** can be a problem at this time. Use a systemic fungicide.

**Net strawberries** if this has not already been done.

**Spray pears** with a fungicide to control scab once the petals fall.

**Thin early apples.**

**Thin out raspberry canes** if they are becoming overcrowded. Six to eight canes is enough for one plant. Remove all suckers appearing some distance away from the plant.

## THE FLOWER GARDEN

**Check standard roses** to ensure they are well secured to their stakes. Use proprietary ties or even old tights around the stem to prevent chaffing against the stake.

**Cytisus** (broom) tends to get very leggy if left unpruned. After flowering cut back slightly, but never into old wood.

**Daffodil bulbs** can be lifted and divided every three or four years. Dry off the bulbs after the foliage has died down, remove the loose skins, leaves and roots, and place them in a dry, vermin-proof shed until they can be replanted in the autumn.

**Dahlia plants** can now be planted in mild areas, but in cold districts it is best to wait another few weeks. They will not tolerate frost. Bedding types can be set about 45 cm (1½ ft) apart, but all others are best spaced 0.9–1.2 m (3–4 ft) apart.

**Hardy primulas** such as *P. denticulata* can be divided as soon as they have finished flowering. The crowns can be split into several parts.

**Tie delphiniums** to their supports. The shoots are easily damaged by wind and heavy rain.

**Michaelmas daisies and delphiniums** sometimes form large clumps. They will often be better if you thin the shoots. Young delphiniums for exhibition are often thinned to just one shoot to a plant, whereas two-year-old plants are left with three shoots and three-year-old plants with five or six shoots.

**Sweet peas** should never be allowed to become dry. They will also respond to a well-balanced liquid feed.

### THE WATER GARDEN

**Fish** will need more food during the summer, but do not give them more than they can eat in 10 minutes.

### LAWNS

**Water** lawns when the weather is dry, preferably using a sprinkler.

## THE GREENHOUSE

**Arum lilies** can be stood outside, but keep them watered and fed until the foliage dies down.

**Aubergines** will need misting with water twice a day to keep the atmosphere humid and to discourage red spider mites. Do not allow a plant to carry more than about four fruits.

**Azaleas** that have provided winter and spring flowers are best put out for the summer. Choose a sheltered and lightly shaded position and bury the pots to the rim. Keep moist but do not use hard water.

**Cacti** can often be raised from cuttings taken during the next few months.

**Chrysanthemums** for growing in pots can be moved into 20–23 cm (8–9 in) pots. After potting, water and stand the plants outside.

**Feed pot-plants** regularly once the roots fill the pots. Follow the manufacturer's instructions.

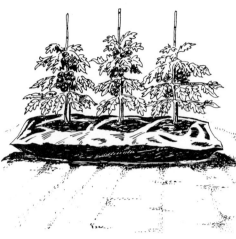

**Hydrangea cuttings** that are well rooted can be potted up individually into small pots.

**Orchids** will need shading during the summer months. Roller blinds are the best method, but a white shading wash is also satisfactory.

**Plants in growing bags** must be checked daily to ensure that the compost does not dry out. An automatic watering tray designed for growing bags is useful if you do not use a trickle watering system.

**Slugs** will often invade a greenhouse, where conditions are usually to their liking. Use a slug bait to control them.

**Stem-rooting lilies** being grown in pots may need a top-dressing of compost. Space should have been left for this.

**Tidy up the greenhouse** now that there is more space with bedding plants being moved into frames. There is often a lot of debris left after a period of greenhouse activity, and this should be cleared up before it encourages pests and diseases. Hygiene is an important part of greenhouse management.

**WEEKEND PROJECTS**

## Make a jungle stump or bromeliad tree

In their native jungle habitat, urn plants, or more properly bromeliads, literally grow on trees. You can use this habit to good effect indoors by making a bromeliad tree. All you need is a suitable piece of tree branch with a number of smaller branch forks to which the urn plants can be wired.

The branch must be held upright using timber struts (as often found in a rustic bird-table) or by standing the branch in a large tub or half barrel and surrounding it with large pebbles or more permanently by setting it into a weak cement mortar. In the latter case, decorate the surface of the mortar with pebbles, or cover it with peat compost in which houseplants can be grown.

Urn plants have quite small root systems, so knock them out of their pots, remove some of the surplus compost and then wrap the root ball in moist sphagnum moss. Attach the moss-covered root system to a fork in the tree using fine plastic mesh stapled to the branch, or by criss-crossing nylon fishing line or plastic-covered wire over the moss. Try to keep the plants as upright as possible because to water them you need to keep the 'urn' full of water.

Keep the tree in a light place, such as close to a patio door or, ideally, in a warm conservatory or sun room.

Water the plants very carefully so as not to damage surrounding carpets, and be careful of decorations when the moss is sprayed with water daily.

Suitable urn plants for the tree treatment include aechmeas, cryptanthus, neoregelia, tillandsia and vriesea. If you can get hold of some Spanish moss, drape if over the branches to get an authentic jungle look. In this case, though, the tree must be in a conservatory or there will not be enough humidity to make the 'moss' flourish.

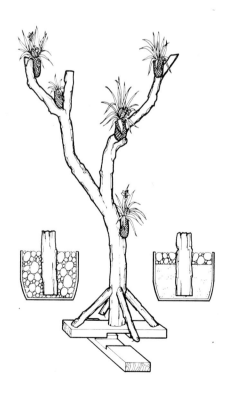

## THE KITCHEN GARDEN

**Beetroot** for storing should be sown now, soaking the seed for a few hours first.

**Endive** can be sown for an early crop.

**French beans** for the main crop can be sown safely in most areas.

**Gather broad beans** and early peas.

**Hoe** between rows after thinning or walking on the soil for any other reason.

**'Japanese' onions** are likely to be ready for harvesting any time now. As it is not wise to attempt to overwinter these in store, lift some to use even if they have not fully ripened. You will be using them when stored bulbs are expensive to buy and clearing the ground for a late sowing of turnips or carrots.

**Outdoor tomatoes** can be planted out.

**Plant winter greens.** If you are buying in the plants, be sure to dip the roots in a club-root preparation. If you have your own growing in a seedbed, water thoroughly the day before if the ground

is dry, and lift with a fork.

**Runner beans** should be safe if the seeds are sown outdoors now without protection, but be prepared to cover them (with old newspapers if necessary) if a late frost occurs.

**Sow marrows** if not already done.

**Thin** all seedlings sown recently before

they become too crowded, but always do it in stages rather than attempting to thin to the final spacings initially.

## FRAMES AND CLOCHES

**Plant frame cucumbers** as space becomes available in frames.

**Plant ridge cucumbers and sweetcorn** in cold districts, covering the plants with cloches if these are available.

**Under cloches** it should be safe to plant aubergines and capsicums.

## FRUIT

**Raspberry beetles** are the insects responsible for maggoty raspberries. Spray or dust with a suitable insecticide about ten days after full bloom. Repeat later as the manufacturer suggests.

**Wall-trained** plums that have set a heavy crop will have larger and better-shaped fruit if you thin them to about 7.5 cm (3 in) apart.

## THE FLOWER GARDEN

**Aphids** (greenfly or blackfly) are a common problem at this time. Use a suitable insecticide at regular intervals to control them. On suitable plants a systemic preparation is likely to give more effective control.

**Hardy perennials** can be sown now in a prepared seedbed.

**Outdoor-flowering chrysanthemums** must have the terminal shoot nipped out by the end of the first week in June. Nip out the shoot by bending it sideways. It is best done when the plants are 15–20 cm (6–8 in) high. Some of the large-flowered greenhouse varieties should also be 'stopped', but consult a specialist book or catalogue as much depends on variety.

**Philadelphus** (mock orange) shrubs can easily be increased by taking half-ripe 10 cm (4 in) cuttings from now until the end of July. Insert them in sandy soil in a propagator with bottom heat.

**Plant out bedding plants** in all but cold districts.

**Prune forsythias** if this has not been

done. Cut out flowered shoots back to young sideshoots. At the same time, cut out all dead, thin and straggly shoots.

**Prune** *Kerria japonica* (Jew's mallow) after flowering. Cut out shoots that have flowered.

**Remove faded pyrethrum flowers** as this will encourage a further flush of bloom later in the year.

**Cotoneasters** can be increased by taking

10–15 cm (4–6 in) half-ripe cuttings from now to the end of July. Root them in a garden frame. Sow biennials such as Canterbury bells, wallflowers and sweet williams, that need a long growing season, but wait for another few weeks before sowing forget-me-nots and Brompton stocks.

**Tulips** that have been lifted and set temporarily in a trench can be lifted again and the bulbs placed in boxes. Remove the stems and leaves, and store them in a cool place until planting time next autumn.

## THE ROCK GARDEN

**Dead-head** *Iberis sempervirens* regularly to extend the flowering period. Increase aethionemas and helianthemums from softwood cuttings of non-flowering shoots, preferably rooting them in a garden frame.

## FRAMES AND CLOCHES

**Pansies** for flowering next March can be sown now in garden frames.

## THE GREENHOUSE

**Arum lilies** in pots should be rested if this has not already been started. Lay the pots on their sides beneath the staging.

**Asparagus densiflorus** (usually known as *A. sprengeri*), the asparagus fern, will need plenty of water during the summer. Keep it moist and not too warm.

**Hydrangeas** in pots will need 'stopping' if the plants are growing strongly. Nip out the terminal shoots to encourage the development of sideshoots.

**Orchids** require a moist atmosphere. If you are growing these plants, damp down and mist the plants with water twice a day during hot weather.

*Philodendron scandens* (sweetheart plant) and *Ficus benjamina* (weeping fig) can be increased from 10 cm (4 in) cuttings inserted in a peaty compost. They should root quickly if you can provide a temperature of 15°C (60°F).

**Prick off cinerarias** sown earlier.

**Regal pelargoniums** can be propagated from cuttings.

They will root easily in a peat-based compost.

**Repot** any plants that have become too large for their pots (if in doubt, knock them out of the pot and see if roots are densely packed in the compost).

**Repot** cyclamen into their final pots. Use John Innes potting compost No. 2, and stand them in a cool part of the greenhouse, shaded from strong sunlight.

**Sow cinerarias** now for a bright spring display in a frostproof greenhouse.

**Tuberous-rooted begonias** have two small single female flowers behind the behind the large double male one. Pinch out these 'wing' buds at an early stage.

**Water gloxinias and African violets** (saintpaulias) carefully, trying to keep water off the leaves, which may develop white blotches if they get splashed in bright weather.

**Winter cherries** (*Solanum capsicastrum*) can be put in the garden frame for the summer, but make sure they do not dry out.

---

**WEEKEND PROJECTS**

### Make a pergola

The instructions here show how to make a rustic pergola, but a similar technique can be used to make a pergola from square sawn timber. In the latter case, preservative treated larch as sold for fencing is ideal. Various poles can be used for a rustic pergola, but the best are peeled chestnut poles, used for fencing and as tree stakes.

The uprights and main horizontal poles should be 7.5–10 cm (3–4 in) in diameter. The cross pieces can be about 5 cm (2 in) in diameter. The pergola should have at least 2.1 m (7 ft) headroom, and the uprights should be long enough to allow at least 45 cm (1½ ft) in the ground.

Arrange the uprights so they are about 2.4 m (8 ft) apart along the length of the pergola and about 1.2 m (4 ft) apart in width to allow a pathway to be easily accommodated below the pergola even when the uprights are clothed in climbing plants. Make sure the lower 60 cm (2 ft) portion of each upright is soaked in wood preservative before erection.

With a string line to get the uprights in a straight row, dig out the post holes at least 45 cm (1½ ft) deep. Drop a half brick into each hole on which the base of each pole can be rested. Check that the top of each post is level with the rest and that the post is upright before filling in around each post with rammed hardcore. A collar of concrete at soil level can be used to hold each post, but it is not a good idea to set each post in solid concrete because this encourages water to collect in the socket around each post, hastening rotting.

Next the main horizontal poles are fitted. Using a saw and chisel, curve the top of each upright to make a simple saddle joint. Check that the poles are level and fix them using a waterproof wood glue, like Cascamite, and a long galvanized nail. The horizontal poles can be extended by making simple half-lap joints to coincide with upright positions.

The pergola is given rigidity by fixing diagonal bracing poles as shown in the diagram. Finally, fix the cross pieces by

simply glueing and nailing them in position. Treat the pergola with wood preservative and then varnish if required.

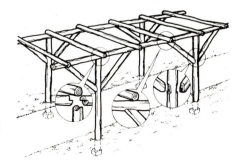

## THE KITCHEN GARDEN

**Apply a nitrogenous fertilizer**, such as nitrate of soda or sulphate of ammonia, to beetroot and onions after thinning.

**Brussels sprouts** should be moved to their final positions if not already done. Make sure the ground is moist before lifting the young plants.

**Cabbages** sown in seedbeds in April will now be ready for transplanting to their final positions. Water the bed thoroughly the day before lifting if the ground is dry.

**Carrots** can still be sown if you have space and should make reasonable roots by the end of the season—but you should not delay.

**Celery** can safely be planted now if not already done. Put down slug bait as a precaution.

**Cut cauliflowers, cabbages and lettuces.**

**Expose shallot bulbs** round the base to allow them to swell more freely and to encourage ripening.

**Lettuces** can be sown again for succession. Select varieties suitable for successional sowing—in the warmer weather germination is often more uncertain.

**Potatoes** may need further earthing up—use a draw-hoe to pull more soil around the stems.

**Sow chicory** on rich ground manured for a previous crop.

**Sow parsley** for succession.

**Stake runner beans** if this has not been done.

**Watch for blackfly** on broad beans and spray at first sign of an infestation.

**Water potatoes,** beans and peas generously if the weather is dry.

### FRAMES AND CLOCHES

**Frame cucumbers** that have had their growing tips pinched out will be forming sideshoots, and these should now be trained to each corner of the frame.

Those under cloches should only be allowed two sideshoots and one trained in either direction.

**Melons** should be planted in frames if not already done (only one to a frame). If they have been planted earlier pinch out the growing tip just beyond the fifth or sixth good leaf (four sideshoots will be trained to the corners of the frame).

**Remove cloches** from strawberries once they have finished fruiting. Weed the row, hoe round the plants, and water them. This will help them revive and make stronger plants for next year.

**Syringe cucumbers** with water occasionally.

**Stack cloches** away if they are not in use. Most kinds will stack neatly on end and by 'nesting' them they will take up less room.

### FRUIT

**Apricots** are sometimes infested with aphids at this time. Spray with an insecticide at the first sign.

**Summer-prune gooseberries** by removing the ends of sideshoots more than 15 cm (6 in) long, cutting back to about 7.5 cm (3 in).

**Water strawberries** generously if the weather is at all dry.

## THE FLOWER GARDEN

**Antirrhinums** infected with rust can be sprayed from now until the end of August using a suitable fungicide. If you are troubled with antirrhinum rust disease, make a note to choose rust-resistant varieties next year.

**Ants** often appear on plants suddenly. They are usually in search of honeydew, which is secreted by aphids. Spray with a suitable insecticide and use an ant bait if necessary.

**Disbud exhibition roses** to encourage big blooms. Remove all flower buds around the central terminal one, snapping them off sideways.

**Flea beetles** often attack wallflower seedlings. Spray or dust with an insecticide as soon as the tiny holes in the leaves are noticed.

**Plant out half-hardy annuals** if this has not already been done and the weather is not too cold or wet.

**Propagate honeysuckle** (lonicera) from 10 cm (4 in) cuttings inserted in a propagator. You can take them from now until the end of August.

**Pyrethrums** can be divided now if the clumps have become too large.

**Ulex europaeus** (gorse) can be clipped back lightly after flowering to encourage shoots to develop from around the base.

### THE ROCK GARDEN

**Propagate** phlox, arabis, aubrieta, and mossy saxifrages any time during the next few months.

### LAWNS

**Mow regularly.** If the grass is left to become too long, it is very difficult to cut. The mowings can be placed on the compost heap if the lawn has not recently been treated with a hormone weedkiller.

**Trim lawn edges** every week to keep them looking neat and tidy. Pick up the grass clippings afterwards to give a neat appearance to the lawn.

## THE GREENHOUSE

**Cacti** will need more water now.
**Melons** like a humid atmosphere, so keep the soil and atmosphere moist.
**Move established cyclamen into a cold-frame.** Shade them from strong sunlight and syringe with water morning and evening.
**Pests and diseases** are always likely to be a problem in the warm environment of a greenhouse. Make a point of looking for them occasionally. You will become more aware of the state of your plants and be able to control problems before they become serious.
**Prick off cineraria seedlings** into boxes or individual 7.5 cm (3 in) pots.
**Repot peperomias**, but be careful not to overpot as they often grow well in a small size. Use a peat-based compost.

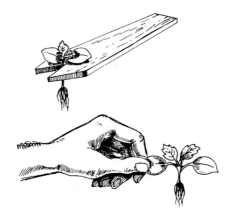

Seedlings should always be handled with care.

**Shade the greenhouse** if this has not already been done, and there are no greenhouse climbers to provide natural shade.
**Stake large-flowered begonias** as unobtrusively as possible. Feed the plants every 10–14 days.
**Thin grapes** any time during the next few weeks.
**Tomatoes** may need a little help if they are not setting fruit naturally. Although you can use sprays for the job, it may be sufficient to tap each plant from time to time, or you can use a fine brush to distribute pollen among the flowers.
**Ventilate** the greenhouse freely on hot days.
**Water hanging baskets** thoroughly every day, and feed once a week from now on.

### Make a bubble fountain

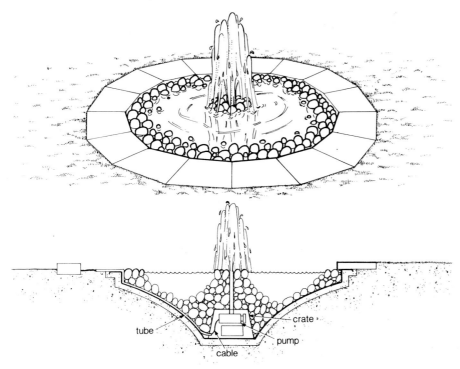

tube
crate
pump
cable

Irrespective of its shape or size, and whether round, square or oblong, a bubble fountain can be built using exactly the same method.

Excavate a saucer-shaped hole sloping down to a flat base which is 38 cm (15 in) square. The size of vinyl liner required is calculated by adding double the depth to each dimension. So, for a 180 × 60 cm (6 × 2 ft) pool you will need 240 × 120 cm (8 × 4 ft) liner—assuming the depth to be 30 cm (1 ft).

Before laying the liner remove any stones or sharp objects from the soil, which could damage the liner. Then lay sand on the base and sides.

This fountain uses cobbles laid in mortar on the liner. Tubing of 13 mm (½ in) diameter is embedded in the mortar for the pump cable to be passed through. A large planting crate is placed upside down over the pump and strainer both to protect the equipment and to support the loose cobbles in the centre.

A piece of 13 mm (½ in) tubing along with a flow adjuster is attached to the outlet of the pump and is cut off just below the water surface level. The required flow of water is then established with the flow adjuster before the final cobbles are placed around and over the crate to form the centre piece.

If preferred, weldmesh could be used to cover any recess with cobbles simply laid on top.

# Week 25

## THE KITCHEN GARDEN

**Cabbage root fly** can be a problem at this time. Burn affected plants (including the roots), then dust around remaining plants with a suitable soil insecticide.
**Finish cutting asparagus** and allow the plants to make foliage, otherwise the plants will not make good crowns for next year.
**Gather spinach** regularly to keep it cropping.
**Hoe** regularly to keep down weeds.
**Kale**, winter cauliflower and savoy cabbage seedlings sown in April or May should be ready for moving to their final positions. Water the ground thoroughly the day before lifting the young plants if it is at all dry.
**Leeks** can be planted out at any time now. Trim off the top few centimetres of leaves before you plant.
**Pinch out the tops of broad beans** in full flower, to deter blackfly.
**Pull radishes** and salad onions before they become too large.

**Runner beans** need a long growing season so they should be sown without delay if you do not already have them in. Alternatively you can buy plants and save yourself a week or two.
**Swedes** should be sown now in the milder districts. In cold areas they should already have been sown.
**Turnips and kohl-rabi** can be sown for successional cropping.

### FRAMES AND CLOCHES

**Cloches** can be removed from early-sown carrots if not already done, as they will not benefit from protection now.

### FRUIT

**Examine blackcurrants** for reversion disease if the bushes have been cropping poorly. Normal leaves have five sub-veins on both sides of the main vein, 'reverted' leaves have less than five. Dig up and burn affected bushes, although you can wait until you have picked any berries.
**Spray apples** against codlin moth. You will need to repeat the treatment in three weeks' time.
**Thin plums** if they have set a heavy crop and you want fruits of good size.

## THE FLOWER GARDEN

**Continue to hoe** regularly to keep down the weeds and to keep the borders looking neat.
**Dahlias** must be staked if this was not done at planting time. Set a firm stake by the side of each plant and use strong garden twine to secure the plant to the stake. Leave enough room for the stem to grow.
**Flag irises** that have finished flowering can be lifted and divided.
**Garryas** can be layered now.
**Hardy annuals** sown in May will need thinning to ensure that the seedlings do not overcrowd each other. Small types can be thinned to 10–12.5 cm (4–5 in) apart, medium ones to 20–30 cm (8–12 in), and tall-growing ones to 45 cm (1½ ft) or more.
**Increase garden pinks** by taking cuttings now.
**Outdoor chrysanthemums** will need feeding with a high-potash fertilizer now.
**Privet hedges** will need regular clipping to keep them tidy.

**Prune deutzias**, diervillas and escallonias as soon as the flowers fade.
**Roses** can be budded from June until early September, while the bark can easily be peeled from the wood beneath.

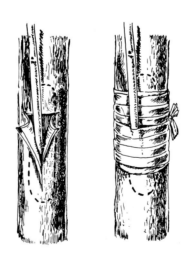

Budding roses (*see* p. 76).

### THE ROCK GARDEN

**Cut back** plants such as aubrieta, arabis, and perennial candytuft, if this has not been done. It will keep them under control and make the rock garden look tidier.
**Increase** *Haberlea ferdinandi-coburgii* during the next month. Take leaf cuttings from leaves from the centre of each rosette of leaves.
**Polygonum vacciniifolium** can be increased from stem cuttings taken any time until September.
**Sow seed** of rock plants now. Many kinds can be sown at this time; consult a good seed catalogue or sow your own seed as it ripens.

### LAWNS

**Mow** in a different direction occasionally. This will prevent ridges.
**Water** your lawn if there has been a prolonged dry spell. Give it a thorough soaking—enough to penetrate several centimetres.

## THE GREENHOUSE

**Carnations** are susceptible to red spider mites. Serious infestations produce webbing around the foliage, which may also become mottled. Misting the plants with water regularly will help, but do not hesitate to use a suitable systemic insecticide spray to control them.

**Continue to damp down** the greenhouse to maintain a humid atmosphere. Do it in the morning and afternoon on hot days, but not in late evening.

**Cucumbers** need to kept well watered. They also need a humid atmosphere. Damp down the greenhouse whenever possible. Feed the plants regularly with a proprietary liquid feed.

**Melons** that have reached the top wire need to have the tip of the growing shoot pinched out to encourage the development of lateral shoots.

**Pests and diseases** often start to build up during early summer. Watch out for them, especially on the undersides of leaves, and spray or fumigate at first sign.

**Pot cyclamen** already in small individual pots into their flowering pots—usually about 12.5 cm (5 in). Be careful not to bury the corm. Cyclamen can spend the summer in a garden frame. **Sow greenhouse calceolarias** to flower next spring.

**Sow** *Primula malacoides* now to produce plants for flowering next year. Sow thinly in boxes or pots.

**Stake and tie** plants in pots if they become too large and floppy.

**Streptocarpus** make attractive greenhouse plants—especially the newer hybrids. They can be sown now to flower next year.

**Tomatoes** will be growing rapidly now. On plants given an early start, the fruits will be ripening and should be picked regularly. If some of the fruits show an area of hard, green skin on top, it is likely to be a disorder called 'greenback'. Use a high potash feed and shade the plants from strong sunlight.

**Tradescantias and zebrinas** will root easily from cuttings taken any time during the next few months. Insert three or four cuttings around the edge of a 10-cm (4-in) pot. Grow on several to a pot; they will soon make a full display.

## WEEKEND PROJECTS

### Make a bird-bath feature

By attracting birds to the garden a bird-bath can bring a lot of pleasure, and in addition if it is properly constructed it will be a focal point in its own right. A good example of this is shown in the photograph. Here a bird-bath with an eye-catching surround has been built in a corner of a lawn close to the house so that the birds can be watched easily from indoors.

The pedestal for the bath is made from reconstructed stone and it stands on a reconstructed stone plinth. A bird-bath like this can be bought, of course, but it is possible to cast one from concrete using suitable moulds, such as a dustbin lid for the bath part. The concrete can be made to look like stone by colouring the cement with colouring powder. It is best to buy the pedestal—a pilaster from concrete balustrading is suitable. The plinth can be moulded in a suitable box.

To make the surrounding area, mark out a circle in the grass. Dig out the soil in a 23 cm (9 in) wide ring around the circumference of the circle to a depth of about 15 cm (6 in). Put a 7.5 cm (3 in) deep layer of rubble in the base and bang it down. Scatter some sand on the surface of the rubble and then lay a ring of bricks around the circle as shown in the photograph.

The rest of the area can have the turf lifted to a depth of 7.5 cm (3 in). At the centre the soil is dug out to a depth of 15 cm (6 in) and then filled up with rubble to act as a firm foundation for the pedestal.

The soil in the remaining part of the area is forked over, trodden firm, and then covered with a 7.5 cm (3 in) deep layer of washed pebbles or small stone chippings, which are also spread between the bricks.

The chippings help to stop weeds from growing and also can be planted with clump-forming rock garden plants, like saxifrages.

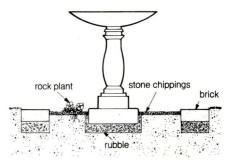

rock plant  stone chippings  brick

rubble

## THE KITCHEN GARDEN

**Cabbage white butterflies** can be around in force, and once their caterpillars hatch they can soon ruin a crop of cabbages or related plants. Spray or dust early with a suitable insecticide.

**Cauliflower curds** should be protected from sun or rain by bending the centre leaves over.

**Chicory** can be sown now if you choose suitable varieties. French beans can still be sown, but if you leave it any later you may need to provide cloche protection at the end of the season.

**Lettuces** can still be sown to provide succession, but you should choose a variety suitable for autumn maturing.

**Parsnips and celery** are often attacked by leaf miner maggots, which cause unsightly white tunnels in the leaves. Use a suitable insecticide to control them.

**Tomatoes** should be tied in to the stake regularly, and any sideshoots removed from non-bush varieties.

**Water** if the weather is dry, but avoid just wetting the surface—you should leave a sprinkler on or apply about 2

gallons to a square yard if using a watering-can. Celery and runner beans particularly benefit from generous amounts of water, as do peas during and after flowering.

**When using insecticides or fungicides** always make a note of the interval which should elapse between spraying and harvesting.

### FRAMES AND CLOCHES

**Stack away cloches** if they are not needed. Most will stack on end, but it is always wise to tie them together and fix them firmly in a sheltered place so that they do not blow over in strong winds.

### FRUIT

**Dust raspberries** with a suitable insecticide against raspberry beetle maggots.

**Gooseberry mildew** can become troublesome at this time, and it is not easy to control. Try a systemic fungicide —but even then you will probably have to repeat the dose later (but never eat the fruit unless the time to eating stated on the bottle has elapsed).

**Thin** crowded or badly placed branches of stone fruits. If you pinch out the tips of most sideshoots of trained plums and apricots you should encourage fruiting spurs to form.

**Tortrix moth caterpillars** may need to be controlled on apples, but an insecticide used against codlin moth is also likely to control these.

## THE FLOWER GARDEN

**Black spot** is a serious disease of roses, causing characteristic black spots on the leaves. Spray the plants with a suitable fungicide as soon as the spots are noticed, and repeat a fortnight later. If you have had trouble in previous seasons, it is probably worth spraying as a routine precaution anyway.

**Continue to feed chrysanthemums** with a liquid fertilizer.

**Dead-head** all plants with flowers that have faded. This will make them look tidier, and sometimes encourages the development of further flowers.

**Half-hardy annuals** of a floppy habit, such as gaillardias, can be supported by inserting twiggy pea sticks around them. The sticks will soon be covered by flowers.

**Herbaceous borders** should be weeded and hoed regularly. In very dry weather herbaceous plants will also respond to watering, but you must apply enough to soak well into the soil. Just dampening

the surface soil may do more harm by causing the roots to search for moisture near the surface rather than exploring deeper.

**Look for rose suckers** growing up from below soil level. Remove soil from around them and cut each sucker off close to the main stem.

**Prune** *Clematis montana*. Thin out overcrowded stems, and if the climber is overcrowded cut some stems back to the base.

**Sow biennials** if not already done, including Brompton stocks and forget-me-nots.

### THE ROCK GARDEN

**Cut back aubrieta** after flowering, to keep the growth compact. Do not trim back plants growing on a wall.

**Arabis** (white rock cress) should have dead flower heads removed. Peg down the shoots into the soil to keep the growth neat and tidy.

### LAWNS

**Keep the edges trimmed** with long-handled shears or a mechanical edge-trimmer. It can make all the difference to the finish of a lawn.

## THE GREENHOUSE

**Air layer** *Ficus elastica* (rubber plants) if they have become leggy at the base.

**Begonias** in flower now should not be allowed to dry out, otherwise buds are likely to drop off.

**Cacti** require plenty of air during the summer, so ventilate the greenhouse freely without creating strong draughts. Cacti will stand plenty of full sun, but in a mixed house you will probably have to use some shading.

**Climbers** such as hoyas and plumbagos will be growing strongly and may need support. Try to ensure they do not cast too much shade over other plants.

**Divide African violets** (saintpaulias) that have finished flowering. Only do this if the plants have become large.

**Foliage houseplants** seriously infected by pests can be held upside down in a bucket of insecticidal solution. Do not do this to plants with hairy leaves, and always wear rubber gloves.

**Feed foliage pot-plants** regularly.

**Freesia corms** in pots that have been dried off can be separated from the compost and stored ready for repotting later in the year.

**Gloxinias and begonias** raised from seed sown earlier in the year can be moved on into larger pots.

**Heaters** should not be needed now unless it turns unusually cold. Clean out paraffin heaters and put them away in a dry, safe place for the summer. Empty any paraffin out of them first. It is worth making sure other types of heaters are satisfactory, and putting any repairs in hand now.

**Pot cinerarias** into individual pots as soon as they can be handled safely if this has not been done.

**Saxifraga stolonifera** (mother of thousands) is easily propagated by pegging its little plantlets into pots of compost. They will soon form roots.

**Spray chrysanthemums** regularly to control aphids and capsid bags.

**The Christmas cactus** (*Zygocactus truncatus*, otherwise known as *Schlumbergera truncata*) can be propagated now from segments of the flattened stems.

## WEEKEND PROJECTS

### Make a fruit cage

By protecting soft fruit bushes from fruit and bud-eating birds, it is possible to get twice as much fruit from crops like gooseberries, currants and raspberries. Soft fruits are long-lasting crops so the best way to protect them from birds is to build a semi-permanent fruit cage covered with plastic bird protection netting. The usual mesh size of this is about 19 mm ($\frac{3}{4}$ in) square. The netting is normally supplied in 2, 4, or 8 m widths, so mark out the area to be protected in units of 2 m (6 ft 6 in) to make it easy to spread the netting over the supporting posts.

Posts are needed at each corner of the area and at 2 m intervals around the sides. The tops of the posts should be about 2 m above ground level to make it easy to walk into the cage.

A quick way to support a fruit cage is to use stout bamboo canes with an upturned jam jar over the top of each cane to prevent the canes from pushing through the netting.

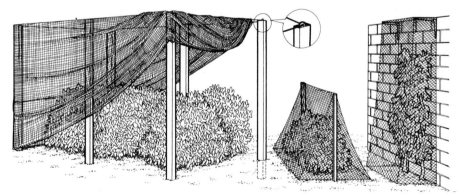

A better method is to use chestnut or sawn fencing posts to support the netting. Before use the posts should be treated with wood preservative. Make sure they are set at least 60 cm (2 ft) into the soil and while they are held upright pack around the base with rammed hardcore. To prevent the netting from sagging between the posts, stretch plastic-covered or galvanized wires between the post tops holding this in place with wire staples.

Next the netting is pulled over the supporting framework and allowed to fall over the sides. Lengths of netting can be joined together by lacing with rot-proof twine. Get the netting tight at the top and tie it to the line wires. At the bottom edge, simply bury the netting in the soil.

Make sure that joins in the sides are properly laced, except at the entrance point where the netting can be overlapped and secured with clothes pegs.

## THE KITCHEN GARDEN

**Cabbages** sown on prepared seedbeds in May should be ready for transplanting. Water the ground thoroughly before lifting the plants if it is at all dry.

**Celery** should be earthed up in stages, starting any time in the next couple of weeks. You may prefer to use collars (corrugated paper is a popular material) before drawing up the soil. A light dressing of sulphate of ammonia or nitrate of soda will give them a boost.

**Continue to plant winter greens** as you clear ground of early crops. It is best to choose showery weather, but if the weather is dry and settled do not delay planting for too long but water in thoroughly.

**Continue to thin** seedlings—those sown last month will soon be ready for an initial thinning.

**Feed tomatoes** regularly using a tomato fertilizer. Repeat liquid feeds every week (or as the manufacturer suggests).

**Hoe regularly** between rows to keep down weeds. Leeks sown in March can

be planted any time during the next couple of weeks.

**Potatoes** are particularly at risk from blight from now on. Be prepared to spray at the first sign of brown patches on the leaves.

**Turnips** for pulling to eat fresh should be sown for the last time during the next week.

### FRUIT

**Check plums** for silverleaf disease; you will see a tell-tale silvery sheen on the leaves (but do not confuse it with mildew, which produces a white mealy growth on the leaves). If you suspect the disease you must cut out and burn the affected branch well back into healthy wood. Paint with a wound paint.

**Finish thinning** apples and pears, reducing the fruit to one (at most two) on a spur.

**Strawberry runners** can be pegged down into pots of good soil plunged into the ground. It is best to use the plantlet nearest the parent plant and to pinch off the runners beyond these unless you need a lot of new plants.

**Summer-prune wall-trained cherries and plums** during the next few weeks. Just shorten the sideshoots that have grown since May by about one-third, but do not touch the leaders on main branches. Spread the work over the next month so that the tree does not receive a check to growth.

## THE FLOWER GARDEN

**Chimonanthus** (wintersweet) can be increased from half-ripe cuttings inserted in a sandy compost in a propagator.

**Chrysanthemums** should be watered regularly unless the weather is damp.

**Earwigs** can be troublesome, chewing and tearing the leaves and petals of many plants, including dahlias. An insecticidal dust or spray can be used, but among dahlias you can easily use pots filled with straw upturned on top of the stakes as traps.

**Layer border carnations.** Select strong, healthy, shoots.

**Early-flowering chrysanthemums** will need support, as their stems are easily broken by rain and wind.

**Mulch** plants such as dahlias with grass cuttings to help conserve moisture

in the soil. Try to water the soil beforehand.

### THE ROCK GARDEN

**Alyssum saxatile** is best cut back hard after flowering to retain a compact habit.

**Divide Anemone nemorosa** now, or any time during the next few months.

**Pulsatilla vulgaris** can be increased from root cuttings about 2.5 cm (1 in) long taken during the next few weeks.

### THE WATER GARDEN

**Remove floating debris** on the surface of the pool by over-filling it with water so that it is washed over the sides.

**Waterlily beetles** can also be a pest at this time when their larvae chew holes in the leaves. Treat as suggested for

waterlily blackfly below.

**Waterlily blackfly** can become a nuisance on various water plants, such as sagittarias, in warm weather. If you cannot dislodge them by submerging the leaves, use a jet of water. Once in the water the fish will do the rest. Do not use insecticides on water plants.

### FRAMES AND CLOCHES

**Cyclamen** in frames should be sprayed with water daily during the summer, but do it in the morning or evening, not in the heat of midday.

**Plant anemones** in frames, or in a position where you can cover them with cloches from mid-September. They should provide invaluable cut flowers for the home in winter and spring.

## THE GREENHOUSE

**Cinerarias and calceolarias** can still be sown to provide a succession of bloom next spring.

**Cyclamen** growing in 7.5 cm (3 in) pots should be ready for moving into 12.5 cm (5 in) pots.

**Dead-head hydrangeas** that have flowered.

**Disbud tuberous-rooted begonias,** removing the small buds behind the main flowers.

**Late-flowering chrysanthemums** should now be moved outside if this has not already been done. Make sure they are well staked, and the flowering shoots securely tied to a stake.

**Limit the number of fruits on aubergines** and capsicums (sweet peppers), if you want good-sized fruit. With large-fruited aubergines, it may be best to settle for three or four fruits;

with peppers it is more a matter of judgement, as much depends on variety (some are prolific).

**Melons** with long lateral shoots should have them nipped out when they have developed five leaves. Melons are best restricted to three or four fruits.

**Perpetual-flowering carnations** raised from cuttings earlier in the year will need to be 'stopped' by removing the tip of each plant.

**Propagate** *Begonia rex* from leaf blade cuttings, selecting strong, healthy leaves.

**Regal pelargoniums** can be placed in a garden frame, or the pots plunged in the soil outside, once they have finished their peak of flowering and if you need the space.

**Whitefly** on tomatoes can soon build up to become a serious problem if not controlled quickly. Be prepared to repeat the treatment as the manufacturer instructs, as it is difficult to achieve complete control with one spray or fumigation.

## WEEKEND PROJECTS

### Make a planter from old car tyres

Scrap car tyres make long-lasting plant containers that cost next to nothing. A single tyre placed on the ground and filled with potting compost makes a good container to decorate an area of plain concrete. For larger plants and even small trees, or where you prefer to garden without stooping, pile three or four tyres one on top of the other. If the tyres are of differing sizes, pile them in a conical fashion with the smallest on the top of the pile.

With a sharp trimming knife, make holes through the tread at random intervals so that trailing plants can be inserted. Give the planter an attractive finish with a coat of paint in white or a colour of your choice—exterior wall paint is ideal, and exterior quality emulsion paint is also suitable.

For economy, rather than using expensive potting compost, fill the planter with a mixture consisting of 7 parts of good soil, 3 parts of peat or shredded bark, and 2 parts of clean, sharp sand—not soft yellow builders' sand plus a dusting of general fertilizer.

A 15 cm (6 in) layer of stones or broken bricks in the bottom of a large planter will improve drainage.

If you want to be even more creative, turn a tyre inside out and fit it to the rim of an old wheel to make an urn-like planter.

## THE KITCHEN GARDEN

**Blanch leeks** when they have made 10–15 cm (4–6 in) of growth if you are using corrugated cardboard collars. Cut the cardboard into strips about 10 cm (4 in) wide and 15–20 cm (6–8 in) long. Wrap them *loosely* round the base of the plants and tie them with raffia or twine, then draw soil about half-way up the collars.

**Early potatoes** may be ready for lifting soon. Lift just sufficient plants for immediate use and leave the rest to get bigger.

**Kohl-rabi** can still be sown for a late crop.

**Lettuces** can be sown again if you choose a suitable variety for maturing in the autumn.

**Ridge cucumbers** sometimes fail to set fruits at this time, the flowers just falling off without setting. If this happens it is worth pollinating the female flowers by hand—just pick off a fully opened male flower and gently tap it over a fully opened female (which will have a miniature cucumber-shaped swelling at the back).

**Runner beans** should not go short of water, and they will benefit from a thick mulch of well-rotted compost or manure applied after watering.

**Sow endive** for the maincrop supply.

**Sprouting broccoli** plants will probably be ready for moving to their final positions. Make sure the ground is moist before lifting them.

**Tomatoes** will benefit from having a few of the lower leaves removed if they are shading the lower trusses.

**Winter radishes** can be sown now. The large roots of this vegetable are left in the ground until required during the winter.

### FRUIT

**Propagate loganberries and blackberries** by tip layering. Bend over and peg into the soil the tips of vigorous and healthy canes produced this year. Lay the tip in a shallow trench about 15 cm (6 in) deep and cover with soil. If the cane tends to spring up you will have to peg it down with a cane or wire.

**Spray apples** again against codlin moth.

**Summer prune** trained apples and pears during the next few weeks, shortening newly-formed sideshoots by about one-third of their length. This will encourage spurs to form for next year's fruit.

## THE FLOWER GARDEN

**Biennials and perennials** sown in early July should be ready for pricking out into nursery beds. Make sure they they are well watered before and after transplanting.

**Choisya** (Mexican grange blossom) can be increased by softwood cuttings 10–15 cm (4–6 in) long, inserted in a garden frame.

**Floribunda roses** do not need to be disbudded, but remove faded flowers. When trusses have finished, they can be cut out completely.

**Forget-me-nots and Brompton stocks** can still be sown.

**Half-hardy annuals** sown late will need support from twiggy sticks. The annuals will grow through them and eventually cover the sticks.

**Outdoor hydrangeas** of the hortensia type can be treated with a colorant if blue flowers are required next year. Do not try to 'blue' white types.

**Polygonum baldshuanicum** (mile-a-minute or Russian vine) can be increased from half-ripe cuttings with a heel, taken during the next couple of months. Insert them in sandy soil in a propagator.

**Propagate** *Hibiscus syriacus* from half-ripe cuttings taken with a heel. Insert them in a garden frame.

**Spray roses** against mildew. This disease can be a problem during very damp spells.

## THE GREENHOUSE

**Coleus** should not be allowed to flower. Pick off any spikes that appear. Better still, nip them off in the bud.

**Cucumbers** will need plenty of water now. Do not allow the soil to dry out.

**Dracaenas and crotons** that have grown too high can be air layered.

**Feed gloxinias and fuchsias** to keep them growing strongly.

**Feed tomatoes regularly.** Use a high potash feed once the first truss of flowers has set.

**Fuchsias** should have long shoots pinched back to form bushy plants. Cuttings can be taken now, and if you choose unflowered shoots about 7.5 cm (3 in) long they should root quickly.

**Melons** will need generous watering and should be fed regularly. You can

Give liquid feed to tomatoes.

support developing fruits by suspending pieces of net or muslin to take the strain.

**Mignonette** can be sown now for winter flowering in pots.

**Pot on cinerarias** singly into 7.5 cm (3 in) pots as soon as they are large enough to be handled.

**Pot up** *Primula obconica* seedlings.

**Regal pelargoniums** can still be propagated.

**Stand suitable plants outside** for the summer if not already done. Indian azaleas, heaths and camellias are among the candidates for standing in a partially shaded place until September.

**Syringe winter cherries** (*Solanum capsicastrum*) every day to encourage the fruits to set.

**Thin grapes** in an unheated greenhouse.

---

**WEEKEND PROJECTS**

### Plan a patio

Essentially a patio is simply a paved area; however it should be planned and designed carefully so that it will be both interesting and functional.

*Materials*   Crazy paving is busy and eye-catching. Paving slabs can be square, shaped, hexagonal or round. Bricks are also popular.

As much or as little colour as desired can be used. However, excessive colour can be unsightly, whereas very little colour can be drab—especially where formal paving is used. If the patio is to have a curved border then crazy paving or bricks are easier to use.

*Shape*   A plain rectangular patio can be enlivened by including features such as differing levels, steps leading up or down to the garden, dwarf walls, raised planters, a water feature and so on. However the main function of the area is for sitting and relaxing, so it should not be overcrowded.

The minimum front to back depth of the patio should be 2.4 m (8 ft). This allows for furniture with room for people to pass by. The width is optional. If slabs are used then the final plan and

size should be calculated to using full-size slabs and so avoiding time-consuming and wasteful cutting work. The patio should slope away from the house—a fall of about 2.5 cm (1 in) in 3 m (10 ft) being sufficient for rainwater drainage. The finished surface should be at least 15 cm (6 in) below the house damp-proof course or airbricks.

Any steps should be broad and shallow with uniform treads and risers. Narrow, steep steps of inconsistent dimensions look unsightly and are dangerous.

Outdoor lighting enhances a patio at night and is a boon at party or barbecue time. Decide where you want your lighting points to be so that armoured outdoor cable can be laid below the patio.

Allow for in-ground planting by digging out 60 cm (2 ft) deep and square holes. Fork the base and fill the holes with good soil enriched with peat or shredded bark.

Any drain inspection cover that falls within the area must not be paved over. It can be hidden under a tub or urn, or by planting a horizontal growing conifer in a soil pocket beside the cover.

Finally, and most importantly, make

sure that the patio is sited where a large part of it will be in the sun for much of the day. Shade and privacy can be provided by a screen block wall, awning or pergola.

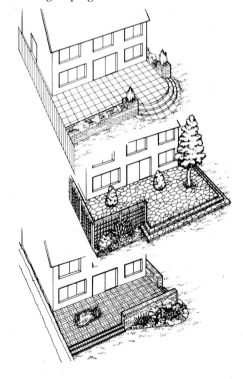

# Week 29

## THE KITCHEN GARDEN

**Cabbage white butterfly** caterpillars can cause extensive damage at this time. You can pick them off and drop them in a strong salt solution to kill them, but this is only practicable with a few plants and you will probably have to use an insecticidal dust or spray intended for caterpillars.

**Feed tomatoes** regularly, and remove any sideshoots.

**Hoe regularly** to keep down weeds.

**Lift autumn-sown onions** if this has not already been done.

**Potatoes** are still at risk from blight. Spray with a suitable fungicide at the first sign of attack.

**Turnips** for winter storage can be sown now. Choose a variety recommended for the purpose.

**Winter spinach** sown now should provide a crop in November. It is worth soaking the seeds in a saucer of water for a few hours before sowing.

### FRAMES AND CLOCHES

**Feed melons** regularly with a liquid fertilizer.

### FRUIT

**Early apples and pears** may be ready for eating about now. Only pick enough for immediate use as very early varieties do not keep well off the tree. Test an apple for ripeness by lifting it without twisting it off the branch. If it comes away with its stalk it is ready for picking. If it tears or is reluctant to come off, wait another week and try again. Test pears by pressing a few fruits gently at the stalk end; they will be ready if they yield to pressure.

**Gooseberry mildew** can be a serious and disfiguring disease. Cut off and burn shoots showing a bad attack of the whitish mealy growth, then spray with a suitable fungicide.

**Keep weeds down** around fruit trees by hoeing and mulching. Alternatively you can use one of the persistent weedkillers that kill off new weeds as they emerge but that will not harm the established trees.

**Pick blackberries**, ideally when the fruit is dry and not damp from dew or rain. Avoid damaging this year's new shoots as these will carry next year's fruit.

## THE FLOWER GARDEN

**Autumn-flowering bulbs** such as autumn crocuses, sternbergias and colchicums should be planted now if you get hold of them as early as this.

**Bud roses** if you fancy tackling this method of propagation.

**Dahlias** will be growing rapidly. If you want to encourage bushiness, pinch out the growing tip when the plants are about 35–45 cm (15–18 in) high. As the lateral shoots grow they will need tying to the stake with soft garden string. Dahlias will also benefit from a regular liquid feed from now on.

**Feed chrysanthemums** regularly from now on.

**Gather sweet peas** regularly and do not allow them to die on the plant. Once they start to set seed the plants will be discouraged from further flowering.

**Layer border carnations**, selecting non-flowering shoots. They should be ready for severing from the parent plant by early September.

**Lobelia cardinalis and Lobelia fulgens** will need staking. Use bamboo canes and soft string.

**Plant the madonna lily** (*Lilium candidum*). The bulbs should not be planted too deeply; cover with about 5 cm (2 in) of soil.

### FRAMES AND CLOCHES

**Ivy cuttings** should root readily in a garden frame.

**Pansies** can be sown in boxes in a frame. These will provide plants that will flower in the spring and early summer next year.

**Propagate cistus** from 5–7.5 cm (2–3 in) long half-ripe cuttings inserted in sandy soil in a garden frame. This can be done any time during the next few weeks.

**Remove faded flower heads** from plants such as delphiniums, phlox and anchusas to encourage them to give a further flush of flowers later in the season.

**Root cuttings** of shrubby plants such as camellias, heathers, hebes, and rosemary in the garden frame.

**Sow polyanthus** in boxes in the frame.

**Syringe cyclamen** plants in frames daily. This will help to keep the corms soft and discourage red spider mites.

**Winter cherries** (*Solanum capsicastrum*) standing in frames for the summer should be watered and misted regularly. Add Epsom salts to the water occasionally (14 g to 4.5 litres/$\frac{1}{2}$ oz to 1 gallon).

**Stake tall autumn-flowering plants** such as sunflowers, heleniums, and Michaelmas daisies.

**Summer-prune established wisterias** if they are as large as you want them.

**Tidy up the shrub border.** Hoe or shallowly fork over the soil, but watch out for self-sown seedlings or foxgloves or other plants you may wish to retain.

**Trim laurel hedges**, using a pair of secateurs.

### THE ROCK GARDEN

**Arabis** can be increased from cuttings taken now.

**Saponaria ocymoides** can be increased from now until the end of August from softwood cuttings of non-flowering shoots, preferably near the roots.

**Helianthemums** can be clipped back to size any time now.

**Silene schafta** can be increased from cuttings taken this month.

**Take cuttings** of early-flowering rock plants, such as *Alyssum saxatile*. Most will root fairly easily in a garden frame.

## THE GREENHOUSE

**Crotons and dracaenas** can be air layered if the plants have become too tall and lanky.

**Greenfly** (aphids) are an ever-present threat. Act at first sign to prevent a build-up.

**Mist** *Solanum capsicastrum* (winter cherry) plants with water every day to encourage the flowers to set.

**Pelargonium cuttings** that have rooted recently should be potted singly into 7.5–9 cm (3–3½ in) pots.

**Pot up** *Primula obconica* seedlings if this has not been done and they are large enough to be handled.

**Red spider mites** can become a pest on perpetual-flowering carnations. Symptoms include mottled leaves, and webbing among the shoots. Use a suitable insecticide and mist the plants

with water regularly to maintain a humid atmosphere, which this pest does not like.

**Scale insects** are not always obvious unless you look carefully, but they can be a serious pest on greenhouse plants. Make a point of looking for them occasionally, and spray with a systemic insecticide if you find any.

**To prevent the temperature rising too high**, ventilate the greenhouse every morning if you do not have automatic ventilators.

**When melon fruits** are about 7 cm (just under 3 in) in diameter the plants will need feeding with liquid fertilizer every week. The fruits will also need support (possibly from suspended nets) otherwise the weight of them may break the lateral stems.

## WEEKEND PROJECTS

### Build a raised bed

A raised bed enlivens a flat patio and makes for pleasurable gardening, especially for the disabled or wheelchair gardener, since stooping is eliminated.

You can build such a bed from brick or stone; old materials will blend better with the mature patio. Rendered blockwork with a pebbledash finish is another possibility. The shape, length and width is determined by the location; the height is governed not only by the situation but also whether it is being built onto a solid base or around a gap purposely left on the patio. If the bed is built on a solid floor it is best to go up to at least 45 cm (18 in) high in order to widen the planting variations. A single skin of brickwork is suitable up to 1 m (3 ft) high; above this a double thickness 23 cm (9 in) of bricks should be considered.

The techniques for building brick walls and barbecues (*see* pp. 151 and 179) are applied here. A decorative finish can be given to the top course by laying bricks on edge or at a 45 degree angle. On top of stonework, coping slabs can be used to finish.

If two or more interlocking beds are

to be constructed as shown, then construct them at different heights for best effect.

Drainage is an important consideration. Without this the soil can become waterlogged and the plants adversely affected. Leave half brick gaps at regular intervals in the second course of bricks above ground level. At the bottom of the bed place a layer of stones,

followed by a few centimetres of gravel and a layer of coarse peat.

Use only top quality garden soil to fill the raised bed—such as soft loam. Peat or garden compost added to the soil also improves it.

When planting it is a good idea to choose plants which will spill over the edges of the bed and so soften the hard outlines of the building materials.

## THE KITCHEN GARDEN

**Cabbages** for spring use should be sown now in cold districts.

**Celery** should be earthed up again.

**Celery fly**, whose maggots tunnel into the leaves, can be a problem now. Pinch off affected leaves and spray with a suitable insecticide.

**Early potatoes** can usually be enjoyed now. You do not have to wait until the haulms (tops) die down. Pull the soil away gently to check progress.

**Hoe regularly** to keep down weeds, but make a special effort to hoe the vegetable plot before you go on holiday, otherwise weed seedlings will have made a surprising amount of growth by the time you get back.

**Lettuces** can be sown again for succession, but this will probably be the last sowing to mature without protection.

**Pests and diseases** can become established if you are away for a few weeks, so check your plants carefully before you go—by spraying now you

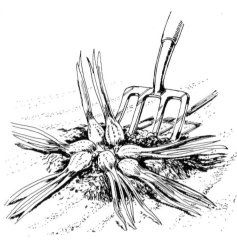

might prevent losses later (though there is no point in spraying *unless* you find a problem).

**Runner beans** should have the leading shoot pinched out once they have reached the top of their supports.

**Shallots** will be ready for lifting any time now. Lift the clumps with a fork and leave on the surface to dry for a few days, before storing. Put aside some bulbs the size of a 5p piece (2 cm/$\frac{3}{4}$ in) to plant next year.

**Support sweetcorn** with canes if just a small block has been planted in an exposed place, and tie each plant loosely to its stake.

### FRUIT

**Examine grape supports** to make sure the weight of the crop is not putting undue strain on them. Reinforce if necessary.

**Perpetual-fruiting strawberries** will need watering whenever the weather is dry. You will also need to make sure the fruits are raised on straw or lifted on wire supports.

**Pick early plums.** If you let early varieties go too soft on the tree they will be attacked by wasps.

## THE FLOWER GARDEN

**Cordon sweet peas** that have reached the top of the supports can be lowered and re-tied into position. Release the stems from the supports, trail them along the ground for about 90 cm (3 ft) and then retie to the supports.

**Dead-head** flowers that have faded. If left on the plant they will tend to sap its strength.

**Olearias** can be increased now from half-ripe cuttings inserted in a propagator during the next two months.

**Osmanthus** shrubs can be increased from 7.5–10 cm (3–4 in) half-ripe cuttings from the end of July through to late August. Insert the cuttings in a propagator.

**Philadelphus** (mock orange) shrubs need to be pruned after flowering. Cut flowered growth back to young shoots, but do not cut into the new growths. Remove a few old stems each year.

**Top-dress chrysanthemums** in pots outdoors. Use a rich compost with a room has been left at the top of the pot to allow this top-dressing, just use the chrysanthemum fertilizer.

**Winter-flowering pansies** that were sown outside earlier in the year will now need pricking out into nursery beds (a piece of spare ground), setting the seedlings 7.5 cm (3 in) apart.

### THE ROCK GARDEN

**Newly planted pot-grown plants** may require plenty of water during dry spells.

### THE WATER GARDEN

**Plants that have become too invasive** and have swamped their neighbours will need to be cut back now. Open space must be left for the benefit of the fish.

### LAWNS

**Apply a summer lawn fertilizer** to established lawns. It is helpful to water it in if the weather is dry.

**Keep cutting** the lawn regularly. Do not allow the grass to become too long before cutting it, and keep the edges well trimmed to give a neat appearance.

## THE GREENHOUSE

**Cactus seeds** can be sown in a pot of well-drained compost. Sow the seeds thinly, and cover them with 3 mm ($\frac{1}{8}$ in) of sifted compost.

**Carnations** will produce better blooms if disbudded, so that only the prime buds are allowed to flower.

**Continue to feed tomatoes** regularly now that the plants are carrying fruit. This applies for whatever growing method you are using; feeding can be the difference between a poor crop and a good one.

**Damp down regularly** to keep the humidity high. Sprinkle water on the floor and staging (unless you are using a capillary watering system).

**Early tomatoes** may be ready to have the growing tip removed if they have reached as high as you want them to go. This will concentrate the plant's energy into producing good-sized fruit.

**Feed azaleas and camellias,** and repeat every fortnight during the next

few months. This will help to produce strong flowering plants next year.

**Gloxinias** can be placed in the garden frame once they have finished their main flush of flowers.

**Ivies** can be rooted from cuttings taken now from mature plants. Insert four or

five 7.5 cm (3 in) cuttings into a 7.5 cm (3 in) pot of equal parts peat and sand, or a seed compost. They should root very quickly at this time of the year.

**Old cyclamen corms** can be repotted.

**Peaches and nectarines** being grown in a greenhouse will need constant watering. Syringe the foliage every evening to help deter red spider mites.

**Tie and stake carnations.**

**Transplant into small pots primulas and cinerarias** sown last month. They can spend the next few months in the garden frame.

**Tuberous-rooted begonias** may need staking with split canes.

**Whitefly on tomatoes** can be a serious problem and it should be sprayed with one of the insecticides recommended for this pest, which can be difficult to control.

**Young hydrangea plants** can be stood outside in a relatively cool place.

## WEEKEND PROJECTS

### A sandpit

A sandpit for the children can be as simple or as involved as you like. Where in the garden it is sited is very important; ideally it should be a good way from the house so that any sand will be discarded before being brought into the house on shoes and clothes.

A paved surround makes it easier to brush up and collect sand which finds its way out of the pit. It also lessens the amount of dirt which is brought into the pit. The pit should not be overlarge —120–180 cm (4–6 ft) in length by 90 cm (3 ft) wide is a reasonable size. Remember, the larger the pit the greater the cost of the sand needed to fill it. You could eliminate a lot of effort by buying a paddling pool and filling this with sand. This way you would avoid leaving a large hole in the lawn needing to be filled in when the children have outgrown the sandpit.

An above-ground sandpit also avoids digging a hole. The sides could be made of bricks or timber with a vinyl liner added to ensure that the sand does not

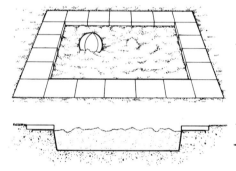

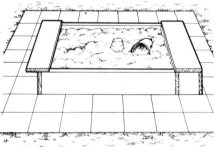

become contaminated with soil. The walls of the pit need not be more than 45–60 cm ($1\frac{1}{2}$–2 ft) high. A 30 cm (1 ft) depth of sand is adequate for play.

An in-ground pit dug to the dimensions above leaves a lot of soil to be disposed of elsewhere; if you could combine the effort with building a rockery, for example, then you would have a ready-made solution for earth disposal.

Remove all sharp stones from around the excavation and from the base— these would cut through the liner.

Insert the liner into the excavation leaving about 30 cm (1 ft) or so lapping on to the ground around the pit. The edges can be secured below paving slabs laid on a sand bed.

Excavate the soil around the pit so that the slabs will lie flush with the lawn. This eliminates a 'dangerous' edge for children to trip over and will also facilitate lawn cutting.

Looking to the future, a sandpit constructed on the above principle could easily be turned into a fish pond when the children grow older.

## THE KITCHEN GARDEN

**Carrots** from early sowings are likely to be progressing well, but all sowings will benefit from a preventive dusting with a soil insecticide.

**Continue to blanch leeks** until sufficient length of stem is prepared.

**Continue to thin** seedlings as necessary. Late-sown crops can soon become overcrowded, especially if neglected before you go on holiday.

**Early potatoes** can be lifted this month as required.

**Endive** sown in April should be ready for blanching about now. Blanch a few plants at a time, covering them with something lightproof. A large, inverted plant pot is effective, but you must cover the drainage holes otherwise they will let light in. Blanching may take several weeks.

**Feed tomatoes** regularly, and remember to remove any sideshoots before they become too large.

**Gather runner and French beans** regularly before the pods become too large.

**Slugs** can be very active after heavy dews or warm, damp weather, so sprinkle slug pellets around plants like celery and lettuces. Turnips and swedes are also particularly prone to attack.

**Spray celery** with a fungicide to control leaf spot.

**Water** runner beans, celery and marrows generously if the weather is dry.

### FRAMES AND CLOCHES

**Cucumbers** in frames should have the main shoot tips pinched out when they reach the corners of the frames.

**Melons** in frames may benefit from having a few leaves removed if they are casting shadows on developing fruit. Do not allow more than three melons to set on each plant.

### FRUIT

**Woolly aphids** (also known as American blight) are often seen on apple trees at this time. The insects, which tend to gather in cracks in twigs and branches, have a cotton-wool-like protective covering. A small attack can be treated by brushing them with methylated spirit, but for a large infestation you will need to spray with a suitable insecticide.

## THE FLOWER GARDEN

**Bracken** is worth collecting if you have a local source. It can be composted or used as a mulch, or to protect the crowns of slightly tender plants being overwintered outside.

**Earwigs** often trouble dahlias during late July, August and September, so set earwig traps by inverting pots filled with straw on top of stakes. Every morning, the earwigs that have taken refuge in the straw can be shaken out and killed.

**Everlasting flowers** such as statice, helichrysum and acroclinium can be cut now for drying to provide winter decoration indoors. Tie the stems together and hang in bunches upside down in a cool, dry airy shed. Achillea flower heads can also be treated in the same way.

**Examine budded roses.** If a bud looks dry and shrivelled, it probably has not taken, but you still have time to try again.

**Geranium cuttings** taken now will root in the open borders if you select a shady position and sandy soil. Take the cuttings from flowering plants, but remove them carefully so that the plants are not spoilt. Trim the cutting immediately below a leaf-joint, and remove the lowest.

**Hardy annuals** sown early will have been in bloom for several weeks. Remove dead flowers, to encourage the development of other blooms.

**Mealy bugs** attack a wide range of plants, including trees and shrubs such as ribes (flowering currant), laburnum and ceanothus. If not controlled, their sap-sucking activities will result in a loss of vigour, and the yellowing leaves may eventually fall. Spray with a suitable insecticide at first sight.

**Order bulbs** early if you want to include sternbergias, autumn-flowering crocuses, colchicums and hardy cyclamen.

**Plant the madonna lily** (*Lilium candidum*), and *L. testaceum*, covering the bulbs with not more than 5 cm (2 in) of soil.

**Rose suckers** must be removed. Cut them off with a sharp knife close to the roots. If necessary remove soil from around the roots, and replace it afterwards.

**Slugs and snails** can be a problem during very wet spells. Keep the soil well hoed and pull up weeds. Use a slug bait.

### THE ROCK GARDEN

**Increase** *Lithospermum diffusum* from softwood cuttings any time during the next month.

**Remove dead flower heads** from rock garden plants to keep them tidy.

**Trim back long stems** on helianthemums that have finished flowering.

## THE GREENHOUSE

*Begonia rex* leaf-cuttings can still be taken. Choose a healthy, mature leaf, and follow the advice on page 42.

**Coleus** plants should not be allowed to produce flowers, so pull off the flower buds as soon as they are seen. Do not allow the compost to become dry, otherwise the foliage will suffer badly.

**Cucumbers** should not be allowed to become dry. Keep the roots moist and maintain a humid atmosphere. If too many cucumbers are being produced at once, it is worth thinning them out.

**Damp down the greenhouse** regularly to create a humid atmosphere. It will also help to deter red spider mites.

**Feed gloxinias** to keep them growing strongly.

**Feed tomatoes** regularly.

**Grapes in an unheated greenhouse** will need thinning.

**Perpetual-flowering carnations** raised from cuttings earlier in the year must be 'stopped' now by nipping out the growing tips of the shoots.

**Pot on cinerarias** into 7.5 cm (3 in) pots as soon as they are large enough to be handled.

**Pot up primula seedlings** as they become ready.

**Regal pelargoniums** can be propagated from cuttings taken now.

**Regular watering** is necessary. If you are finding it difficult to keep the compost moist, it is well worth considering an automatic watering system (*see* page 63). If you install one now, you will have the immediate benefit from it throughout the summer when watering can be more of a chore. It will also ease the holiday care problem.

**Ventilate** the greenhouse freely whenever the weather is warm.

---

### WEEKEND PROJECTS

## Steps in the garden

Garden steps must be built with good, weather-resistant materials and be safe. The maximum height for risers should be about 19 cm ($7\frac{1}{2}$ in); treads should be at least 30 cm (12 in) deep with 38–45 cm (15–18 in) being a reasonable average.

If the land is to be raised to introduce steps then the dimensions of treads and risers can be planned in advance. However, where steps are being built into a slope, careful measuring is needed. To measure the height and width of the slope, lay a plank horizontally from the top of the slope to meet a vertical plank standing on the ground at the base of the slope. The vertical plank will give you the height of the steps and this can be divided to leave an equal number of treads. Similarly the horizontal plank will give the width of the steps.

Although concrete steps can be cast *in situ*, it is far easier to use paving slabs or, as here, crazy paving for the treads with brick or stones for the risers. If bricks are used, choose the very durable engineering bricks. Textured, non-slip paving is best for the treads.

First, the shape of the steps should be cut out roughly into the bank. Start at the bottom, working upwards and check each shaped tread and riser for size. The treads should be about 13 mm ($\frac{1}{2}$ in) or so less than the depth of each slab to be formed, so that the treads will overhang the risers by about 2.5 cm (1 in).

The first brick riser requires a foundation, so dig a trench about 15 cm (6 in) deep, lay a couple of inches of well-compacted hardcore, add 10 cm (4 in) of levelled concrete (one part cement to five parts ballast).

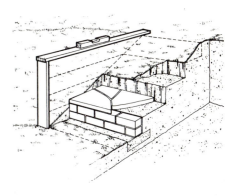

Build the first riser using the brickwork techniques described for wall building (*see* page 179). Bed down the slabs or crazy paving as described on pp. 103 and 115; remember to leave a slight projection over each riser and build in a very light fall for rainwater drainage.

Lay the next course of riser bricks on the back edge of the first tread and continue in this way until the steps are completed. Finally point the joints between the paving treads.

# Week 32

## THE KITCHEN GARDEN

**Cabbages** for spring use should be sown now in milder areas. Cabbage seedlings already coming through the ground are likely to be attacked by flea beetle (which can severely damage the plants by puncturing the leaves with small holes) so dust the rows with a suitable insecticide.

**Green manuring** (*see* page 15) is a useful way of improving soil cleared of potatoes and other early crops. If you sow the seed now you should be able to dig in the crop by the end of September.

**Lift beetroots** before they become too large. They store well in just-moist sand.

**Parsley** will germinate readily at this time and if sown now will crop steadily next spring and early summer.

**Protect cauliflower curds** by breaking and bending over outer leaves.

Sow spring onions to overwinter. They should produce salad onions for pulling next spring.
Spray tomatoes with a fungicide against blight.

**Tomatoes** will ripen better if any leaves shading the maturing trusses are removed to let in the light.

### FRAMES AND CLOCHES

**Cucumbers** in frames should be cut regularly before they become too big. Feed the plants regularly.

### FRUIT

**Blackcurrants** may suffer from a shortage of potash. If the edges of the leaves are turning brown, hoe in sulphate of potash around the bushes at 70 g per m² (2 oz per sq yd).

**Complete summer pruning** of cordon apples and pears.

**Prune summer-fruiting raspberries**, which should have finished cropping now. Cut out all the canes that have just fruited right down to ground level.

## THE FLOWER GARDEN

**Dahlias** need a great amount of water. During dry spells soak the soil thoroughly. Do not just dampen the surface, as this can do more damage than good. After soaking the soil, place a mulch of well-rotted compost, straw, or even grass cuttings around the plants.

**Deutzias** are best pruned after they have finished flowering. Cut out all the old wood close to soil level.

**Early-flowering chrysanthemums** forming buds should be disbudded by retaining the main bud and removing smaller buds below it, together with any sideshoots.

**Hanging baskets** and all plants in containers must be watered regularly —every day in warm weather.

**Mulches** conserve moisture in the soil and can be particularly useful if there are restrictions on the use of hose-pipes.

**Pansies and violas** can be propagated from cuttings taken in the autumn, and if you want to try this cut the plants back now by shortening flowering stems back to about 2.5–5 cm (1–2 in).

New shoots will be encouraged, especially if you sprinkle some sieved soil or compost over the plants.

**Rose bushes** need to be kept free of weeds. The weeds are likely to harbour pests and diseases.

**The crown imperial** (*Fritillaria imperialis*) can be planted now. In all but well-drained soils, the bulbs are best set on their sides, on a bed of sand, as they are prone to rotting.

**Zonal pelargonium** (geranium) cuttings can be taken now to provide bedding plants for next year.

### THE ROCK GARDEN

**Aubrieta** can be increased from cuttings taken between now and the end of September.

**Propagate** *Dianthus deltoides* from softwood cuttings taken after the plants have finished flowering.

### THE WATER GARDEN

**Fish** can sometimes suffer from lack of oxygen at this time, especially in thundery weather and if the pond is 'out of balance'. If you see the fish gulping for air at the surface, agitate the water violently for a few minutes with a jet from a hose-pipe. You may have to repeat the operation a few times but the problem is usually a short-term one.

**Unwelcome insects** such as the water boatman and great water beetle are best netted and removed.

### FRAMES AND CLOCHES

**Lavender cuttings** 5–10 cm (2–4 in) long, can be inserted in sandy soil in a garden frame. Take them from ripened wood, and either cut just below a leaf joint or take them with a 'heel'.

### LAWNS

**Prepare for new lawns** to be sown later this month or early next. The ground should be dug thoroughly and all perennial weed roots removed. Level roughly and allow the ground to settle for a few weeks.

## THE GREENHOUSE

**Aphids**, such as greenfly and whitefly, can be a problem at this time. Spray as soon as they are noticed, and repeat the treatment a week later (or as the manufacturer recommends). It is not always possible to control whitefly at the first attempt, although a systemic insecticide is more likely to succeed (but there are some plants on which you should not use them).

**Cyclamen** plants will still need to be sprayed with water every day.

**De-leaf tomato plants.** Remove the old lower leaves covering the lower trusses, but do not remove healthy leaves further up the plant.

**Exacums** can be sown now to flower during late winter and spring. Although they are treated as annuals they do make a pretty pot plant.

**Extra shading** may be necessary where a shading paint has been washed away.

**Fatsias** can be increased by cuttings taken during the next two months, selecting young, healthy shoots.

**Ficus, dracaenas and crotons** can be air layered if they have grown too tall or have lost a lot of lower leaves.

**Insect pests** can multiply rapidly. If you are planning to go on holiday, check your plants carefully first, making sure you look under the leaves too. Spraying or fumigating before you go away (provided it is necessary) will reduce the risk of pests and diseases having a couple of weeks start on you when you return.

**Leaf miners** may attack some soft-leaved plants such as cinerarias. The maggots bore into the leaves and leave unsightly tunnels in the process. Remove and burn badly affected leaves and spray the plants with a suitable insecticide. One of the systemic type can be particularly useful.

**On hot days** it may be necessary to use the doors as well as the windows to provide adequate ventilation.

**Pot up** *Primula malacoides, Primula obconica* and calceolaria seedlings as they become large enough to be handled. Do not allow the seedlings to become overcrowded.

**WEEKEND PROJECTS**

## Ideas to keep houseplants watered at holiday times

cross-section of bath

If you are going away for only a few days, simple precautions will suffice. Take houseplants away from windowsills and hot sunny places, such as porches and south-facing rooms. Water them thoroughly, remove yellowing leaves and flower buds that are about to open as well as fully developed flowers, then enclose the entire plant in an upturned, clear polythene bag which should be tightly secured just below the rim of the pot, using an elastic band. Next, place the plants in the centre of a fairly cool room with a north or east-facing window.

If the holiday is longer than about a week, and you cannot arrange for a neighbour or friend to do the watering, then make a self-watering system. Depending on how many plants you have, a very simple method is to lay some capillary matting (available from garden centres and shops) in the bottom of the kitchen sink and run it up on to the draining board where it is laid in a bowl of water. The water makes its way down into the sink by capillary action. Now simply stand the house houseplants on the matting and as long as they are growing in modern plastic pots in a peat compost (or do not have crocks at the bottom if a loam-based compost is used) they will take up water from the matting as and when they need it.

If there are too many plants to put in a sink, an alternative is to stand a bucket of water on a few bricks and then run capillary wicks from the bucket to each plant where the wick is held on the surface of the compost with a stone. It is worth testing any method before going on holiday because it can take some modifications to get the system to work properly.

If you prefer not to move your plants, then the only thing to do is to buy a proprietary automatic watering gadget for each one. These gadgets usually have water reservoirs and they are simply pushed into the compost in the pot.

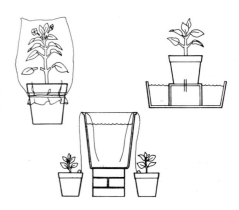

## THE KITCHEN GARDEN

**Celery** should be earthed up again. It is best to do this when the soil is moist.

**Feed tomatoes** regularly.

**Hoe regularly** to keep down weeds and to avoid a hard crust forming on the soil, especially where it is walked on frequently.

**Onions** will be ripening well, but the process can be hastened by bending over the tops to expose the bulbs to more sunshine.

**Ridge cucumbers** should be cropping now. Keep them picked as they are not so nice if they become too large and old. This kind is always smaller and chunkier than greenhouse cucumbers.

**Sow winter spinach,** the sooner the better in cold districts.

**Stop tomatoes** when four trusses have set. Also remove sideshoots.

**Sweetcorn** may be maturing now. Test for ripening by pressing a grain with a

fingernail; if it is ripe it will exude a milky fluid.

**Water** celery, runner beans and marrows generously if the weather is dry.

### FRAMES AND CLOCHES

**Cucumbers** in frames often suffer from mildew about this time—the leaves become covered with a whitish powdery coating. Spray with a suitable fungicide.

### FRUIT

**Strawberry runners** pegged down last month should have made good roots by now and can be severed from the parent plant. If you do this now they should be ready for moving from next week onwards.

If you want early strawberries in the greenhouse next year, pot up some of the plant now into 15 cm (6 in) pots, using a good compost. Stand in frames or a sheltered position outdoors until they need to be taken in.

## THE FLOWER GARDEN

**Box** (buxus) grown as an edging can be trimmed back but not too severely. Cuttings can be taken now. Choose 7.5–12.5 cm (3–5 in) cuttings from ripe sideshoots, inserting them in a garden frame. Try to ensure that each cutting has a 'heel' (part of the stem from which the cutting is taken) attached to it.

**Daffodil bulbs** can be planted from now on. Make the holes about three times the depth of the bulbs. Planting in irregular groups produces the best effect.

**Border carnations** layered in July should have produced roots by now and can be transplanted to their permanent positions.

**Dahlias** need feeding every 10 days with a liquid fertilizer. To encourage the plant to produce larger blooms, on large flowered types reduce the number of shoots branching from the base of the plant. Disbud dahlias intended for exhibition. Make sure you have earwig traps (upturned pots filled with straw placed on top of the stakes), and empty

these every day if you can.

**Hardy annuals** for overwintering in favourable districts can be sown during the next few weeks. They include alyssum, asperula, calendula, candytuft, clarkia, cornflower, eschscholzia, godetia, larkspur, nigella, sweet scabious and viscaria. They may need cloche protection in cold districts or a bad winter, but are worth trying for an early display next year.

**Polyanthus seedlings** should be large enough to transplant to a partially shaded (but not dry) border.

### THE ROCK GARDEN

**Sempervivums** can be increased simply by severing some of the offsets and planting them in sandy soil.

### THE WATER GARDEN

**Blanket weed,** which can form a green filament over the water, should be removed with a rake. Take the opportunity to clear any other water or waterside weeds, and deposit them on the compost heap.

### FRAMES AND CLOCHES

**Many tree and shrub cuttings** can be taken now for rooting in a garden frame. Use a hormone rooting powder, and keep the frame closed for a few weeks, misting the cuttings regularly; but do not keep them too wet otherwise they may start to rot. Among the cuttings you can try now are aucuba, berberis, ceanothus, cotoneaster, escallonia, garrya, hibiscus, hypericum, ilex (holly), kalmia, lavender, lonicera, olearia, ribes (flowering currant), roses, rubus and *Viburnum tinus.*

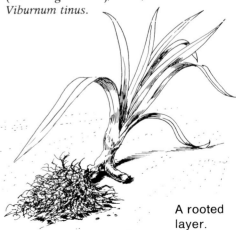

A rooted layer.

## THE GREENHOUSE

**Check cinerarias** and other soft-leaved plants for leaf miners. They are easily controlled on ornamental plants by a systemic insecticide.

**Continue to damp down** to create a humid atmosphere.

**Continue to feed** all plants growing actively.

**Cucumbers** must be kept moist. Check for red spider mites. Mist the plants with water regularly.

**De-leaf tomato plants** by removing any old leaves that are shading fruit about to ripen. Do not remove the upper leaves or any healthy leaves.

**Ivy cuttings** will root easily if taken now.

**Old cyclamen corms** repotted a few weeks ago may benefit from an

occasional misting with water. Keep the compost moist but not too wet.

**Pot up pelargonium cuttings** into 9 cm (3½ in) pots.

**Red spider and whitefly** can be a problem on tomatoes, so watch out for them.

**Schizanthus** can be sown now for flowering in the spring. Sow the seed thinly as they usually germinate well.

**Sow cyclamen.** They should make good, flowering-sized plants for the Christmas after next.

**Sow exacums** to flower next spring.

**Take fuchsia cuttings,** which will root readily at this time.

## WEEKEND PROJECTS

### A simple barbecue

Barbecue parties have become a popular patio pastime. You can buy a ready-made barbecue complete with legs or trolley, or build a base to take a portable barbecue or a metal grill from an oven. The base can be as simple or ambitious as you want to make it. It can be a permanent feature of the patio or planned as a quick assembly project for just before the party.

1) This one is made from loose-laid walling blocks with paving slabs enclosing the back (to contain the heat) and another slab to act as a base for the charcoal. A metal grill can be 'borrowed' from the oven for the evening.

Decorative walling blocks are laid on firm foundations (*see* brick wall building, page 179) using a mix of 1 part masonry cement to 4 parts soft sand. These blocks are available in two sizes: full blocks, 53 × 15 × 10 cm (21 × 6 × 4 in), and half blocks, 27 × 15 × 10 cm (10½ × 6 × 4 in). Mortar joints should be about 6 mm (¼ in) thick and the blocks laid with the frog (indentation) upwards. Only build up four courses before allowing 48 hours for the mortar to harden. Plan your project around full size and half block complete dimensions as it is extremely difficult to cut blocks cleanly.

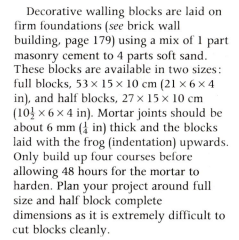

2) Here, bricks or building blocks can be used for the base and be rendered over. A pebbledash finish could be used if you want to match the house walls. For the top a concrete slab is needed —this will serve as a base for quarry or exterior quality ceramic tiles.

3) Concrete walling blocks and paving slabs provide a more ambitious project. This design provides plenty of useful preparation and serving surfaces. Walling blocks such as these are used in much the same way as bricks.

## THE KITCHEN GARDEN

**Batavian endive** may be sown to provide a winter salad.

**Cabbage aphids** can be particularly bad on brassicas such as Brussels sprouts and cauliflowers at this time. Because they are often well camouflaged you may need to look closely. Spray with a suitable insecticide as soon as they are noticed.

**Earth up maincrop celery.** It is useful to tie the stems loosely with raffia before you do this. Herbs of many kinds can usefully be picked for drying now. Choose a warm, dry day and gather them in the afternoon.

**'Japanese' onions** for harvesting next June and July can be sown any time during the next month.

**Potato blight** can still be a problem. Cut off any affected haulms to avoid it spreading to the tubers, and spray with a suitable fungicide.

Peas should be ready for picking now.

**Spinach** for winter picking can be sown during the next month, provided a winter variety is chosen.

### FRAMES AND CLOCHES

**Lettuces** can be sown under glass during the next two months to provide heads for cutting from late November to early March, but special varieties bred for cropping under glass must be used.

**Sow Batavian endive** for winter use.

### FRUIT

**Blackberries and loganberries** can still be tip-layered (*see* pp. 42–3).

**Early pears** usually remain at their best for a very short time. Pick them as soon as they are soft and try to eat them as soon as possible.

**Pick damaged plums** off the tree, otherwise wasps will be further encouraged and diseases will take hold.

**Prepare the fruit store** for apples and pears in plenty of time.

## THE FLOWER GARDEN

**Dahlias** required for exhibition should have the wing buds (those produced just beneath terminal flowers) removed. For really large blooms, you will also need to remove any sideshoots.

**Herbaceous perennial seedlings** that have been growing in a nursery bed for the last summer or two can be moved to the border now, unless you prefer to do this in the spring.

**Herbaceous plants** that have flowered should be dead-headed. This may encourage further flowers to develop, and will keep the border looking tidy.

**Hyacinths** for flowering at Christmas can be potted up now. Use bulb-fibre in 20–25 cm (8–10 in) wide bowls or compost in pots, and place them in a cool, dark place, in a temperature of 5–10°C (41–50°F). Ensure that the bulb-fibre is moist. Use specially prepared bulbs.

**Michaelmas daisies** should be well staked if they are tall varieties. Water generously if the soil is dry.

**Rambler roses** that have finished flowering can be pruned. Cut all the ties holding the stems to the trellis-work and lay the shoots on the ground. Cut out at ground level those that have produced flowers. The new stems produced this year will bear flowers next season.

**Tidy up border carnations,** which will probably be practically over by now. Trim them back, removing old flower stems and straggly leaves. You should also be able to put supports away for the winter. If the plants have been layered, these will probably be ready for severing and transplanting.

**Trim lavender hedges** to tidy them up after flowering.

**Keep flower beds hoed,** to eliminate weeds and improve the general appearance.

**Winter aconites** should be planted as soon as possible. The tubers are not always easy to start, and it is worth soaking them for a day first: incorporate plenty of *moist* peat when you plant.

### THE ROCK GARDEN

**Small rock garden bulbs** can be planted now. Set them in small groups around the sides of the rocks. In this way, they will gain some protection from the rocks.

### THE WATER GARDEN

**Tidy up the pool** during late summer and early autumn.

### LAWNS

**Keep the edges trimmed**; it really does give a neat outline to the lawn.

**Prepare to sow a new lawn** in the next few weeks. Dig the ground thoroughly, removing all perennial weeds. Break down large lumps of soil to leave a friable surface.

## THE GREENHOUSE

**Annuals** can now be sown to provide flowering pot plants in the spring. Among those to try are, calendulas (choose a dwarf variety), godetia, mesembryanthemums, nemophilas, and salpiglossis. East Lothian stocks can also be sown for spring flowering— ideally in the greenhouse border. They can be used for greenhouse display or for cutting.

**Botrytis** (grey mould) can attack a wide range of plants. Although usually worse in cool, damp, and badly ventilated conditions, it is always a risk in greenhouses. It can easily start up on dead or dying flowers and on soft-leaved plants. Remove dead or dying flowers or leaves regularly, and spray

with a suitable fungicide as soon as the disease is seen.

**Cyclamen** can still be sown for flowering at the end of next year.

**Order Christmas-flowering bulbs** as soon as possible. These need to be available to pot up at the right time if they are to flower at the time you want.

**Pot on large cineraria plants** and take the opportunity to make sure the plants are free of diseases or pests (especially greenfly).

**Pot up freesia corms,** five or six to a 15 cm (6 in) pot.

**Pot up lachenalia** bulbs now.

**Take cuttings** of greenhouse plants such as tradescantias, zebrinas, pileas, busy lizzies (impatiens) and coleus. In the case of coleus it is only worth propagating and overwintering those plants with the very best colouring, as they are so easy to raise from seed.

**Tomato plants** that have exhausted themselves are best cleared from the greenhouse. However, late-sown crops will still be carrying a good crop.

## WEEKEND PROJECTS

### Preserving garden timber

All the timber in the garden will gradually deteriorate and rot unless it is protected from the elements. Most susceptible to decay is timber which is in direct contact with the ground—fence posts, cold frames etc.

Timber that has been coated with wood primer, undercoat and gloss paint will be well protected but this is costly, time-consuming and not always desirable. The normal way to protect unpainted timber is to cover it with a water repellent wood preservative, or, in the case of garden furniture and so on, with a polyurethane varnish which gives a top quality appearance.

Wood preservatives are generally sold in various grades. There is a clear type, and various timber shades—red cedar and green. Preservatives are harmful to plant life, so care must be taken to avoid splashing plants or allowing excessive amounts to soak into soil near roots. Some preservatives are not harmful to plant life when they have dried and these should be used on greenhouses, seed boxes and so on. Green

preservatives are particularly recommended in the above situations.

Preservatives can be applied by a large brush or spray. Spraying is far easier over large areas such as fences but

should not be attempted on blustery days when the spray can be blown around. Use the preservative only on dry timber and when rain is not expected for a day or so; this will give the liquid plenty of time to soak in. Apply one or two coats as advised on the container.

Treat fence posts every two years at least. The vulnerable part is below or at ground level. Dig a hole around the post so that the base in the ground can be well soaked.

Small items such as seed boxes can be treated by brush or by dipping them in preservative for about 15 seconds.

Polyurethane varnish comes in a clear finish and various timber colours. The surface of the item being treated should be rubbed down with glasspaper, wiped clean, and the varnish applied with a clean, good quality brush. Use a flowing coat and apply it in the direction of the grain. Apply at least two, preferably three coats, allowing each coat to dry before continuing with the next. Repeat the treatment each year.

## THE KITCHEN GARDEN

**Brussels sprouts** that are becoming very tall can be encouraged to produce sprouts by pinching out the tops and applying a dressing of sulphate of potash at 35 g per m² (1 oz per sq yd).
**Continue to hoe** between the rows to keep an open soil and to prevent weeds seeding.
**Earth up** round the base of winter cauliflowers and kales to provide a good anchorage for the stormy weather ahead. It will be more effective if done now than left until the bad weather arrives.
**Feed tomatoes** regularly.
**Onions** that have been ripening ought to be lifted with a fork and left to dry off in a dry, sunny place.
**Sow turnips** for turnip tops any time

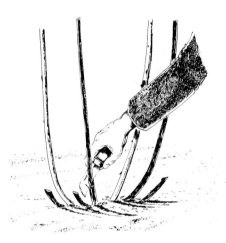

within the next month. The seed is usually sown broadcast for turnip tops.
**Wind** could easily cause damage to tall Brussels sprouts plants during the next

few months, and it is worth staking these varieties in exposed areas.

### FRAMES AND CLOCHES

**Sow lettuces** in frames, but choose a suitable variety.

### FRUIT

**Blackcurrants** should not be allowed to become short of water, otherwise growth will be stunted and this may affect next year's crop. Water generously if the weather is very dry, and it is not too late to apply a mulch.
**Prune loganberries and blackberries** once all the fruit has been picked. Cut out fruited shoots at ground level and tie in the current year's growth.

## THE FLOWER GARDEN

**Eremurus** can be planted now if you have a suitable site for these stately border plants, with their tall spikes. They can look particularly impressive against a background of conifers.
**Large-flowered, tuberous begonias** grown as bedding plants must be dead-headed continuously. Wet, faded flowers soon become diseased and healthy parts of the plant may become infected.
**Lavender cuttings** can be put in now. These root quite easily, and are best inserted in a shallow trench with sand in the base. Firm the soil around the base of the cuttings.
**Plant spring-flowering bulbs** any time during the next month. The sooner you can get them in the better, but it is not worth clearing summer bedding for a few weeks if it is still showing useful colour.
**Plant erythroniums** (dog's tooth violets) as soon as possible. They do not store well out of the ground.
**Plant leucojum** (snowflake) bulbs as soon as they are available in the

autumn. Set them 5–7.5 cm (2–3 in) deep in small clusters.
**Propagate bedding geraniums and fuchsias.** Insert the cuttings in boxes in a garden frame.
**Rose cuttings** can be taken now. Insert them in sand-filled trenches in a sheltered part of the garden.
**Scillas** are best planted as soon as they become available, setting them 5–7.5 cm (2–3 in) deep, in little groups.

### THE ROCK GARDEN

**This is a good time to carry out alterations** to the rock garden, while the problems of the current season are still fresh in the mind's eye. Choose a time when the soil is moist, then you should be able to move the plants and reposition rocks without too much of a setback to the plants.

### THE WATER GARDEN

**Plants in the pool** may need to be trimmed back to keep them tidy during the autumn.

### FRAMES AND CLOCHES

**Anemones** can be planted in frames or cloches between now and the end of next month for a succession of bloom.
**Pansy and viola cuttings** can be taken now. Plants cut back a few weeks ago should have produced plenty of shoots from the base. Take the healthiest shoots about 5–7.5 cm (2–3 in) long, and cut off just below ground level. It might even be possible to remove some pieces complete with roots forming. Plant in the garden frame.
**Take hardwood cuttings** of camellias, heathers, hydrangeas, lavender and rosemary to root in the frame.

### LAWNS

**Sow a new lawn** if the ground has already been prepared.
**Turf** can also be laid at this time of year.
**Worms** sometimes become a problem about this time. Use a wormkiller if they are particularly troublesome, otherwise brush casts away with a broom.

## THE GREENHOUSE

**Botrytis** (grey mould) is a disease that attacks soft-leaved plants, covering them with a grey mould. It often gets a start on dead flowers or rotting fruit, and is encouraged by a damp atmosphere. Pick off all dead or dying leaves and flowers, and try to maintain a drier atmosphere now that the season is advancing.

**Cineraria plants** that have become too large for their small pots should be moved on into 12.5 cm (5 in) pots. Take the opportunity to check the leaves for greenfly and leaf miner.

**Freesia corms** can be potted up now. Plant five or six corms in a 15 cm (6 in) pot of John Innes potting compost.

**Keep the greenhouse clean** and tidy. Dead or dying vegetation encourages

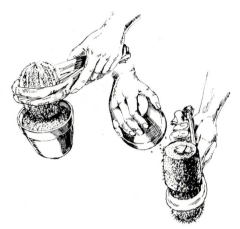

pests and diseases. Keep plants picked over as they begin to age, and clear out beneath staging. Sweep the path clean.

**Lachenalia bulbs** can be potted up now, in the same way as freesias.

**Repot cacti** if they need it, but remember that cacti do not need large pots for their size. If the plants have very prickly spines, fold a piece of newspaper over into a thick, narrow strip, and use this in a clamp-like action to hold the plant while repotting.

**Rest gloxinias** that have finished flowering by gradually giving less water. Once the top growth has died back and the compost is dry, the tubers can be stored in their pots, which are best placed on their side out of the way.

**Sow annuals** for spring flowering in pots.

**Take cuttings** of coleus, pileas, tradescantias, zebrinas, heliotrope, begonias and busy lizzies (impatiens).

---

**WEEKEND PROJECTS**

### Make an onion rope

Rub dead roots and loose skin off the dried bulbs. Take two bulbs with sturdy necks and knot them together with thick string. Keep the dead leaves pointing upwards and tie more bulbs, two or three at a time, to the string until the rope of onions is any convenient length. Onions are not damaged by cold, but they must be kept dry, so hang the rope in a shed, garage, greenhouse or loft.

The rope lets plenty of air circulate around each bulb. As a bulb is needed it is cut off at the neck and the onions can be removed one by one without damaging the rope. It is best to use the onions from the top of the rope downwards.

Other ways of storing onions are in nylon tights, net bags, or on shallow trays (*see* project on page 157), although none of these methods lets air circulate around the bulbs in the way that an onion rope does.

## THE KITCHEN GARDEN

**Blanch endive**—a few at a time on a regular basis.

**Cabbage caterpillars** may still cause problems. Catching them early, dusting or spraying with a suitable insecticide, will make control more effective and prevent too much damage to the crops.

**Celery** should be earthed up a little more if necessary. Remove any suckers appearing from the base. Leeks can also be earthed up.

**Hoe regularly** between all vegetable crops.

**Lift maincrop carrots and beetroot.** They are likely to deteriorate if left in the ground much longer.

**Second early and maincrop potatoes** should soon be ready for lifting. Wait until the haulms (stems) die down. Burn any top growth that appears diseased.

**Sow winter-hardy lettuces** outdoors

during the next few weeks. Suitable varieties sown now and wintered outdoors or with slight protection should be ready in May.

**Spray celery** with a fungicide if leaf spot shows signs of being troublesome.

**Water runner beans** thoroughly if the weather is dry.

### FRAMES AND CLOCHES

**It is not too late to sow** a few radishes and forcing varieties of carrot in a frame. It is also worth sowing some parsley.

**Pick melons** if the skin has begun to crack or if they smell ripe. The end furthest from the stalk will give a little when pressed with the thumb if it is ripe.

### FRUIT

**Container-grown trees,** bushes, and canes can be planted this month.

**Mildew** is likely to be a problem on many fruits this month (particularly gooseberries) so be prepared to use a fungicide regularly during September.

**Pick apples and pears** as they mature.

**Strawberries** should be planted as soon as possible if not already done.

## THE FLOWER GARDEN

**Bearded irises** can be divided in September after flowering. Lift the roots with a garden fork and cut off pieces from the outside of each clump. Replant each piece, which must have one or two fans of leaves, with 2.5–5 cm (1–2 in) of soil over the roots. It is best to divide clumps every three or four years.

**Buy sweet pea seeds** for autumn sowing now if you have not already done so.

**Canterbury bells** sown earlier in the year can now be planted in their flowering positions. This job can be done during September and October.

**Chinese lanterns** (*Physalis alkekengi*) can easily become spoilt during autumn gales. Provide support for them until the bottom lanterns have coloured, then you can cut them and hang them upside down in a cool place to dry off.

**Late-flowering chrysanthemums** should be fed once a fortnight, until colour shows in the buds.

**Ornamental gourds** grown for winter decoration should be harvested as soon as the stalks begin to wither. Pick them on a dry day and store in a cool, dry place until you want to use or varnish them.

**Plant bulbs for naturalizing.** Apart from daffodils, you can also naturalize snowdrops, crocuses, chionodoxas, *Fritillaria meleagris* (the snake's-head fritillary), as well as miniature narcissi such as *N. cyclamineus*, and *N. triandrus.*

**Prepare the shrub border** for autumn planting. It is best to get all the thorough digging done before you buy the plants, incorporating as much rotted compost or manure as you can spare.

**Rake up fallen leaves** in rose beds, to reduce the risk of black spot being carried over the winter.

### THE ROCK GARDEN

**Campanula carpatica** should have all dead flowers removed.

**Sedums** can be divided this month.

**Thymus serpyllum** should have its dead flower heads removed with sharp shears as soon as flowering is finished.

### THE WATER GARDEN

**Fish** should be built up for the winter by giving them a rich and varied diet. Do not overfeed (it should all be eaten within 10 minutes), but make sure they are fed regularly.

**Remove dead leaves and flowers** before they have a chance to pollute the water.

**Thin out aquatic plants** that have become overgrown. Make a note of any water lilies have become too large and will need dividing next spring.

### LAWNS

**Sow lawn seed** on soil previously prepared.

**Raise the cutting height** by about 6 mm ($\frac{1}{4}$ in) now that the end of summer growth is in sight.

## THE GREENHOUSE

**Aspidistras** often look better if you clean the leaves occasionally. Use a proprietary leaf-cleaner or a mixture of milk and water.

**Cacti** can still be repotted.

**Clean off summer shading** washes from the outside of the house.

**Cuttings** can still be taken of plants such as pileas, zebrinas, tradescantias, coleus and busy lizzies.

**Cyclamen** coming into flower early should have the flowers pulled off. It is better to allow the plant to build itself up first, then you should have a bolder display later.

**Dwarf bulbs** grown in pans can make a wonderfully refreshing display in a cold or cool greenhouse in spring. Pot them up now.

**Feed winter-flowering pot-plants** and do not allow the soil to become dry.

**Heliotrope cuttings** can be rooted now

in a sandy compost in a propagator.

**Ivies** can still be increased from cuttings.

**Paraffin heaters** need to be cleaned and new wicks bought if you use these

heaters during the winter. In some areas frost is a possibility from now on. It is unlikely to be severe, and may not happen for weeks, but it is wise to be prepared if you have tender plants.

**Pot up lachenalia bulbs** now.

**Regal pelargoniums** that have been in garden frames for the summer should be producing new shoots. These can be used as cuttings. After taking cuttings the old plants can be repotted.

**Repot large cinerarias** into 12.5 cm (5 in) pots if not already done.

**Schizanthus** should not be given too much warmth. They will make sturdier and better plants if grown cool.

**Ventilate** the greenhouse more carefully now. Avoid draughts striking the plants on cool evenings.

**Water** more carefully now. Avoid saturating the compost and see that water does not fall on the leaves.

### Make a storage rack for fruit and vegetables

Fruit and vegetables need plenty of air around them and cool, not too dry, conditions if they are to store well. A well ventilated cellar is ideal, but a garage or shed is often suitable. By storing the crops in single layers in slatted trays there will be the necessary air circulation around them. Should rotting set in, then the affected fruits can be seen and removed before the adjacent fruits are affected.

If you have only a few fruits or vegetables to store, place them in Dutch type tomato trays which have raised corners and can be stacked, yet still allow air to circulate.

For larger quantities, make a storage rack consisting of slatted timber trays which can slide like drawers in an outer framework.

Make the rack to fit the space available and to suit the anticipated size of the crops. Typical dimensions are shown in the diagram. The main framework is 38 × 25 mm (1½ × 1 in) timber. The sides are simple rectangles

joined at the corners with half-lap joints. The side frames are glued and nailed to a hardboard base and linked at the top with two 38 × 25 mm cross pieces. Two more 38 × 25 mm vertical pieces nailed to the back of the rack at each side strengthen the framework and prevent the storage trays from being pushed right through.

The front is stiffened with two triangular pieces of hardboard glued and nailed to the top corners. The tray runners are 25 × 25 mm (1 × 1 in) battens.

The trays themselves are simply boxes made from 75 × 19 mm (3 × ¾ in) timber. The bases are 38 × 13 mm (1½ × ½ in) slats. Air can circulate between the trays and also through the slats.

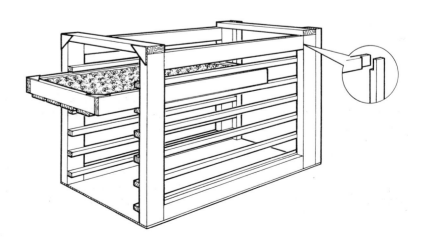

## THE KITCHEN GARDEN

**Beetroot** for storing can be lifted at any time during the next month. Lift with a fork, carefully wipe away the soil, twist off the tops and after allowing the roots to dry store the sound ones in boxes of dry sand or peat, or in a clamp in the open. Late sowings can be left in the ground until required in favourable areas.

**Brussels sprouts** will be developing well on the early varieties, and will probably be ready for picking in about a month's time. Pinch out any buttons low down that have split open, to encourage better ones above. Tread the soil around all Brussels sprout plants to make sure it is firm.

**Celery leaf miner** can cause unsightly damage with its white tunnels and blisters. Spray with a suitable insecticide at first sign.

**Continue to feed tomatoes;** they will still benefit from a special tomato fertilizer.

**Feed late crops** of lettuces, carrots and beetroot with a light dressing of nitrogenous fertilizer such as nitrate of soda or Nitro-chalk—being careful to keep it off the leaves.

**Globe artichokes** should be given a liquid feed if they appear weak. You need to build up strong plants for next season. Cut to ground level any stems that have had flower-heads cut.

**Spinach** for winter picking should be sown within the next week if it has not already been done.

**Thin winter spinach** sown last month.

**Water celery** generously if the weather is dry.

### FRUIT

**Prune blackcurrants** by cutting out old branches to reduce the over-all number by about one-third. Remove the branches at ground level if possible.

**Sow grass** round established fruit trees if you prefer to manage a grassed orchard. Grass sown now should be established by next summer.

**Water-shoots** (long, sappy growths sprouting from the trunk) on apples and pears should be cut cleanly off with a pair of secateurs as soon as possible. Left to get large, they will have to be sawn off and this can stimulate further growth.

## THE FLOWER GARDEN

**Bellis perennis** (double daisy) plants sown earlier in the year and grown on in a nursery bed can now be planted out into their flowering positions.

**Bulbous irises** can be planted 10–15 cm (4–6 in) deep during the next month or two. Choose a light, fertile soil in full sun.

**Daffodil bulbs** can still be naturalized in grass for flowering next year. Use a special bulb planter, which takes out a core of soil, or make holes with a trowel. Scatter the bulbs on the grass, in small groups, and plant each bulb where it has fallen.

**Daffodils for flowering indoors** can now be planted in pots of compost or deep bowls of bulb-fibre. Stand the potted bulbs outdoors on a firm but well-drained base and cover with a 23 cm (9 in) layer of moist peat.

**Plant evergreen trees and shrubs** during the next few weeks.

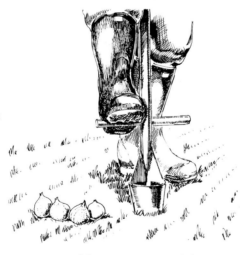

**Prune rambler roses.** Some of them will probably have made a lot of new growth, in which case you can cut out all the old growth that has flowered (but, if there is not much new wood, save some of the old shoots for another year).

**Trim hedges** for the last time before winter.

**Wallflowers** sown earlier in the year will now need to be set in their flowering positions. The sooner they are put in the better. In case some of the plants die during the winter, plant a few extra ones at the end of the bed or on a spare piece of soil, so that they can be used to fill any gaps.

### THE ROCK GARDEN

**Divide alpines.** Many kinds can be divided successfully at this time.

**Plant dwarf evergreen shrubs and conifers.** These can add interest to a rock garden, but be careful in the choice of varieties, as you want real dwarfs.

**Plant spring-flowering bulbs,** but try to bear in mind what will be in flower next to them next spring. As it is best to leave bulbs for the rock garden undisturbed for several years, bear this in mind too.

## THE GREENHOUSE

**Arum lilies** can be divided now.

**Bring in plants from the frame** that have been spending the summer outdoors. Make sure they are clean and healthy *before* you bring them in. Spray them first if they show signs of pests or diseases.

**Feed winter-flowering pot-plants** as they continue to grow actively.

**Keep the greenhouse free from rubbish,** which encourages pests and diseases. Rubbish often accumulates under greenhouse staging and the conditions there are often ideal for woodlice and the like. An 'autumn clean' will not come amiss.

**Mice** sometimes try to set up home for the winter in a greenhouse. If you suspect that they are going to be a

Sow lettuce seed in drills, for subsequent thinning.

problem, use baits or traps, placed where they cannot harm children or pets.

**Pot up schizanthus** seedlings if this needs to be done.

**Remove shading** from the outside of the greenhouse if the weather has turned dull.

**Repot cacti** if the pots are full of roots.

**Sow a winter lettuce** variety in the greenhouse border. You will need to thin them to about 23 cm (9 in) apart later. Make sure you can maintain an adequate temperature for the variety; there are several to choose from but you are likely to need to provide a winter temperature of 7°C (45°F).

**Ventilate** greenhouses very carefully, making sure the plants are not in a cold draught.

**WEEKEND PROJECTS**

### Drying and preserving flowers

Many flower and seed heads can be preserved simply by hanging them up to dry. The best flowers to dry are the so-called everlasting—helichrysums or strawflowers, and statice, for example. You can also dry flower heads of delphiniums, larkspur and acanthus, but in this case make sure that all the flowers on each head are fully open or the tips of the flower spikes will hang over after drying. Helichrysums also tend to nod their heads on drying, but this can be prevented by pushing a short length of florists' wire through the flower head and into the stem.

Seed heads that can be dried include all the grasses and cereal crops, as well as the seed heads of many flowers. Even some vegetable seed heads can be dried. For example, the rounded seed heads of onions and leeks can be very striking.

The secret of drying is to ensure that the material dries as quickly as possible. After cutting, remove all the leaves and hang the stems upside down in small bunches in a really dry and airy place, such as over a boiler. In summer, a conservatory or porch is a suitable

place. Some stems, like onion and yellow achillea heads, may be damaged by hanging them in bunches, so dry these singly. By hanging the bunches upside down, the sap runs into the head and after drying they are less easily damaged.

Many leaves and branches can be preserved in glycerine. Leaves of beech and mahonia are particularly good for preserving by this method. The mixture is 1 part glycerine to 2 parts of hot water. Pour the solution into a tall container so it goes well up the stems of

the branches being preserved. Hammer the bases of the stems so they absorb the glycerine solution. Also wipe the leaves with the glycerine solution. Leave them in the solution for about two weeks until all the leaves have changed colour as the glycerine is absorbed.

The best way to preserve ferns, brackens and all kinds of autumn leaves is by pressing. Spread out the leaves and press them between sheets of blotting paper or newspapers under heavy books or other weight. Leave them for a few weeks until dry.

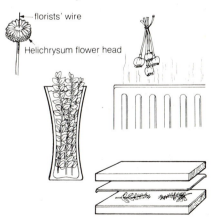

florists' wire

Helichrysum flower head

## THE KITCHEN GARDEN

**Cabbages** sown in July for spring use should now be ready for transplanting.
**Continue to hoe** regularly to maintain good soil structure and to keep down weeds.
**Carrots** should be lifted once the leaves have started to turn yellow. Do not store any with small holes made by carrot fly maggots.
**Cauliflowers** can be protected from sun or rain by breaking and bending over two or three outside leaves to cover the curd.
**Harvest ripe marrows** if this has not already been done.
**Lift and store beetroot** if they are still in the ground and they are almost the size of a tennis ball. If left too long beyond that stage they tend to become 'woody'. Lift with a fork to avoid damaging the roots.
**Onion ropes** are an attractive way to store onions. When the bulbs are dry, make them into ropes or store on slatted trays in a cool, dry place.

## FRAMES AND CLOCHES

**High winds** are often a problem at this time, so make sure you have a way of securing the lights (tops) of frames. On wooden frames you can knock a large staple into the light and one into the main frame (or screw in stout eyes) and use strong string to tie the top down in very bad weather.

**Lettuces** for January cutting can be sown under glass if some heat can be provided. A suitable variety must be used.

## FRUIT

**Apples** for store can be dipped into a proprietary sugar-based protective coating to extend storage life.
**Grease-band fruit trees,** especially apples. You can buy these from a garden centre or shop. They will catch all kinds of insects that crawl over the sticky surface and reduce many insect problems next year.
**Perpetual strawberries** will rot unless the fruit is held clear of the soil. Use straw or wire supports.
**Prune loganberries** if this has not already been done, cutting out fruited canes to the base and tying in new ones.

## THE FLOWER GARDEN

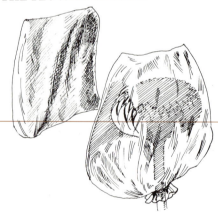

**Chrysanthemum blooms** still to flower outdoors will need protection against wet weather. Greaseproof-paper bags placed over the blooms provide an excellent method of protection. Damaged bags are easily replaced.
**Hardy annuals** that have finished flowering can be forked up, the soil shaken off, and placed on the compost heap.
**Hyacinth bulbs** can be planted in the garden as soon as summer-bedding

plants are removed. Plant the bulbs 12.5–15 cm (5–6 in) deep and 20 cm (8 in) apart. Small-sized bulbs are usually adequate for outdoor flowering.
**Plant allium bulbs.** Make the holes three times the bulb depth, and choose a well-drained soil in a sunny position.
**Window boxes** need not be bleak in winter. Apart from the spring bulbs and dwarf wallflowers that can be planted now, do not overlook the possibility of some evergreen plants to add interest during the cold months. Small-leaved ivies are useful, but young or dwarf shrubs such as heathers can be very effective. You can always plant them out in the garden if they become too large, or if you want to fill the boxes with summer bedding plants next year. Some of the dwarf conifers can also make an attractive feature for a year to two.

## THE WATER GARDEN

**Autumn leaves** from trees can be a nuisance. Keep them raked up regularly,

and scoop them off the water if possible. Spreading plastic netting over the pool may help.
**Clean out the pond** if it is looking dirty and neglected. There will be plenty of dead leaves and other decaying matter to be removed, and this should be done even if the water is not lowered for a more serious 'autumn clean'.

## LAWNS

**Diseases** sometimes become obvious this month. Most of the fungus diseases will respond to a suitable fungicide, but you may have to repeat the treatment.
**Mow less frequently** from now on, and cut the grass 6–13 mm ($\frac{1}{4}$–$\frac{1}{2}$ in) higher than during the summer.
**Spike (aerate) the lawn** during the next few weeks, if this has not already been done, and brush in a lawn top-dressing.

## THE GREENHOUSE

**Crocuses**, scillas, chionodoxa and other early-flowering bulbs can be potted up now.

**Divide arum lilies** in pots.

**Erica hiemalis** can be raised from cuttings taken now. Use the tips of sideshoots, trimming them to about 19 mm (¾ in) long.

**Insulate your greenhouse** if you are planning to heat it for the winter. Polythene sheeting can be stapled to the framework of a wooden greenhouse and there are several devices for fixing it to a metal-framed structure (ask at your garden centre). Do not seal off the ventilators.

**Pot up schizanthus seedlings** if not already done. Those potted up earlier may be ready for potting on into larger pots (if they become potbound they will flower too soon). Keep them growing

Place bulbs carefully in compost before covering over.

and give a weak liquid feed.

**Remove shading** from the glass if this has not already been done.

**Tomato plants** that have finished fruiting can be cleared away. Unripened fruit can be taken indoors to ripen on a window-sill or in a drawer.

**Chrysanthemums** to flower in the greehouse can be brought inside now.

**Ventilate** greenhouses carefully and avoid cold draughts. Keep the atmosphere dry now. At this time of year very high humidity can cause problems through fungal diseases.

**Water pot-plants** cautiously, being careful not to splash the leaves and flowers.

**Winter lettuces** can be sown in the greenhouse border, but make sure you choose a suitable variety and can provide the temperature recommended on the packet.

---

## WEEKEND PROJECTS

### Make a cold frame

The best cold frames are covered with glass lights. Plastic and clear polythene covers can be used, but these do not retain heat as well as glass frames, and they are also more prone to wind damage. If you decide to use polythene, use the wire reinforced type, which can be tacked to a simple timber frame, or use ordinary heavy gauge sheet which can be wrapped around a timber frame.

The suggested dimensions for a cold frame are shown in the diagram. It is a good idea to have a cold frame that can be moved around to cover various crops, and in this case make the frame from preservative-treated timber boards. Secondhand floor joists are ideal and these can be bought from demolition contractors. A permanently sited frame can be made from bricks, or even better from lightweight building blocks, although the latter do not look as attractive as bricks.

If old window frames are available for the lights of the frames, it may be necessary to alter the dimensions to suit them. If you have to buy glass for the frames choose horticultural glass which

can be obtained in a single sheet measuring 1220 × 710 × 3 mm (48 × 28 × ⅛ in). Check dimensions with your glass supplier before making the frames. The sheets can be set without putty in simple timber frames and each unit is

termed a 'Dutch light'.

The front of a frame should be about 25 cm (10 in) high and the rear about 30–35 cm (12–14 in). This allows the glass to slope from back to front to throw rainwater clear and to catch the sun (a frame should face south if possible). If the frame is made from bricks or blocks, see the project on p. 179 for details of foundations and laying.

A timber frame can be made simply by resting the front and back timbers on edge between pairs of pegs which are hammered into the ground. The end walls can be made of sawn timber which is also held in place with timber pegs.

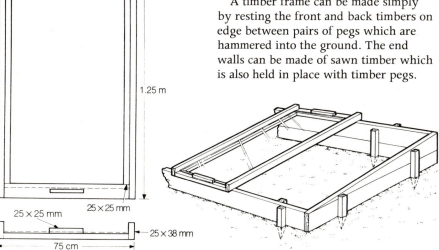

25 × 38 mm

1.25 m

25 × 25 mm

25 × 25 mm

25 × 38 mm

75 cm

## THE KITCHEN GARDEN

**Continue to feed tomatoes** if they are still showing a good crop and seem to be growing actively. You can stop, however, once the weather turns too cold for much active growth.

**Green manure** sown in August (*see* page 15) should be dug in now if this has not already been done.

**Harvest** any remaining marrows, squashes or pumpkins before the weather deteriorates too much.

**Lift potatoes** for storing. Put damaged tubers on one side for immediate use.

**Slugs and snails** will still be very active, probably encouraged by damp weather. Sprinkle slug pellets wherever they are likely to congregate round crops still in the ground.

**Sow turnips** for turnip tops without delay if not already done.

**Thin vegetable seedlings** sown last month, such as lettuces and spinach.

### FRUIT

**Late-maturing apples** should be protected from scab by spraying with a suitable fungicide.

**Peach leaf curl** is always a problem, so it is worth spraying peaches, nectarines and almonds with a suitable fungicide as soon as the leaves start to fall.

**Plant container-grown fruit trees,** but prepare the ground well first.

**Propagate gooseberries and currants** from hardwood cuttings any time during the next month.

## THE FLOWER GARDEN

**Basal-rooting lilies** such as *Lilium candidum* (madonna lily) are best planted in the autumn. Plant madonna lily bulbs with their noses just below soil level. Stem-rooters would be set deeper.

**Border perennials** raised from seed, such as hollyhocks and lupins, can be moved from the nursery bed into their flowering positions.

**Chionodoxa** bulbs can be planted 5–7.5 cm (2–3 in) deep in large groups. A well-drained soil in full sun suits them best.

**Climbing roses** may have produced long shoots that will need tying in to the support.

**Cyclamen neapolitanum** (*C. hederifolium*) and *C. coum* can be naturalized in a shady part of the garden if you add plenty of peat to the soil. The corms should only just be covered with soil or leafmould.

**Dahlias** are still likely to be in bloom, and disbudding and tying should not be neglected. Continue to trap earwigs.

**Ensure michaelmas daisies are staked** securely.

**Established polyanthus** plants can be divided and replanted; although another year it is worth growing a fresh supply from seed.

**Lift gladioli** and allow them to dry off in a garden shed or garage before storing for the winter in paper bags or tins in a cool, frostproof place.

**Rampant climbers** that have grown out of bounds should be cut back. The mile-a-minute vine (*Polygonum baldschuanicum*) can become a tangled mass of shoots, and will benefit from being cut back to shape.

**Red-hot pokers** (kniphofias) look unattractive after they have finished flowering, so cut the dead spikes off with a sharp pair of secateurs.

**Tidy up stakes** that are no longer required, and stack them in a dry place for a few weeks before storing them away for the winter.

### FRAMES AND CLOCHES

**Root cuttings of evergreen shrubs** such as aucuba, laurel, lavender, *Lonicera nitida* and privet.

**Viola and pansy cuttings** can be taken from young, non-flowering shoots and rooted in sandy soil in the frame.

### THE WATER GARDEN

**This is a good time to check pumps,** fountains and cables (but make sure the electricity supply is switched off and disconnected before tackling this job). Pump filters will need particular attention. Clean them, and renew if necessary. If any pipes are in an exposed position where they are likely to freeze, it is best to drain them before the cold weather arrives.

### LAWNS

**Diseases** such as fusarium patch and red thread should be treated with a suitable fungicide as soon as you notice them.

**Spike (aerate) and top-dress** if this has not already been done.

## THE GREENHOUSE

**Cinerarias** should be watered carefully; do not over-water, and do not splash the leaves. Watch for greenfly and other pests.

**Chrysanthemums** to flower in the greenhouse should be brought in if not already done.

**Crocuses,** scillas, chionodoxa and other early-flowering bulbs can be potted up now.

**Freesias** that have been standing outside in a frame can be brought into the greenhouse. Water regularly to encourage them into growth.

**Perpetual-flowering carnations** that have spent the summer outside should be brought into the greenhouse. They need plenty of light and a rather dry atmosphere.

**Plan for spring colour** in an unheated greenhouse. You can have a superb

Covering bulbs with compost.

display of winter and spring colour in an unheated greenhouse. Many bulbs and winter- or spring-flowering shrubs can be used to create continuing interest. Bulbs with double flowers that may get spoilt outdoors in bad weather are often better with the protection a greenhouse provides. The delicate fragrance of some of the small-flowered bulbs, such as *Iris danfordiae*, can also be appreciated much more readily in an enclosed environment. Winter-flowering heathers grown in pots can also be very attractive.

**Tomato plants** that have finished fruiting should be cleared away before they have chance to harbour pests and diseases. Any remaining green tomatoes can be ripened indoors.

**Winter cherries** (*Solanum capsicastrum*) should be brought into the greenhouse if they have been in frames.

## WEEKEND PROJECTS

### Build a retaining wall

It is quite easy to build a wall to retain a bank of soil up to about 1.2 m (4 ft) high. Above this height it is best to take professional advice as the weight of soil may push over a conventional retaining wall.

A retaining wall can be built with random stone blocks as shown in the photograph, with broken paving slabs, decorative concrete wall blocks, facing bricks or rubble—odd pieces of stone, flint, paving slabs or broken bricks.

A retaining wall up to about 60 cm (2 ft) high can be made simply by sprinkling sifted soil between the stones (called a dry stone wall), but for maximum durability and for walls over 60 cm (2 ft) high, cement mortar should be used between the stones.

Low dry stone walls need a gravel or ballast foundation. Simply dig out the top soil in a level, 40 cm (15 in) wide strip until firm ground is reached. Ram at least 10 cm (4 in) of rubble into the base of the trench and lay the first blocks on this foundation. Start with the largest blocks and grade the blocks so that the smallest are at the top of the wall. The first blocks should be laid with their

bases slightly below the surrounding soil level. Make sure that the blocks are level and firmly bedded on soil, and also ensure that the vertical joints between blocks are staggered in brickwork fashion. For extra stability lay the blocks so that the face of the wall slopes back about 5 degrees from the vertical towards the soil bank.

For walls up to 1.2 m (4 ft) high, dig out the foundation trench, as before (it should be as wide as twice the thickness of the wall) and then lay at least a 10–15 cm (4–6 in) thick layer of concrete, allowing at least the first course of

blocks to be below soil level. Lay the blocks using a mortar mix of 1 part cement to 5 parts of builders' sand, and add a squirt of washing-up liquid to improve the workability of the mix.

For neatness, keep the mortar joints as narrow as possible: 6–13 mm ($\frac{1}{4}$–$\frac{1}{2}$ in) is about right. To allow water in the soil bank to drain away, at one course above ground level leave an open vertical joint between the bricks or blockwork at 1 m (3 ft) intervals. If the soil bank is very wet build sections of circular land drainage pipes into the wall at the same intervals.

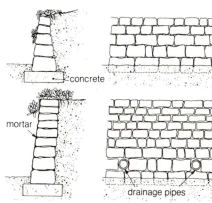

concrete

mortar

drainage pipes

## THE KITCHEN GARDEN

**Brussels sprouts** are likely to be ready for picking from early varieties this month. Harvest the buttons while they are still tight.

**Continue to blanch endive** by covering with a light-proof container.

**Hoe** between winter crops whenever the weather is suitable. A surprising number of weed seedlings can germinate in spells of mild autumn weather.

**Lift the roots of chicory** and leave exposed for a few days to check growth, then cut off foliage 2.5 cm (1 in) above the crown and store in sand or peat in a cool place. They will provide forced chicons for the winter.

**Maincrop potatoes** should be lifted as soon as possible as they will not grow any more and leaving them in the ground only provides food for the slugs.

**Outdoor tomatoes** will not be ripening so well in cold areas. If you have barn cloches available, remove the stakes and lay the plants down over straw before covering them to prolong the season.

**Pick tomatoes** to ripen indoors unless the weather is still particularly fine. Pick them with stalk attached and wrap in tissue paper and place in a drawer.

**Plant cabbages** for spring cutting.

**Plant rhubarb.** You can lift and divide old clumps that have been in the ground for about four years. Make sure each piece has a thonged root and two or three strong buds. Rhubarb clumps can be tough to cut, but a half-moon edger or a spade should solve the problem.

**Thin winter spinach** if it has not already been done.

### FRUIT

**Check tree ties.** Make sure they are not constricting the stem but are tight

enough to withstand autumn and winter winds.

**Examine stored fruit** and remove any rotting specimens.

## THE FLOWER GARDEN

**As gladioli die down** they can be lifted and stored in a frost-proof, light, and airy place. If you collect the young cormlets from the bases of corms, you can plant these in a spare piece of ground next year. It is a good way to increase your stock if you are prepared to wait a few years for them to flower.

**Cornus alba** (dogwood) is easily increased from 25–30 cm (10–12 in) cuttings inserted in sandy soil in a sheltered part of the garden.

**Early-flowering chrysanthemums** should be lifted and the stools (clumps of roots with cut-down stems) placed in a garden frame to provide propagation material later.

**Prune shrub roses** at any time between now and March. Thin out the shoots and remove all those that are dead or diseased. Keep a well-spaced framework of branches.

**Sow sweet peas** in pots in a frame if you want early blooms next year.

## THE ROCK GARDEN

**Alpines raised from cuttings** earlier in the year can now be planted out in the rock garden. If they are not really established, place them in their pots in a cold frame, and plant them out in spring.

## FRAMES AND CLOCHES

**For early cut flowers** next year, it is worth providing cloche protection for pyrethrums, scabious and gaillardias.

**Overwintering annuals** will also benefit from cloches in all but the mildest areas (and even then it is worth using them if you have spare cloches not in use).

## LAWNS

**Aerate lawns** by spiking the surface with either a garden fork or a lawn spiker. A garden fork will just produce a series of holes in the lawn, but many lawn spikers will take out cores of soil. Brush a top-dressing of finely-granulated peat and sand into the holes.

## THE GREENHOUSE

**Arum lilies** will now need more water. They will also benefit from a liquid fertilizer.

**Check heating equipment** and thermostats if not already done. Thermostats may need resetting. Use a thermometer while the heater is on to determine accuracy; do not depend on the figures on the dial. If you use a hot-water system, check for leaks.

**Check perpetual-flowering carnations** for red spider mite.

**Chrysanthemums** for flowering in the greenhouse should be brought in if this has not already been done. Watch for botrytis (grey mould) and earwigs, both of which can be troublesome. An insecticidal dust is likely to be more successful than a spray, for earwigs.

**Crocuses** and other small-flowered spring bulbs can be potted up now.

**Plant spring-flowering gladioli**, such as *G. colvillei*, *G. byzantinus*, and *G. nanus*. Plant three corms to a 12.5 cm (5 in) pot, and keep in a frost-free frame until late February.

**Prune passion flowers** (*Passiflora*

*caerulea*) as soon as the flowers fade. Thin out the shoots to prevent overcrowding, but leave sufficient lateral shoots to provide a good display next year.

**Reglaze loose or cracked glass**; do not leave this job until winter. Try using a mastic rather than a hard-setting putty.

**Rest** gloxinias, begonias, gloriosas and achimenes by withholding water

gradually. Gloxinias can be left in the pot once they have dried off, but place the pots on their sides somewhere out of the way, such as beneath the greenhouse staging if this is reasonably dry. If you remove achimenes tubers to store in bags in a cool but frost-free place, handle them carefully as they are easily damaged.

**Tulips** can still be potted up for spring flowering in the greenhouse (but put them in a garden frame until they are ready for increased warmth early next spring).

**Ventilate** the greenhouse whenever the weather is suitable, but close the house up in time to conserve warmth in the evening.

**Water pot-plants carefully.** Waterlogged compost will soon kill plants now that the colder weather and shorter days are here. Do not let moisture fall on the leaves or flowers.

**Winter cherries** (*Solanum capsicastrum*) should now be in the greenhouse and protected from frost.

---

## WEEKEND PROJECTS

### Save your own seeds

Home-saved seed can give rather variable results, but as long as you are prepared to go by trial and error the results can be rewarding. The basic point to remember is that seeds from hybrid plants ($F_1$, $F_2$ and so on) are unlikely to resemble the parent plants, and it is also a waste of time saving seed from plants which hybridize easily, such as members of the cabbage family.

Having said that, it is often worth watching for plants that are forming seed pods with a view to saving the seed. In the vegetable garden it can be worth saving seed from non-hybrid tomatoes, leeks, onions, peas, beans and marrows. In the flower garden look out for seed heads on shrubs, alpines and annuals. Many herbaceous plants, particularly lupins, delphiniums, irises and dahlias, will produce seed that is worth saving, although the seedlings

will come up in a variety of colours and not necessarily the same as the parents.

In all cases, take the seeds from the strongest and best plants. With plants that produce small seeds, place clear plastic bags over the best seed heads and tie it to canes to prevent the seeds from being lost. With many flowers, the stems with the seed heads can be cut just before the pods are fully ripe and can be hung upside down in bundles with the heads in paper bags so the seeds are not lost. Keep the heads in a cool, dry place.

With peas and beans, allow the pods

holes
sand
seeds

more or less to ripen on the plants, then pick the pods and bring them into a cool dry place to dry off properly.

Marrow seeds can be scraped out of the pulp and left to dry on paper. Allow tomato fruits to ripen fully, then scrape out the seeds and pulp into a sieve and wash under a tap to remove the pulp, then dry the seeds on paper.

As soon as the seeds are dry, clean them from the husks and store them in a cool dry place in envelopes placed in an airtight container and stored in a cool dry place until the correct sowing time. Seeds of berried shrubs, like cotoneaster, should be mixed with damp sand and stored in the open in perforated tins or in plant pots until the sand and seed mixture can be sown in spring. This period of cold conditions, which is necessary to ensure good germination, is called stratification.

# Week 41

## THE KITCHEN GARDEN

**Cabbages** sown in August for spring use should be ready for transplanting to their final positions.

**Carrots for store** should be lifted now, apart from late sowings. Twist the tops off, clean the roots, and do not put into store any that are not sound. Store them in boxes of sand, or in clamps in the open.

**Celery** sometimes shows signs of rust disease at this time—remove affected leaves or plants, and spray the rest with a suitable fungicide.

**Earth up late celery and leeks** without delay.

**Gather up stakes** and canes before they start rotting. Dip the bases into creosote or some other wood preservative once they have been dried out—but do it now rather than in the spring to allow time for any fumes to have worn off.

Tie sticks and canes into bundles and store them in a dry place.

**Lift self-blanching celery** and use up as soon as possible. The ordinary type will carry on the season.

**Scorzonera** can be lifted as required from now on.

FRUIT

**Harvest remaining apples and pears** as soon as possible. You can store them in trays or boxes (never pile pears on top of each other) and keep them cool. You can use a proprietary sugar-based dip to prolong the storage life; it acts by putting a protective coat around the fruit.

**Order fruit trees** now if you want to be sure of getting your first choice of varieties and rootstocks. Do not order or buy apples unless you know the rootstock used—and always try to buy virus-free stock of plants like raspberries and strawberries. It will be worth paying a little more for quality plants.

## THE FLOWER GARDEN

**Bonfires** are a part of the autumn scene, and not without reason. Now that many plants have been cleared, there is both the space and the need. Do not try to compost woody material, and avoid putting diseased plants on the compost heap. All such material can be burnt on a slow fire. Keep the ash dry and store when cold, then you can use it as a potash fertilizer.

**Check tree ties and stakes.** Make sure they are adequate for the coming winter.

**Colchicums** can be naturalized quite easily, setting them 5–7.5 cm (2–3 in) deep. Plant them in turf by lifting the grass and placing the bulbs underneath. Replace and firm the turf. (Remember to put the bulbs where their bold foliage can be left to grow unchecked in spring.)

**Deutzias** can be increased from hardwood cuttings 20–25 cm (8–10 in) long, inserted in sandy soil in a sheltered part of the garden.

**Empty outside water butts** where practical, and turn them upside down so that they are not damaged by ice.

**Garden chrysanthemums** that have flowered can be cut down to within 15–20 cm (6–8 in) of soil level. Lift the stools (roots) and place them in boxes

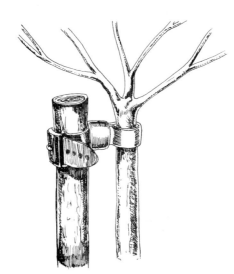

of damp soil in a garden frame. Ensure each plant is labelled.

**New hedges** can be planted now from either container-grown or bare-root plants. Be prepared to look beyond privet. Flowering hedges include lavender, potentilla, berberis and spiraea. Among the evergreens you can consider conifers, holly and laurel.

**Plant erythronium** (dog's-tooth violet) bulbs about 5 cm (2 in) deep in rich soil on a north-facing slope. They can be left undisturbed for several years.

LAWNS

**Mowing** is coming to an end for another year. If the lawn is not too wet, try to give it a cut before the weather deteriorates. Do not forget to trim the edges to finish off.

**Turfing** is still feasible, but the ground should be prepared and levelled as soon as possible. It is wise to let the ground settle for a few weeks before laying.

## THE GREENHOUSE

**Conserve heat.** If your greenhouse is not already insulated, line it with polythene. If you do not have many plants to overwinter, try lining just one end and partition it off with more polythene. This can look unattractive, but that may be less important than keeping the plants alive through the winter. Do not seal over the ventilators.

**Cyclamen** should be checked every few days to ensure that damaged or dying flowers have not been infected by botrytis. Pull off and burn any infected blooms, making sure you remove the complete flower stem.

**Feed** plants that you expect to bloom at Christmas, such as cyclamen, but do not allow them to flower yet—remove any premature flowers that form.

**Houseplants** that have spent the summer outside in the garden frame can now be brought inside.

**Lettuces** can still be sown in the greenhouse border if you select a

suitable variety. Consult a good seed catalogue.

**Pest and disease control** can be a major part of greenhouse management. During the colder months fumigating has the advantage of not wetting the leaves.

**Pot on rooted geranium cuttings** and pot-grown annuals as soon as they are large enough, if this has not already been done.

**Rest fuchsias and hydrangeas** by gradually withholding water.

**Shrubs for a cold or cool greenhouse** include *Nerium oleander* (oleander), *Daphne odora*, *Euonymus fortunei* 'Silver Queen', *Hebe armstrongii*, the bottle-brush tree (*Callistemon linearis*), camellias and *Fatsia japonica*. Some of these will become very large in time if planted in the greenhouse border, but will grow satisfactorily for a number of years in large pots.

**Turn on the heating** whenever it is likely to turn cold in the evening, if you need to provide frost protection.

**Ventilate** the greenhouse carefully and avoid cold draughts. These can kill sensitive plants, and cause buds to drop on others.

**Water with care** from now on. Try to water in the morning so that the plants have chance to dry out a little before it turns cool in the evening.

## WEEKEND PROJECTS

### Lay a gravel (or stone chipping) path

Gravel is a hard-wearing material but uncomfortable to walk on if it is not properly compacted.

Set string lines as a guide to both sides of the path, then dig out to a depth of about 7.5 cm (3 in). Set concrete kerbs on either side so that their top edges are either flush with or slightly below the lawn. For the foundations use either 5 cm (2 in) of well compacted ashes or hardcore. Over this pour a 2.5 cm (1 in) layer of gravel and roll thoroughly. You will find that the surface of the gravel roughs up in use and will have to be raked and rolled occasionally to keep it flat.

*Stone chippings*  These are laid on bitumen emulsion. Any firm, compacted surface makes an ideal base. For a new path use a 7.5–10 cm (3–4 in) excavation filled with hardcore, placing larger pieces at the bottom and covering them with finer pieces. Cover this with

ballast, rolled flat. Ensure there are no depressions and a fall is built in for rainwater drainage. Concrete kerbs can be laid to give a neat edge. The bitumen emulsion is poured from a watering can over an area of about 5 m² (5 sq yds) to form a 2–3 mm thick film. Fitting a dessert spoon in the spout of the can ensures an even spread. Sprinkle the chippings over the emulsion immediately, covering it in a single layer. After each two or three sections are completed, roll them lightly. When the path is complete, give a final roll.

Cold macadam is available in bags. On concrete and loose surfaces a coating of bitumen emulsion is required to act as a binder for the macadam. When the emulsion changes in colour from brown to black, the macadam is emptied on to it and raked out to a 19 mm (¾ in) thickness. A water dampened roller is then used to compact the area.

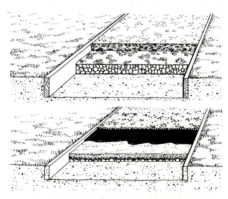

## THE KITCHEN GARDEN

**Burn garden debris**, including the stumps and roots of cabbages and cauliflowers.

**Globe artichoke** plants should be cleaned up. Remove any old flowered stems, together with dead leaves, and sprinkle sharp sand or grit around the base of each plant.

**Lift celeriac** and store in a frost-proof place.

**Outdoor tomatoes** will not ripen much now, unless protected with cloches. If frost is forecast and you do not have protection, be prepared to pick the fruit for ripening in a warm place indoors.

**Pigeons and rabbits** can become a problem from now on in some areas, and plants like spring cabbages can soon be

destroyed. If either of these pests are a problem you have little option but to fence off or net the most vulnerable crops.

**Rats and mice** can be a problem among stored root vegetables, and here the solution is traps or bait.

### FRUIT

**Apples damaged by birds or earwigs**, or that are bruised, should be used up promptly. Do not try to store imperfect fruit.

**Take cuttings** of red, white and blackcurrants and gooseberries. They should be about 20–25 cm (8–10 in) long, taken from well-ripened year-old wood. It is usual to rub off the lower buds of all except blackcurrants. Insert the cuttings outdoors, burying them to two-thirds their length in well drained soil.

## THE FLOWER GARDEN

**Alstroemerias** (Peruvian lilies) can be increased by dividing the clumps. Replant with the healthy, young tuberous roots from the outside of the clump.

**Carnation layers** not already severed should be separated from the parent plant now.

**Dig over** any areas of vacant ground and leave them rough for the winter.

*Fritillaria imperialis* (crown imperial) bulbs can be planted 20 cm (8 in) deep in well-drained fertile soil. Plant on their sides to avoid the hollow crowns retaining moisture. Alternatively, set the crowns in sand.

**Herbaceous plants** can still be planted, and established plants in borders can be rearranged and replanted if necessary.

**Lift begonias and cannas** that have been grown outdoors. Dry them off to store in a frostproof place for the winter.

**Once dahlias have been cut down by frost** they can be lifted and placed in a greenhouse or other dry and frostproof place for a few weeks before storing for

the winter. Stand them with the stalks down, so that moisture does not affect the crown. If the plants are still flowering, leave them until blackened by frost.

**Peonies** can still be divided or planted.

**Plant out spring bedding plants**, such as polyanthus, wallflowers, forget-me-nots, sweet williams, and Canterbury bells. Clear the remaining summer

bedding if this has not been done, fork over the soil, and dust it with bonemeal. Plant firmly and water them well if it is dry.

**Plant roses** any time during the next few months.

**Plant spring-flowering bulbs** as soon as possible. Some kinds can be planted for another month yet, but it is sensible to plant by the end of October.

**Summer bedding** can be cleared if this has not been done, although it is best to leave the plants a little longer if there is still a little colour and the ground is not needed for bulbs.

### THE ROCK GARDEN

**Aubrieta** can still be divided. Replant with young parts from the outside of the clump.

**Brush up fallen leaves** from the rock garden. Fallen leaves harbour slugs and can smother dwarf plants.

**Half-ripe cuttings** that were inserted in a frame during July and August may have rooted. If they have, pot up into 7.5 cm (3 in) pots and grow them on in a garden frame. Keep the compost moist.

## THE GREENHOUSE

**Be prepared for night frosts,** and provide sufficient heat whenever the weather turns cold. If you depend on paraffin or bottled gas, now is the time to make sure you have an adequate supply. It is always wise to have two cylinders of gas, preferably with an automatic change-over, and it is prudent to keep a spare can of paraffin in a safe place. This at least avoids the consequences of running out at an inconvenient time.

**Cinerarias** still in a garden frame should be brought in as soon as possible.

**Disbud** perpetual-flowering carnations and chrysanthemums.

**Pot on** *Primula malacoides* into their final pots.

**Rest fuchsias** by gradually withholding water, but do not let the compost dry out completely.

**Prune passion flowers** (*Passiflora caerulea*) if the flowers have faded and it has not been done. Thin the shoots to prevent overcrowding, but leave sufficient lateral shoots to provide a good display next year.

**'Stop' schizanthus,** and plants such as clarkia, by pinching out the tops to encourage bushiness.

**Store begonia tubers** that have been dried off. Keep them in paper bags or dry peat in a cool but frost-free place.

**Thin climbers** on the greenhouse wall and any that are climbing into the roof. Tall climbers should not cast too much shade during the dark months.

**Water carefully now,** keeping the compost moist but not wet for those plants that are still growing actively.

**WEEKEND PROJECTS**

### Plant a hedge

Because a hedge will be in position for many years it is important to prepare the soil properly by double-digging a trench about 50 cm (20 in) wide along where the hedge is to be planted. Start the trench by taking out a 60 cm (2 ft) section to the full depth of the spade. Take this soil to the far end of the area ready to fill in the trench when the end is reached.

As each section of trench is opened up, put plenty of well-rotted manure or garden compost into the base and fork this in. Dig back another 60 cm section, turning this soil on to the forked base. Continue in this manner until the trench is completed. If possible, leave the soil for at least a week to settle. If planting is to take place immediately, shuffle over the soil to tread it firm.

Rake in a general fertilizer at about 110 g (4 oz) per metre (yard) run of trench just before planting.

Most hedging plants should be set 45–60 cm (1½–2 ft) apart. Take out holes at these spacings large enough to take the soil clumps or bare roots of the plants without cramping them. The holes should be deep enough to allow the

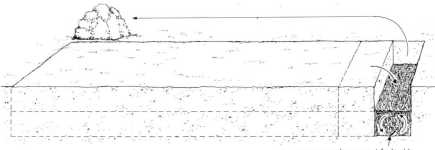

manure and compost forked in

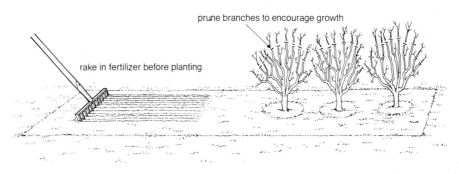

prune branches to encourage growth

rake in fertilizer before planting

plants to be set only fractionally deeper than they were growing in the nursery —indicated by a soil mark on the stem.

Replace the soil carefully and tread it firm. Loosely tie whippy plants to bamboo canes and keep the plants well watered, especially in dry weather.

## THE KITCHEN GARDEN

**Blanch endive** with large inverted plant-pots (hole blocked) or blackened cloches. Alternatively use darkened frames to blanch them.

**Celery** may benefit from a little more soil being drawn up around the stems.

**Cut back asparagus** growth, which will have started to turn yellow. You can use garden shears for this, but cut the shoots off close to the ground.

**Hoe** between crops that are to stand for the winter, such as spring cabbages, overwintering onions and spinach.

**Jerusalem artichokes** should be cut down to within about 15 cm (6 in) of the ground. You do not need to lift the tubers immediately as they are hardy and you can harvest them as required.

**Late cauliflowers** should have the curds protected by breaking large outer leaves over the centre.

FRAMES AND CLOCHES

**Clean glass.** The plants will need all the light they can get during the shortening days, so scrub the glass with a strong soda solution.

**Overwinter flowers** such as pelargoniums if you can provide frost protection in the frames. It may be cheaper than heating a greenhouse, and even if the greenhouse is heated it is sometimes useful to keep overwintering plants that are not attractive somewhere less conspicuous.

FRUIT

**Hoe round soft fruit,** but be prepared to hand weed around the stems of plants; the hoe will miss weeds growing in among the plants but these should be removed before they become too entangled with the crop.

**Pick up fallen fruit** before it rots and acts as a reservoir of diseases for next year. Take the opportunity to clear any weeds that are taking hold around fruit trees and bushes.

## THE FLOWER GARDEN

**Conifers** such as *Cupressus lawsoniana* can be increased from cuttings. They may take up to a year to root, so use a spare piece of land where they can be left undisturbed.

**Fences** will need repairing eventually. This is a good time to tackle these jobs, when the plants have been cleared yet the weather is not too cold for comfort.

**Paint the fence** with a preservative if this has not been done in recent years (be careful with creosote, which will probably kill plants growing nearby). If plants are secured to the fence, it will be necessary to undo all the ties and lay the plants on the ground, re-securing them afterwards.

**Heathers** can be planted now. Plant firmly and try to incorporate peat into the soil. A mulch of damp peat is also beneficial.

**Large-flowered tuberous-rooted begonias** used for bedding purposes are not hardy and must be lifted before frosts damage them. Dry them slowly,

and when top growth has withered removed it and store the tubers.

**Muscari** (grape hyacinths) are easy plants to grow, and multiply rapidly. Plant the bulbs 7.5 cm (3 in) deep in small groups in a sunny position.

**Philadelphus** (mock orange) shrubs

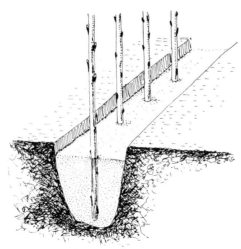

can be increased easily from 20–25 cm (8–10 in) hardwood cuttings inserted in sandy soil in a sheltered part of the garden.

**Plant hardy ferns,** unless the site is very exposed and windy (in which case it is best to wait until spring).

**Tidy up leaves and weeds,** and place them on the compost heap. They harbour insects and diseases.

**Tigridia** bulbs should be lifted as soon as the foliage yellows. Keep them in a frostproof place until the leaves and stems have withered, then clean the bulbs and store them in a dry, cool place indoors.

## THE ROCK GARDEN

**Divide** *Gypsophila repens.*

**Remove leaves** which may have fallen from nearby trees. If left they encourage pests and may cause the leaves of some plants to rot. A spiked stick is useful for removing leaves from crevices.

## THE GREENHOUSE

**Autumn-sown pot-plants** should be kept near to the glass, where they will get the most light. But on cold nights ensure that there is enough heat to prevent frost damage.

**Check ventilators** to ensure they rest evenly on their frames, and do not let out too much warm air. If there are any cracked or broken panes of glass in the greenhouse, replace these now before winter sets in.

**Christmas pot-plants** such as winter cherries (*Solanum capsicastrum*) and Indian azaleas are often on sale from now on. Do not allow them to dry out, and try to water the azaleas with rainwater, or some other relatively lime-free source. If you have had these plants in the frame for the summer, bring them in without delay.

**Cyclamen and primulas** should be fed regularly.

**Ferns** will need less water now, but never let them become too dry.

**Fuchsias** will gradually require less water now that their flowering period is coming to an end.

**Grapes** will ripen more successfully if the leaves immediately above ripening bunches are removed.

**Hippeastrums** are impressive greenhouse and houseplants. They can be potted up now for flowering from Christmas onwards. For the earliest flowers you will need to buy 'prepared' bulbs. Established hippeastrums that have been in flower should be dried off, and if this has not been done withhold water gradually.

**Mice** can be a problem at this time. You can use bait or traps, but place them where they cannot be reached by children or pets. It is a good idea to place them in drainpipes in a suitable position.

**Pot on** *Primula malacoides* into their final pots.

**Schizanthus seedlings** should be 'stopped' by pinching out the growing tips to induce bushiness.

**The Christmas cactus** (*Zygocactus truncatus*, otherwise known as *Schlumbergera truncata*) should also be kept well watered now (unlike other cacti). Try to avoid turning the pot round, as this can cause the developing buds to drop.

## WEEKEND PROJECTS

### Lighting in the garden

Garden lighting can be installed for either or both practical and decorative purposes. On the practical side, and with safety and security in mind, it is a good idea to illuminate drives, side entrances, steps and so on—especially where there may be obstacles which could cause accidents. On the decorative side, fish pools and fountains can be transformed into eye-catching night-time features; patios can be illuminated for summer evening parties; and dramatic effects can be brought to trees and shrubs with strategically placed, concealed lighting.

Bear in mind, always, that an 80 watt lamp, for example, will look far brighter outside than it does inside. So generally only low wattage lights are needed outdoors.

A good range of garden lights is available. There are spotlamps for mounting on the ground, in trees or on walls; these can be selected to throw a narrow, defined beam of light on to a chosen spot, or you can get a type which will cast a splash of light over a wide area. There are downlights intended to illuminate an area immediately below —perhaps a plant or steps. There is also a good selection of ornamental lamps on pillars which are used for general illumination.

For pools and ponds there are submersible and floating lighting sets. All outside lights can be fitted with coloured bulbs to increase decorative possibilities.

Installing an outside power supply requires a sound knowledge of electrical work. All fittings and cables must be waterproofed. Although cables can be run on the surface it is far better to bury them below ground.

The simplest way to install the lighting is to buy a kit from a reputable manufacturer which will include cable and decorative lamps. These low voltage systems (12 or 24 volts) incorporate a step-down transformer to ensure that power is run safely from the house mains to the lights without creating danger to anyone through accidental severing of the cables.

If you are in any doubt about installation then do not fail to seek the advice or practical help of a qualified electrician.

## THE KITCHEN GARDEN

**Broad beans** for an early crop can be sown now in favourable areas to overwinter. Choose a well-drained, sheltered site and only sow a variety recommended for October or November sowing. Many ordinary varieties are unsuitable.

**Double-dig** any ground you are reclaiming for next year, to allow plenty of time for the soil to settle and weathering to break it down.

**Make onion ropes** if you have ripe onions to store for winter use.

## FRUIT

**Apply grease-bands** to apple trees if you have not already done so. The bands and grease can be bought from garden centres and shops; ready-greased bands make the job easier.

**Order fruit trees** if you have not already done so.

**Plant fruit trees** within the next month if possible. The sooner they can be planted once they have shed their leaves the better. Container-grown plants can be planted at any time of course, but even these can well be planted now as it gives the plants chance to have settled down by spring.

If bare-root plants arrive and you are not ready to plant them, protect the roots and keep them moist until you can.

**Plums and damsons** that are not fruiting well can be root-pruned (*see* drawing) after leaf-fall. It is best to spread this job over two years (half each year) to avoid too much shock to the tree.

## THE FLOWER GARDEN

**Agapanthus** may need protection in cold areas. Place straw or bracken over the crowns.

**Annuals** sown last month for overwintering to provide early flowers next year should be thinned. Take the opportunity to ensure the ground is also cleared of weeds.

**Hose-pipes** need to be checked and packed away for the winter. Roll them up, making sure all water is drained out of them. Wipe sprinklers clean and dry, giving them a rub with an oily rag to prevent bright parts rusting.

**Hydrangeas** may require some protection in cold areas. Leave old flower heads on the plants to protect the tender flower buds, which will produce next year's blooms.

**Lift gladioli and montbretias** if not already done. Hang them up in a dry place for a week or two, then store in a frostproof place. Montbretias will often overwinter outside in all but the coldest areas, especially if given a little protection.

**Plant tulips** if not already done.

**Protect** slightly tender bulbs, such as *Amaryllis belladonna* and *Crinum powellii*, that are to be overwintered outdoors. Cover them loosely with

straw, leaves or bracken if you cannot provide cloche protection (which often looks odd in the border anyway).

**Spring bedding plants** can still be planted, but any not put in this week are best planted in the spring instead.

**Store dahlia tubers** after lifting and drying off for a week or two. Cut away dead stems, leaving a short stump. After removing old soil, label carefully and store in a frostproof place in boxes.

## THE ROCK GARDEN

**Alpines** from seed often germinate better if exposed to a period of frost. For this reason it is worth sowing them now and leaving them outdoors for the winter, but protect the pots from heavy rain (a piece of glass positioned above the pots is adequate).

## THE WATER GARDEN

**Remove leaves** that have fallen into the garden pool. If left, they will cause discoloration and contamination of the water.

## THE GREENHOUSE

**Do not feed late-flowering chrysanthemums** any more. Too much food from now on is likely to be detrimental.

**Draughts** can soon kill tender plants; see that the ventilators fit properly, and repair any broken panes of glass.

**Empty greenhouses** not being used for the winter should be cleaned thoroughly. Scrub all the brickwork and staging. Remove all debris that may be harbouring pests and diseases.

**Finish off any repotting** that needs to be done.

**Foliage houseplants** in the home will benefit from a respite in the better light of a greenhouse, provided that they are not going to be subjected to a significant drop in temperature.

**Hippeastrums** dried off a month or two ago may be showing signs of regrowth. As soon as you can see evidence of a new shoot, start to water them again.

Houseplants will enjoy the extra light provided in the greenhouse.

**If you want mint for Christmas**, lift a few roots now and lay them thinly on potting compost in deep seed trays, and cover with about 2.5 cm (1 in) of the same compost. Provided you can maintain a temperature of 10°C (50°F) the plants should grow if you keep the compost moist, but water cautiously until the shoots are growing.

**Kalanchoes** need a minimum winter temperature of 15°C (60°F) for the buds to form, but once this has happened they will grow satisfactorily at 7°C (45°F).

**Pot up** *Erica hiemalis* cuttings into 7.5 cm (3 in) pots of a peaty compost.

**Primula obconica and P. malacoides** need a minimum winter temperature of 10°C (50°F), although 13°C (55°F) suits them better. Do not allow the compost to dry out.

**Some of the hardy annuals** sown for a greenhouse display are likely to give a better show if three or four plants are put in a pot—nemophila and mignonette being examples. They will, however, still put on a good display in individual pots.

## Repairs to paths and drives

Tackle concrete repairs when the danger of frost has passed. If working in hot weather then any fresh concrete repairs should be protected by damp sacking for a day or two.

Cracks in a concrete slab are caused mostly by settlement on inadequate foundations. Minor cracks should be filled only after it is certain that all movement has ceased.

Use a mortar mix of one part cement to three parts sand. For small repairs use a bag of dry mixed mortar.

First, undercut the crack with a bolster chisel and club hammer to widen it below surface and to ensure that the filling mortar gets a good grip. Brush away any dust then dampen the crack with water before forcing in the mortar with a small trowel and bringing it flush with the surface before smoothing it off.

A crack in the edge of a concrete drive should be cut back with a cold chisel and club hammer to sound material. Fix a stout board, supported by pegs, alongside the formwork; the top edge of the board should be level with the surface of the concrete.

Use a concrete mix of one part cement to five parts of ballast. To improve adhesion, add a little pva adhesive to the mix. Diluted pva adhesive brushed over the repair area will also improve adhesion.

Press the mix well down into the formwork, making sure that no air pockets are trapped. Bring the mix to the surface then level it by using a float in a semi-circular motion. Allow at least a week before removing the formwork.

A cracked slab or brick can be broken into smaller pieces for removal. A new slab should be bedded down on five dabs of mortar (one part cement to five parts sand). Tap down the slab with the shaft of a club hammer and use a straight-edge to check that it is flush with the surrounding slabs. If the joints are to be pointed use a mix of one part cement, 1½ sharp sand and 1½ soft sand.

A cracked brick and its old bedding down mortar should be removed and repaired as for a slab. Use a mix of one part cement to three parts sand for both bedding down and pointing the joints. Point the joints after the bedding mortar has set.

Broken concrete

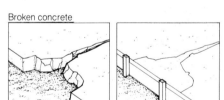

Broken slab

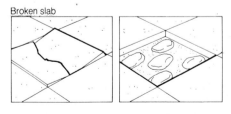

Broken brick

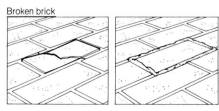

# Week 45

## THE KITCHEN GARDEN

**Dig over vacant ground.** It is especially important to dig heavy soils as soon as possible, so that the winter weather can help to break them down.
**Harvest Brussels sprouts** and spinach beet regularly.
**Peas** can also be sown if a suitable winter-hardy variety is chosen. It is no use sowing ordinary summer varieties; a sheltered position should be chosen. Obviously cloche protection helps, but it is not essential in mild districts. It will pay to use a seed dressing to prevent diseases affecting the seeds before they germinate, and wire-netting or black cotton stretched over the rows will keep them protected from birds.
**Remove yellow leaves** from Brussels

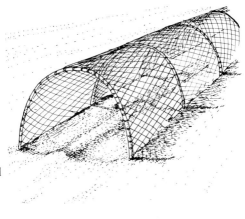

sprouts and other plants and put them on the compost heap.
**Sow broad beans** now if you have a sheltered spot and live in a mild area. Otherwise raise the plants in a greenhouse in February or wait until the maincrop spring sowings.

### FRUIT

**Check apples and pears** in store and remove any showing signs of disease.
**Winter prune apple and pear trees** that were summer pruned earlier in the year. Cut back the unpruned leading shoot by one-third, and the sideshoots back to two buds. This plan may have to be modified according to the way the trees are being trained (*see* page 54).

## THE FLOWER GARDEN

**Check supports** for climbers. Those supports concreted into brick must be firm; reconcrete them if necessary. Straining bolts often become so rusty that the screw part cannot be moved. Use penetrating oil to release them. Check that the wires are sound.
**Finish planting tulips** as soon as possible.
**Heel in trees and shrubs** that arrive when you are not able to plant them immediately. Take out a hole on a spare piece of ground and lay the plants with their roots in it. Replace the soil over the roots and firm lightly. They should be safe until you are able to plant them, but do not delay needlessly.
**Labels** usually need replacing at some time, so make a note of any that clearly will not last another season, and write new ones.
**Large windbreaks** can be planted now. If your garden is in a very exposed area and your plants frequently suffer from wind damage, consider a windbreak of two rows of the fast-growing × *Cupressocyparis leylandii* — but you need a large garden. Plant about 1.5 m (5 ft) apart in the rows, with the staggered rows the same distance apart. A hedge like this will

filter the wind effectively and provide a useful screen at the same time. These trees grow very rapidly, however, so only plant them in a suitable place.
**New herbaceous borders** should be prepared now for spring planting. Thoroughly dig the soil, incorporating well-rotted compost or manure, and removing perennial weeds.
**Store stakes** in a dry place. Tie them up into neat bundles.
**Tidy up the herbaceous border**, and lightly fork over or hoe the surface to keep down the weeds that invariably germinate in the autumn, and to improve appearances.

**Tie in shoots of climbers.** These will probably have made substantial growth during the summer, and ought to be tied in before winter gales start blowing.

### FRAMES AND CLOCHES

**Root-cuttings** can be taken of anchusas, gaillardias, hollyhocks, phlox (perennial kind), *Primula denticulata*, oriental poppies and *Romneya coulteri*, if you place them in a garden frame.

### THE WATER GARDEN

**Marginal plants**, which grow in the damp surrounds of the pool, can be tidied up by pulling off damaged leaves, picking up leaves from the surface of the soil, and hoeing around plants. Make sure you remove weeds.
**Remove fallen leaves** from the pool. Left in they will decompose and pollute the pool.

### LAWNS

**It is not too late to mow** once more with the blades set high, provided that the weather is not frosty or wet.
**Wormkillers** can still be used if wormcasts are particularly troublesome, although it is not worth bothering for just a few that are easy to brush away.

## THE GREENHOUSE

**Azaleas** will need regular watering, ensuring that the compost is well saturated each time.

**Cyclamen** and winter-flowering primulas will be coming into flower. Feed them once a week with a weak liquid fertilizer.

**Flowering plants** should be as near to the glass as possible so that they receive maximum light. Keep them away from the glass at night, however, unless you can provide sufficient warmth to ensure that they will not be damaged.

**Clean the glass** on the outside of the greenhouse. You want as much light as possible for the next few months.

**Freesias** should be growing strongly now. Give them a position in good light, near the glass, and be prepared to insert small canes or twigs as support. Watch out for greenfly.

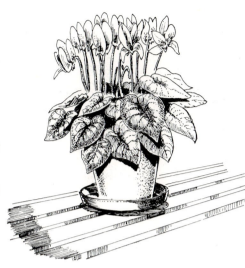

**Lilies** can be potted up as soon as the bulbs become available. *Lilium henryi*, *L. regale*, and *L. rubellum* can all be grown in pots: one bulb to a 15 cm

(6 in) pot, three to a 23 cm (9 in) pot. Always leave room for top-dressing afterwards. They can be placed in a garden frame until growth starts.

**Lily of the valley** crowns can now be bought and potted up, just covering them with compost. Give the pots a light watering and place in a cool part of the greenhouse.

**Pot up more freesia corms**, five or six in a 15 cm (6 in) pot.

**Watering** plants in pots is always a difficult matter of judgement in the winter. It is better to err on the side of underwatering rather than overwatering, especially if temperatures are low. Try not to splash the water about.

**Winter-flowering begonias** will need good light and a regular weak liquid fertilizer.

## WEEKEND PROJECTS

### Build a screen block wall

A firm level foundation is needed. The height of the wall and the soil firmness govern foundation depth. Normally a 30 cm (1 ft) wide strip should be dug 25 cm (10 in) deep to allow for 13 cm (5 in) of well compacted hardcore topped with 13 cm of concrete. A low wall of 60–90 cm (2–3 ft) requires 10 cm (4 in) of hardcore and 10 cm of concrete. Use a concrete mix of one part cement to five parts 1 cm ($\frac{3}{8}$ in) ballast.

On a sloping site, a base wall of bricks or decorative walling blocks is needed to create a level base and to ensure, for best appearance, that no part of the screen walling disappears below ground level.

The pilaster blocks (which are the hollow, upright pieces that provide the pillars between the blocks) can be reinforced with angle iron inserted in the foundation concrete before it sets. The angle iron should extend to within a centimetre or so of the top of the pilasters and should be vertical. Accurate positioning of these angle irons is essential to ensure that they coincide with the centre of each pilaster column. This reinforcement is essential where a

gate is to be hung from a pilaster.

Screen blocks are 30 cm (1 ft) wide and pilaster blocks are 20 cm (8 in) wide. Neither can be cut so the wall must be designed to these full-size dimensions.

Before laying blocks, position the first course of pilasters and screen blocks; when satisfied, stretch a string line between the end pilasters as a guide to building the wall.

The mortar mix for both screen blocks and pilaster blocks should be one part cement to five parts builder's sand and should be pliable. White cement and a light coloured sand will produce joints to blend with the colour of the blocks.

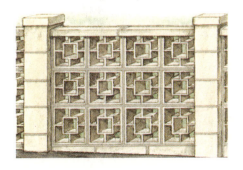

Lay the end pilaster columns first up to three courses high and fill each one as it is laid using a fluid mix of one part cement to three parts sand. Check that each block is vertical and horizontal and is aligned with the string line. Repeat this process for each intermediate pier.

The first walling block is then laid on mortar and its end is tucked into the groove of the pilaster block which should have also been filled with mortar. To avoid breakages while tapping down each block with the shaft of a club hammer, place a piece of wood on the block. Check the block for horizontal and vertical alignment. Repeat this process for the first block in the next pilaster column. Lay a straight-edge across these two blocks and check that they are level. Set up a string line between the blocks.

With subsequent blocks work towards the middle. At the required finished height, bed down coping slabs and pilaster caps. Do not lay more than four courses of blocks per day. In higher walls, reinforce the joints in every second course of blocks by laying wire mesh in the mortar.

# Week 46

## THE KITCHEN GARDEN

**Brussels sprouts** often have some yellowing leaves at this time. Simply pull them off and place them on the compost heap.
**Celery** should be ready for its final earthing up.
**Clear runner bean haulms** (stems) and put them on the compost heap. Clean and store canes and stack in a dry place.
**Peas** are normally sown in spring, but you can have an early crop in May or June by sowing a *round-seeded* variety any time now. Do not attempt to sow the sweeter wrinkle-seeded kinds.
**Protect late cauliflowers** from frost by bending outer leaves over the curds.
**Wind protection** can be of great benefit in the vegetable garden, and it is worth creating a temporary windbreak near winter crops if they are not grown

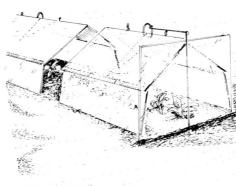

where you are worried about the visual appearance. You can buy specially-designed plastic windbreaks, or you can improvise something with polythene or sacking well secured to stout stakes on the windward side of the crops.

## THE FLOWER GARDEN

**Dahlia borders** can be prepared for next year. Dig the soil at least one spit (spade depth) deep, remove all perennial weeds, and incorporate plenty of bulky organic material such as garden compost. Dahlias need a sunny position that is not too exposed.
**Protect Christmas roses** from rain and mud splashes during the winter by covering them with a piece of glass suitably supported; or you can use a cloche. This does not look attractive, but it is well worth while if you want to pick the flowers for indoor decoration.
**Rabbits and squirrels** often come into gardens at this time of year, in search of food, and can severely damage the bark of trees. Proprietary tree guards can be wrapped around trunks, or you can use

## FRAMES AND CLOCHES

**Slugs** are often attracted to the combination of a succulent meal and a protected environment. Keep a few slug pellets sprinkled along cloches and in frames.
**Ventilate frames** on mild days, but close them up in early afternoon, to store up the heat for the night.

## FRUIT

**Canker** on apple trees should be cut or gouged out; use a chisel if necessary. Then paint over the area with a wound-treating compound.
**Plant vines** in a sheltered position. They are best trained against a wall in less favourable areas, but in mild districts grow them along wires in an open situation.
**Prune apples and pears** if it has not already been done.

wire-netting round the base of valuable trees.
**Trees and shrubs** with bare roots can be planted from now until early spring, provided that the soil is not frozen or waterlogged. Evergreen types are best transplanted in late autumn or early spring, when the soil is warmer. Plants growing in containers can be planted at any time of the year if the soil is in a suitable condition.

## THE WATER GARDEN

**Tender water plants** should be lifted from the pool and stored in their containers in a frostproof greenhouse for the winter. Cut back the foliage and keep the soil moist.

## THE GREENHOUSE

**Avoid too much humidity** at this time of year. Try to keep the air dry. Do not splash water about, especially if the greenhouse is lined with polythene.
**Azaleas** for flowering at Christmas should not be allowed to become dry at their roots at any time.
**Clean out the gutters** if you collect water from them. After the autumn they are often clogged with leaves and other rubbish. A piece of perforated zinc will keep leaves out of the down-pipe.
**Feed cyclamen and primulas**, and do not allow the compost to become dry.
**Force rhubarb** by packing the roots closely together under the greenhouse staging, providing darkness with black polythene. Alternatively the roots can be placed in black polythene sacks, with a few canes inside to hold the bag off the crowns.
**Greenhouse chrysanthemums** that have already flowered can now be cut down to about 45 cm (1½ ft) above the soil.
**Keep the glass clean** to ensure that the maximum amount of light reaches the

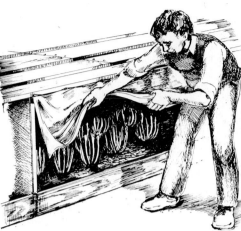

plants. If grime has gathered where the panes overlap, use a thin plastic label or an old toothbrush and soapy water to get the worst of it out.
**Late chrysanthemums** should be given plenty of ventilation if the weather is mild, and do not forget to watch for greenfly and leaf-miners, which can still be a problem.
**Lily of the valley** crowns can be potted up now if not already done.
**Mid-season chrysanthemum** varieties

that have flowered can be cut down to about 23 cm (9 in) and the stools (roots with remaining top-growth) planted close together in boxes of peat and sand.
**Orchids** enjoy shade from direct sun, but at this time of year they need full light, so make sure that summer shading has been removed from the glass.
**Trailing plants** with a lot of foliage can be stood on top of an upturned pot to keep the leaves off damp staging and to provide better circulation of air.
**Unheated greenhouses** are useful for alpine plants in pots. It is not too late to pot some up for a spring display. Use round seed pans or half-pots, and dress the surface with stone chippings to finish it off and encourage free drainage round the neck of the plant.
**Water calceolarias** carefully, and do not splash the foliage.
**Winter-maturing lettuces** may need thinning or transplanting. Water the soil or compost about an hour before moving them, and water lightly afterwards, but try to avoid splashing the leaves.

## WEEKEND PROJECTS

### Build a soakaway

Often an area in a low lying part of the garden stays waterlogged after a wet spell. The problem can be solved by building a soakaway. This simply comprises a hole about 1 m (3 ft) square dug sufficiently deep to reach porous subsoil. The hole should be at least 1 m (3 ft) deep.

Fill the bottom 60 cm (2 ft) of the hole with large pieces of hardcore and cover this with a 13–15 cm (5–6 in) layer of gravel. Fill the remainder of the hole with topsoil.

When water drains into the hole, the gravel will serve as a filter to trap silt and soil and so prevent the hardcore in the base from becoming blocked.

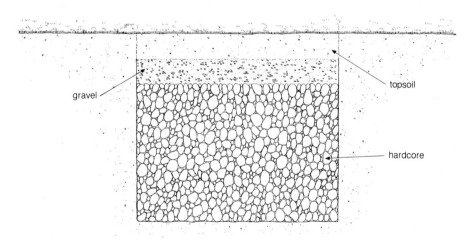

topsoil

gravel

hardcore

## THE KITCHEN GARDEN

**Asparagus beds** will benefit from a 5 cm (2 in) layer of well-rotted manure or compost.

**Clean up the herb bed.** Clear plants of dill, basil and chervil and dig over the ground. Parsley sown last year but still being grown on is best discarded in favour of new plants.

**Cut celery** as required.

**Lift leeks** as you need them.

**Lift winter radishes** if they are ready, and store in boxes of sand or peat.

**Rhubarb roots** for forcing later can be lifted now and left on the surface exposed to frost. They will then be ready when required.

**Runner bean trenches** can be prepared now, ready for next year.

Salsify can also be lifted as required from now on.

## FRUIT

**Blackcurrants** can have some old wood removed, but leave as much new growth as possible. Do not prune the first season after planting.

**Check fruit in store** and remove without delay any showing signs of disease.

**Check tree ties** and stakes; the stakes should be strong enough to stand up to winter gales and the ties should be firm but not biting into the tree.

**Continue to plant fruit trees** whenever the weather is not too cold and the ground is not frozen or waterlogged.

**Prune gooseberries**, redcurrants and whitecurrants, if not already done.

## THE FLOWER GARDEN

**Check bulbs** being forced for spring or Christmas flowering to ensure that the compost or bulb-fibre has not become too dry.

**Dry stone walls** are always attractive and winter is a good time to make them. They do need a great deal of skill in construction, as the stones have to be fitted together rather like a jigsaw. As the wall is constructed, plants can be set in soil between the stones. Walls over 90 cm (3 ft) high should slope backwards slightly.

**Garden paths** can be hazardous at any time if they are in need of attention, but especially so in winter. Try to attend to them now before the bad weather sets in.

**Gunnera manicata** and eremurus will need protection from severe frosts. Rake away all dead leaves and shoots, then cover the crowns with wire-netting and place bracken or straw on top. You may need to use more netting to keep this in place. Eremurus species can also be protected by covering the crowns with well-weathered ashes.

**Protect plants** that are not quite hardy, or whose winter blooms benefit from protection from the worst of the weather, such as the Christmas rose (*Helleborus niger*). The blooms of the Christmas rose will be much better for cutting, less splashed by the rain, if covered with a sheet of glass or a

cloche. Some fuchsias are hardy in mild districts, but in colder areas will need some protection (tender kinds should be taken indoors). Some of the more tender kinds will survive in mild areas if given some protection, even though the top growth will be cut back. A 15 cm (6 in) layer of leaves, straw or peat may be all that is required. Camellias and any newly-planted evergreens may benefit from the protection afforded by a simple framework of stout canes around which you can wrap a sheet of polythene as protection from biting winds.

## FRAMES AND CLOCHES

**Chrysanthemum stools** being stored in the frame should not be allowed to become drawn or forced through lack of light. Keep the glass clean, and ventilate whenever the weather is reasonably mild.

**Sweet peas** sown in the autumn and growing in pots should be 'stopped' (the growing tip pinched out) when the seedlings are about 10 cm (4 in) high.

## THE GREENHOUSE

**Automatic watering equipment** is most conveniently installed during the winter when most greenhouses are either empty or contain comparatively few plants. As there are many different makes and systems available, it is worth spending a weekend or two looking at the various options.

**Cacti** should be kept dry during the next couple of months. Provided that they are not kept too moist, most of them will tolerate quite low temperatures, if they are not subjected to frost. The Christmas cactus is an exception at this time, and should be given enough water to keep the compost just moist; and they should have a temperature of about 10°C (50°F) as a minimum. Do not turn the plant round, otherwise the buds may start to drop.

**Dahlia tubers** that have not been stored away for the winter until

required for cuttings should be packed in dry peat or vermiculite and stored in a frostproof place.

**Force rhubarb**, providing a combination of darkness and some warmth.

**Greenhouse** lighting may seem a luxury, but it will give you many more hours of enjoyment from your greenhouse during the winter.

**Cut down chrysanthemum** plants that have flowered. Chop them back to about 23 cm (9 in).

**Lettuces** sown earlier in the greenhouse border should be thinned to about 23 cm (9 in) apart, if this has not already been done.

**Poinsettias** should not be allowed to dry out at any time from now on. Try to maintain 10°C (50°F).

**Mice** can be troublesome in the winter. If they are, do not hesitate to put down traps or bait. Choose a safe place away from pets and children (a good place is in a short length of drainpipe laid in a safe position).

## Build a brick wall

A dwarf wall, perhaps to enclose a patio, is a good starting point for bricklaying. New bricks can be used though second-hand bricks often merge better with a garden setting. Bricks measure 215 × 102 × 65 mm (8½ × 4 × 2½ in)—add a nominal 10 mm (½ in) to each dimension when planning the overall size of the wall. A single skin of bricks laid to a stretcher bond requires 60 bricks per m².

When the bricks are delivered, stack them carefully and cover them with polythene to keep them dry—saturated bricks are more difficult to lay.

For a stretcher bond wall up to 1 m high, incorporate piers 330 × 215 mm (13 × 8½ in) at 1.8 m (6 ft) centres. There must also be a pier at the start and end of the wall. It is a good idea to lay out the bricks 'dry' to get into the habit of laying bricks to a bond pattern.

Build a wall on a firm, level concrete foundation (one part cement to five parts ballast). For a low wall, lay 15 cm (6 in) of concrete in a 30 cm (1 ft) wide trench with a hardcore base. Set up

string lines as a guide to the outline of the trench and the wall. Lay the concrete and let it set before laying the bricks.

*Mortar* Use a mix of one part cement, one part lime and six parts of clean, sharp sand. Suitable mixes are available in dry mix bags and these save having to remember to mix uniform mortar.

The first course of bricks must be laid accurately as the alignment of the complete wall depends on it. To lay the first corner brick, use a bricklayer's trowel to spread a 1.5 cm (⅝ in) bed of mortar. Place the brick on the mortar ensuring that it is aligned with the string lines. Lay a spirit level on top and tap down the brick with a trowel handle until it is level. The first course of bricks should be completed, remembering to build in the base course for any piers.

The ends or corners are then built up to about six or seven courses high. Check for horizontal and vertical using a spirit level as work proceeds. Each complete course of bricks then can be

filled in. As a guide to each course use a taut string line attached to steel pins. Clean up each joint with a trowel and draw a rounded piece of metal through the joint to leave a concave finish.

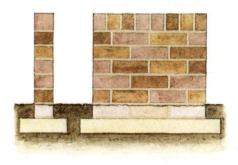

## THE KITCHEN GARDEN

**Autumn-sown peas and beans** coming through will benefit from having a little soil drawn up into a 7.5 cm (3 in) ridge both sides of the row to provide a degree of wind protection. Straw laid between the rows will have a similar effect.

**Beetroot and turnips** from a July sowing should be ready for lifting and putting into store.

**Double-dig** any part of the vegetable plot that is clear of crops and which would benefit from deep digging and a dressing of manure or garden compost.

**Lift parsnips** as you need them.

**Outside water taps** should be well lagged. Standpipes should have straw or sacking wrapped round, with a final covering of polythene to keep out the wet.

**Rhubarb** will be required for forcing. If some roots have not already been

lifted and exposed to the weather for about a fortnight, lift some now.

### FRAMES AND CLOCHES

**Cover frames** with sacking or some other material that will provide extra insulation on cold nights. Cloches can be covered in a similar way. Always remember to remove the protective material in the morning.

**Water lettuces carefully**, trying to keep the water off the leaves. Remove and burn any leaves that show signs of decay.

### FRUIT

**Blackberry and loganberry tip layers** should be separated from the parent plant (if not already done) and moved to their growing positions.

**Check pears in store**; they can soon go over-ripe if neglected. Gently press the neck end. If the flesh yields to the pressure, they will soon need eating.

**Collect up leaves** and put them on the compost heap.

## THE FLOWER GARDEN

**Dig over** vacant ground whenever the weather is suitable. Remove all perennial weeds, but dig in annual weeds. You can leave the surface rough to allow the weather to break down large lumps. Almost all soils will benefit from plenty of bulky, well-rotted compost, but if you do not have enough to go round, concentrate it where you intend to grow plants that need it most, such as sweet peas.

**Order manure** for digging in during the winter. If stable manure is not available locally, spent hops and spent mushroom compost are also very useful.

**Plant** deciduous trees and shrubs.

**Protect outside taps.** It is best to cut off the supply and drain the pipes if possible. If water has to remain in the pipework, lag all exposed areas. Use sacking or straw, and cover with polythene to keep it dry.

**Roses** can be planted whenever the weather and ground are suitable.

**Soil-testing** kits can be used to check the acidity of the soil. Several kinds are available, and most of them are likely to give a reasonably accurate reading of the pH. Always test the soil from several places as it can change significantly even in a small garden. If the soil needs more lime, winter is the

best time to put it on.

**Tulips** can still be planted, although you should not delay beyond this week.

**Turn the compost heap**, making sure unrotted material on the outside is placed in the centre.

### FRAMES AND CLOCHES

**Anemones** planted outdoors for winter and spring flowering should be covered with cloches.

**Autumn-sown hardy annuals** will need cloche protection in cold districts.

### LAWNS

**Brush leaves off** the lawn if more have blown on to the grass. A besom or a wire-tined rake will help to remove them.

**Clean the mower** thoroughly if this has not been done. After removing all traces of soil and grass, wipe it over with an oily rag to reduce the risk of rusting.

## THE GREENHOUSE

**Bulbs for Christmas flowering** should be checked to see that they have not dried out, and to see whether they are ready to bring into slight warmth yet.

**Cacti** should be kept almost bone dry now, except the 'leaf' cacti such as the Christmas cactus.

**Chives** can be induced into early growth. Just pot up a few roots and place them in a cool or warm greenhouse.

**Geranium cuttings** taken earlier should have rooted and can be potted up.

**Pick off dead and diseased leaves** from pot-plants, making sure you remove the stalks too.

**Pot-plants for indoor decoration** should be checked first to ensure they are not harbouring pests or diseases. Use a suitable insecticide or fungicide

if necessary, and wait until the plants are clean before taking them indoors.

**Spray over rhubarb crowns** brought in for forcing beneath the staging.

**The Christmas cactus** should be kept moist and fed once a week with a liquid fertilizer. Avoid draughts and

dryness at the roots, and do not keep moving the plant around, otherwise the buds are likely to drop.

**Vines** can be pruned any time during the next month or two.

**Christmas Cherries** (*Solanum capsicastrum*) should have set their berries ready for a Christmas display. As the plants often produce vigorous leafy growth beyond the position of the berries on the stems, appearances can be improved by cutting back some of the long growths to display the berries to best advantage.

**Winter lettuces** are particularly vulnerable to damp, cool conditions. Try not to splash the leaves when watering, and pick off any decaying or damaged leaves as soon as you notice them.

**WEEKEND PROJECTS**

## Erecting a fence

The simplest fence to erect is a panel type with timber posts. Use a taut string line first to denote the exact line of the fence and leave this in place until the fence has been erected. The first post is usually fixed to the house wall since there is often a patio which prevents the post being sunk in the ground. Here the posts should be bolted to the house wall ensuring that the bolts lie below the surface of the post. The first panel can then be nailed to this post using non-rusting galvanized nails (three nails on each side of the fence). Check that the top of the panel is horizontal.

Mark out the position of the first post hole accurately. A piece of wood cut to the length of the panels makes a handy measuring stick for post spacings. It is also worth hiring a post hole borer to make the post holes; this resembles a large corkscrew and is turned into the ground down to the required depth. Waste earth is lifted out as boring progresses.

The post is positioned in the hole and hardcore rammed around its base to

keep it vertical (check with a spirit level). Next, nail the panel to the post. Then knock a nail into each side of the post and prop it upright using struts below the nails.

The remainder of the fence is erected in the same way, keeping each post wedged upright with struts. Finally, fill the holes with alternate layers of stones and concrete (one part cement to five parts sand); mix the concrete fairly dry. Finish the concrete with a rounded collar to ensure that rainwater flows away from the hole. Leave the struts

holding the posts upright for 48 hours.

In really firm ground it is often possible for the posts to be inserted in the ground and supported only by hardcore and still remain stable.

Panel fences can be erected using concrete posts. These should either be grooved to contain the edges of the panels, or be pre-drilled and supplied with brackets and screws which are used to secure the panels. The positioning of the posts again is critical and they should be supported with hardcore and concrete.

## THE KITCHEN GARDEN

**Brussels sprouts** and spinach beet should be cropped regularly.
**Celeriac** to be overwintered in the ground should have a layer of soil drawn over the swollen stems as protection against the worst frosts.
**Lift some Jerusalem artichokes** before the ground becomes frozen. The tubers will remain in good condition in the ground, but lifting enough for two or three weeks at a time will save having to try digging them up in frosty weather.
**Swedes** can be lifted as required once they have been touched by a few sharp frosts. If you lift them for storing, place them in boxes of dry sand or peat in a cool, dry place.

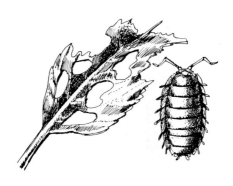

### FRAMES AND CLOCHES

**Woodlice** can be troublesome in frames. Dust round the edges of the frame with a suitable insect powder if they are seen.

**Pot up a few chives.** In the protection of a frame they will soon produce a crop of new leaves.

### FRUIT

**Apple shoots** whitened with mildew are best cut off. If the disease overwinters it is likely to start a bad infestation next year.
**Gather quinces** before they deteriorate any further. They can be made into marmalade or wine.
**Tie in canes of raspberries and blackberries**, and shoots of wall-trained fruit trees. Use proper wall nails if you have to fix any to the wall.

## THE FLOWER GARDEN

**Canes and stakes** are often taken for granted, yet there never seem to be enough of them when you actually need them, and the cost of buying canes can be substantial if you have to renew them regularly. Take care of those you have by cutting off any rotten parts and soaking the ends of the canes in a wood preservative. Store them in a dry place, neatly bundled.
**Check dahlia tubers** stored in boxes, to ensure that the tubers have not become shrivelled or diseased. If necessary, lightly syringe them with water.
**Roses** with a great deal of top growth can be trimmed back to avoid wind-rock. Full pruning can be completed in spring.
**Slugs and snails** may attack soft plants during winter, so clear up all leaves the remove weeds that are likely to harbour them. Place slug bait around susceptible plants. Grit or weathered ashes sprinkled around sensitive plants can also be effective. Slugs do not like travelling over a rough surface.

**Spring bedding plants** such as wallflowers will usually look better if you hoe around them. Take the opportunity to refirm any that have been loosened by frost. If the plants are interplanted with bulbs, it is best not to hoe, otherwise the developing shoots may be damaged.

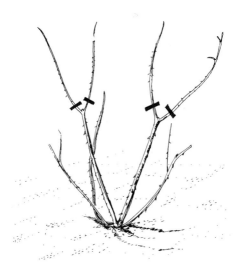

**Sweet pea** enthusiasts like to grow these plants in ground that has been well prepared the previous year. You can do this now by taking out trenches 60 cm (2 ft) wide and one spit (spade depth) deep. Dig manure or compost into the bottom of the trench, then return the topsoil. Leave rough until nearer planting time.

### FRAMES AND CLOCHES

**Ventilate frames** whenever you can, provided that there is no frost about. In very windy weather, secure the lights (tops) firmly with rope to make sure they cannot be blown off. If cloches have to be ventilated, remove one or two from along the run rather than removing the ends, which would provide a kind of wind tunnel.

### THE WATER GARDEN

**Shallow pools** in water-cascades and waterfalls are best emptied and cleaned, as they are very likely to become frozen solid if water is left in, and may crack concrete.

## THE GREENHOUSE

**Avoid too much heat** unless the plants really require it. Most greenhouse plants can survive relatively cool temperatures if they are kept fairly dry. Too much heat not balanced by adequate light can produce unseasonal and unhealthy growth. If you have just a few plants that do need extra warmth, try moving them into the home for a couple of months, or partition off part of the greenhouse and maintain the warmer temperature in that part. Most plants will be happy with 13°C (55°F), although chrysanthemums and perpetual-flowering carnations will tolerate less. With care, many plants can be overwintered satisfactorily at 7°C (45°F).

**Azaleas** need to be kept moist and will benefit from a regular misting with water.

**Chrysanthemums** that have finished flowering should be cut back to about 23 cm (9 in) if this has not already been done. Make sure that they are all individually labelled.

**Clay pots** should be scrubbed clean to remove soil and pests. Wash them in warm water and stack them to dry before storing in a garden shed or garage. Plastic pots can be cleaned and stored at the same time.

**Cyclamen** should be watered with

A simple way to provide a humid atmosphere for cuttings is to put them in a polythene bag.

great care. Try not to get the corms too wet and do not splash water on the leaves or flowers. Remove dead flowers regularly, complete with stalk.

**Fan-trained peaches** in a greenhouse are a bit of a speciality these days, but if you do have one release it from the support and prune it if this has not already been done. Tie in the new growth to maintain the attractive fan shape.

**Seed catalogues** will be advertised about this time, and if you want to spend a pleasant few hours planning how to use the delights within their pages over the Christmas holiday, send off for them now. You will find that some seedsmen have a much better selection of greenhouse plants than others, so it may be worth ordering from a few firms if you do not already know their specialities. Be careful, however, of the really exotic seeds—they *may* germinate, but some kinds that are offered are likely to be of doubtful viability. If you only want one or two plants, though, you may think it is worth the risk.

**Take perpetual-flowering carnation cuttings** any time during the next few months, choosing strong, free-flowering plants.

**Ventilate** whenever possible, but only if it does not mean very low temperatures or icy draughts. Always open the ventilators on the leeward side. Greenhouses containing only chrysanthemums, carnations, peaches or grape vines can be ventilated most of the time.

**Water carefully**, ensuring that you do not splash the leaves. It is best to water in the morning, so that excess water has more chance to drain or evaporate by the evening.

## WEEKEND PROJECTS

### Build a garden compost container

A compost container can be built from old bricks, wire netting or wood. The important thing is to allow for plenty of air to pass through the sides and reach the composting material. It is useful to have a couple of compost containers in the garden so that one load can be allowed to decompose completely while another load is being brought on. Site the containers in a concealed spot but do not choose a place which is too shaded or rotting down will not take place completely.

A honeycomb brick container is built in exactly the same way as a wall (*see* page 179). A wooden slatted container can comprise old feather-edged fence

boards nailed to four corner posts driven into the ground. Leave 7.5 cm (3 in) spaces between the boards.

A simpler construction is made by driving four sections of fence post into the ground and stretching wire netting around them. Secure the netting to the posts with staples.

Even simpler is to bend some netting in a circle and fix it with wire ties to a single stake or post driven below ground.

Suitable compost materials are clean straw, leaves and non-woody plant remains; noxious weeds, such as docks, or any diseased materials should not be used for garden compost.

## THE KITCHEN GARDEN

**Badly drained ground** can be improved by digging out a trench about 60 cm (2 ft) deep with a slight fall towards a soakaway. Take out side trenches to feed into the main channel and place rubble or bundles of brushwood in the bottom of the trenches and then return the soil.
**Continue digging** whenever the weather is suitable. Late celery can be damaged by hard frosts, so cover them with bracken or dry straw held in place with netting or wire-netting pegged into the soil.
**Protect marrows from frost**, bringing them indoors if necessary.
**Winter cabbages and savoys** should be ready for harvesting.

### FRUIT

**Continue to prune fruit trees** not already tackled.
**Plant fruit trees** as soon as possible provided that the soil is not frozen or waterlogged.
**Rabbits** are a problem in some areas; they gnaw the bark of young trees, and if they girdle the tree it may die. Making the whole plot rabbit-proof may be expensive, but you can always protect an individual tree with a column of wire-netting or a spiral plastic rabbit guard.
**Spray fruit trees** with a tar oil winter wash to kill off the eggs of pests such as aphids.

## THE FLOWER GARDEN

**Bulbs in bowls** for bringing into the house should be checked if they are plunged in peat or some other material outside. As soon as the shoots are a couple of centimetres high, bring them into the light—but do not move them directly into a warm place. Keep them in a cool position until the actual flower buds are showing good signs of development.
**Collect up rubbish** from around the garden and burn or compost it.
**Continue to dig** vacant ground, including beds that are to take dahlias and chrysanthemums next year.
**Cut** *Jasminum nudiflorum* shoots now and place them in water to flower for Christmas. If the buds start to open too quickly, place them in a cool garden shed to slow development.
**Heel in** any trees and shrubs that have arrived but cannot be planted because of the weather. Take out a trench or hole in a sheltered part of the garden and place the roots in it. Cover with soil and firm gently (do not press heavily otherwise the roots may be broken or damaged). The plants should

be safe until suitable planting weather arrives.
**Land drains** sound an uninteresting aspect of gardening, but if your ground is very poorly drained then winter is a good time to put them in. Pipe land drains can be used, or the deep trenches can be filled with rubble where drainage

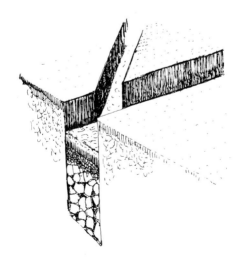

is not too much of a problem or the area to be drained is not great.
 If the rubble drain method is used, dig a trench and fill the bottom with 23 cm (9 in) of rubble, topping with inverted turves to prevent the rubble filling up with soil. Subsoil and then topsoil should be returned to the trench in the right order.
**Rake up fallen leaves** and put them on the compost heap. Leaves left to rot around plants may cause them to rot, and will encourage slugs.
**Tidy up bamboo canes**, cutting off pieces that have rotted during the summer. Ensure that they do not harbour pests and diseases by washing them thoroughly in hot water. Dry before storing in a shed or other dry place.

### FRAMES AND CLOCHES

**Christmas roses** (*Helleborus niger*) will benefit from the protection of a cloche if you have a spare one.
**Slugs and snails** can be a problem in cloches and frames in the winter. Put down slug bait.

## THE GREENHOUSE

**Bring in bulbs** for early flowering that have been plunged in peat or some other material outside, provided they have made good root growth and the shoots are at least a couple of centimetres high. If you want to use grass to set off hyacinths, sow the seed now on the surface of the compost surrounding the bulbs. Lightly prick over the surface of the compost first. If the grass becomes a little high by the time they are in bloom, it is a simple matter to trim it with scissors.

**Check stored tubers and plants,** looking for signs of disease that will need immediate attention. Begonia and dahlia tubers, and gladioli corms, are all worth checking over.

**Clean algae off paintwork,** staging and glass.

**Clean old pots and boxes,** scrubbing them in warm, soapy water. Rinse and dry thoroughly. It is a good idea to soak them in a disinfectant suitable for greenhouse use first.

**Cyclamen** do not need a lot of warmth —about 10°C (50°F) is right—but it should be steady. Do not overwater, and try not to wet the corms.
**Do not splash water about** the greenhouse as it will encourage diseases such as botrytis (grey mould).

**Exhibition onions** can be sown now if you can provide a temperature of 13°C (55°F). You have plenty of time to sow onions for an ordinary crop next year.
**Force vegetables** such as chicory, seakale and rhubarb, lifted from the garden.
**Keep the glass clean.** It can become dirty in a surprisingly short time in winter, and it is worth cleaning the outside about once a month until the better weather and light returns.
**Order plants** such as carnations and chrysanthemums in plenty of time. It is best to do these jobs now while there is not a lot to do in the greenhouse, rather than wait until the busy spring season.
**Perpetual-flowering carnation cuttings** can be taken any time now. They will need a temperature of about 15°C (60°F) until they have rooted.
**Spray azaleas** regularly with tepid water.

### WEEKEND PROJECTS

### Insulate a greenhouse

By lining the inside of a greenhouse with clear medium grade polythene sheeting, heating bills can be reduced with only a small reduction in the amount of light entering the greenhouse. Lining with polythene is, in fact, a form of double glazing, and it can be even more effective if the cellular bubble-type polythene quilt is used. It is important to fix the polythene so an air gap is created between the sheeting and the glass. The polythene will eliminate draughts and it will also increase humidity, so make sure the vents are not sealed as they may be needed to reduce humidity.

In a timber-framed greenhouse fixing is very easy. Stretch the polythene between the glazing bars and pin it in place with drawing pins or by using a staple gun. To prevent the polythene sheeting from tearing, reinforce each fixing with a small square of cardboard. Fix the polythene in horizontal strips, starting at the apex of the greenhouse

and finishing at floor level. In this way, any condensation that forms on the plastic sheeting will trickle down to floor level without dripping on to the plants. Keeping the polythene tight will also minimise dripping.

With a metal frame greenhouse, fixing the polythene can be more of a problem. Some greenhouse manufacturers and accessory firms sell special clips for holding the polythene in place. The clips attach to the glazing bars. If a do-it-yourself system is preferred it may be possible to wedge narrow flexible timber battens between the sides and ends of the greenhouse. The battens can

either be fixed under the polythene so they hold it up, or the battens can be positioned and the polythene stapled to the battens as it would be in a timber house.

Another method is to fix small drilled metal plates to the glazing bars at each end of the house using self-tapping screws, available from hardware and motor accessory shops. Horizontal wires can be stretched between these plates and then the polythene lining can be draped over the wires.

The lining should be removed in spring and summer so that light transmission is not hindered.

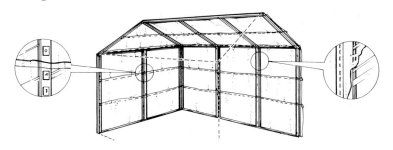

# Week 51

## THE KITCHEN GARDEN

**Firm vegetables** loosened by severe frost once the ground has thawed. The most recently planted vegetables are the most at risk.

**Lettuces** sown in frames in October for maturing in April and May should be thinned to about 23 cm (9 in) square.

**Lift** artichokes, parsnips, celery, and leeks as required. If bad weather threatens, lift a few extra plants to have in the house.

**Manure and garden compost** can most easily be barrowed into position when the ground is frozen. Leave it in small heaps ready for digging in when the soil is workable again.

**Protect swedes and turnips** still in the ground by drawing soil up around the roots, but leave the stem and leaves exposed.

### FRUIT

**Brown rot disease** will soon spread if rotting fruit is not picked up off the ground. These should have been cleared already, but go round again to pick up any still remaining. Bury rotted fruit deeply, or burn them.

**Burn prunings** that have accumulated. If you have the fire on a piece of concrete or sheet of something like corrugated iron, the ash can be collected and kept dry until required for use as a potash fertilizer.

**Spray fruit trees** with a tar-oil winter wash if this has not already been done. Do not spray peaches with it after the end of December.

## THE FLOWER GARDEN

**Christmas roses** (*Helleborus niger*) are popular cut flowers at this time (if urged on with cloches), but they do not normally last long when cut. However, if you immerse the bottom 5 cm (2 in) in hot water as soon as they are cut, then plunge them in cold water after about five minutes, they should last longer. If slugs have been causing damage, sprinkle slug bait around the plants.

**Evergreens** such as holly and ivy used for Christmas decorations should be cut with sharp secateurs. Try to cut branches carefully so that you do not spoil the shape of the plant.

**Inspect straw or bracken over tender plants.** Make sure it is still in position and is doing its job properly.

**Refirm soil around hardwood cuttings** where it has been loosened by frost.

### THE ROCK GARDEN

**Protect lewisias** from too much water. Rest a piece of glass on wire supports to cover them.

**Small glass tents** placed over tender rock plants should be checked to see that they are sound and that leaves have not blown under them and lodged against the plants.

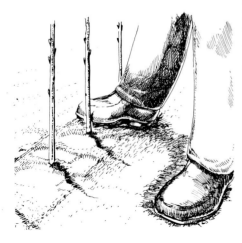

### LAWNS

**Mowers** will need overhauling during the winter. It is a useful job to do over the holiday if the weather is too bad to get out in the garden. Clean off any old grass cuttings still adhering, and clean all metal parts, wiping them with an oily rag. A cylinder mower may need sharpening, so make a note to take it along to a specialist shop if you think it needs attention. If you wait until spring it is often difficult to get the mower back quickly. It is worth having an electric mower checked by an electrician to reassure yourself that it is electrically safe.

**New lawns** to be sown or laid next spring will get off to a better start if the ground has been prepared well in advance. It is not too early to do the initial clearing and digging if there is a suitable break in the weather.

## THE GREENHOUSE

**As this is about the time of the shortest day**, there is every reason to keep the glass clean and let through as much light as possible.

**Botrytis (grey mould)** is one of the greatest disease problems in the winter. It can be particularly troublesome in a cold, damp atmosphere. If it is a problem, give more heat and increase ventilation on mild days. It is best to treat the disease by fumigating rather than using a spray at this time of year.

**Chrysanthemums** should have been cut down to about 23 cm (9 in) after flowering. Act now if this has not been done.

**Cinerarias and primulas** should be coming into flower, so make sure they are given a light position near the glass.

**Clean any brickwork** on the inside of the greenhouse. Paint it white to reflect as much light as possible.

**Continue to force rhubarb.** Place roots from the garden in black plastic bags, using a few canes to keep the plastic off the sprouting crowns, or place the crowns beneath the greenhouse staging and black out the area with sacking or black plastic.

**Flowering pot-plants** bought for Christmas decoration can be placed in a frostproof greenhouse until required. The lower temperature and better light will keep them in good condition until the holiday.

**Forced strawberries** are always a delight, to look at and to eat. Bring in the first batch of plants, which ideally will have been standing in a garden frame in pots.

**Grape vines** can be pruned now. On established vines cut all side growths (laterals) back to two buds.

**Peaches and vines** should be kept cool, which is one reason why they do not mix well with many of the more exotic greenhouse plants.

**Prune peach trees** under glass if not already done.

**Rhubarb crowns** being forced can be given more heat; about 10°C (50°F) will be adequate.

**Send for seed catalogues.** You will need to get your order in as soon as possible after Christmas.

**Tidy up the area around the greenhouse**, which often becomes neglected during the rush of activity in the growing season. It is worth cleaning out the water butt too, as this can become an unhealthy reservoir of diseases.

**Water very cautiously** at this time of year; most plants are best kept almost dry during dull, cold weather.

## WEEKEND PROJECTS

### Make a cheap shed from fencing panels

A simple and cheap shed can be built using 2 × 2 m (6 × 6 ft) fencing panels for three walls, together with a basic framework clad with feather-edged boards for the front. The fence panels should be of the solid, peep-proof type such as vertical or horizontal close boards.

A solid base is needed for a shed—use either concrete or paving slabs and aim for a thickness of 7.5–10 cm (3–4 in).

Four fence posts, 7.5 × 7.5 cm (3 × 3 in), set in the ground (*see* erecting a fence, page 181) provide the anchor points for the walls of the shed. When the three fence panels have been nailed to the posts, the front framework can be built. This framework can be made from 5 × 5 cm (2 × 2 in) sawn softwood which is cheaper than planed wood. Into the framework a door and window frame should be built. The positions of these is optional.

Make the door frame about 75 cm (2½ ft) wide from 5 × 5 cm (2 × 2 in) softwood, and include a diagonal cross member pointing to the hinge side to stabilize the door and prevent future warping. Clad the door with feather edged boards.

The window can be of glass or plastic sheet, 3–4 mm thick. Pin wood beading to the main window frame to form a rebate for the glass. Run a bead of putty or mastic around the beading and press the glazing panel into position. Add another layer of mastic or putty to the edges of the glass, then pin in place a further frame of wood beading. The glass will then be weatherproofed.

The roof can be made from 19 mm (¾ in) chipboard, or plywood. Although it is better to use a more expensive exterior grade board, a standard board will prove adequate if well protected with roofing felt.

A slight fall is needed from the front to back of the roof to shed rainwater. To do this, cut firring strips from 50 × 25 mm (2 × 1 in) softwood and nail these to the tops of the side 'walls' of the shed. Also cut infill strips as needed for the top edges of the front and rear walls. A

central roof beam should also be fixed to the side walls to support the roof panels.

The chipboard roof sheets can then be screwed or nailed into place and be covered with roofing felt. Overlap the edges of the felt by at least 5 cm (2 in) and use bitumastic adhesive to seal down all seams. The edges of the felt should be secured to the wood with clout nails inserted at 5–7.5 cm (2–3 in) centres.

Finally treat the whole shed with wood preservative (*see* page 153).

## THE KITCHEN GARDEN

**Check stored vegetables** (including potatoes and onions) and remove any that show signs of disease or rots.

**Digging** can be quite exhilarating, and is one way to get plenty of exercise over the holiday. Dig deeply for root-crops, but you need not incorporate any manure at this time.

**Lift and store swedes** and carrots sown in late summer if the weather is suitable for working the ground.

**Order your seeds**—surely one of the most pleasurable of all jobs. Do not abandon well-tried varieties lightly for the sake of novelties, but do try a few new vegetables or varieties each year: it is what helps to make each season a new experience.

**Plan next year's plot.** It always pays

to plan the vegetable plot on paper, even if you have to modify your plan to suit the season as it progresses. It enables you to plant early crops allowing space for those sown or planted later. Careful planning now will often enable you to work in catch crops (quick-growing vegetables, usually salads) and intercrops (quick-maturing vegetables planted or sown close to slow-maturing vegetables that can be cleared before the later ones need the extra space). These are often more difficult to fit in if you just decide where you will plant things as you go along.

Bear in mind the need for crop rotation (see page 48).

## THE FLOWER GARDEN

**Check supports for climbers.** Repair them if they are not sound enough to last another year.

**Christmas-flowering bulbs** in bowls can often be improved by covering the compost with freshly-gathered moss. Simply pack it around the plants, completely covering the surface.

**Compost heaps** sometimes become untidy. You can put this right now and repair any containers that have succumbed after years of use.

**Fences** should be treated with a wood preservative regularly, and this is a good time to do the job. If the fence is in close proximity to plants, use one intended for use near plants—not creosote.

**Rustic fences and arches,** which often become overburdened with foliage during the summer, may have been weakened. Now is the time to refirm uprights and repair any joints.

**Relax with the seed catalogues.** If you write out your order now you will stand a good chance of getting all the varieties you order—in good time.

**Snow** can break branches off choice trees and shrubs, if it lies thickly. Sweep it off with a soft broom, as soon as possible after it has fallen.

**Tool sheds** will need an annual check. Rearranging the tools is a good job to finish the year with, as they often get put away too quickly during the busy months. Wash any soil off the tools,

wipe them over with an oily rag, and hang them up.

**Virginia creeper** and ivy growing over the house wall can be trimmed back from around window frames and away from gutters. If the weather is too bad to use a ladder safely, however, wait for a more suitable time.

### THE ROCK GARDEN

**Check that rock plants have not been lifted** by the frost, and firm back any that are loose.

**If slugs appear to be a problem,** sprinkle a little slug bait around particularly vulnerable plants.

**Protect tender alpines** (or those that do not like to become too wet) with a sheet of glass, if this has not already been done. Make sure, however, that it is not in such a position, or fixed in such a way, that it can be lifted by a gust of wind and broken.

# Week 52

## THE GREENHOUSE

**Check paraffin heaters.** Make sure they are clean, and the wick is trimmed. If it smokes, fit a new wick.

**Chrysanthemum cuttings** of late-flowering large and medium exhibition varieties can be taken from now on.

**Clean all greenhouse equipment,** including watering-cans, and repair seedboxes.

**Continue to bring in bulbs** that have been plunged outdoors. Do not let the shoots become too long before bringing them into a light position, but do not move them straight into a warm greenhouse. If you are maintaining a warm temperature, it is best to place the pots and bowls in a garden frame for a few weeks until flower buds are developing well.

**Continue to take cuttings** of perpetual-flowering carnations.

**Dead-head cyclamen** by pulling off the flowers and stalks together.

**Empty greenhouses** should be given a thorough clean before the next season, and this is a useful holiday job. Scrub all the brickwork and woodwork, using

a disinfectant. Clean the glass inside and out, paying attention to grime lodged between overlapping panes. A thin plastic label or an old toothbrush can come in useful for this job.

**Keep aspidistras** on the dry side, and wipe over the leaves with a damp cloth occasionally.

**Old geranium plants** can be cut back,

shortening the shoots to about 20 cm (8 in) above the pot. They can then be removed from the pot, shaken free of soil, and repotted into the smallest pots into which they will fit.

**Pests** such as greenfly will not go away for the holiday. Do not forget to keep an eye open for them, and act as soon as you notice them.

**Pick over pot-plants,** removing dead or yellowing leaves, and all flowers that have passed their best.

**Pot up crowns of lily of the valley** for forcing; if you want them for cutting, simply plant them quite close together in boxes. Cover the crowns with damp peat, and place in a warm part of the greenhouse.

**Support daffodils and hyacinths** that have been brought into the greenhouse to flower, using split canes and soft, green string.

**Wash old pots,** clean seed trays and labels, and generally tidy up the path and staging, ready for the busy weekends that lie ahead in the coming season.

**WEEKEND PROJECTS**

## Make an indoor pot plant stand

Pot-plants look better and grow better if grouped together, and a neat way to do this is to place them in a plant stand. Each plant is kept in its original pot and pots are stood on a tray of gravel which increases humidity around the plants and catches any drips from excessive watering. Start by buying a plastic drip tray of a suitable size for the number of plants to be displayed and then make the stand around this component.

Cut the side pieces from 200 × 25 mm (8 × 1 in) planed timber, the length the same as the drip tray. The end pieces are also cut from 200 × 25 mm timber and shaped as shown in the diagram. Battens to match the width of the drip tray are cut from 25 × 25 mm (1 × 1 in) timber and are glued and screwed to the bottom of the end pieces. For strength, use a pva woodworking adhesive at all joins. Next glue and screw the two

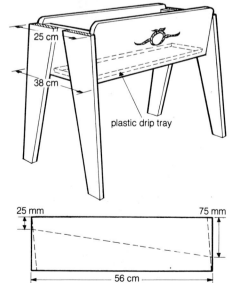

plastic drip tray

75 × 25 mm (3 × 1 in) base pieces between the end pieces. Now fix the side pieces into place after rounding off the top corners with a plane or wood rasp. The sides can be fixed by screwing through the end pieces into the ends of the sides.

Each pair of legs is made from one piece of 100 × 25 mm (4 × 1 in) timber, 60 cm (2 ft) long. The legs taper and are made by sawing as shown in the cutting plan. They are simply screwed to the end pieces and the top edges are rounded over using a plane.

Before painting, fill all the screw heads with a filler suitable for wood. If desired, glue a plastic whitewood furniture decoration to each side. Finish the stand with primer, undercoat and two coats of gloss or silk finish paint.

# Acknowledgements

## CONTRIBUTORS

Site and Design: David Stevens
Tools and Equipment: Andrew Kaye
Soil Care: Peter McHoy
Weed Control: Ann Bonar
Pests, Diseases and Disorders: Patrick Johns
Lawns: Robert Palin
Pruning and Training: Graham Rice
Bedding Plants: Janet Browne
Buying Seeds and Plants: Roy Hay
Irrigation: Roy Hay
Border Plants: Alan Bloom
Propagation: Peter McHoy
Container Gardening: Graham Rice
Vegetables: Joy Larkcom
Fruit: Ray Procter
Rock Gardening: Will Ingwersen
Cloches and Frames: Peter McHoy
Greenhouse Gardening: Peter McHoy
Water Gardening: Bill Heritage
Bulbs: Frederic Doerflinger
Shrubs: Richard Gorer
Trees: Richard Gorer
Roses: Henry Edland
Climbers and Wall Plants: Peter Q. Rose
Houseplants: Brian and Valerie Proudley
Diary section: Peter McHoy (text) and Roger duBern (projects).

## ILLUSTRATION CREDITS

The publishers are grateful to the following for supplying illustrations for this book.

### Colour photographs

Peter McHoy: pp. 14, 15, 22, 23 (top), 26, 27, 35, 43, 46, 47, 50, 51, 54, 55, 71, 87, 107, 111, 115, 123, 135, 139, 147, 155, 159, 163, 167
Michael Warren: pp. 23 (centre and bottom), 30, 31, 38, 127, 131
Gordon Procter: p. 63
Robin Fletcher: pp. 2, 58, 59, 70, 78, 79
Brian and Valerie Proudley: pp. 82, 83

### Black and white photographs

Peter McHoy: pp. 21 (centre), 24 (left), 25, 61
George E. Hyde: pp. 20. 21 (left)
Michael Warren: pp. 21 (right), 24 (right)
Sutton Seeds: pp. 28, 29
Pat Brindley: p. 36

### Colour artwork

Anita Lawrence

### Line drawings

John MacAulay/Halcyon Illustrators and Anita Lawrence

# Index

# Index